NEXUS TOEFL® iBT
Reading

2 Level

NEXUS TOEFL *i*BT Reading Level 2

지은이 넥서스영어교육연구소, 박종현, Jeffrey S. Zeter,
  JoAnn Woods, Virginia Hanslien, Mary French,
  David Desmond O'Flaherty, Yvonne Raub
펴낸이 임상진
펴낸곳 (주)넥서스

출판신고 1992년 4월 3일 제311-2002-2호
10880 경기도 파주시 지목로 5
Tel (02)330-5500 Fax (02)330-5555
ISBN 978-89-6000-617-1 54740

출판사의 허락 없이 내용의 일부를
인용하거나 발췌하는 것을 금합니다.

가격은 뒤표지에 있습니다.
잘못 만들어진 책은 구입처에서 바꾸어 드립니다.

www.nexusEDU.kr

성공적인 학습을 위한 단계별 전략!
Development & Progress for Completion

NEXUS TOEFL® iBT

Reading

2

Level

NEXUS Edu

머리말

영어를 배우는 데 있어서, 네 가지 언어 영역을 균형 있게 학습해야 할 필요성은 오랫동안 인지되어 왔다. 하지만 국내 영어 학습 현실 속에서 그런 학습을 진행하기에는 현실적 여건이 따라 주질 못했다. 먼저 말하기나 쓰기 부분의 공인된 평가가 많지 않았던 탓도 있겠지만, 현실적으로 수업시간에 활용할 수 있는 다양한 학습 모델이 많지 않았기 때문이기도 하다.

그러나 CBT 토플이 iBT로 바뀌어 speaking과 writing이 새롭게 추가되면서 여러 변화가 생겼다. 전반적인 문제 유형이 일차원적 문제 풀이 방식에서 벗어나 제공되는 정보를 잘 정리하여 이해하고, 이해한 내용을 다시 정리하여 표현할 수 있는 능력이 더 중요하게 되었다. 이런 능력 향상은 영어를 배울 때 암기와 반복에 의존하는 학습 방식보다는 절제된 문장 구조 속에서 "organized thoughts"를 할 수 있도록 유도하는 학습 방식을 통해 더 효과적으로 향상될 수 있다. 말하기나 쓰기의 통합적인 영역에서만 이런 능력이 필요한 것이 아니라, 독해 및 청취 영역에서도 마찬가지이다. 문제에 근거한 내용만을 맞히는 것이 아니라, 문단 간의 정보 관계를 전체적으로(global understanding) 훑을 수 있는 훈련이 되어야 한다. 따라서 토플을 단기간에 한 권으로 끝을 내려한다거나 한 학기의 강의 수업 방식으로 짧은 시간에 높은 성적을 올리기에 급급하기보다는 위와 같은 학습 방식에 초점을 맞춰 체계적인 계획을 가지고 접근하게 되면, 토플 성적 이외에도 전반적인 영어 실력을 키워갈 수 있으리라 생각된다.

넥서스 토플은 전반적으로 위와 같은 취지로 기획되었다. 다시 말해, 각 단원마다 주어진 스킬만 배우고 끝내는 것이 아니라 앞서 학습한 스킬을 다시 반복학습할 수 있게 하고, 지문을 통합적으로 활용하며, "speed reading" 같은 짧은 시간 안에 정보의 구조를 파악하는 능력을 훈련할 수 있도록 구성하였다.

짧은 시간에 점수를 올리려는 전략적인 학습 방식을 선호하기보다는 체계적인 학습 계획과 그에 맞는 적절한 교재를 활용하여 토플 점수 향상 이외에도 영어로 생각하고 정리하는 표현 기술을 잘 연마할 수 있도록 학습하는 데 있어 이 교재가 많은 도움이 되기를 바란다.

| 넥서스영어교육연구소 |

이 책의 특징

1 지문을 분석, 정리하는 학습 훈련 강조
- 독해 지문의 "Global understanding" 능력을 향상시키기 위해 지문의 구조, 전개 방식, 문단 간의 관계, 주제, 요지 학습 등의 기본 학습 장치를 단계별로 구성

2 학습 스킬의 체계적인 구성
- 새롭게 바뀌는 iBT Reading Section에 나오는 질문 유형을 철저히 분석하고, 질문 유형이 요구하는 기본적인 strategies를 바탕으로 reading skill을 체계적으로 습득할 수 있도록 구성

3 다양한 테마의 독해 지문 및 관련 어휘 학습
- 토플에 자주 쓰이는 테마와 관련된 어휘 학습 강조 (동의어, 반의어, 영영 해석)

4 중요한 리딩 스킬의 누적 활용
- 앞서 학습한 스킬을 반복적으로 노출시켜 학습 효과 강화

5 iBT 실전에 맞춘 단계별 연습 문제
- Exercise, Practice, Progress Test, Final Test 등 다양한 실전 연습 문제

이 책의 구성

Overview

본격적인 학습에 들어가기 전, 학습할 질문 유형이 요하는 기술을 미리 접할 수 있는 맛보기 테스트를 제시하였다.

해당 chapter에서 학습할 질문 유형이 요하는 기술을 향상시키기 위한 세부 전략 등 구체적인 내용을 정리하였다.

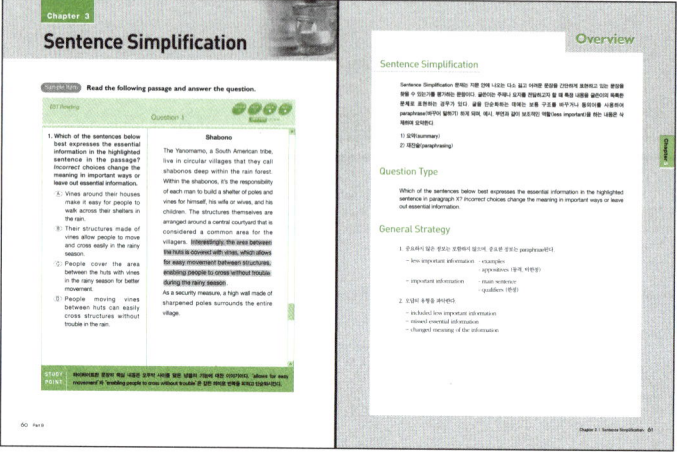

Basic Drill

Overview에서 정리한 전략을 바탕으로 기술을 습득할 수 있는 단계별 훈련을 제공하였다.

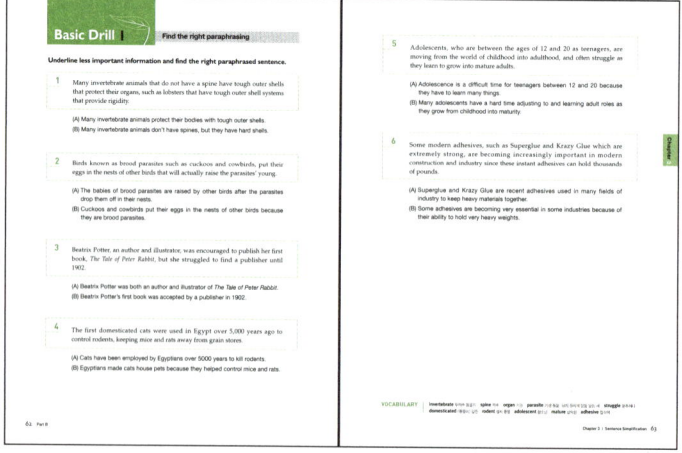

Vocabulary Preview

Exercise에 들어가기 전에 중요 어휘와 구를 미리 제시하고 이를 응용한 어휘 activity를 제공하여 학습 어휘의 습득을 도모하였다.

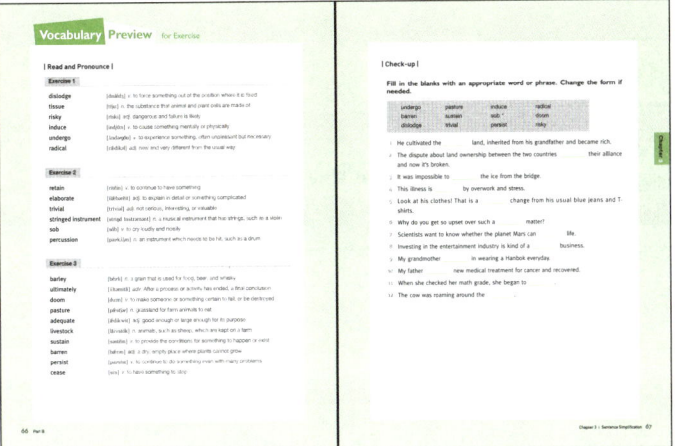

Exercise

실전 감각을 높일 수 있도록 테스트 화면과 유사하게 페이지를 구성하였다.

지문의 세부 구조를 묻는 [Text Outline] 문제도 제시하였다.

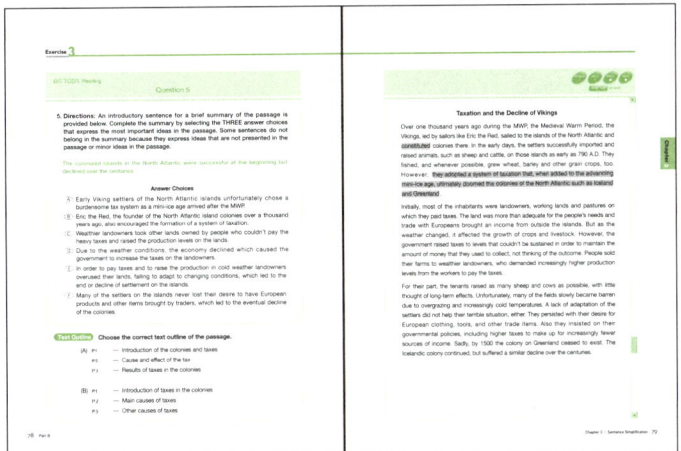

Vocabulary Test

해당 chapter의 중요 어휘나 어구의 동의어를 고르는 문제를 제공하여 어휘력의 확장을 도모하였다.

Progress Test

Part가 끝날 때마다 앞에서 학습한 skill들을 누적 출제하여 각각의 skill들을 복습할 수 있도록 구성하였다.

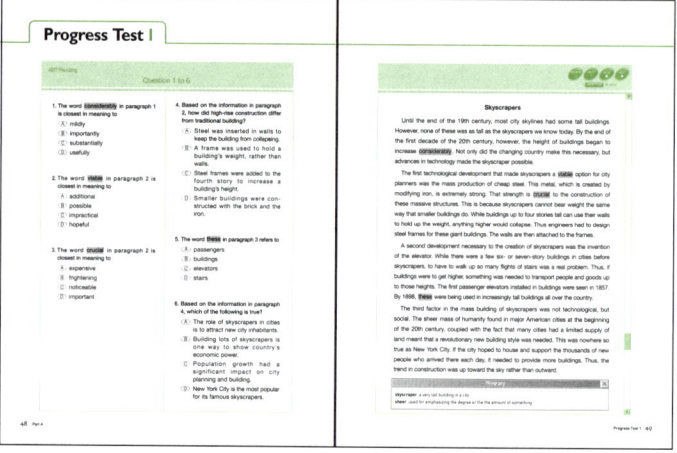

Final Test

Chapter 1~9를 아우르는 모든 skill을 종합적으로 평가해 skill을 마스터했는지 점검해 볼 수 있다.

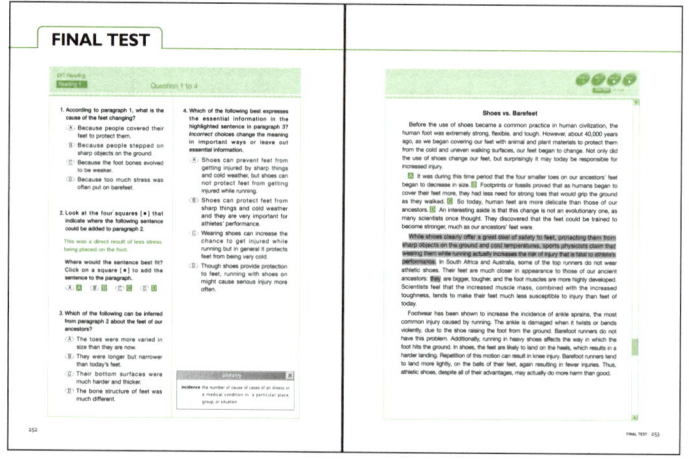

목차

Introduction to *i*BT TOEFL

Part A — Reading to Learn Questions

- **CHAPTER 1** Prose Summary • 13
- **CHAPTER 2** Schematic Table • 31
- Progress Test 1-2 • 47

Part B — Basic Comprehension Questions

- **CHAPTER 3** Sentence Simplification • 59
- **CHAPTER 4** Vocabulary • 81
- **CHAPTER 5** Reference • 103
- **CHAPTER 6** Details • 125
- Progress Test 3-4 • 149

Part C — Inferencing Reading Questions

- **CHAPTER 7** Rhetorical Purpose • 165
- **CHAPTER 8** Insertion • 189
- **CHAPTER 9** Inference • 213
- Progress Test 5-6 • 237

Final Test • 251

Introduction to iBT TOEFL

iBT (Internet-based Test) TOEFL이란?

iBT는 Internet-based Test의 약자로 인터넷을 통해 시험을 치르게 하는 차세대 토플이다. 기존의 CBT가 미국으로 유학 오는 외국 학생들의 실제 영어구사능력을 제대로 측정하지 못한다는 비판에 대한 대안으로 새롭게 만들어졌으며 특히 말하기 능력에 대한 평가를 요구하는 미국 대학들의 요청에 따라 Speaking Section을 신설했다. 기존 CBT와는 달리 언어영역간의 통합을 접목시킨 것이 특징이며 학생들이 얼마나 빠르게, 제대로 미국 대학 생활에 적응해 갈 수 있을지에 대한 지표를 대학에 제공해 준다.

미국에서는 2005년 9월부터 시작되었고, 한국에서는 2006년 5월부터 실시되며, iBT가 실시되면 기존의 CBT 방식으로는 더 이상 시험이 치러지지 않는다.

CBT에서 iBT는 어떻게 달라졌나?

	CBT	iBT
Skills Test	Reading Listening Grammar * Writing은 별도	Reading Listening Writing Speaking
Test time	3.5 hours	4 hours
Reading	4~5 지문 (250~350 words) 각 지문당 11개 문제 (시간 70~90분)	3~5 지문 (700 words) 각 지문당 12~14개 문제 (시간 60~100 분)
Listening	1. 11~17개 대화 　(각 지문당 1개의 질문) 2. 2~3개 짧은 대화 　(각 지문당 2~3개의 질문) 3. 4~6개 미니 강의와 토론 　(각각 3~6 개 문제) (시간 40~60분)	1. 4~6개의 강의 및 교실토론 　(각 지문당 5~6개의 질문) 2. 2~3개의 대화 　(각 5~6개의 질문) (시간 60~100분)
Speaking	없음	1. 2개의 independent tasks 　일반 토픽에 대한 개인의 의견 발표 2. 4개의 integrated tasks 　읽고 들었던 것을 근거하여 말하기 (시간 20분)

Writing	One independent task 토픽에 대한 의견을 개진하기 (시간 30분)	1. 1개의 integrated task 　읽고 들은 내용에 근거하여 쓰기 (20분) 2. 1개의 independent task 　토픽에 대한 의견을 개진하기 (30분)
Structure (Grammar)	20~25개의 문제 (시간 15~20분)	없음
전체 점수	300	120
피드백	점수만 제공	Section별 점수와 총점제공

iBT 시험 유형 세부 분석

iBT의 전체 시험 구성과 문항 수, 제한 시간은 다음과 같다.

Section	지문종류	지문	새로 추가된 특징
Reading		3~5 지문 (각 지문 당 12~14문제)	- 전문용어를 설명하는 Glossary - Multiple focus 정보를 분류하거나 summary를 완성 하는 문제 추가
Listening	Lecture	4~6 지문 (각 지문 당 6문제)	- Replay 문제 추가 - note-taking 허락
	Conversation	2~3 지문 (각 지문 당 5문제)	
Break		10분	
Speaking	Speaking	2문제	경험 또는 의견 말하기
	Reading → Listening → Speaking	2문제	- 제시된 안건을 읽고 그 안건에 대한 강의를 듣고 정리해서 말하기 - 제시된 안건을 읽고 안건에 대한 대화를 듣고 정리해서 말하기
	Listening → Speaking	2문제	- 강의를 듣고 요약하여 말하기 - 대화를 듣고 요약해서 말하기
Writing	Writing on topic	1개의 토픽	제시된 안건에 대한 의견 쓰기
	Reading → Listening → Writing	1개의 토픽	읽고 들은 내용에 근거하여 요점을 정리하여 논리적으로 쓰기

iBT Total Score Range Comparisons

Internet-based Total	Computer-based Total	Percentile Rank
111 - 120	273 - 300	97.6 - 100
96 - 110	243 - 270	85.9 - 96.8
79 - 95	213 - 240	64.8 - 85.0
65 - 78	183 - 210	45.6 - 63.6
53 - 64	153 - 180	29.9 - 44.3
41 - 52	123 - 150	16.7 - 28.6
30 - 40	93 - 120	7.4 - 15.8
19 - 29	63 - 90	1.7 - 6.5
9 - 18	33 - 60	0.1 - 1.2
0 - 8	0 - 30	0.04

iBT Reading Section의 구성

- **문제 유형으로 본 Reading Section에서 요하는 Reading Skills**

1. Basic Comprehension Questions
- 핵심 내용 또는 중요한 정보를 지문 내에서 빨리 효과적으로 찾아내는 능력
- 주제 또는 요지, 중요한 사실과 세부 내용, 문맥상의 어휘의 뜻, 지시어가 지칭하는 것이 무엇인지 파악하는 능력
- 복잡한 문법 구조를 가진 긴 문장의 해당 핵심 내용을 파악하는 능력

2. Inferencing Reading Questions
- 특정 소재를 언급한 작가의 의도, 특정 소재가 단락/지문 내에서 하는 역할, 작가의 주장을 전개해나가는 글의 구조를 파악할 줄 아는 능력
- 글의 논리적 전개에 따라 특정 문장을 올바르게 삽입하여 글의 유기적 통일성을 완성하는 능력
- 암시되어 있는 내용이 무엇인지 유추하는 능력

3. Reading to Learn Questions
- 지문의 전체적인 구조와 단락간의 관계를 인식하는 능력
- 지문 내에 표출되는 여러 내용 간의 관계를 이해하는 능력(접속사의 역할을 제대로 이해하는 것이 필요)
- 주어진 여러 개의 정보를 올바르게 분류하는 능력
- 지문 내의 중요한 정보와 핵심적인 세부 사항을 기억하여 간략히 요약할 줄 아는 능력

Reading Section의 형식과 특징

지문 길이	지문 수와 문제 수	시간
600~700단어	3-5개 지문 지문 당 12~14개 문제	60~100분

1. 각 지문마다 제목이 제시되기 때문에 main topic 고르는 문제는 출제되지 않는다. main idea 구하는 문제도 출제되지 않을 확률이 높다.

2. 새로운 문제 유형이 생겨났다.
    ▶ **Prose Summary** : introductory sentence를 제시해주고, 지문을 잘 요약할 수 있는 문장 3개를 6개의 보기 안에서 드래그하여 완성하기 (부분 점수 있음)
    ▶ **Schematic Table** : 지문에 제시되는 두 개의 대상에 대해 맞는 이야기를 하는 phrases를 올바르게 분류하여 차트 완성하기. 7개에서 5개 고르는 유형(2개는 지문에 언급되지 않는 내용)과 9개에서 7개 고르는 유형(2개는 지문에 언급되지 않는 내용)이 있음. 지문 전체의 구조와 세부 내용 간의 관계를 이해할 필요가 있음.(부분 점수 있음)
    ▶ **Sentence Simplification** : 지문에 하이라이트된 문장의 핵심 정보를 가장 적절히 paraphrase한 문장 고르기. 처리해야하는 문장이 문법적으로 복잡한 구조를 가지고 있다는 것이 특징임.
    ▶ **Rhetorical Purpose** : 단어 또는 소개하는 내용이 갖는 수사학적인 목적을 파악하는 문제. 저자가 어떤 의도 및 목적으로 그 단어 또는 내용을 사용하는 지를 이해해야 함.

3. CBT에 없는 새로운 기능이 첨가되었다.
    ▶ **Glossary** : 지문에 파란색으로 밑줄 그어진 단어를 클릭하면 그 단어에 대한 영문 설명이 나오는 팝업창 뜸.
    ▶ **Review** : 문항에 대한 응답 상태를 확인할 수 있고, Go To Question 아이콘들을 이용하여 Review 화면에서 미응답 문제로 바로 이동 가능.

4. 기타
    ▶ 문제 배점은 대부분 1점씩, Prose Summary와 Schematic Table 문제에는 2~4점이 주어짐.
    ▶ 한 지문 내에 Prose Summary 문제와 Schematic Table 문제가 동시에 출제되지 않음.

PART A
Reading to Learn Questions

Chapter 01 Prose Summary
Chapter 02 Schematic Table

Progress Test 1-2

Chapter 01
PROSE SUMMARY

Chapter 1

Prose Summary

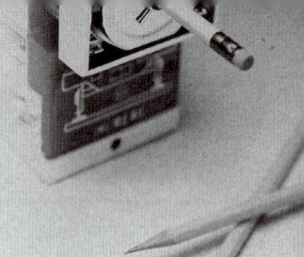

Sample Item Read the following passage and answer the question.

In 1622, first European colonists brought honeybees to North America since they had imported many of the crops that depend on honeybees for pollination. Lots of them escaped and spread rapidly as far as the Great Plains, the broad prairie which lies east of the Rocky Mountains. Honeybees did not naturally cross the Rocky Mountains; they were carried by ship to California in the early 1850s.

Of all the insects, honeybees are the most commercially valuable since they are insects that can be moved for the purpose of pollination. There are about fifty crops known to depend on these pollinators, including such crops as vegetables, fruits, nuts, and animal feeds, as well as non-cultivated plants which help prevent erosion.

Honeybees are also valued for many other reasons. Honey that they produce itself is a delicious food and also has various uses in the food industry. Other honeybee products, such as beeswax, pollen, propolis, and royal jelly, are marketed for medical and other purposes. Beeswax and propolis, for example, are used in lotions, candles and varnishes.

---

*i*BT TOEFL Reading

Question 1

REVIEW HELP BACK NEXT

HIDE TIME 02:10:00

---

1. **Directions:** An introductory sentence for a brief summary of the passage is provided below. Complete the summary by selecting the THREE answer choices that express the most important ideas in the passage. Some sentences do not belong in the summary because they express ideas that are not presented in the passage or are minor ideas in the passage.

   The honeybee is a commercially important insect that performs a vital function in agriculture.

   - •
   - •
   - •

   Ⓐ It took long time to spread honeybees all over the North America since honeybees couldn't cross the Rocky mountains.

   Ⓑ Since the first honeybees were brought to North America for pollination, they quickly spread all around the nation.

   Ⓒ Honeybees are the only insects that can pollinate many kinds of crops human beings consume in everyday life.

   Ⓓ Royal jelly produced by honeybees is the most useful product because it has many medicinal and other uses.

   Ⓔ The primary commercial importance of honeybees lies in their necessity for the pollination of fifty crops.

   Ⓕ Besides pollination, the honeybee produces honey and beeswax, among other useful products.

Overview

Prose Summary

Prose Summary 문제는 전체 주제와 중심 주제를 몇 개의 문장으로 요약할 수 있는가를 평가하는 유형이다. 지문 요약문제(Prose summary)는 iBT TOEFL에서 새롭게 출제되는 문제로 글의 내용을 정확히 이해해야 하며 문제의 난이도가 높은 유형이다. 수험자가 전체 글을 제대로 이해하고 또한 요약할 수 있는가를 측정하는 것이 이 유형의 주목적이다.

Question Type

Directions: An introductory sentence for a brief summary of the passage is provided below. Complete the summary by selecting the THREE answer choices that express the most important ideas in the passage. Some sentences do not belong in the summary because they express ideas that are not presented in the passage or are minor ideas in the passage. **This question is worth 2 points.**

Drag your answer choices to the spaces where they belong. To review the passage, click on View Text.

Introductory sentence will be given here

-
-
-

General Strategy

1. 각 단락별 핵심적인 내용을 파악한다.
2. 보기가 잘못된 내용(false)을 말하고 있지 않은지, 중요한 정보(main information)를 언급하고 있는지 부연 내용(minor information)인지를 판별한다.
   - 보기의 내용이 지문에 나온 것인지 없는 것인지를 판단한다.
   - 지문에 나온 소재를 다루고는 있지만 잘못 언급하고 있는 보기는 제거한다.
   - 지문에 근거하여 사실인 내용을 다루는 보기들 중에서 예나 부연 설명을 하는 주변 내용은 summary에 포함되지 않는다.

Tips

1. 실제 화면에서는 컴퓨터 마우스를 이용해 주어진 표에 답을 드래그해야 한다. 다른 문제들과는 다르게 요약 문제는 문제가 화면 전체를 다 차지하지만 답을 푸는 도중에 다시 지문 화면으로 돌아갈 수 있다.
2. 부분 점수가 있다. 올바른 수의 답을 선택하면 총 2점을 얻지만 만약 세 개의 답을 골라야 하는데 두 개만 올바르게 고르면 1점을 받고, 세 개의 답 중 한 개만 정답이거나 아무것도 제대로 고르지 못하면 0점 처리된다.

Basic Drill

Choose the best summary of each paragraph

Find the major point of each paragraph.

1

P1 Play therapy is a recent discipline in mental health. It has its roots in psychotherapy, Rogerian counseling, and Axline's methods. It attempts to help people, regardless of age, with life's problems through play. It has been proven to be especially effective for those people who have difficulty expressing themselves through language.

(A) Play therapy has been used for a long time in mental health practices for those having problems in their life.

(B) Play therapy is a fairly new mental health discipline with its roots in Rogerian counseling and Axline's methods.

(C) Play therapy can effectively help people who have difficulty expressing themselves through language.

P2 Most people associate play therapy with children because often they are the ones least able to communicate their thoughts well and are helped the most by this therapy. Play therapy allows children to explore thoughts and feelings with the help of a trained therapist. Through repeating the actions from TV shows or stories, a play therapist can help children successfully face previously overwhelming emotions and problems.

(A) Children are the ones who can get successfully helped by play therapy since they often lack of communication skills.

(B) Play therapy allows children to experiment with the therapist's thoughts and feelings to learn how to face their problems.

(C) Children can be helped by a well-trained therapist who knows how to provoke children's feelings through plays.

P3 The key to successful treatment is the therapist's ability to gain the trust of the children, which allows the therapist to get enough information from the children during the sessions to be able to help them. Those children are reluctant to express a problem because they are afraid or ashamed. Then they won't talk to the therapist at all. During play therapy, reality seems to be suspended and the children feel safe as they start to trust the therapist and talk about their individual problems.

(A) Play therapists should trust children in order to access children's information.

(B) Information that is important for future treatment can be gained from the children.

(C) Earning the trust of the children is the most important element, prior to opening up their mind.

VOCABULARY   **therapy** 치료, 요법   **discipline** 학과, 학문 분야   **psychotherapy** 심리요법   **regardless of** ~을 개의치 않고   **explore** 탐구하다, 조사하다   **face** 직시하다   **previously** 이전에   **overwhelming** 압도하는   **gain** 얻다, 획득하다   **reluctant (to)** 내키지 않는   **ashamed** 부끄러워   **suspend** 일시 중지하다

Basic Drill

Choose the best summary of each paragraph

Find the major point of each paragraph.

2

P1 Medical researchers have known for years that plant foods contain lifesaving ingredients including vitamins and minerals. But recently, they discovered phytochemicals, a series of chemical compounds found only in plants. While they can be found in some grains and nuts, they are especially abundant in brightly colored fruits and vegetables. These chemicals are what make cherries red and broccoli green. However, they do much more than make plants pretty; they also protect human beings from disease.	(A) Phytochemicals are found in fruits and vegetables but are most prevalent in nuts and grains. (B) Phytochemicals add color to some plants as well as provide health benefits to humans. (C) Beyond vitamins and minerals in plant foods, other chemicals that color the food were found.
P2 In clinical tests, phytochemicals have been shown to prevent diseases. Some phytochemicals, called antioxidants, are known to protect cells against damage and therefore help prevent certain kinds of cancers. Another type of phytochemical found in cabbages reduces the damaging effects of estrogen, a hormone linked to breast cancer in women. Other phytochemicals have been shown to prevent high blood pressure, diabetes and heart disease. They have even been shown to slow down the affects of aging.	(A) The chemicals have been proven to prevent various health problems. (B) Many cancers have been closely tied to high levels of estrogen in women. (C) Similar phytochemicals that fruits and vegetables contain are revealed to exist in human body as well.

P3 With all the health benefits of phytochemicals, it's no surprise that doctors are recommending a diet with more fruits and vegetables. To benefit from as many naturally occurring phytochemicals as possible, it's best to eat a variety of different colored plants. Yellow, orange, red, green, blue and purple fruits and vegetables all have different types of phytochemicals which add to the potential health benefits when combined together.

(A) The chemicals create a variety of colors in fruits and vegetables, including yellow, orange, red, and green.

(B) To benefit most from the chemicals' effects, a variety of colored fruits and vegetables should be eaten.

(C) Different colors represent different phytochemicals contained in fruits and vegetables.

P4 Phytochemicals are thought to be destroyed or removed by cooking. For this reason, it is believed that industrially processed foods are less beneficial and contain fewer phytochemicals than unprocessed foods. It is claimed that the absence or deficiency of phytochemicals has increased rates of disease in contemporary society.

(A) Unprocessed plant foods are more beneficial because more phytochemicals are not removed during cooking.

(B) Beneficial phytochemicals will be likely to be destroyed by processing the food because of the heat.

(C) Absence of phytochemicals in many instant foods may increase the risk of disease that occur today.

VOCABULARY | ingredient 성분   phytochemical 파이토케미컬(식물성 화학물질)   abundant 풍부한   antioxidant 산화 방지제
prevent 막다; 예방하다   breast cancer 유방암   diabetes 당뇨병   recommend 추천하다   process 화학적으로 가공처리하다   deficiency 부족, 결핍

Vocabulary Preview for Exercise

Read and Pronounce

Exercise 1

demonstrate	[démənstrèit]	*v.* to prove or make a fact clear, especially by reasoning or examples
deny	[dinái]	*v.* to say that something is not true; to refuse to admit something
autobiographical	[ɔ̀:toubáiəgrǽfikəl]	*adj.* relating to someone's life
enthusiasm	[enθú:ziæ̀zəm]	*n.* the feeling of being interested in or excited by something
struggle	[strʌ́gəl]	*v.* to try hard to do something, even though there are some obstacles to succeed
literary	[lítərèri]	*adj.* relating to books that have value as art
fictionalize	[fíkʃənəlàiz]	*v.* to use a real story by changing some details

Exercise 2

unforeseen	[ʌ̀nfɔːrsíːn]	*adj.* not expected to happen or known about beforehand
swallow	[swálou]	*v.* to make food or drink go from the mouth into the stomach
conversely	[kənvə́:rsli]	*adv.* used for introducing part of a sentence that says something that is the opposite of the first part
disruption	[disrʌ́pʃən]	*n.* a situation in which something cannot continue due to a problem
alter	[ɔ́:ltər]	*v.* to change something or someone significantly
fragile	[frǽdʒəl]	*adj.* will break easily, or easily damaged

Exercise 3

primarily	[praimérəli]	*adv.* what is mainly true in a certain situation
man-made	[mǽnméid]	*adj.* something that is made by people, rather than existing naturally
agricultural	[æ̀grikʌ́ltʃərəl]	*adj.* relating to farming
crisis	[kráisis]	*n.* an urgent, dangerous situation
productive	[prədʌ́ktiv]	*adj.* producing or doing in large quantities for the amount of resources used
collapse	[kəlǽps]	*v.* to fail or come to the end completely and suddenly
exhaust	[igzɔ́:st]	*v.* to use all that someone or something has

resident [rézidənt] *n.* someone who lives in a place
livelihood [láivlihùd] *n.* work or other source of income that provides the money to live
migrate [maigréit] *v.* to move to other place to find work or to live
remain [riméin] *v.* to stay in a particular place and not leave there
replenish [riplénis] *v.* make something full and complete again
tactic [tǽktik] *n.* a particular method for achieving something in a particular situation
adopt [ədápt] *v.* to use a particular method or idea

| Check-up |

Fill in the blanks with an appropriate word or phrase. Change the form if needed.

disruption	primarily	alter	deny
agricultural	crisis	demonstrate	exhaust
enthusiasm	tactic	collapse	conversely

1. The play is _____ targeted at families with young children.
2. Paul has repeatedly _____ the rumors that he is getting special treatment.
3. Gallileo couldn't _____ the idea that the earth goes around the sun in his lifetime.
4. I bought this land to use for _____ purposes, not for industrial purposes.
5. The two countries negotiated only to fail to resolve the _____.
6. After Lisa graduated from college, she _____ her face with plastic surgery.
7. The airline strikes caused major _____ for hundreds of people going abroad.
8. Henry's _____ for music has stayed strong throughout his life.
9. The troops could not help turning back to their country when they _____ their food supply.
10. Well, situations that happen in our life are not always bad, _____ they are not always good.
11. Because of the continual earthquakes and floods, the country's tourist industry _____.
12. Her _____ of threatening to quit her job was very effective.

Exercise 1

*i*BT Reading

Question 1 to 3

1. According to paragraph 1, why were slave narratives written?
   - Ⓐ They were written specifically to influence American literature.
   - Ⓑ They contributed money to former slaves.
   - Ⓒ They had a goal of contributing to the end of slavery.
   - Ⓓ They were the histories of African-Americans in pre-slave days.

2. According to paragraph 1, what is known about slave narratives?
   - Ⓐ Slave narratives were printed mostly in the United States.
   - Ⓑ Most of the narratives written by slaves were informative about their lives.
   - Ⓒ They were written yearly over a period of one hundred years, from 1760 to 1860.
   - Ⓓ Because they were written so long ago, the stories mean less now.

3. **Directions:** An introductory sentence for a brief summary of the passage is provided below. Complete the summary by selecting the THREE answer choices that express the most important ideas in the passage. Some sentences do not belong in the summary because they express ideas that are not presented in the passage or are minor ideas in the passage.

   As one of its lasting contributions, the slave narrative helped to cause the end of slavery.

   Answer Choices
   - Ⓐ Slave narratives continue to be written in America, today.
   - Ⓑ The American slave narrative described the life of the slave and helped defeat slavery, while remaining influential in American literature, today.
   - Ⓒ Supporters of slavery believed slaves were intelligent.
   - Ⓓ Slave auctions, disintegration of slave families and escapes were common features of the narratives.
   - Ⓔ The purpose of the writings was to help people see slaves as people who were smart and had feelings just like they did.
   - Ⓕ Around 1825 the autobiographical form became prevalent and fictionalized narratives were introduced to further the Abolitionist cause.

The Slave Narrative

The slave narrative is a kind of story that continues to influence American literature, today. Between the years 1760 and 1860 about 150 narratives written by former slaves were published in the U.S. and England, in large part to help the Abolitionist Movement — the movement to end slavery. These narratives also tell a lot about the lives of African-Americans during that period of time .

The most immediate function of the genre was showing the writer's humanity and intelligence. Not only did the act of telling the story of one's own life demonstrate that the slave or former slave was smart, but it also showed that he or she had an emotional life similar to that of any white person — facts which were denied by supporters of slavery.

From the mid-1820s the genre consciously used much more of the autobiographical form to create enthusiasm for the Abolitionist struggle. They became more literary in form often with the introduction of fictionalized dialogue. Between 1835 and 1865 over 80 such narratives were published. Slave auctions, the break-up of families and frequent escapes were common features of those narratives.

Glossary

Abolitionist a person who campaigns for the end of a particular system

auction a public occasion where things are sold to the person who offers the highest price for them

Exercise 2

*i*BT Reading

Question 1 to 3

1. According to paragraph 1, which of the following is NOT mentioned as a benefit of building dams?
   - Ⓐ Electricity generated from water
   - Ⓑ Creation of jobs and investment
   - Ⓒ Sufficient water supply for farms
   - Ⓓ River control during rainy seasons

2. The word reproduce in paragraph 3 is closest in meaning to
   - Ⓐ feed
   - Ⓑ die
   - Ⓒ breed
   - Ⓓ create homes

3. **Directions**: An introductory sentence for a brief summary of the passage is provided below. Complete the summary by selecting the THREE answer choices that express the most important ideas in the passage. Some sentences do not belong in the summary because they express ideas that are not presented in the passage or are minor ideas in the passage.

   Dams have long been used to manage rivers and streams.

   Answer Choices
   - Ⓐ Environmental problems regarding dams are often the result of hydroelectric power generation.
   - Ⓑ Dams, although beneficial, can cause lasting environmental problems.
   - Ⓒ Sediments are the tiny particles of earth that are moved about by the water's currents.
   - Ⓓ Some animals find it very hard to migrate in the area after a dam has been built.
   - Ⓔ The area around the dams can be negatively impacted from either a lack of, or too much sediment deposition.
   - Ⓕ A number of species of salmon are now on the endangered species list in North America.

Effects of Building Dams

For centuries, humans have tried to control rivers and streams by building dams. A dam can bring benefits to a region by preventing floods, storing water for irrigation and generating hydroelectric power. As a result, most countries invest large amounts of money and manpower in building dams. However, it is necessary to weigh the benefits of building a dam against the negative impacts. Environmental problems associated with the building of dams are often unforeseen and can cause lasting damage.

The land surrounding a dam can be negatively affected in many ways. First of all, the reservoir created behind the dam can swallow large areas of land, causing valleys, farms and forests to go underwater. Secondly, a river carries sediment — fine particles of dirt or sand — along its path and out to sea. But dam building changes the amount of this carried away. Much of the river's sediment will collect behind the dam, causing problems with sediment in the reservoir over time. Conversely, below the dam, the lack of natural sediment deposits can lead to erosion along river banks, extending all the way to the coast. Clearly, dams can have a lasting negative effect on the surrounding land. Furthermore, the effects of the dam often extend to the habitats of plants and animals.

The erection of a dam can split a habitat in two, preventing the natural migration of species within the area. This can especially be a problem for fish, which may need to swim upstream to reproduce. Since the construction of major dams in North America, several species of salmon have been put on the endangered species list. Another problem is the disruption of ecosystems along the river as water flows and sediment deposits are altered. Most river ecosystems are very fragile and support diverse forms of wildlife. Without these habitats, entire species of plants and animals will become extinct.

Glossary
reservoir lake that is used for storing water before it is supplied to people
erosion the gradual destruction and removal of rock or soil in a particular area by weather, rivers and the sea
habitat a place where an animal or a plant normally lives or grows
erection building something or placing something in an upright position
upstream moving against the current or towards the source of a river

Exercise 3

*i*BT Reading

Question 1 to 4

1. The word **fertile** in paragraph 1 is closest in meaning to
   - Ⓐ barren
   - Ⓑ rich
   - Ⓒ germless
   - Ⓓ weedy

2. Based on the information in paragraph 2, which of the following is true about the region?
   - Ⓐ A drought that had lasted for a long time ruined the soil's nutrients.
   - Ⓑ People who had other types of businesses stayed in the region.
   - Ⓒ There was no more land left to develop into farms.
   - Ⓓ Farmers added fertilizer in an attempt to improve the soil.

3. The word **tactic** in paragraph 3 is closest in meaning to
   - Ⓐ method
   - Ⓑ tool
   - Ⓒ farm
   - Ⓓ crop

4. According to paragraph 4, the wind and rain
   - Ⓐ are only a concern in farming if there is a major drought.
   - Ⓑ provided farmers with the inspiration to begin terrace farming.
   - Ⓒ are less likely to destroy soil if crops are not planted in straight lines.
   - Ⓓ have no effect on crops planted in a circular terrace formation.

The Dust Bowl

The name "Dust Bowl" refers to a primarily man-made agricultural crisis that occurred in the southern central part of the United States during the 1930s. Though this part of the country had long been known for its extremely fertile soil and highly productive farms, during the 1930s, the agricultural industry in this region collapsed.

Farmers there had overused the fields, exhausting the soil's nutrients to the point that it was no longer able to support plant life. The soil became extremely poor, and the lack of nutrients, combined with a long drought, caused much of the soil to blow away. The majority of the region's residents lost their livelihoods and were forced to migrate to other parts of the country to find jobs.

The farmers who remained in the area were left to repair the damage and replenish the soil. They learned about different types of sustainable agriculture — that is, ways of farming that did not ruin the soil. One tactic they adopted was crop rotation. In traditional farming, farmers would plant the same crop in their field every year. These crops would take the same nutrients from the soil, and there was not time for them to be replaced before the next growing season. With crop rotation, however, the farmers would put different crops in the fields each year. This way, there was time for nature to replace the nutrients between growing seasons.

Another sustainable farming method that farmers began using was terrace farming. In the past, the farmers had planted their crops in straight lines across the field. This made the soil easy for the wind and rain to wash away. However, farmers realized if they planted the crops in circles, or on hillsides, this process of erosion was much less likely to occur.

Glossary

crop rotation the practice of growing two or more different type of crops in the same space in sequence
terrace a levelled section of a hilly cultivated area, designed to slow or prevent the rapid run-off of irrigation water

Exercise 3

iBT Reading

Question 5

5. Directions: An introductory sentence for a brief summary of the passage is provided below. Complete the summary by selecting the THREE answer choices that express the most important ideas in the passage. Some sentences do not belong in the summary because they express ideas that are not presented in the passage or are minor ideas in the passage.

The Dust Bowl taught American farmers some important lessons about sustainable agriculture.

Answer Choices

Ⓐ The quality of the soil and farms in the southern central part of the United States was well known.

Ⓑ Overuse of the land in combination with a long drought resulted in poor soil, much of which was blown away.

Ⓒ The farmers learned that planting different crops each year helped keep the soil healthy.

Ⓓ The farmers realized that a long drought could blow away much of unhealthy soil.

Ⓔ While most of the farmers left the region, few of them stayed there to repair damages.

Ⓕ Another way to sustain the farm was changing the formation that crops were planted in.

Text Outline Choose the correct text outline of the passage.

(A) P1 — Definition of Dust Bowl
P2 — Background of the problem
P3 — Solutions attempted to recover
P4 — Additional solution to the problem

(B) P1 — Main result of Dust Bowl
P2 — Various causes of the problem
P3 — Development of agriculture
P4 — Occurrence of new agricultural method

The Dust Bowl

The name "Dust Bowl" refers to a primarily man-made agricultural crisis that occurred in the southern central part of the United States during the 1930s. Though this part of the country had long been known for its extremely fertile soil and highly productive farms, during the 1930s, the agricultural industry in this region collapsed.

Farmers there had overused the fields, exhausting the soil's nutrients to the point that it was no longer able to support plant life. The soil became extremely poor, and the lack of nutrients, combined with a long drought, caused much of the soil to blow away. The majority of the region's residents lost their livelihoods and were forced to migrate to other parts of the country to find jobs.

The farmers who remained in the area were left to repair the damage and replenish the soil. They learned about different types of sustainable agriculture — that is, ways of farming that did not ruin the soil. One tactic they adopted was crop rotation. In traditional farming, farmers would plant the same crop in their field every year. These crops would take the same nutrients from the soil, and there was not time for them to be replaced before the next growing season. With crop rotation, however, the farmers would put different crops in the fields each year. This way, there was time for nature to replace the nutrients between growing seasons.

Another sustainable farming method that farmers began using was terrace farming. In the past, the farmers had planted their crops in straight lines across the field. This made the soil easy for the wind and rain to wash away. However, farmers realized if they planted the crops in circles, or on hillsides, this process of erosion was much less likely to occur.

Vocabulary Test

Choose the closest meaning of each underlined word or phrase.

1. He decided to <u>adopt</u> a more careful approach to the problem.
   (A) adapt   (B) contact   (C) take up   (D) put out

2. I was <u>reluctant</u> to ask for help finishing my assignment.
   (A) acute   (B) unwilling   (C) peculiar   (D) ready

3. The play <u>explores</u> the relationship between art and money.
   (A) reflects   (B) describes   (C) integrates   (D) probes

4. Anemia is caused when the body has an iron <u>deficiency</u>.
   (A) sufficiency   (B) surplus   (C) want   (D) defect

5. The person who gets this job should be knowledgable in a wide range of <u>disciplines</u>.
   (A) research   (B) subjects   (C) investigation   (D) certificates

6. As a result of the strike, lots of employees were fired; namely, they lost their means of <u>livelihood</u>.
   (A) outcome   (B) money   (C) home   (D) occupation

7. The man I met there yesterday was so rude and I had the <u>overwhelming</u> desire to leave.
   (A) sensitive   (B) shocking   (C) dreadful   (D) strong

8. The country has an <u>abundant</u> supply of oil and tourist attractions.
   (A) plentiful   (B) insufficient   (C) keen   (D) sterile

9. The sculpture is very <u>fragile</u> and you have to treat it carefully.
   (A) ponderous   (B) unstable   (C) random   (D) important

10. James was <u>previously</u> employed as a part-timer.
    (A) precisely   (B) preciously   (C) once   (D) compatibly

11. The technology has advanced, and it's very difficult to tell real flowers from the <u>man-made</u> ones now.
    (A) permanent   (B) brilliant   (C) rough   (D) artificial

12. Any one can run for election <u>regardless of</u> age or sex.
    (A) in general   (B) irrespective of   (C) fond of   (D) according to

30   Part A

Chapter 02
SCHEMATIC TABLE

Chapter 2
Schematic Table

Sample Item **Read the following passage and answer the question.**

New developments in genetic engineering may make it possible for scientists to commercially grow meat in a laboratory. Laboratory-meat production would involve removing muscle tissue from cattle or other animals presently used for meat. This tissue would be cultured and then later used to create the texture of "real" meat.

This would, ultimately, lessen the dependence on meat producing animals, like cattle, and the resulting environmental problems. Cattle herds, for example, damage the environment by over-grazing and emitting methane gas into the atmosphere. Laboratory-meat production may help to slow global warming and protect grasslands from further destruction.

In addition to benefiting the environment, meat-eaters might benefit from eating laboratory-produced meat as well. Scientists could control the nutrients in the meat, replacing the unhealthy or less-healthy fats with healthier choices. It could stop the use of drugs and antibiotics being used on meat producing animals. This would be healthier for consumers.

However, laboratory-grown meat may initially be more expensive due to problems with the development process. The cost of setting up and operating meat laboratories may discourage development. Beef muscle is more difficult to grow than fish or chicken because beef muscle needs to exercise or stretch to have almost the same texture as natural meat. Fortunately, fish and chicken have grown fairly well in laboratories.

*i*BT Reading

Question 1

1. **Directions:** Select the appropriate phrases from the answer choices and match them to the types of meat to which they relate. TWO of the answer choices will NOT be used. **This question is worth 3 points.**

   Answer Choices

   Ⓐ Can be more healthy with selective nutrients
   Ⓑ Uses antibiotics and drugs for better meat
   Ⓒ Can cause some problems in certain cultures
   Ⓓ Can reduce or remove possible diseases
   Ⓔ Can lessen the dependence on fish or chicken
   Ⓕ Can contain unnecessary nutrients for humans
   Ⓖ Can cost a lot of money to produce it at first

   Laboratory Meat
   •
   •
   •

   Natural Meat
   •
   •

Overview

Schematic Table

지문에서 분류, 비교/대조, 또는 논쟁하는 내용을 이해하고 주어진 문장들 중에서 관련있는 내용을 골라 2~3가지 분류 중에 어디에 해당하는지를 선택하는 문제이다.

Question Type

- **Directions:** Select the appropriate phrases/statements from the answer choices and match them to the types of X to which they relate. TWO of the answer choices will NOT be used. **This question is worth 3 points.**

General Strategy

1. Principles or Features
   어떤 기준 또는 특징들에 의한 분류 또는 비교/대조인지를 파악한다. 예를 들어, 크기에 의한 분류인가, 서식지에 따른 분류인가를 파악하고, 비교/대조의 경우에는 어떤 특징들을 비교 또는 대조하고 있는지 파악한다.

2. Relationship between features
   분류 또는 비교/대조되는 특징들 사이의 관계에 주목한다. 예를 들어, 습지가 서식지인 동물들은 습지에 산다는 특징 때문에 나타날 수 있는 또다른 특징을 열거하게 되므로 그 관계에 의한 특징을 파악하도록 한다.

Tips

9개의 answer choices에서 7개의 정답을 알맞게 분류하거나 7개의 answer choices에서 5개의 정답을 알맞게 분류하도록 한다. Answer choices에서 정답을 click and drag하여 해당 column에 drop하여 넣는다.

Partial Credits

* 5 answer table: 0–3점
  (0–2 correct: 0, 3 correct: 1, 4 correct: 2, 5 correct: 3)
* 7 answer table: 0–4
  (0–3 correct: 0, 4 correct: 1, 5 correct: 2, 6 correct: 3, 7 correct: 4)

Basic Drill

Recognize features compared

Read the following passage and complete the outline.

1

P1 Tundra regions, extremely cold regions, have no trees and are characterized by a lack of rain or snow, lack of diversity of animal life, and simplicity of plant life. There are two types of tundra regions on earth: Arctic and alpine. While both share the previously mentioned characteristics, each also has its own unique features.

P2 The arctic tundra circles the North Pole and goes south to the forests of northern Europe and Asia while the alpine tundra regions are located at the tops of high mountains all over the world. The arctic tundra has an extremely short period when plants can grow — only about 50 days per year, and winter temperatures can go as low as minus 30 degrees Celsius. But, because the summer temperatures can get as high as 55 degrees, this region can sustain life. For the alpine tundra areas, there are longer days of growing seasons, about 180 days. But the nighttime temperature is usually below freezing, no matter what time of year it is.

P3 Though there is little rain or snow falls in the arctic tundra regions, the poor drainage allows the ground to stay moist — there are many small ponds and bogs here. This nourishes the plants that grow there. These plants, while simple, are adapted to the climate; for instance, they don't need much sun to make food for themselves. And despite their shallow roots, they can withstand the strong winds. Unlike in the arctic tundra, the soil in alpine tundra regions is much better drained. Also the plants are well adapted to the climate as well. As with the Arctic tundra plants, alpine tundra plants such as grasses, mosses, and lichens, which are the dominant vegetation in both types of tundra, have evolved to not only survive, but actually thrive in the harsh conditions that would kill other plants. And here, as well as in the Arctic tundra, the plants have shallow roots and possess the ability to withstand extremes of temperature.

P2	Tundra Region	Arctic tundra	Alpine tundra
Location		Circles the North Pole- goes south to the forests of northern Europe and Asia	① _____
Plant's growing season		② _____ per year	③ About _____
Temperature		Extreme weather between winter and summer Winter - ④ _____ Summer - ⑤ _____	Extreme weather between day and night Night temperature is ⑥ _____ at any time of year

P3	Tundra Region	Arctic tundra	Alpine tundra
⑦ _____		⑧ _____	Much better drained
Plant adaptation		well adapted to the climate - many small ⑨ _____ and ⑩ _____ nourish plants	well adapted to the climate - thrive in the harsh conditions
⑪ _____		Shallow but withstand the strong winds	Shallow but withstand ⑫ _____

VOCABULARY arctic 북극의 alpine 고산 지대의, 산악의 characteristic 특질, 특성 drainage 배수 moist 축축한, 습기 있는 bog 습지, 늪 adapt 적응하다 despite ~에도 불구하고 shallow 얕은 withstand 견디어내다, 버티다 freezing 어는 moss 이끼 lichen 지의, 이끼 vegetation 식물 evolve 진화(발달)시키다 thrive 잘 자라다, 무성해지다 harsh 거친

Vocabulary Preview for Exercise

Read and Pronounce

Exercise 1

visible	[vízəbəl]	*adj.* something seen
obscure	[əbskjúər]	*v.* to cover something so that it cannot be seen

Exercise 2

figure	[fígjər]	*n.* an important person in a certain capacity
passively	[pǽsivli]	*adv.* accepting what happens without trying to control or change events or to react things
slogan	[slóugən]	*n.* a short phrase used in advertising
curious	[kjúəriəs]	*adj.* be interested in something, wanting to know more about it
strict	[strikt]	*adj.* exact and accurate
alternative	[ɔːltə́ːrnətiv]	*adj.* another possibility, usually different from the first option
site	[sait]	*n.* a piece of ground is used for a particular purpose or where a particular thing happens
immensity	[iménsəti]	*n.* large size
memorable	[mémərəbəl]	*adj.* something worth remembering because it is special in someway

Exercise 3

characterize	[kǽriktəràiz]	*v.* to describe someone or something as a particular kind of person or thing
generate	[dʒénərèit]	*v.* to cause something to develop, start or grow
standardize	[stǽndərdàiz]	*v.* to change things so that they have the same or similar features
interpretation	[intə̀ːrprətéiʃən]	*n.* an explanation of the meaning or importance of something
screen	[skriːn]	*v.* to question people in order to find out ability, health, loyalty, etc.
normally	[nɔ́ːrməli]	*adv.* in most situations or in the usual way
gauge	[geidʒ]	*v.* to consider and weigh people's actions, feelings, or intentions

| Check-up |

Fill in the blanks with an appropriate word or phrase. Change the form if needed.

characterize	visible	standardize	passively
curious	figure	screen	slogan
immensity	alternative		

1. Ronald doesn't pay attention in classes. He just stares at the blackboard _____.
2. There should be _____ methods of getting there.
3. The signboard was so big that it was _____ from the great distance.
4. He was the dominant _____ in biotechnology in this century.
5. Steve is _____ about the language and the culture in my country.
6. How would you _____ yourself?
7. I think we have to make a _____ test for entrance exam.
8. The _____ of stars you can see at night is incredible.
9. This new test will _____ people at risk for cancer.
10. Our company's new advertising _____ cost 1,000,000 won to create.

Exercise 1

iBT Reading

Question 1 to 4

1. The word **inclined** in paragraph 1 is closest in meaning to
   - Ⓐ tilted
   - Ⓑ located
   - Ⓒ cast
   - Ⓓ lowered

2. The word **circular** in paragraph 2 is closest in meaning to
   - Ⓐ dark
   - Ⓑ traveling
   - Ⓒ spherical
   - Ⓓ hanging

3. The word **it** in paragraph 2 refers to
   - Ⓐ Sun
   - Ⓑ Moon
   - Ⓒ Earth
   - Ⓓ eclipse

4. **Directions:** Select the appropriate statements from the answer choices and match them to the type of eclipses to which they relate. TWO of the answer choices will NOT be used.

   Answer choices
   - Ⓐ The Earth lies between the Sun and the Moon.
   - Ⓑ The Moon lies between the Earth and the Sun.
   - Ⓒ It can be seen from any part of the Earth.
   - Ⓓ It reflects light from the Moon back to the Sun.
   - Ⓔ It gives a chance to observe curving light rays.
   - Ⓕ It can be only viewed in certain areas of the Earth.
   - Ⓖ It helps to study the Moon's disk more effectively.

   Lunar Eclipse
   •
   •

   Solar Eclipse
   •
   •
   •

Eclipses

An eclipse occurs whenever the Sun, Earth and Moon line up exactly. If this occurrence is at the time of a full moon where the Moon passes through the Earth's shadow, it is called a lunar eclipse. A full moon is the lunar phase that occurs when the Moon lies on the opposite side of the Earth from the Sun. A full moon is the only time when a lunar eclipse is possible; at that time the moon may move through the shadow cast by the Earth. However, because the Moon's orbit around the Earth is inclined by 5°, the Moon may pass above or below the shadow, so a lunar eclipse does not occur at every full moon.

Every year there are at least two lunar eclipses. Unlike a solar eclipse, which can only be viewed in a certain relatively small area of the world, a lunar eclipse may be viewed from anywhere on the night side of the Earth. The lunar eclipse was the first hint that the earth was round, as scientists safely observed Earth's circular shadow crossing the surface of it.

A solar eclipse occurs when the Moon passes in front of the Sun and obscures it totally or partially. A solar eclipse is not as widely visible as a lunar eclipse. A solar eclipse can only be seen in a band across the Earth as the Moon's shadow moves across its surface. During a solar eclipse, scientists observe parts of the Sun, such as solar flares, sunspots, the size and composition of the Sun's corona, and how light rays bend as they near the Sun's gravitational field.

Glossary

full moon the moon when the shape of it is like a complete circle
lunar relating to the Moon
solar flare a violent explosion in the Sun's atmosphere with an energy equivalent to tens of millions of hydrogen bombs
corona the circle of light around the Sun when the Moon passes in front of it during an eclipse

Exercise 2

*i*BT Reading

Question 1 to 3

1. The word hands-on in paragraph 2 is closest in meaning to
   - Ⓐ useful
   - Ⓑ passive
   - Ⓒ active
   - Ⓓ transformed

2. According to paragraph 1, which of the following is true about Dewey's effective learning style?
   - Ⓐ A student should bring their materials to study in the classroom.
   - Ⓑ A teacher should guide the learning process using his own questions.
   - Ⓒ It has changed traditional thoughts about the way students should study.
   - Ⓓ A student learns best by participating in activities during the class.

3. **Directions:** Select the appropriate statements from the answer choices and match them to the type of views to which they relate. TWO of the answer choices will NOT be used.

   Answer choices

   - Ⓐ Students can benefit much from the immensity of information.
   - Ⓑ Students should learn by participating in experiments.
   - Ⓒ Students might not know which information is important.
   - Ⓓ Teachers shouldn't restrict children's natural characteristics.
   - Ⓔ Teachers cover age-appropriate materials for the students.
   - Ⓕ Too much information might not be useful without a guidance.
   - Ⓖ Students' learning should not be limited to the classrooms.

   Dewey's Views
   •
   •
   •

   Other Views
   •
   •

Applications of John Dewey's Educational Philosophy

John Dewey, a major figure in 20th century U.S. education, had a major impact on educational philosophy in general. Dewey believed a student learned best by being active, that is a teacher lecturing while a student sits passively was not an effective learning style. His slogan was that schools should encourage children to "Learn by doing." He wanted people to realize that children are naturally active and curious. Many students have benefited greatly from a more practical involvement in their own learning through laboratory courses and hands-on types of learning sessions in schools.

His ideas, while quite popular, were never broadly and deeply integrated into the practices of American public schools, though some of his values and terms were widespread. Many schools and teachers thought that effective education can not be done without the strict control and guidance of the teacher and retained limited and controlled teaching styles. Creativity and active, practical student involvement was to be reserved for a time and place like recess or a writing exercise.

Dewey believed the role of education is to broaden the learning experience. This part of his philosophy has most influenced alternative learning sites, where his overall philosophy has been best reflected in places such as museums and libraries. These sites have applied Dewey's less formal methods of education by changing the way they educate visitors to their sites.

Unfortunately, if a museum's student-guided learning experience becomes too broad, learning gets lost in the immensity of data being experienced. In those cases when a teacher is not present, students may find interesting, memorable material, but it might not be helpful to the present or future academic success of the students.

Glossary

retain to maintain something
recess (Am E) a period of time between school classes when students can eat, rest, or play

Exercise 3

*i*BT Reading

Question 1 to 4

1. The word **ambiguous** in paragraph 1 is closest in meaning to
   - Ⓐ plain
   - Ⓑ aspiring
   - Ⓒ deceptive
   - Ⓓ indefinite

2. Based on the information in paragraph 1, which of the following can be true about the Rorschach Inkblot Test?
   - Ⓐ It consists of 10 different images with various stories.
   - Ⓑ It is a sequence of thirty-one inkblot pictures.
   - Ⓒ It uses the images of inkblot that are not clearly known what they are.
   - Ⓓ It requires a story, including thoughts and feelings of characters.

3. The word **yield** in paragraph 2 is closest in meaning to
   - Ⓐ resist
   - Ⓑ produce
   - Ⓒ resign
   - Ⓓ abandon

4. The word **diagnose** in paragraph 3 is closest in meaning to
   - Ⓐ separate
   - Ⓑ picture
   - Ⓒ determine
   - Ⓓ compose

Psychological Testing

There are a number of psychological tests that help psychologists and psychiatrists learn more about people. Two popular projective tests are the Rorschach Inkblot Test and the Thematic Apperception Test (TAT). The Rorschach Inkblot Test is a sequence of ten inkblots, each of which the participant is asked to observe and then characterize. The TAT is a series of thirty-one pictures of people in ambiguous relationships. The participant's task is to generate a story to accompany each picture, including the thoughts and feelings of the people in each picture.

Different aspects of a participant's descriptions or explanation are scored to yield an evaluation of the individual's personality. No standardized answers exist to aid in the interpretation of these tests. More recently the TAT has been used primarily as a research tool, for example, to study dreams, and, to a lesser degree, to screen workers for high-stress jobs.

The second type of tests, the inventory-type, contains fixed answers to questions. These tests typically do not allow the "free" responses of projective tests. A classic example is the Minnesota Multi-Phasic Personality Inventory-2 (MMPI-2). This test presents the participant with a variety of statements. The participant's task is to answer "true," "false" or "can't say" to each question. This test, too, yields a characterization of the personality of the test-taker. It is normally used to diagnose abnormalities in personality, such as psychosis.

Other examples of inventory-type psychological tests are power tests that gauge abilities in certain areas through the use of extremely difficult questions, and speed tests that have very easy items to answer, but in a limited time.

Glossary

psychologist a person who has studied the human mind and tries to explain why people behave in a certain way
psychiatrist a doctor who treats people suffering from mental disorders
abnormality an unusual feature of a person's body or in a person's behavior
psychosis mental illness which make people lose contact with reality

Exercise 3

*i*BT Reading

Question 5

5. Directions: Select the appropriate statements from the answer choices and match them to the type of tests to which they relate. TWO of the answer choices will NOT be used.

Answer choices

- (A) Images are shown to participants.
- (B) Answers should be based on the given statements.
- (C) Some participants can get a perfect score on a test.
- (D) A numbered score can be used to tell about the personality.
- (E) Time spent on finishing a test is counted as the score.
- (F) Interpretations of a response can be different.
- (G) Most employees are required to take one of the tests.

Projective Test
-
-

Inventory-Type
-
-

Text Outline Choose the correct text outline of the passage.

(A) P1 — Projective tests: Definition and classification into two types
   P2 — Projective tests: Uses and the reason
   P3 — Inventory of tests: Definition and examples and use
   P4 — Inventory of tests: Other examples

(B) P1 — Projective tests: Description and examples
   P2 — Projective tests: Evaluation and uses
   P3 — Inventory of tests: Description and examples and use
   P4 — Inventory of tests: Other examples

Psychological Testing

There are a number of psychological tests that help psychologists and psychiatrists learn more about people. Two popular projective tests are the Rorschach Inkblot Test and the Thematic Apperception Test (TAT). The Rorschach Inkblot Test is a sequence of ten inkblots, each of which the participant is asked to observe and then characterize. The TAT is a series of thirty-one pictures of people in ambiguous relationships. The participant's task is to generate a story to accompany each picture, including the thoughts and feelings of the people in each picture.

Different aspects of a participant's descriptions or explanation are scored to yield an evaluation of the individual's personality. No standardized answers exist to aid in the interpretation of these tests. More recently the TAT has been used primarily as a research tool, for example, to study dreams, and, to a lesser degree, to screen workers for high-stress jobs.

The second type of tests, the inventory-type, contains fixed answers to questions. These tests typically do not allow the "free" responses of projective tests. A classic example is the Minnesota Multi-Phasic Personality Inventory-2 (MMPI-2). This test presents the participant with a variety of statements. The participant's task is to answer "true," "false" or "can't say" to each question. This test, too, yields a characterization of the personality of the test-taker. It is normally used to diagnose abnormalities in personality, such as psychosis.

Other examples of inventory-type psychological tests are power tests that gauge abilities in certain areas through the use of extremely difficult questions, and speed tests that have very easy items to answer, but in a limited time.

Vocabulary Test

Choose the closest meaning of each underlined word or phrase.

1. When winter comes, we have to withstand the harsh coldness in Norway.
   (A) mild (B) severe (C) outstanding (D) massive

2. It's normally much colder in December.
   (A) considerably (B) usually (C) absolutely (D) probably

3. The warning lights were clearly visible.
   (A) observable (B) bright (C) visual (D) optical

4. The building was not designed to withstand the weight of the frame.
   (A) add (B) measure (C) endure (D) lower

5. Thanks to strong sunlight and plentiful water, flowers in my garden are thriving.
   (A) withering (B) growing (C) falling (D) bearing

6. They were reacting passively toward the notice.
   (A) submissively (B) abnormally (C) decisively (D) thoroughly

7. I'm curious to know her reaction at the news.
   (A) uninterested (B) anxious (C) confident (D) inquisitive

8. The excitement was generated by changes in relationships with my classmates.
   (A) ended (B) engendered (C) recovered (D) disappeared

9. I can't accept the idea that human beings have evolved from apes.
   (A) survived (B) resembled (C) developed (D) declined

10. Dense fog obscured everything so we can't see anything.
    (A) hid (B) exposed (C) lit (D) cleared

PROGRESS TEST

READING SECTION DIRECTIONS

In this section you will read two passages and answer reading comprehension questions about each passage. Most questions are worth one point, but the last question in each set is worth more than one point. The directions indicate how many points you may receive.

You will have 30 minutes to read all of the passages and answer the questions. Some passages include a word or phrase that is underlined in blue. Click on the word or phrase to see a definition or an explanation.

When you want to move on to the next question, click on **Next**. You can skip questions and go back to them later as long as long as there is time remaining. If you want to return to previous questions, click on **Back**. You can click on **Review** at any time and the review screen will show you which questions you have answered and which you have not. From this review screen, you may go directly to any question you have already seen in the reading section.

When you are ready to continue, click on the Dismiss Directions icon.

Progress Test 1

*i*BT Reading

Question 1 to 6

1. The word **considerably** in paragraph 1 is closest in meaning to
   - (A) mildly
   - (B) importantly
   - (C) substantially
   - (D) usefully

2. The word **viable** in paragraph 2 is closest in meaning to
   - (A) additional
   - (B) possible
   - (C) impractical
   - (D) hopeful

3. The word **crucial** in paragraph 2 is closest in meaning to
   - (A) expensive
   - (B) frightening
   - (C) noticeable
   - (D) important

4. Based on the information in paragraph 2, how did high-rise construction differ from traditional building?
   - (A) Steel was inserted in walls to keep the building from collapsing.
   - (B) A frame was used to hold a building's weight, rather than walls.
   - (C) Steel frames were added to the fourth story to increase a building's height.
   - (D) Smaller buildings were constructed with the brick and the iron.

5. The word **these** in paragraph 3 refers to
   - (A) passengers
   - (B) buildings
   - (C) elevators
   - (D) stairs

6. Based on the information in paragraph 4, which of the following is true?
   - (A) The role of skyscrapers in cities is to attract new city inhabitants.
   - (B) Building lots of skyscrapers is one way to show country's economic power.
   - (C) Population growth had a significant impact on city planning and building.
   - (D) New York City is the most popular for its famous skyscrapers.

Skyscrapers

Until the end of the 19th century, most city skylines had some tall buildings. However, none of these was as tall as the skyscrapers we know today. By the end of the first decade of the 20th century, however, the height of buildings began to increase considerably. Not only did the changing country make this necessary, but advances in technology made the skyscraper possible.

The first technological development that made skyscrapers a viable option for city planners was the mass production of cheap steel. This metal, which is created by modifying iron, is extremely strong. That strength is crucial to the construction of these massive structures. This is because skyscrapers cannot bear weight the same way that smaller buildings do. While buildings up to four stories tall can use their walls to hold up the weight, anything higher would collapse. Thus engineers had to design steel frames for these giant buildings. The walls are then attached to the frames.

A second development necessary to the creation of skyscrapers was the invention of the elevator. While there were a few six- or seven-story buildings in cities before skyscrapers, to have to walk up so many flights of stairs was a real problem. Thus, if buildings were to get higher, something was needed to transport people and goods up to those heights. The first passenger elevators installed in buildings were seen in 1857. By 1898, these were being used in increasingly tall buildings all over the country.

The third factor in the mass building of skyscrapers was not technological, but social. The sheer mass of humanity found in major American cities at the beginning of the 20th century, coupled with the fact that many cities had a limited supply of land meant that a revolutionary new building style was needed. This was nowhere so true as New York City. If the city hoped to house and support the thousands of new people who arrived there each day, it needed to provide more buildings. Thus, the trend in construction was up toward the sky rather than outward.

Glossary

skyscraper a very tall building in a city
sheer used for emphasizing the degree or the the amount of something

Progress Test 1

*i*BT Reading

Question 7

7. **Directions:** An introductory sentence for a brief summary of the passage is provided below. Complete the summary by selecting the THREE answer choices that do not belong in the summary because they express ideas that are not presented in the passage or are minor ideas in the passage.

For a number of reasons, cities needed a new way of building in the 20th century.

-
-
-

Answer Choices

(A) Steel, with its high strength and low cost to produce was a major factor in the development of the skyscraper.

(B) To keep down the cost of steel, it was mixed with various other metals and then used in skyscrapers.

(C) Population growth and limited land in major cities demanded tall buildings like skyscrapers.

(D) Big cities had to build tall buildings and expand the residential areas for workers in the cities.

(E) The advance of elevator had much to do with skyscraper development.

(F) The technology used in creating elevators for the skyscrapers is now used in most of buildings in the world.

Skyscrapers

Until the end of the 19th century, most city skylines had some tall buildings. However, none of these was as tall as the skyscrapers we know today. By the end of the first decade of the 20th century, however, the height of buildings began to increase considerably. Not only did the changing country make this necessary, but advances in technology made the skyscraper possible.

The first technological development that made skyscrapers a viable option for city planners was the mass production of cheap steel. This metal, which is created by modifying iron, is extremely strong. That strength is crucial to the construction of these massive structures. This is because skyscrapers cannot bear weight the same way that smaller buildings do. While buildings up to four stories tall can use their walls to hold up the weight, anything higher would collapse. Thus engineers had to design steel frames for these giant buildings. The walls are then attached to the frames.

A second development necessary to the creation of skyscrapers was the invention of the elevator. While there were a few six- or seven-story buildings in cities before skyscrapers, to have to walk up so many flights of stairs was a real problem. Thus, if buildings were to get higher, something was needed to transport people and goods up to those heights. The first passenger elevators installed in buildings were seen in 1857. By 1898, these were being used in increasingly tall buildings all over the country.

The third factor in the mass building of skyscrapers was not technological, but social. The sheer mass of humanity found in major American cities at the beginning of the 20th century, coupled with the fact that many cities had a limited supply of land meant that a revolutionary new building style was needed. This was nowhere so true as New York City. If the city hoped to house and support the thousands of new people who arrived there each day, it needed to provide more buildings. Thus, the trend in construction was up toward the sky rather than outward.

Progress Test 2

*i*BT Reading

Question 1 to 6

1. The word **criteria** in paragraph 1 is closest in meaning to
   - Ⓐ measurements
   - Ⓑ criticisms
   - Ⓒ roles
   - Ⓓ standards

2. According to paragraph 1, which of the following is NOT true about financial aid?
   - Ⓐ Financial aid is an award to an individual student.
   - Ⓑ Financial aid helps students pay for tuition or other higher education costs, such as room and board.
   - Ⓒ Financial aid is not considered the way the government funds public education.
   - Ⓓ Financial aid is classified based on the organizations by whom it is given.

3. The word **potential** in paragraph 2 is closest in meaning to
   - Ⓐ accomplishment
   - Ⓑ claim
   - Ⓒ possibility
   - Ⓓ power

4. According to paragraph 2, what is true of merit-based scholarships?
   - Ⓐ Financial need is not required when deciding a scholarship student.
   - Ⓑ They are considered need-based awards.
   - Ⓒ Only organizations may give them.
   - Ⓓ Poor athletes with financial needs can not qualify.

5. The phrase **their parents** in paragraph 3 refers to
   - Ⓐ parents of students filing a FAFSA form
   - Ⓑ parents of U.S. students
   - Ⓒ parents who want to return to college
   - Ⓓ parents qualifying for financial aid

6. According to paragraph 3, what role does FAFSA play in college funding?
   - Ⓐ FAFSA determines if a student should be funded throughout the college years.
   - Ⓑ Without filing out a FAFSA form, no U.S. student can receive a college education.
   - Ⓒ FAFSA determines who meets the criteria for federal student aid.
   - Ⓓ FAFSA allows students and their families to access merit-based organizations.

52 Part A

Two Types of Financial Aid

Financial aid, in the United States, is funding intended to help students pay for college, university, or private school tuition or other costs, such as room and board. This aid is not considered general governmental funding for public education. Financial aid refers to an award to a specific individual student. This aid may be classified based on the criteria by which it is awarded. Two types of financial aid are available to college students: merit-based awards or need-based awards.

Merit-based awards include scholarships given by individual colleges or universities and scholarships awarded by outside organizations. Such scholarships are usually given because of high academic achievements, although some merit-based scholarships may be awarded for special talents, leadership potential or other characteristics. Merit-based scholarships are sometimes awarded regardless of the financial need of the applicant. At many universities, every student is considered for a merit-based scholarship. At other universities, however, a student must apply for such a scholarship. Athletic scholarships are a form of merit-based awards that consider athletic talent as a special criterion.

Need-based awards are given based on the financial need of the student. To receive federal need-based financial aid, a student must file a special form, the Free Application for Federal Student Aid (FAFSA). This form must be filled out yearly by all U.S. college students and their parents to determine if they qualify for federal financial aid. Need-based financial aid can come in the form of grants, loans and work-study programs. Grants and work-study programs do not have to be repaid. Many students also apply for government and private loans, since grants and work-study programs generally can not cover the total cost of a college or university education. Federal education loan programs offer low interest rates and flexible repayment plans, which make them an attractive way to finance a college education.

Progress Test 2

iBT Reading

Question 7

7. **Directions:** Select the appropriate phrases from the answer choices and match them to the type of awards to which they relate. TWO of the answer choices will NOT be used.

Answer Choices

- (A) Is given to the parents to support their children
- (B) Is awarded for special talents or skills
- (C) Is awarded based on the financial statement
- (D) Needs to be repaid
- (E) Provides a part time job to support themselves
- (F) Is lent to the students at low interest rate
- (G) Is depending on a student's achievement

Merit-Based Award
-
-

Need-Based Award
-
-
-

Two Types of Financial Aid

Financial aid, in the United States, is funding intended to help students pay for college, university, or private school tuition or other costs, such as room and board. This aid is not considered general governmental funding for public education. Financial aid refers to an award to a specific individual student. This aid may be classified based on the criteria by which it is awarded. Two types of financial aid are available to college students: merit-based awards or need-based awards.

Merit-based awards include scholarships given by individual colleges or universities and scholarships awarded by outside organizations. Such scholarships are usually given because of high academic achievements, although some merit-based scholarships may be awarded for special talents, leadership potential or other characteristics. Merit-based scholarships are sometimes awarded regardless of the financial need of the applicant. At many universities, every student is considered for a merit-based scholarship. At other universities, however, a student must apply for such a scholarship. Athletic scholarships are a form of merit-based awards that consider athletic talent as a special criterion.

Need-based awards are given based on the financial need of the student. To receive federal need-based financial aid, a student must file a special form, the Free Application for Federal Student Aid (FAFSA). This form must be filled out yearly by all U.S. college students and their parents to determine if they qualify for federal financial aid. Need-based financial aid can come in the form of grants, loans and work-study programs. Grants and work-study programs do not have to be repaid. Many students also apply for government and private loans, since grants and work-study programs generally can not cover the total cost of a college or university education. Federal education loan programs offer low interest rates and flexible repayment plans, which make them an attractive way to finance a college education.

PART B
Basic Comprehension Questions

Chapter 03 Sentence Simplification
Chapter 04 Vocabulary
Chapter 05 Reference
Chapter 06 Details

Progress Test 3-4

Chapter 03
SENTENCE SIMPLIFICATION

Chapter 3

Sentence Simplification

Sample Item Read the following passage and answer the question.

Question 1

1. Which of the sentences below best expresses the essential information in the highlighted sentence in the passage? *Incorrect* choices change the meaning in important ways or leave out essential information.

   Ⓐ Vines around their houses make it easy for people to walk across their shelters in the rain.

   Ⓑ Their structures made of vines allow people to move and cross easily in the rainy season.

   Ⓒ People cover the area between the huts with vines in the rainy season for better movement.

   Ⓓ People moving vines between huts can easily cross structures without trouble in the rain.

Shabono

The Yanomamo, a South American tribe, live in circular villages that they call shabonos deep within the rain forest. Within the shabonos, it's the responsibility of each man to build a shelter of poles and vines for himself, his wife or wives, and his children. The structures themselves are arranged around a central courtyard that is considered a common area for the villagers. ==Interestingly, the area between the huts is covered with vines, which allows for easy movement between structures, enabling people to cross without trouble during the rainy season.== As a security measure, a high wall made of sharpened poles surrounds the entire village.

STUDY POINT 하이라이트된 문장의 핵심 내용은 오두막 사이를 덮은 넝쿨의 기능에 대한 이야기이다. "allows for easy movement"와 "enabling people to cross without trouble"은 같은 의미로 반복을 피하고 단순화시킨다.

Overview

Sentence Simplification

Sentence Simplification 문제는 지문 안에 나오는 다소 길고 어려운 문장을 간단하게 표현하고 있는 문장을 찾을 수 있는가를 평가하는 문항이다. 글쓴이는 주제나 요지를 전달하고자 할 때 특정 내용을 글쓴이의 독특한 문체로 표현하는 경우가 있다. 글을 단순화하는 데에는 보통 구조를 바꾸거나 동의어를 사용하여 paraphrase(바꾸어 말하기) 하게 되며, 예시, 부연과 같이 보조적인 역할(less important)을 하는 내용은 삭제하며 요약한다.

1) 요약(summary)
2) 재진술(paraphrasing)

Question Type

Which of the sentences below best expresses the essential information in the highlighted sentence in paragraph X? *Incorrect* choices change the meaning in important ways or leave out essential information.

General Strategy

1. 중요하지 않은 정보는 포함하지 않으며, 중요한 정보는 paraphrase된다.

    – less important information
    - examples
    - appositives (동격, 비한정)

    – important information
    - main sentence
    - qualifiers (한정)

2. 오답의 유형을 파악한다.

    – included less important information
    – missed essential information
    – changed meaning of the information

Basic Drill | Find the right paraphrasing

Underline less important information and find the right paraphrased sentence.

1 Many invertebrate animals that do not have a spine have tough outer shells that protect their organs, such as lobsters that have tough outer shell systems that provide rigidity.

(A) Many invertebrate animals protect their bodies with tough outer shells.
(B) Many invertebrate animals don't have spines, but they have hard shells.

2 Birds known as brood parasites such as cuckoos and cowbirds, put their eggs in the nests of other birds that will actually raise the parasites' young.

(A) The babies of brood parasites are raised by other birds after the parasites drop them off in their nests.
(B) Cuckoos and cowbirds put their eggs in the nests of other birds because they are brood parasites.

3 Beatrix Potter, an author and illustrator, was encouraged to publish her first book, *The Tale of Peter Rabbit*, but she struggled to find a publisher until 1902.

(A) Beatrix Potter was both an author and illustrator of *The Tale of Peter Rabbit*.
(B) Beatrix Potter's first book was accepted by a publisher in 1902.

4 The first domesticated cats were used in Egypt over 5,000 years ago to control rodents, keeping mice and rats away from grain stores.

(A) Cats have been employed by Egyptians over 5000 years to kill rodents.
(B) Egyptians made cats house pets because they helped control mice and rats.

5 Adolescents, who are between the ages of 12 and 20 as teenagers, are moving from the world of childhood into adulthood, and often struggle as they learn to grow into mature adults.

(A) Adolescence is a difficult time for teenagers between 12 and 20 because they have to learn many things.
(B) Many adolescents have a hard time adjusting to and learning adult roles as they grow from childhood into maturity.

6 Some modern adhesives, such as Superglue and Krazy Glue which are extremely strong, are becoming increasingly important in modern construction and industry since these instant adhesives can hold thousands of pounds.

(A) Superglue and Krazy Glue are recent adhesives used in many fields of industry to keep heavy materials together.
(B) Some adhesives are becoming very essential in some industries because of their ability to hold very heavy weights.

VOCABULARY   invertebrate 무척추 동물의   spine 척추   organ 기관   parasite 기생 동물; 남의 둥지에 알을 낳는 새   struggle 분투하다
domesticated (동물이) 길든   rodent 설치 동물   adolescent 청소년   mature 성숙한   adhesive 접착제

Basic Drill 2

Analyze the wrong paraphrasing

Choose the right paraphrase and analyze wrong paraphrases. Put **1** for missing essential information / Put **2** for focusing only on examples / Put **3** for changed information.

1 In the United States in the second half of the 20th century, the practice of exchanging cards was extended to include the giving of all manner of gifts including roses and chocolate.

(A) In the 20th century in the United States, roses and chocolate were exchanged with cards. _____

(B) People started to give gifts with cards in the United States in the 20th century. _____

(C) All types of gifts began to be exchanged in the beginning of the 20th century in the United States. _____

2 Chinese foot binding probably originated when a prince's wife in the Sung Dynasty had her feet bound to aid in her performance of a special dance.

(A) A Sung Dynasty woman had her feet bound after performing a special dance. _____

(B) A wife of a prince in the Sung Dynasty used to perform a particular dance. _____

(C) Foot binding was likely started when a prince's wife danced with her feet bound. _____

3 While the Baroque's details were often hideous and ugly, Rococo's details showed curving leaves, swirling clouds and other curves found in nature.

(A) The Rococo style imitated the decoration of Baroque art but didn't use monsters. _____

(B) Unlike ugly details of Baroque, Rococo showed curved forms found in nature. _____

(C) Rococo arts are usually ornamented in a style that can be seen in nature. _____

4 By considering the effect each plant has on encouraging or discouraging insects, the gardener can use plant combinations to attract beneficial insects and repel harmful ones.

(A) Gardeners can use certain plants to control wanted or unwanted insects. _____

(B) Various kinds of plants are used to control the number of insects in the garden. _____

(C) A gardener would use certain kinds of plants to discourage or repel insects. _____

5 Old Faithful is perhaps the most popular U.S. geyser, a pressurized spring of hot water that wells up from underground, for the water shoots out to a height of 100 feet or more.

(A) The hot water forced out very high has made Old Faithful the most liked geyser in the United States. _____

(B) Old Faithful is one of many 100 foot geysers found on the earth, shooting hot water from pressurized streams. _____

(C) Old Faithful is a geyser where hot water comes up through the ground and shoots up to 100 feet. _____

6 An octopus' self-protective mechanisms allow it to squeeze into small places, like the crack of a rock and also to squirt blinding dark ink at its predator, so the predator can only see ink.

(A) An octopus can innately squeeze into small cracks of an underwater rock to keep itself safe when a predator appears. _____

(B) An octopus can protect itself with the ability to squash itself and hide in a narrow space and to blind its attacker with dark ink. _____

(C) An octopus uses dark ink to blur itself so it can earn some time to run into a crack of a rock. _____

VOCABULARY **hideous** 끔찍한, 무시무시한 **swirling** 소용돌이 치는 **repel** 쫓아버리다 **old Faithful** 올드 페이스풀(미국 옐로스톤 국립공원에 있는 간헐천) **geyser** 간헐천 **pressurized** 가압된 **well (up)** 솟아 나오다, 분출하다 **mechanism** 수법, 기교 **squeeze** 밀어넣다, 쑤셔넣다 **crack** 갈라진 틈 **squirt** 뿜어대다, 분출시키다

Vocabulary Preview for Exercise

Read and Pronounce

Exercise 1

dislodge	[dislédʒ]	*v.* to force something out of the position where it is fixed
tissue	[tíʃuː]	*n.* the substance that animal and plant cells are made of
risky	[ríski]	*adj.* dangerous and failure is likely
induce	[indjúːs]	*v.* to cause something mentally or physically
undergo	[ʌndərgóu]	*v.* to experience something, often unpleasant but necessary
radical	[rǽdikəl]	*adj.* new and very different from the usual way

Exercise 2

retain	[ritéin]	*v.* to continue to have something
elaborate	[ilǽbərèit]	*adj.* to explain in detail or something complicated
trivial	[tríviəl]	*adj.* not serious, interesting, or valuable
stringed instrument	[striŋd ínstrəmənt]	*n.* a musical instrument that has strings, such as a violin
sob	[sáb]	*v.* to cry loudly and noisily
percussion	[pəːrkʌ́ʃən]	*n.* an instrument which needs to be hit, such as a drum

Exercise 3

barley	[báːrli]	*n.* a grain that is used for food, beer, and whisky
ultimately	[ʌ́ltəmitli]	*adv.* After a process or activity has ended, a final conclusion
doom	[duːm]	*v.* to make someone or something certain to fail, or be destroyed
pasture	[pǽstʃər]	*n.* grassland for farm animals to eat
adequate	[ǽdikwit]	*adj.* good enough or large enough for its purpose
livestock	[láivstòk]	*n.* animals, such as sheep, which are kept on a farm
sustain	[səstéin]	*v.* to provide the conditions for something to happen or exist
barren	[bǽrən]	*adj.* a dry, empty place where plants cannot grow
persist	[pəːrsíst]	*v.* to continue to do something even with many problems
cease	[siːs]	*v.* to have something to stop

| Check-up |

Fill in the blanks with an appropriate word or phrase. Change the form if needed.

undergo	pasture	induce	radical
barren	sustain	sob	doom
dislodge	trivial	persist	risky

1. He cultivated the _____ land, inherited from his grandfather and became rich.
2. The dispute about land ownership between the two countries _____ their alliance and now it's broken.
3. It was impossible to _____ the ice from the bridge.
4. This illness is _____ by overwork and stress.
5. Look at his clothes! That is a _____ change from his usual blue jeans and T-shirts.
6. Why do you get so upset over such a _____ matter?
7. Scientists want to know whether the planet Mars can _____ life.
8. Investing in the entertainment industry is kind of a _____ business.
9. My grandmother _____ in wearing a Hanbok everyday.
10. My father _____ new medical treatment for cancer and recovered.
11. When she checked her math grade, she began to _____.
12. The cow was roaming around the _____.

Exercise 1

*i*BT Reading

Question 1 to 4

1. The word **devastating** in paragraph 1 is closest in meaning to
   - Ⓐ paralyzing
   - Ⓑ damaging
   - Ⓒ temporary
   - Ⓓ long-lasting

2. The phrase **this problem** in paragraph 1 refers to
   - Ⓐ a variety of measures
   - Ⓑ recovery time
   - Ⓒ a physical event
   - Ⓓ a stroke

3. According to paragraph 1, which of the following is true about doctors?
   - Ⓐ They have many suggestions to prevent strokes.
   - Ⓑ They discovered various methods to treat strokes.
   - Ⓒ They suggest diets and exercises during treatment.
   - Ⓓ They treat strokes with many exceptional surgeries.

4. Which of the following best expresses the essential information in the highlighted sentence in paragraph 3? *Incorrect* choices change the meaning in important ways or leave out essential information.
   - Ⓐ This is effective in most cases of new medical treatments because it can give doctors enough time for surgery.
   - Ⓑ This increases the chance to save more lives of stroke victims and for them to recover without any disabilities.
   - Ⓒ This saves time for doctors to treat damaged vessels and for victims to recover without major disabilities.
   - Ⓓ This allows doctors to raise the possibilities of curing more patients who suffer from significant strokes.

Strokes

When a blood vessel in the brain explodes or is suddenly blocked by a floating blood clot or dislodged tissue called plaque inside the blood vessels, it causes what is termed a stroke. A stroke can be mild in its effects, but more often than not, a stroke is a devastating physical event resulting in loss of movement, speech, or even life. Doctors suggest a variety of measures, including a healthy diet and exercise, to prevent this problem. However, up until now, there has been very little, except supportive therapy and risky surgery, that could be done for people once a stroke has occurred.

A recent development in stroke treatment, however, may enable stroke victims to suffer fewer and improve their chances for recovery and survival. In the new treatment, doctors induce hypothermia — an extremely low body temperature that slows a person's metabolism — within no more than three hours of a stroke. Patients who have undergone this radical new treatment survived, on average, twice as long as those who didn't receive it.

Hypothermia itself can be a very dangerous condition, which, if left untreated, can lead to death. However, in a tightly controlled medical environment, it appears that decreased metabolism slows the progress of brain tissue destruction. This gives doctors more time to provide lifesaving medical treatment, repairing damaged blood vessels, and the stroke victim, in turn, has a much higher rate of recovery without significant mental or physical disabilities.

Glossary

blood vessel the narrow tubes through which blood flows
clot a sticky lump that forms when blood dries up or becomes thick
metabolism the chemical processes in the body that cause food into energy

Exercise 1

iBT Reading

Question 5

5. Directions: An introductory sentence for a brief summary of the passage is provided below. Complete the summary by selecting the THREE answer choices that express the most important ideas in the passage. Some sentences do not belong in the summary because they express ideas that are not presented in the passage or are minor ideas in the passage.

A blocked or exploding blood vessel leads to a devastating stroke.

Answer Choices

- (A) Doctors suggest a healthy diet and a lot of exercise for the victims of strokes that often cause loss of movement, speech, or even life.
- (B) Tragic strokes have had very few treatment options and only some preventive support up to now.
- (C) In a radical new treatment, hypothermia induced to slow the metabolism improves the chances for recovery and survival.
- (D) Hypothermia raised the body's metabolism, which led to the survival of twice as many people.
- (E) Hypothermia, by itself, can be a very dangerous condition for people in an unsupervised situation.
- (F) With hypothermia, more strokes can be treated without any serious disabilities because of slow brain tissue destruction that gives more time for treatment.

Strokes

When a blood vessel in the brain explodes or is suddenly blocked by a floating blood clot or dislodged tissue called plaque inside the blood vessels, it causes what is termed a stroke. A stroke can be mild in its effects, but more often than not, a stroke is a <mark>devastating</mark> physical event resulting in loss of movement, speech, or even life. Doctors suggest a variety of measures, including a healthy diet and exercise, to prevent <mark>this problem</mark>. However, up until now, there has been very little, except supportive therapy and risky surgery, that could be done for people once a stroke has occurred.

A recent development in stroke treatment, however, may enable stroke victims to suffer fewer and improve their chances for recovery and survival. In the new treatment, doctors induce hypothermia — an extremely low body temperature that slows a person's metabolism — within no more than three hours of a stroke. Patients who have undergone this radical new treatment survived, on average, twice as long as those who didn't receive it.

Hypothermia itself can be a very dangerous condition, which, if left untreated, can lead to death. However, in a tightly controlled medical environment, it appears that decreased metabolism slows the progress of brain tissue destruction. <mark>This gives doctors more time to provide lifesaving medical treatment, repairing damaged blood vessels, and the stroke victim, in turn, has a much higher rate of recovery without significant mental or physical disabilities.</mark>

Exercise 2

iBT Reading

Question 1 to 4

1. The word flourishing in paragraph 1 is closest in meaning to
   - Ⓐ developing
   - Ⓑ prospering
   - Ⓒ spreading
   - Ⓓ changing

2. The word integral in paragraph 2 is closest in meaning to
   - Ⓐ essential
   - Ⓑ unconnected
   - Ⓒ beneficial
   - Ⓓ related

3. According to paragraph 2, the role of a degatari musician is
   - Ⓐ to observe the actions of the performers on stage
   - Ⓑ to conduct the music played by offstage musicians
   - Ⓒ to comfort the actors who are performing on stage
   - Ⓓ to enhance and explain the story being performed

4. Which of the following best expresses the essential information in the highlighted sentence in paragraph 3? *Incorrect* choices change the meaning in important ways or leave out essential information.
   - Ⓐ The geza musicians only produce sound effects of rain or wind.
   - Ⓑ Geza musicians perform on the stage with some instruments.
   - Ⓒ The geza musicians play percussion and bells to produce the sounds of rain and wind.
   - Ⓓ Geza musicians function by making some effects using percussion and bells to go along with the action.

Musicians in Kabuki Theater

Kabuki is one of Japan's traditional theatrical arts. The first Kabuki goes back to the latter part of the 16th century. Though not as flourishing as it once was, the Kabuki theater retains a wide popularity among the people, and is in fact drawing quite large audiences even now. Kabuki is mostly known for elaborate costumes of performers and for the movement of the actors on stage. Even in the realistic Kabuki play, the most trivial gestures are frequently closer to "dancing" than to "acting." Since most of those gesticulation is accompanied by music, many musicians take part in the productions. Some of them appear on stage throughout the Kabuki, while others remain offstage for the entire performance.

The onstage musicians are called *degatari*. While they are not actors who are the most important in the performance, they are integral to the story being told. These people primarily use a stringed instrument to help tell the story that is taking place on stage. For example, imagine that one of the actors is crying. One of the degatari musicians will use his instrument to imitate the sobbing of the actor, making the action more dramatic and easier for the audience to understand. These onstage musicians will also act as narrators for the story, explaining the plot of the play, as needed, to the audience.

Offstage musicians in Kabuki theater are called *geza* musicians. They usually sit in a room off to the right side of the stage. They are able to see the action of the play, but the audience cannot see them. The *geza* musicians primarily use percussion and bells to produce sound effects to accompany the action occurring on the stage, such as the sounds of rain or wind.

Glossary

Kabuki a traditional Japanese form of theater; plays about historical events, moral conflict in love relationships and so on; male actors on the stage

Exercise 2

*i*BT Reading

Question 5

5. Directions: Select the appropriate phrases from the answer choices and match them to the type of musicians to which they relate. TWO of the answer choices will NOT be used.

Answer Choices

- (A) Can be seen by the audience and the actors.
- (B) Trains for several years in a special school.
- (C) Has in-depth knowledge of weather.
- (D) Is able to observe the actors, unseen by other people.
- (E) Mainly uses a stringed instrument.
- (F) Produces special effects of weather during the play.
- (G) Uses bells and percussion a lot in a play.

Degatari
-
-

Geza
-
-
-

Musicians in Kabuki Theater

Kabuki is one of Japan's traditional theatrical arts. The first Kabuki goes back to the latter part of the 16th century. Though not as flourishing as it once was, the Kabuki theater retains a wide popularity among the people, and is in fact drawing quite large audiences even now. Kabuki is mostly known for elaborate costumes of performers and for the movement of the actors on stage. Even in the realistic Kabuki play, the most trivial gestures are frequently closer to "dancing" than to "acting." Since most of those gesticulation is accompanied by music, many musicians take part in the productions. Some of them appear on stage throughout the Kabuki, while others remain offstage for the entire performance.

The onstage musicians are called *degatari*. While they are not actors who are the most important in the performance, they are integral to the story being told. These people primarily use a stringed instrument to help tell the story that is taking place on stage. For example, imagine that one of the actors is crying. One of the degatari musicians will use his instrument to imitate the sobbing of the actor, making the action more dramatic and easier for the audience to understand. These onstage musicians will also act as narrators for the story, explaining the plot of the play, as needed, to the audience.

Offstage musicians in Kabuki theater are called *geza* musicians. They usually sit in a room off to the right side of the stage. They are able to see the action of the play, but the audience cannot see them. The *geza* musicians primarily use percussion and bells to produce sound effects to accompany the action occurring on the stage, such as the sounds of rain or wind.

Exercise 3

*i*BT Reading

Question 1 to 4

1. The word **constituted** in paragraph 1 is closest in meaning to
   - Ⓐ threatened
   - Ⓑ stayed with
   - Ⓒ established
   - Ⓓ destroyed

2. Which of the following best expresses the essential information in the highlighted sentence in paragraph 1? *Incorrect* choices change the meaning in important ways or leave out essential information.
   - Ⓐ Iceland and Greenland initiated the end fate of the colonies of the North Atlantic because of their imposition of tax.
   - Ⓑ Taxation system they adopted had resulted in the advance of ice age in the colonies of the North Atlantic.
   - Ⓒ The adoption of a tax system and cold weather led to failure of the colonies of the North Atlantic.
   - Ⓓ Cold weather due to mini ice age influenced the taxation system in colonies of the North Atlantic.

3. According to paragraph 2, which of the following was the cause of the raised tax?
   - Ⓐ Higher production level estimated by the government
   - Ⓑ Decreased production from crops due to the cold weather
   - Ⓒ Money needed to pay for environmental problems
   - Ⓓ Extended authority the government held

4. According to paragraph 3, which of the following is true about the fields?
   - Ⓐ The wheat had to be used to support the cattle and sheep.
   - Ⓑ They were finally sold to the government to pay the taxes.
   - Ⓒ Tenants failed to manage them efficiently, overusing them.
   - Ⓓ They were ruined but they could still support some animals.

Taxation and the Decline of Vikings

Over one thousand years ago during the MWP, the Medieval Warm Period, the Vikings, led by sailors like Eric the Red, sailed to the islands of the North Atlantic and constituted colonies there. In the early days, the settlers successfully imported and raised animals, such as sheep and cattle, on those islands as early as 790 A.D. They fished, and whenever possible, grew wheat, barley and other grain crops, too. However, they adopted a system of taxation that, when added to the advancing mini-ice age, ultimately doomed the colonies of the North Atlantic such as Iceland and Greenland.

Initially, most of the inhabitants were landowners, working lands and pastures on which they paid taxes. The land was more than adequate for the people's needs and trade with Europeans brought an income from outside the islands. But as the weather changed, it affected the growth of crops and livestock. However, the government raised taxes to levels that couldn't be sustained in order to maintain the amount of money that they used to collect, not thinking of the outcome. People sold their farms to wealthier landowners, who demanded increasingly higher production levels from the workers to pay the taxes.

For their part, the tenants raised as many sheep and cows as possible, with little thought of long-term effects. Unfortunately, many of the fields slowly became barren due to overgrazing and increasingly cold temperatures. A lack of adaptation of the settlers did not help their terrible situation, either. They persisted with their desire for European clothing, tools, and other trade items. Also they insisted on their governmental policies, including higher taxes to make up for increasingly fewer sources of income. Sadly, by 1500 the colony on Greenland ceased to exist. The Icelandic colony continued, but suffered a similar decline over the centuries.

Glossary

Medieval Warm Period an unusually warm period during the European Medieval period, from about the 10th century to the 14th century

taxation the system that a government takes money from people for several uses, such as education, health, and defense

tenant someone who pays rent for the place he lives in, or the land or buildings used

Exercise 3

iBT TOEFL Reading

Question 5

5. Directions: An introductory sentence for a brief summary of the passage is provided below. Complete the summary by selecting the THREE answer choices that express the most important ideas in the passage. Some sentences do not belong in the summary because they express ideas that are not presented in the passage or minor ideas in the passage.

The colonized islands in the North Atlantic were successful at the beginning but declined over the centuries.

Answer Choices

(A) Early Viking settlers of the North Atlantic islands unfortunately chose a burdensome tax system as a mini-ice age arrived after the MWP.

(B) Eric the Red, the founder of the North Atlantic island colonies over a thousand years ago, also encouraged the formation of a system of taxation.

(C) Wealthier landowners took other lands owned by people who couldn't pay the heavy taxes and raised the production levels on the lands.

(D) Due to the weather conditions, the economy declined which caused the government to increase the taxes on the landowners.

(E) In order to pay taxes and to raise the production in cold weather landowners overused their lands, failing to adapt to changing conditions, which led to the end or decline of settlement on the islands.

(F) Many of the settlers on the islands never lost their desire to have European products and other items brought by traders, which led to the eventual decline of the colonies.

Text Outline Choose the correct text outline of the passage.

(A) P1 — Introduction of the colonies and taxes
P2 — Cause and effect of the tax
P3 — Results of taxes in the colonies

(B) P1 — Introduction of taxes in the colonies
P2 — Main causes of taxes
P3 — Other causes of taxes

Taxation and the Decline of Vikings

Over one thousand years ago during the MWP, the Medieval Warm Period, the Vikings, led by sailors like Eric the Red, sailed to the islands of the North Atlantic and constituted colonies there. In the early days, the settlers successfully imported and raised animals, such as sheep and cattle, on those islands as early as 790 A.D. They fished, and whenever possible, grew wheat, barley and other grain crops, too. However, they adopted a system of taxation that, when added to the advancing mini-ice age, ultimately doomed the colonies of the North Atlantic such as Iceland and Greenland.

Initially, most of the inhabitants were landowners, working lands and pastures on which they paid taxes. The land was more than adequate for the people's needs and trade with Europeans brought an income from outside the islands. But as the weather changed, it affected the growth of crops and livestock. However, the government raised taxes to levels that couldn't be sustained in order to maintain the amount of money that they used to collect, not thinking of the outcome. People sold their farms to wealthier landowners, who demanded increasingly higher production levels from the workers to pay the taxes.

For their part, the tenants raised as many sheep and cows as possible, with little thought of long-term effects. Unfortunately, many of the fields slowly became barren due to overgrazing and increasingly cold temperatures. A lack of adaptation of the settlers did not help their terrible situation, either. They persisted with their desire for European clothing, tools, and other trade items. Also they insisted on their governmental policies, including higher taxes to make up for increasingly fewer sources of income. Sadly, by 1500 the colony on Greenland ceased to exist. The Icelandic colony continued, but suffered a similar decline over the centuries.

Vocabulary Test

Choose the closest meaning of each underlined word or phrase.

1. Suddenly, I woke up to see a hideous face at the window.
   (A) mournful   (B) serious   (C) monstrous   (D) gloomy

2. The army was ready near the border of the country, ready to repel any attack.
   (A) fight   (B) reject   (C) launch   (D) drive off

3. Don't behave childishly! You need to be mature!
   (A) grown-up   (B) childlike   (C) anguished   (D) moderate

4. The family struggled a lot to overcome poverty.
   (A) desired   (B) labored   (C) opposed   (D) possessed

5. To irrigate the barren land, he needed to pump water from the river.
   (A) productive   (B) dry   (C) infertile   (D) slant

6. Lots of adolescents tend to be too sensitive or too serious about things they care about.
   (A) adults   (B) boys   (C) pupils   (D) teenagers

7. The argument doomed their contract to failure.
   (A) dismissed   (B) condemned   (C) strengthened   (D) declined

8. Dogs are domesticated animals from early on in human history, and now they are one of mankind's best friends.
   (A) raised   (B) educated   (C) tame   (D) wild

9. The factory needs to maintain an adequate supply of trained workers.
   (A) apparent   (B) actual   (C) multiple   (D) sufficient

10. This country needs a radical reform of the tax system.
    (A) complete   (B) cautious   (C) gradual   (D) inevitable

11. Economic unrest will ultimately lead to even more job losses.
    (A) needlessly   (B) properly   (C) accordingly   (D) eventually

12. The elaborate effort has to be made to complete the plan.
    (A) beneficial   (B) detailed   (C) desperate   (D) fabulous

Chapter 04
VOCABULARY

Chapter 4
Vocabulary

Sample Item Read the following passage and answer the questions.

*i*BT Reading

Question 1 to 2

1. The word **primitive** in the passage is closest in meaning to
   - Ⓐ chief
   - Ⓑ early
   - Ⓒ natural
   - Ⓓ advanced

2. The word **groundbreaking** in the passage is closest in meaning to
   - Ⓐ unusual
   - Ⓑ difficult
   - Ⓒ new
   - Ⓓ immature

Margaret Mead and her Works

Margaret Mead wrote on a variety of subjects, from societies that were considered **primitive** or not at an industrial stage of development to modern issues like war and women's rights that were contemporary and important to people. A prime example of the former was her first major work. There has been controversy surrounding her first book, *Coming of Age in Samoa (1928)*, but her position as a pioneering anthropologist remains firm. This **groundbreaking** anthropological work described the process of adolescent maturation on a Pacific Island. The latter is exemplified by the book *Themes in French Culture*, in which she attempted to apply anthropology to the study of western society.

STUDY POINT 문맥 구조상 from societies that were considered primitive ~ to modern issues...에서 clue를 찾을 수 있다. groundbreaking은 앞에 나오는 'first book'과 'pioneering'에서 clue를 얻을 수 있다.

Overview

Vocabulary

지문에 사용된 특정 어휘와 대체될 수 있는 같은 의미, 또는 유사한 의미의 보기를 고르는 문제이다. 이미 알고 있는 단어라 해도 문맥 속에서 어떤 의미로 사용되었는지를 다시 한 번 확인하고, 선택한 보기를 대입하여 뜻이 제대로 통하는지 살펴야 한다. 평소 글을 읽을 때 모르는 어휘를 바로 사전을 찾는 것보다 signal word를 참고하여 '문맥상 무슨 뜻인가?'를 추론하는 것이 중요하다. 또한 쉬운 단어는 사전적 의미보다 문맥에서 의미를 파악해야 하는 문제가 나오고, 어려운 단어는 대개 동의어를 묻는 문제가 나온다.

Question Type

— The word/phrase X in paragraph X is closest in meaning to

General Strategy

어휘 문제는 주로 문맥 안에 뜻을 가늠할 수 있는 clue가 있고, 그런 clue가 없어도 문맥의 흐름을 통해 답을 유추할 수 있다. 어떤 clue들이 있는지를 파악하고 문맥을 통해 의미를 파악하는 연습을 하도록 하자.

— Exemplifying
— Subordinating
— Comparing
— Explaining (or Elaborating)

Basic Drill I

Clues in the context - Exemplifying

Underline the clues and choose the answer choice that has closest in meaning to the highlighted word or phrase.

1 Animals bred in captivity often exhibit remarkably different behaviors than those found naturally. **For example**, when raised in zoos, lions tend to sleep 4 to 5 hours per day more than they typically do in the wild.

(A) liberally (B) in cages

2 Modern technology made a number of startling astronomical discoveries feasible. **For instance**, in 2003 the latest digital processes enabled scientists to find a heavenly body one, a half times the size of Pluto orbiting the sun at the far reaches of our solar system.

(A) possible (B) valuable

3 Common infectious illnesses often cause fatigue for days, or even weeks. Infectious mononucleosis, **for example**, is a disease seen most commonly in adolescents and young adults, characterized by weariness and sleepiness.

(A) drowsiness (B) weariness

4 A coming-of-age ceremony is an important part of many African cultures and are often formally initiated by the tribal chief. **For example**, when there is an initiation, the chief would start it by giving his speech in the approved manner.

(A) officially begun (B) temporarily stopped
(C) ranked in order (D) responsibly created

VOCABULARY startling 놀랄 만한   infectious mononucleosis 전염성 단구 증가증   adolescent 청소년   coming-of-age ceremony 성인식   initiation 개시

Basic Drill 2 — Clues in the context - Subordinating

Underline the clues and choose the answer choice that has closest in meaning to the highlighted word or phrase.

1 The quality of paper upon which Gutenberg printed his first Bible in 1450 remains **unsurpassed** today, it is so strong and durable **that** nothing today is so unique.

(A) oldest (B) greatest

2 The Romans used **translucent** rocks **that** some light could pass through for their greenhouses because light would be able to enter the building without much heat escaping.

(A) see-through (B) thin

3 Surrounded by others, Socrates **administered toxin**, **which** ultimately took his life.

(A) caused death (B) created the end
(C) took poison (D) followed orders

4 Young people experiencing fever from viral illnesses may take aspirin to **control fever**, **which** can cause a life-threatening disease, Reye's Syndrome. The syndrome can develop after taking aspirin to reduce elevated temperatures.

(A) lower high body heat (B) remove viruses
(C) eliminate disease (D) restrict illness

Basic Drill 3

Clues in the context - Comparing

Underline the clues and choose the answer choice that has closest in meaning to the highlighted word or phrase.

1 Skin normally sheds in microscopic flakes on most people. **But** the skin cells of those who suffer from what is commonly called "fish scale disease" comes off in much larger pieces that resemble the scales of a fish.

(A) remains
(B) falls off

2 Many people consider nuclear power to be a completely inexhaustible source of energy. In truth, **however**, this power source is not actually unending; when radioactive sources such as uranium and plutonium are gone, there will be no more nuclear power.

(A) eternal
(B) transitory

3 **Even though** many people are faced with arthritis, there are not many effective ways developed to stop their suffering from severe joint pain.

(A) refuse to move
(B) endure a painful illness
(C) experience joint disease
(D) use joints to move

4 The DuPont chemical company made public in 1939 that it had produced the first parachutes made from a synthetic material and that it would be producing them for the military. The news had been kept a secret up to that time, **but** was released nationally prior to World War II and was welcomed by many pilots.

(A) announced
(B) hinted
(C) defined
(D) foresaw

VOCABULARY | microscopic 아주 작은, 미세한 flake 얇은 조각 scale 비늘 radioactive 방사성이 있는 joint 관절 synthetic 합성의, 인조의

Basic Drill 4

Clues in the context - Explaining

Underline the clues and choose the answer choice that has closest in meaning to the highlighted word or phrase.

1 A new satellite called 'Messenger' now orbits the planet Mercury. It made that planet perceptible 24 hours a day, allowing scientists a clear view of it.

(A) noticeable (B) permanent

2 Psychologists have discovered that people behave quite differently when they are in a clique, rather than alone. Members of a group quite often repress their own desires and follow that of others, even when the group's action is harmful, or even deadly.

(A) meeting (B) crowd

3 The Hubble Space Telescope was routinely inspected from the time it was launched. Every third month of the year engineering support to check and mend the telescope was provided by NASA.

(A) examined (B) renewed

4 In the past, patients with tuberculosis were confined to an institution for years out of a fear of spreading the disease. They thought that the chain of transmission could be stopped by limiting patients with the active disease to an area where they could start effective anti-tuberculin therapy.

(A) kidnapped (B) restricted
(C) sent away (D) reported

VOCABULARY orbit 궤도를 그리며 돌다 repress 억누르다, 억제하다 deadly 치명적인 routinely 일상적으로, 정기적으로 telescope 망원경 tuberculosis 결핵 transmission 전염 anti-tuberculin 항 투베르쿨린

Vocabulary Preview for Exercise

Read and Pronounce

Exercise 1

wander	[wǻndər]	*v.* to travel from place to place, particularly on foot, without a particular direction or purpose
convert	[kənvə́ːrt]	*v.* to change your beliefs, particularly your religious beliefs
mountainous	[máuntənəs]	*adj.* full of mountains

Exercise 2

operation	[àpəréiʃən]	*n.* the cutting of the body in order to set right or remove a diseased part
addiction	[ədíkʃən]	*n.* a strong need that someone feels to regularly take an illegal or harmful drug
optimistic	[àptəmístik]	*adj.* hopeful about the future and the tendency to expect good things
conscious	[kánʃəs]	*adj.* having all your senses working and able to understand what is happening; knowing, understanding, or recognizing something
uncover	[ʌnkʌ́vər]	*v.* to figure out about something that has been hidden or kept secret
self-destructive	[sélfdistrʌ́ktiv]	*adj.* doing things that are likely to harm you or make you fail
upsetting	[ʌpsétiŋ]	*adj.* making someone feel sad, worried, or angry

Exercise 3

aquatic	[əkwǽtik]	*adj.* growing or living in or near water
solely	[sóulli]	*adv.* involving nothing except the person or thing mentioned
locomotion	[lòukəmóuʃən]	*n.* an ability to move around
apparently	[əpǽrəntli]	*adv.* based primarily on what you have heard, not on what you are certain that it is true

| Check-up |

Fill in the blanks with an appropriate word or phrase. Change the form if needed.

convert	apparently	upsetting	operation
conscious	solely	uncover	optimistic
locomotion	self-destructive		

1. Mary _____ to Catholicism after dreaming of Saint Peter.
2. I became _____ of a sudden change in the atmosphere with Mike's arrival.
3. The surgeon is scheduled to perform a minor _____ at 5.
4. My dad was a very positive man and was always _____ about his future.
5. _____, he gave up his career because his parents forced the family business on him.
6. The police failed to _____ the plot to rob the National Bank.
7. Don't you understand how _____ it is for us to have you resign from the company?
8. A bird uses its wings for _____.
9. Paul's miserable childhood led him to be a sarcastic and _____ person.
10. I am _____ concerned with my family's happiness.

Exercise 1

*i*BT Reading

Question 1 to 4

1. The word integrated in paragraph 1 is closest in meaning to
   - Ⓐ described
   - Ⓑ created
   - Ⓒ mixed
   - Ⓓ took

2. Based on the information in paragraph 2, which of the following is true regarding Queen Isabella?
   - Ⓐ She named Flamenco Spain's national music.
   - Ⓑ She insisted everyone in Spain be the same religion.
   - Ⓒ She demanded the Gypsies move into the mountains.
   - Ⓓ She distrusted the Arabs and the Jews in Spain.

3. The word interacted in paragraph 3 is closest in meaning to
   - Ⓐ engaged
   - Ⓑ responded
   - Ⓒ met up
   - Ⓓ communicated

4. The word incorporate in paragraph 3 is closest in meaning to
   - Ⓐ increase
   - Ⓑ include
   - Ⓒ imitate
   - Ⓓ indicate

The Roots of Flamenco Music

Flamenco music is well known today as the national music of Spain. Its long history dates back to the 15th century. It integrated a wide variety of different musical influences, combining Jewish, Gypsy, and Arab music. This variety of influences is a result of the history of Spain and the people who lived there during this time period.

During the Middle Ages and early Renaissance, many different people lived in Spain. Jews from the Middle East as well as Arabs from North Africa had made a permanent home in Spain. Gypsies, a wandering people from India also made a home in Spain. However, in the year 1492, Isabella, the Queen of Spain, ordered that anyone living in the country was required to either convert to Christianity or leave the country. The Jews and the Arabs did not want to give up their religion, so some moved away, while others moved into the mountainous regions of the country.

It was in the mountains that the Jews, Arabs, and Gypsies interacted. They lived very close and spent much time together. They took the most common music in Spain, which was Christian and religious, and combined it with music from their own cultures. The result was truly unique. When we listen to Flamenco music today, we can still hear the unique rhythms of Arabic music and the repetition of notes and words that is common in Indian music. Additionally, many Flamenco songs incorporate traditional Jewish words and often contain their tunes as well. It is truly a product of many different cultures coming together.

Exercise 1

*i*BT Reading

Question 5 to 6

5. Which of the following best expresses the essential information in the highlighted sentence in paragraph 3? *Incorrect* choices change the meaning in important ways or leave out essential information.

    Ⓐ Religious music was the most common music in Spain and other countries.
    Ⓑ Jews, Arabs and Gypsies have the greatest influence on Spanish music.
    Ⓒ They mixed common Spanish music with their traditional music.
    Ⓓ Christian music in Spain has affected music in many other cultures.

6. **Directions:** An introductory sentence for a brief summary of the passage is provided below. Complete the summary by selecting the THREE answer choices that express the most important ideas in the passage. Some sentences do not belong in the summary because they express ideas that are not presented in the passage or are minor ideas in the passage.

    Flamenco music is a result of a mixture of several different cultures.

    Answer Choices

    Ⓐ Queen Isabella demanded that everyone in Spain become a Christian.
    Ⓑ The different musical influences came together as a result of religious oppression.
    Ⓒ Indian music can be recognized by the same note being played again and again.
    Ⓓ Three distinct and old cultural musical traditions can be clearly heard in today's Flamenco music.
    Ⓔ As the different cultures mixed, each contributed to a unique musical style.
    Ⓕ Some Jews fought against Queen Isabella's decision and declared war.

The Roots of Flamenco Music

Flamenco music is well known today as the national music of Spain. Its long history dates back to the 15th century. It integrated a wide variety of different musical influences, combining Jewish, Gypsy, and Arab music. This variety of influences is a result of the history of Spain and the people who lived there during this time period.

During the Middle Ages and early Renaissance, many different people lived in Spain. Jews from the Middle East as well as Arabs from North Africa had made a permanent home in Spain. Gypsies, a wandering people from India also made a home in Spain. However, in the year 1492, Isabella, the Queen of Spain, ordered that anyone living in the country was required to either convert to Christianity or leave the country. The Jews and the Arabs did not want to give up their religion, so some moved away, while others moved into the mountainous regions of the country.

It was in the mountains that the Jews, Arabs, and Gypsies interacted. They lived very close and spent much time together. They took the most common music in Spain, which was Christian and religious, and combined it with music from their own cultures. The result was truly unique. When we listen to Flamenco music today, we can still hear the unique rhythms of Arabic music and the repetition of notes and words that is common in Indian music. Additionally, many Flamenco songs incorporate traditional Jewish words and often contain their tunes as well. It is truly a product of many different cultures coming together.

Exercise 2

*i*BT Reading

Question 1 to 4

1. Which of the following best expresses the essential information in the highlighted sentence in paragraph 2? *Incorrect* choices change the meaning in important ways or leave out essential information.
    - Ⓐ In cognitive-behavior therapy, negative thoughts are the basic cause of the problems.
    - Ⓑ Cognitive-behavior therapists try to study the problems that lead to negative thoughts.
    - Ⓒ Cognitive-behavior therapists claim bad thoughts cause mild depression, addiction, or fear.
    - Ⓓ A person who seeks for treatment of negative thoughts needs cognitive-behavior therapy.

2. The word undo in paragraph 2 is closest in meaning to
    - Ⓐ listen to
    - Ⓑ obey
    - Ⓒ reverse
    - Ⓓ improve

3. The word drastically in paragraph 2 is closest in meaning to
    - Ⓐ significantly
    - Ⓑ slightly
    - Ⓒ hopefully
    - Ⓓ temporarily

4. The word unresolved in paragraph 3 is closest in meaning to
    - Ⓐ unknown
    - Ⓑ unexpected
    - Ⓒ unsettled
    - Ⓓ unfriendly

Psychoanalysis and Cognitive-Behavioral Therapy

Over the past hundred years, a number of therapies have been developed to help people with a variety of psychological disorders. Two of the most commonly practiced therapies today are cognitive-behavioral therapy and psychoanalysis.

Cognitive-behavioral therapy begins with the idea that the reason a person has the problem such as a mild depression, addiction, or fear is because he has negative thoughts that lead to this problem. Thus, the therapist helps the person learn to undo these thoughts. That is, first, the person becomes aware of the negative thoughts and their impact; then the person learns to replace these negative thoughts with positive ones. This short-term therapy has been very successful for many people, leading them to drastically change their behaviors. The depressed learn to become more optimistic, and so on. This kind of therapy really focuses on the present and the conscious mind.

Psychoanalysis is quite the opposite. It is a longer-term strategy that seeks to help people uncover the root of their inner problems. This kind of therapy begins from the idea that people's problems are a result of unresolved issues deep in their subconscious mind. That is, they aren't even aware of these issues. Yet, these issues cause them to be unhappy or to engage in self-destructive behavior. Thus, the psychoanalyst will frequently ask the person to talk in great depth about his life, especially his childhood, in order to discover and resolve these issues. Psychoanalysts believe that many of adult problems begin in childhood; thus, by going "back in time" and remembering important and possibly upsetting events from the past we can become healthier and happier adults in the present.

Glossary

depression a feeling of sadness and hopelessness; a mental disorder during which people suffer from great sadness, unnatural tiredness and unwillingness to do anything, difficulty in thinking, etc.

Exercise 2

*i*BT Reading

Question 5 to 6

5. The author contrasts the two therapies based on
   - Ⓐ the success rates of each strategy
   - Ⓑ the origination of each kind of therapy
   - Ⓒ the period they last and what they focus on
   - Ⓓ the kinds of patients who are best served by each

6. **Directions:** Select the appropriate phrases from the answer choices and match them to the type of therapy to which they relate. TWO of the answer choices will NOT be used.

   Answer Choices
   - Ⓐ Takes quite long time to treat the patients.
   - Ⓑ Focuses on the present
   - Ⓒ Is best used for people who tend to commit suicide
   - Ⓓ Looks at the past for answers about the present
   - Ⓔ Seeks to retrain a person to think differently
   - Ⓕ Is more effective with young adults
   - Ⓖ Finds out unresolved problems in a person's life

   Cognitive-Behavioral Therapy
   •
   •
   •

   Psychoanalysis
   •
   •
   •

Psychoanalysis and Cognitive-Behavioral Therapy

Over the past hundred years, a number of therapies have been developed to help people with a variety of psychological disorders. Two of the most commonly practiced therapies today are cognitive-behavioral therapy and psychoanalysis.

Cognitive-behavioral therapy begins with the idea that the reason a person has the problem such as a mild depression, addiction, or fear is because he has negative thoughts that lead to this problem. Thus, the therapist helps the person learn to undo these thoughts. That is, first, the person becomes aware of the negative thoughts and their impact; then the person learns to replace these negative thoughts with positive ones. This short-term therapy has been very successful for many people, leading them to drastically change their behaviors. The depressed learn to become more optimistic, and so on. This kind of therapy really focuses on the present and the conscious mind.

Psychoanalysis is quite the opposite. It is a longer-term strategy that seeks to help people uncover the root of their inner problems. This kind of therapy begins from the idea that people's problems are a result of unresolved issues deep in their subconscious mind. That is, they aren't even aware of these issues. Yet, these issues cause them to be unhappy or to engage in self-destructive behavior. Thus, the psychoanalyst will frequently ask the person to talk in great depth about his life, especially his childhood, in order to discover and resolve these issues. Psychoanalysts believe that many of adult problems begin in childhood; thus, by going "back in time" and remembering important and possibly upsetting events from the past we can become healthier and happier adults in the present.

Exercise

*i*BT Reading

Question 1 to 4

1. The word elusive in paragraph 1 is closest in meaning to
   - Ⓐ illusionary
   - Ⓑ superstitious
   - Ⓒ rare
   - Ⓓ evolutionary

2. The word tangible in paragraph 1 is closest in meaning to
   - Ⓐ vague
   - Ⓑ suspicious
   - Ⓒ persuasive
   - Ⓓ concrete

3. The word witnessed in paragraph 3 is closest in meaning to
   - Ⓐ seen
   - Ⓑ proven
   - Ⓒ survived
   - Ⓓ described

4. According to paragraph 3, what reason does the author give for claiming squid fight whales?
   - Ⓐ Photographs fighting each other were taken by sailors.
   - Ⓑ Remains of a squid were found in a whale.
   - Ⓒ Whale parts have been found in a squid's stomach.
   - Ⓓ Whales have been spotted with squids wrapped around them.

The Giant Squid

One of the most mysterious and elusive creatures found in the deep sea is the giant squid. This creature has never been seen alive by scientists and very little is known about its aquatic habits. Once thought to be a figment of mariners' imaginations, we now know they exist for two reasons. One is because sailors and fishermen have supplied photographic documentation of the creatures for many years. The other is more tangible: a few real giant squid have washed up onto beaches around the world.

What exactly is known about these creatures? First, they are mollusks, creatures that have soft bodies and shells that protect them. Clams and snails are examples of other mollusks. Squid have shells, too — however, they are inside their bodies. In addition, they have eight arms, two of which are used to gather food while six are used solely to aid in locomotion through the ocean. Another interesting feature of the giant squid is that its eyes are the biggest of any other animals — they can be as big as eighteen inches across. It isn't only their eyes that are big, though. Giant squid, as their name implies, are huge. Some have been found that were over twenty feet long.

These creatures are so big, in fact, that they frequently get into fights with another giant of the sea: the whale. While no one has ever witnessed a giant squid battling a whale, evidence of their apparently even-matched aquatic struggles exists. Sometimes, giant squid tentacles have been found wrapped around dead whales. Other times, parts of giant squid have been found in the stomachs of whales.

Glossary

a figment of one's imagination something that has been imagined and therefore does not really exist
mollusk a type of animal, usually covered by a hard shell, that has a soft body without bones
even-matched having an equal chance to win
tentacle a long, snakelike, boneless, joint-less limb on certain creatures, used for moving, feeling, seizing, touching, etc.

Exercise 3

iBT Reading
Question 5

5. Directions: An introductory sentence for a brief summary of the passage is provided below. Complete the summary by selecting the THREE answer choices that express the most important ideas in the passage. Some sentences do not belong in the summary because they express ideas that are not presented in the passage or are minor ideas in the passage.

The deep sea living giant squid is one of the most mysterious creatures in nature.

Answer Choices

- (A) Fishermen have said for years that the giant squid exists and they took some photographs of the creature.
- (B) Once thought to be entirely fictitious, the giant squid is now known to be a real oceanic animal.
- (C) The evidence of fighting between giant squid and whales is another thing that proves the existence of giant squid.
- (D) The giant squid is one reason causing the rapid decrease of certain kind of fish.
- (E) Although the giant squid has been proved genuine, many people today still doubt that it's real.
- (F) From the evidence found, it has been learned that giant squid are mollusks and have extremely big eyes and bodies.

Text Outline Choose the correct text outline of the passage.

(A) P1 — Introducing the giant squid: The evidence of its existence
P2 — Elaborating on the description of the giant squid
P3 — Comparing the size between the giant squid and the whale

(B) P1 — Introducing the topic: The giant squid and the evidence of its existence
P2 — Description of the giant squid's appearance
P3 — Evidence of the fight between the giant squid and the whale

The Giant Squid

One of the most mysterious and elusive creatures found in the deep sea is the giant squid. This creature has never been seen alive by scientists and very little is known about its aquatic habits. Once thought to be a figment of mariners' imaginations, we now know they exist for two reasons. One is because sailors and fishermen have supplied photographic documentation of the creatures for many years. The other is more tangible: a few real giant squid have washed up onto beaches around the world.

What exactly is known about these creatures? First, they are mollusks, creatures that have soft bodies and shells that protect them. Clams and snails are examples of other mollusks. Squid have shells, too — however, they are inside their bodies. In addition, they have eight arms, two of which are used to gather food while six are used solely to aid in locomotion through the ocean. Another interesting feature of the giant squid is that its eyes are the biggest of any other animals — they can be as big as eighteen inches across. It isn't only their eyes that are big, though. Giant squid, as their name implies, are huge. Some have been found that were over twenty feet long.

These creatures are so big, in fact, that they frequently get into fights with another giant of the sea: the whale. While no one has ever witnessed a giant squid battling a whale, evidence of their apparently even-matched aquatic struggles exists. Sometimes, giant squid tentacles have been found wrapped around dead whales. Other times, parts of giant squid have been found in the stomachs of whales.

Vocabulary Test

Choose the closest meaning of each underlined word or phrase.

1. The research finally <u>uncovered</u> the composition of the bones.
   (A) solved   (B) revealed   (C) suggested   (D) comprehended

2. <u>Wandering</u> from street to street and taking pictures are one of my hobbies.
   (A) Running   (B) Withering   (C) Drawing   (D) Roaming

3. This dress is made from <u>synthetic</u> material but it can be washed in a washing machine.
   (A) man-made   (B) nylon   (C) raw   (D) analytic

4. Doctors are doing their best to prevent the <u>transmission</u> of the disease.
   (A) control   (B) change   (C) spread   (D) outbreak

5. Jennifer is <u>apparently</u> talented in singing and dancing.
   (A) outstandingly   (B) awkwardly   (C) genuinely   (D) outwardly

6. Don't <u>repress</u> your feelings. Be honest and real.
   (A) release   (B) fake   (C) suppress   (D) oppress

7. Statistics are <u>routinely</u> used in making a marketing plan.
   (A) seldom   (B) usually   (C) practically   (D) directly

8. My father is fighting his <u>addiction</u> to gambling.
   (A) attitude   (B) courage   (C) will   (D) obsession

9. Don't drink the wine! There's a <u>deadly</u> poison in the glass!
   (A) awful   (B) evil   (C) destructive   (D) fatal

10. I'm sure that he is the one who is <u>solely</u> responsible for the failure of the plan.
    (A) firmly   (B) wisely   (C) entirely   (D) incredibly

11. The Soviet Union was the country that launched the first satellite to <u>orbit</u> the Earth.
    (A) unearth   (B) circle   (C) protect   (D) watch

12. At the age of 25, Mike <u>converted</u> to Christianity.
    (A) reformed   (B) transferred   (C) shared   (D) enjoyed

Chapter 05
REFERENCE

Chapter 5
Reference

Sample Item   **Read the following passage and answer the question.**

*i*BT Reading   REVIEW   HELP?   BACK   NEXT

Question 1   HIDE TIME 02:10:00

1. The word **these** in the passage refers to
   - Ⓐ cultures
   - Ⓑ floods
   - Ⓒ myths
   - Ⓓ civilizations

Myths of an Ancient Flood

Myths of an ancient flood that destroyed a large part of civilization are common among many different cultures. There may be a factual basis to **these**. Rather than being a sudden event, though, as is often depicted in the stories, the floods may have been a result of rising sea levels at the end of the last ice age. The rising sea could have claimed hunting grounds and even cities. The recent discovery of what might be a submerged ancient town off the coast of Cuba may provide evidence to support this theory.

STUDY POINT   these 앞에 복수인 명사가 무엇인지 살핀다. myths와 cultures를 각각 대입하여 의미가 맞는 것이 무엇인지 생각해 본다.

Overview

Reference

Reference 문제는 대명사나 지시어가 무엇을 가리키는 지를 평가하는 유형이다. 영어에서는 간결성을 위해 동일한 단어를 사용하지 않고 지시어(reference)를 사용하는데 이는 수험자가 글의 흐름을 제대로 파악하고 있는 가를 측정하는 데 주목적이 있다. 평소 글을 읽을 때 지시어가 나오면 그것이 가리키는 것으로 해석하는 습관을 길러두면 글의 흐름을 놓치지 않고 쉽게 내용을 이해할 수 있을 것이다.

Question Type

– The word / phrase X in the paragraph X refers to

General Strategy

1. 지시어의 성격을 파악하고 지시 대상을 찾는다.
    사람인지, 사물인지, 복수인지, 단수인지 등 지시어의 성격을 파악하고 지시 대상을 찾고, 문장에 대입하여 의미가 올바른 지 확인한다.

    – he, she, it, they
    – this, that, these, those
    – who, which, whose
    – one, then, any, many, each, all, the former, the latter, the other...

2. 지시어가 무엇을 포괄하는 것인지 파악한다.
    앞에서 설명한 내용을 포괄하는 단어가 무엇을 가리키는 지를 파악한다. 대부분 paraphrase되어 있으므로 내용을 잘 이해하도록 한다.

    – this, that, these, those
    – this system, this problem, that effect, that result ...

Basic Drill 1 — Reference - Word

Choose the word or phrase that the highlighted reference refers to.

1 Some frogs have vocal pouches that vary in size and stretch like balloons. **These** allow sounds to echo loudly, which lets the frogs produce mating calls and songs.

*vocal pouch 성낭

(A) Balloons
(B) Pouches
(C) Frogs

2 The increasing trend toward underachievement by school-age males can be tackled from many angles. **One** is to hire more male teachers to serve as role models to help address this problem.

(A) Trend
(B) Angle
(C) Problem

3 Though intended to decrease domestic violence, Prohibition mainly resulted in an upswing in crime. Though alcohol did indeed fuel **it**, banning it was clearly not the way to solve the problem.

(A) domestic violence
(B) upswing in crime
(C) Prohibition

4 Evidence exists that wheat first grew in Mesopotamia and in the Euphrates River Valley. Wheat at the time was originally a wild grass but it was in **the former** that people first realized the potential of this grain.

(A) Mesopotamia
(B) Euphrates River Valley
(C) Evidence

5 Wind, moisture, and atmospheric pressure all collide to create a monsoon. But before the modern era of weather satellites and sophisticated computers, climate scientists had only a basic understanding of how these forces accomplish such a powerful weather pattern.

(A) wind, moisture, pressure
(B) satellites and computers
(C) climate scientists

6 The first half of the 20th century saw an increase in anti-immigrant sentiment. Anger at the influx of Japanese immigrants as well as those from Eastern Europe caused many Americans to call for a halt or a decrease to immigration, ignoring the benefits that, in particular, the latter brought to the country's economy.

(A) Japanese immigrants
(B) Americans
(C) Eastern European immigrants

VOCABULARY vary 다르다 underachievement 낮은 학업 성취 tackle (문제 등을) 다루다 address (어려운 문제 등을) 처리하다, 다루다 domestic violence 가정 내 폭력 Prohibition (미국) 금주법 upswing 상승, 현저한 증가 ban 금지하다 potential 가능성, 잠재력 grain 곡물 collide 충돌하다 monsoon (인도양에서 불어오는) 계절풍, 몬순 sophisticated 정교한 sentiment 감정, 정서 influx 유입 halt 정지, 멈춤 in particular 특히, 그 중에서도

Basic Drill 2

Reference - Phrase

Write what the highlighted references refer to.

---

1 The influence of technology on the music industry cannot be underestimated. Record players enabled people to listen to music without needing live musicians. The same was true for restaurants and bars, as they purchased jukeboxes to play recorded music. While this was perhaps good for consumers and businesses, it did have a negative effect on musicians who wanted work.

① The same _____
② this _____

---

2 In the past, a consumer might need to search used booksellers for months to find a copy of an out-of-print book. And teachers who wanted to assign one to a class were out of luck. Now, however, these print-on-demand publishers are buying copyrights of out-of-print books and making relatively inexpensive copies as they are needed. This way prevents the need for storage of books waiting for sale as well as the need for large print runs.

① one _____
② This one _____

---

3 In the past, people could not buy soap to clean their bodies at a store. Therefore they had to make it at home. Making soap was a two-part process. First, wood ash had to be gathered and processed to make lye. It is a chemical that cleans the dirt off the body. Then the lye was mixed with animal fat which would provide a solid form for the lye. This substance was left to set and soon a bar of soap was created.

① It _____
② This substance _____

4

Having a poisonous bite or large teeth can be very helpful to ensuring an animal's survival. In the absence of these features, however, many animals have characteristics which fool predators into thinking they are more dangerous than they really are. This can be seen in a type of caterpillar that has evolved to have large looking eyespots on its back, making it look more menacing than it really is. Other insects have evolved to resemble stinging wasps, though they themselves actually have no stingers.

① these features _____

② This _____

VOCABULARY | underestimate 과소평가하다 jukebox 주크박스, 자동 전축 assign 할당하다 out of luck 운이 나빠서 ash 재 lye 잿물 predator 포식 동물 caterpillar 모충 evolve 진화시키다, 발달시키다 menace 위협하다 resemble ~을 닮다 stinging 찌르는 wasp 말벌

Vocabulary Preview for Exercise

Read and Pronounce

Exercise 1

access	[ǽkses] *n.* means or right to use, reach, or obtain something
satellite	[sǽtəlàit] *n.* An object sent into space that travels around the Earth in order to receive and send information
incredibly	[inkrédəbli] *adv.* extremely; very
along with	used for mentioning additional people or things that are also included or involved in something
indigenous	[indídʒənəs] *adj.* people who have lived in a place before other people came to live there
reflect	[riflékt] *v.* to show the attitude, nature or existence of something

Exercise 2

spin	[spin] *v.* to turn or go around and around quickly
sticky	[stíki] *adj.* be made of, or covered with a substance which stays fixed to anything it touches, and is used for fastening things together firmly
fiber	[fáibər] *n.* a very thin, thread-like piece of a natural or artificial substance
prey	[prei] *n.* an animal caught and eaten by another animal
ensnare	[ensnέər] *v.* to catch in a trap
remarkable	[rimɛ́ːrkəbəl] *adj.* unusual in a way that impresses or surprises someone

Exercise 3

lawn	[lɔːn] *n.* an area of grass, usually in someone's yard
tidy	[táidi] *adj.* neat and orderly in appearance or habits
admire	[ædmáiər] *v.* to think of or look at with pleasure and respect
prone (to)	[proun] *adj.* likely to do something or be affected by something, particularly something bad
varied	[vέərid] *adj.* includes a wide range of things or people
trim	[trim] *v.* to cut something, such as hair, so that it looks neat

| Check-up |

Fill in the blanks with an appropriate word or phrase. Change the form if needed.

ensnare	prone	trim	along with
spin	incredibly	sticky	tidy
varied	prey	lawn	reflect

1. The test was _____ difficult to pass the first time.
2. She _____ the wheels suddenly in the middle of the highway.
3. My little sister loves strawberry jam; her fingers are always _____ with it.
4. Spiders make webs and catch their _____.
5. Japan is _____ to have earthquakes.
6. The man _____ poor Jane into giving him all of her money she had.
7. I earn my pocket money by mowing the neighbor's _____.
8. I want to be a _____ boy so that my mom can be proud of me.
9. My father is going to _____ the tree in the garden this weekend.
10. The concert hall held _____ performances throughout the year.
11. I could not go to school due to a heavy cold, so my English teacher visited me _____ two other classmates.
12. Dr. Lee insisted that the report did not _____ his own views.

*i*BT Reading

Question 1 to 4

1. The word One in paragraph 2 refers to
   Ⓐ Country
   Ⓑ Network
   Ⓒ Government
   Ⓓ Satellite

2. The word dominated in paragraph 2 is closest in meaning to
   Ⓐ linked
   Ⓑ occupied
   Ⓒ shared
   Ⓓ owned

3. The word these in paragraph 2 refers to
   Ⓐ western satellite stations
   Ⓑ economic policies
   Ⓒ Indian television stations
   Ⓓ Indian contents

4. Which of the following best expresses the essential information in the highlighted sentence in paragraph 4? *Incorrect* choices change the meaning in important ways or leave out essential information.
   Ⓐ The role of women has changed a lot and Indian women have begun to value their work more than marriage.
   Ⓑ Indian parents have begun to adopt the values of their children.
   Ⓒ The principles of young Indians have changed, and now are much different from their parents'.
   Ⓓ Today's young Indians hold values that are as much of a mix between the traditional and the modern, much the same as their parents did.

The Influences of Western Television in India

Countries where television programming was often determined by the state now have access to satellite television networks. Thanks to this, western television programming has expanded far beyond the boundaries of the western world.

One where the influence of western media can be observed is India. Until the early 1990s, Indian television was dominated by Indian content. News programs, Indian movies, and government programming were the main things on Indian TV. However, a change in economic policies allowed the western satellite stations to begin broadcasting. Thus, these were soon replaced by more popular programs.

At first, the only programs broadcast were western news. However, what followed were sports stations, music stations, and entertainment channels featuring American and British TV shows. All of these kinds of stations were incredibly popular with Indian television consumers, and soon western music and television were a big part of Indian youth culture. By the end of the 1990s, over 20 million Indian households had satellite television.

Along with this change in programming has come a change in cultural values. Young Indians today have begun to express different values than those held by their parents, whose values were largely shaped by indigenous cultural norms, such as attitudes about marriage, the role of women and men, and the importance of work and family. These important values have begun to reflect western influences. Fashion has also been affected. Indian teenage girls, for example, are far more likely to mimic the fashions worn by western rock stars rather than the traditional clothes of their mothers. Clearly the influence of western television has been a part of this change.

Exercise 1

*i*BT Reading

Question 5 to 6

5. All of the following are mentioned related to India EXCEPT
   - Ⓐ Indian population who has satellite television
   - Ⓑ The main contents of Indian television programs before the introduction of western programs
   - Ⓒ The influence of western programs on Indian youngsters
   - Ⓓ Kinds of western programs that can be found in India

6. **Directions:** An introductory sentence for a brief summary of the passage is provided below. Complete the summary by selecting the THREE answer choices that express the most important ideas in the passage. Some sentences do not belong in the summary because they express ideas that are not presented in the passage or are minor ideas in the passage.

   The influence of western television is spreading throughout the world.

   Answer Choices
   - Ⓐ India is a good example of a nation affected by western television.
   - Ⓑ Until the 1990s, Indians didn't accept western television as good for their culture.
   - Ⓒ Indian music was heavily influenced by the increase in western entertainment shows.
   - Ⓓ The number and types of western programs found in India expanded a lot during the 1990s.
   - Ⓔ Indian young people have much different values in television programs than their parents do.
   - Ⓕ The difference in the perspectives between young and old Indians is a result of western TV.

The Influences of Western Television in India

Countries where television programming was often determined by the state now have access to satellite television networks. Thanks to this, western television programming has expanded far beyond the boundaries of the western world.

One where the influence of western media can be observed is India. Until the early 1990s, Indian television was dominated by Indian content. News programs, Indian movies, and government programming were the main things on Indian TV. However, a change in economic policies allowed the western satellite stations to begin broadcasting. Thus, these were soon replaced by more popular programs.

At first, the only programs broadcast were western news. However, what followed were sports stations, music stations, and entertainment channels featuring American and British TV shows. All of these kinds of stations were incredibly popular with Indian television consumers, and soon western music and television were a big part of Indian youth culture. By the end of the 1990s, over 20 million Indian households had satellite television.

Along with this change in programming has come a change in cultural values. Young Indians today have begun to express different values than those held by their parents, whose values were largely shaped by indigenous cultural norms, such as attitudes about marriage, the role of women and men, and the importance of work and family. These important values have begun to reflect western influences. Fashion has also been affected. Indian teenage girls, for example, are far more likely to mimic the fashions worn by western rock stars rather than the traditional clothes of their mothers. Clearly the influence of western television has been a part of this change.

Exercise 2

*i*BT Reading

Question 1 to 5

1. The word One in paragraph 1 refers to
   - Ⓐ Web
   - Ⓑ Spider
   - Ⓒ Insect
   - Ⓓ Food

2. The word Unsuspecting in paragraph 2 is closest in meaning to
   - Ⓐ Unaware
   - Ⓑ Unbelievable
   - Ⓒ Unknown
   - Ⓓ Unprepared

3. The word them in paragraph 2 refers to
   - Ⓐ insects
   - Ⓑ spiders
   - Ⓒ webs
   - Ⓓ silk

4. The word hatch in paragraph 3 is closest in meaning to
   - Ⓐ stay safe
   - Ⓑ come out
   - Ⓒ feed
   - Ⓓ protect

5. According to paragraph 3, what do typical spiders do with their egg sacs?
   - Ⓐ They place them under a tree branch or leaf.
   - Ⓑ They attach the sac to a corner of their web.
   - Ⓒ They carry them until the eggs are nearly hatched.
   - Ⓓ They put them in a place protected from danger.

Typical Spiders and Fisher Spiders

When we think of spiders, we most likely imagine small, eight-legged creatures that spin webs primarily for the purposes of catching insects for food. However, this is not true of all spiders. One that is actually different from others in many ways is the fisher spider.

The typical spider web is made of a sticky silk fiber that the spider produces in its abdomen. Unsuspecting insects walk or fly into the web and are unable to escape. The spider then comes and wraps the insect in more silk in order to eat it. Fisher spiders, while they spin webs, use them not for trapping food, but for observation. Instead of relying on their potential prey to get ensnared in the sticky silk web, fisher spiders build webs over water where they can watch the small fish that they live on and strike only when success is probable. They will then use their remarkable speed to catch and kill the prey.

Another difference between typical spiders and fisher spiders is in terms of reproduction. Typical spiders lay thousands of eggs that are then wrapped in the sticky silk for protection. The spider places the egg sac in a secure location and then leaves them to hatch without any further interference. When the baby spiders are born, they go out into the world immediately. However, fisher spiders carry their egg sacs on their body until just a few days before they hatch. Then the fisher spider attaches the sac to a nearby leaf or branch. When the babies are born, they remain near the mother for several weeks before leaving.

Glossary

abdomen the part of the body below a person's waist
sac a part of an animal or plant that is shaped like a small bag and is usually filled with liquid or air

Exercise 2

iBT Reading

Question 6 to 7

6. Which of the following best expresses the essential information in the highlighted sentence in paragraph 2? *Incorrect* choices change the meaning in important ways or leave out essential information.

    (A) Fisher spiders use their webs to catch small fish and to catch other prey that generally live in water.
    (B) Fisher spiders mainly catch small water creatures in the webs they build over water.
    (C) The fisher spider uses its web not as a tool to catch prey but as a place to see its prey and then attack from it at the proper time.
    (D) Fisher spiders build webs so that they can live near the water where their prey lives and therefore attack this prey with a high probability of success.

7. **Directions:** Select the appropriate phrases from the answer choices and match them to the types of spider to which they relate. TWO of the answer choices will NOT be used.

    Answer Choices
    (A) Uses incredible speed to hunt its food
    (B) Catches its food in the web
    (C) Stays near babies for several weeks after birth
    (D) Lives primarily underground when not hunting
    (E) Does not take care of its babies once they are born
    (F) Hunts small rodents and other spiders for food
    (G) Puts its egg sac away from danger

    Typical Spider
    •
    •
    •

    Fisher Spider
    •
    •

Typical Spiders and Fisher Spiders

When we think of spiders, we most likely imagine small, eight-legged creatures that spin webs primarily for the purposes of catching insects for food. However, this is not true of all spiders. One that is actually different from others in many ways is the fisher spider.

The typical spider web is made of a sticky silk fiber that the spider produces in its abdomen. Unsuspecting insects walk or fly into the web and are unable to escape. The spider then comes and wraps the insect in more silk in order to eat it. Fisher spiders, while they spin webs, use them not for trapping food, but for observation. Instead of relying on their potential prey to get ensnared in the sticky silk web, fisher spiders build webs over water where they can watch the small fish that they live on and strike only when success is probable. They will then use their remarkable speed to catch and kill the prey.

Another difference between typical spiders and fisher spiders is in terms of reproduction. Typical spiders lay thousands of eggs that are then wrapped in the sticky silk for protection. The spider places the egg sac in a secure location and then leaves them to hatch without any further interference. When the baby spiders are born, they go out into the world immediately. However, fisher spiders carry their egg sacs on their body until just a few days before they hatch. Then the fisher spider attaches the sac to a nearby leaf or branch. When the babies are born, they remain near the mother for several weeks before leaving.

Exercise 3

iBT Reading

Question 1 to 4

1. The phrase this feature in paragraph 1 refers to
   - Ⓐ a green grass lawn
   - Ⓑ the happy dog
   - Ⓒ the white picket fence
   - Ⓓ the chimney

2. Based on the information in paragraph 1, which of the following is NOT true?
   - Ⓐ During the 17th century, only the wealthy could afford a grassy yard.
   - Ⓑ Prior to grass lawns, many Americans had dirt yards.
   - Ⓒ A grassy yard is often considered as a status symbol today.
   - Ⓓ To complete the image of typical American home, a family should have the white fence.

3. The phrase tended to in paragraph 2 is closest in meaning to
   - Ⓐ planted
   - Ⓑ cared for
   - Ⓒ watered
   - Ⓓ fixed up

4. The word they in paragraph 2 refers to
   - Ⓐ Americans
   - Ⓑ The English
   - Ⓒ native grasses
   - Ⓓ English lawns

The Development of the Grass Lawns in America

Like the white picket fence, the chimney, and the happy dog running around, the green grass lawn is part of the image of the typical American home. However, until the 18th century, most American houses did not have this feature that is now, in most places, considered normal. Until that point, a grass lawn was considered to be the sign of extreme wealth. A family had to be able to afford to hire groundskeepers to take care of such a lawn. Thus, most Americans had either dirt or a vegetable garden outside of their homes.

In addition to the wealth required to keep a green grass lawn, Americans did not have grasses that were easily tended to. Native North American grasses were not soft and tidy like the grass on English lawns. Instead, they were tough and prone to grow out of control quickly. However, a growing interest in keeping lawns caused the U.S. Agriculture Department to begin researching grasses that might suit the Americans' desire for a soft and tidy English-style lawn which would do well in the varied U.S. climate, too. By 1915, the answer was found in the form of Kentucky Bluegrass, a combination of native grasses and ground covers that soon covered the yards of millions of American homes.

Besides changing the look of the American home, grass lawns also had some effects on technology and the economy. The need to keep the grass well watered, even during the heat of summer, resulted in improvements in home irrigation technology to supply the grass with water. Additionally, the need to keep the grass trimmed led to improvements in mechanical lawn mowers. Today, the lawn care industry generates over 20 billion dollars a year.

Glossary

ground cover plants that can be used to cover the ground because they don't need a lot of care and spread easily

irrigation bringing water to land through a system of pipes, etc. in order to make crops grow

Exercise 3

iBT Reading

Question 5

5. Directions: An introductory sentence for a brief summary of the passage is provided below. Complete the summary by selecting the THREE answer choices that express the most important ideas in the passage. Some sentences do not belong in the summary because they express ideas that are not presented in the passage or are minor ideas in the passage.

Though most American homes have grass today, it was not always considered part of a typical yard.

Answer Choices

- (A) Many wealthy American people had very well-taken-care-of yards until the 18th century.
- (B) The cost of taking care of a lawn limited their ownership to the wealthy.
- (C) Growing needs of having lawns in the U.S. led to the development of the quality grasses.
- (D) The lawnmower would never have been invented without Kentucky Bluegrass.
- (E) The introduction of a grass blend that was easy to raise influenced many relevant businesses.
- (F) It was hard for Americans to manage lawns because of the poor quality of the grasses.

Text Outline Choose the correct text outline of the passage.

(A) P1 — History of green grass lawn in the United States
P2 — Comparison of lawns between the United States and England
P3 — Efforts made to solve the problem

(B) P1 — A problem of having green grass lawn in the past in the United States
P2 — Another problem of having a lawn
P3 — Effect of growing interest in lawns

The Development of the Grass Lawns in America

Like the white picket fence, the chimney, and the happy dog running around, the green grass lawn is part of the image of the typical American home. However, until the 18th century, most American houses did not have this feature that is now, in most places, considered normal. Until that point, a grass lawn was considered to be the sign of extreme wealth. A family had to be able to afford to hire groundskeepers to take care of such a lawn. Thus, most Americans had either dirt or a vegetable garden outside of their homes.

In addition to the wealth required to keep a green grass lawn, Americans did not have grasses that were easily tended to. Native North American grasses were not soft and tidy like the grass on English lawns. Instead, they were tough and prone to grow out of control quickly. However, a growing interest in keeping lawns caused the U.S. Agriculture Department to begin researching grasses that might suit the Americans' desire for a soft and tidy English-style lawn which would do well in the varied U.S. climate, too. By 1915, the answer was found in the form of Kentucky Bluegrass, a combination of native grasses and ground covers that soon covered the yards of millions of American homes.

Besides changing the look of the American home, grass lawns also had some effects on technology and the economy. The need to keep the grass well watered, even during the heat of summer, resulted in improvements in home irrigation technology to supply the grass with water. Additionally, the need to keep the grass trimmed led to improvements in mechanical lawn mowers. Today, the lawn care industry generates over 20 billion dollars a year.

Vocabulary Test

Choose the closest meaning of each underlined word or phrase.

1. Western TV programs are changing the traditional values of <u>indigenous</u> Chinese people.
   (A) industrious   (B) intelligent   (C) native   (D) prejudiced

2. I get angry when someone <u>underestimates</u> me. I find it difficult to forgive them.
   (A) undervalues   (B) make fun of   (C) disagree   (D) criticize

3. I want the government to <u>ban</u> smoking in all buildings.
   (A) discourage   (B) block   (C) break   (D) destroy

4. There are few people who look and act the same way. Character is always <u>varied</u>.
   (A) equal   (B) abundant   (C) fluent   (D) different

5. Mr. Johnson's lecture was terrible! His pronunciation was ridiculous, <u>in particular</u>.
   (A) additional   (B) especially   (C) extremely   (D) surprisingly

6. People who enjoy suntanning are <u>prone</u> to develop skin cancer.
   (A) difficult   (B) sensitive   (C) liable   (D) hopeful

7. As I got older, I began to <u>resemble</u> my mother in appearance.
   (A) repent   (B) fit   (C) be similar to   (D) gain

8. The communication system for honeybees is very <u>sophisticated</u>.
   (A) brilliant   (B) simple   (C) superb   (D) advanced

9. The riot <u>reflected</u> the bitterness of the minority groups in the city.
   (A) showed   (B) doubled   (C) proved   (D) settled

10. Lots of social problems are increasing because of the <u>influx</u> of refugees.
    (A) decline   (B) rush   (C) departure   (D) income

11. This copy <u>varies</u> slightly from the original.
    (A) manufactures   (B) is similar   (C) differs   (D) quotes

12. She has to find out how to <u>address</u> her stage fright when she gives speeches at meetings.
    (A) confirm   (B) threaten   (C) amaze   (D) deal with

Chapter 06
DETAILS

Chapter 6
Details

Sample Item — Read the following passage and answer the question.

*i*BT Reading

Question 1

1. According to the passage, which of the following is NOT mentioned as a reason of Abstraction in the U.S.?
   - Ⓐ Influence of European artistic schools
   - Ⓑ Conflict between Communism and Capitalism
   - Ⓒ Desire to develop the unique artistic school
   - Ⓓ Attempts to represent freedom

Development of Abstraction

The 1950s in the U.S. was the golden period of Abstraction, an art form characterized by the use of shapes and forms rather than realistic depictions. Why was this the case? Prior to the 1950s, Americans were strongly influenced by the European school of Realism. However, at mid-century, American artists were anxious to create their own, unique artistic school. Additionally, other reasons why Abstraction was considered so important were both political and ideological. During the fifties, the ideological battle between Communism and Capitalism was perhaps at its peak. Communist societies encouraged realism in art, with recognizable figures. Abstraction then represented the freedom that Capitalist artists had to express themselves.

STUDY POINT 글쓴이는 미국에서 Abstraction이 생겨난 몇 가지의 이유 또는 배경을 설명하고 있다. 이 중에서 유럽 예술의 영향은 그 시대의 상황을 설명하는 것으로 추상주의가 생겨난 이유는 아니다.

Overview

Details(Fact/Negative facts/detail)

지문에서 언급하는 내용에 대한 세부 정보들이다. 질문은 지문에 대한 '사실' 또는 '거짓'을 이야기하거나 '이유', '원인', '결과', '대상' 등에 대한 세부적인 내용을 묻는다.

다음의 정보가 나오는 부분은 주의 깊게 체크할 필요가 있다. 해당 정보가 나올 때 상습적으로 같이 나오는 signal words를 알아두면 더 효율적이다.

- Definition
- Example- for example/for instance, such
- Benefits (and drawbacks)
- Reason- because (of), due to, as a result of
- Evidence
- Cause
- Result - as a result, therefore, accordingly
- Problem
- Solution(suggestion, advice)

Question Type

1. True/False를 묻는 문제

    — According to paragraph X, which of the following is true about Y ~?
    — All of the following are mentioned in paragraph X EXCEPT
    — Which of the following is NOT mentioned as X?

2. Details를 묻는 문제

    — According to/Based on paragraph X, why/who/what/how ...
    — What is the reason of X?
    — Which of the following best describes X?

General Strategy

1. Factual information questions는 문제에서 묻고 있는 단어 또는 동의어가 나온 부분을 지문에서 찾아 그 주변의 내용을 꼼꼼히 읽어야 한다. 문제의 보기들과 지문의 내용을 비교하면서 정답을 찾는다. 대부분의 경우, 보기는 paraphrase되어 있다는 것을 명심한다.

2. Negative facts questions는 넓은 범위에 걸쳐 내용을 파악해야 한다. 지문에서 언급된 사실을 과장하거나 잘못 말하고 있는 오답들에 주의한다.

Basic Drill 1 — Factual information

Read the passages and answer the questions.

1 Modern technological advances like radio telescopes and satellites have helped modern humans to better understand outer space. Yet, humans have been using tools to understand changes and events in the heavens for thousands of years. One example of this is calendars. Some calendars were created by observing changes in the moon. Others used the movements of the sun and stars to mark the passage of time. Evidence of these ancient calendars can still be found on several different continents. Stonehenge, a massive standing stone circle in England is considered to be a kind of calendar. Some think that it measured the passage of time by the sun. Likewise, stone circles were also used to note the changes in the moon by ancient Native North Americans.

(1) What is one evidence of an ancient tool used to study outer space?

   (A) Stone platforms for noting changes in the moon
   (B) Circular formations used to note the passage of time
   (C) A pyramidical structure used to mark the solstice
   (D) A piece of paper noting the position of the stars

(2) Which of the following is true about the tools?

   (A) Modern technologies revealed that ancient calendars were not precise.
   (B) Ancient tools used to study the heavens were much more advanced.
   (C) Judging the distance between stars was possible in ancient times.
   (D) The ancient tools to understand outer space are found in many places.

(3) What are the stone circles used for?

   (A) Observing movement of sun or moon
   (B) Marking the changes of sun
   (C) Understanding the planets near the earth
   (D) Noting the time of a day

2 The intentional manipulation of plants and seeds for food production and for aesthetic appeal is called horticulture. Humans have been practicing horticulture for at least 11,000 years, saving and cultivating the seeds of wild plants in order to better control the final product of the plant — be it fruit, vegetable, or flower. This resulted in major technological innovations, as well as increased planting knowledge. For example, by 2800 B.C., Egyptians had designed extensive and sophisticated irrigation systems to support the pharaoh's gardens. And the Mesopotamians, by 1700 B.C., had completed an almanac, a book that contains information about the best planting times and growing methods.

(1) What is the purpose of horticulture?

   (A) To influence the final result of a plant's progress

   (B) To create justification for new technology

   (C) To invent new species of flowers

   (D) To produce as much food as possible

(2) What is true of the Egyptian gardens?

   (A) They were the first examples of horticulture in ancient times.

   (B) The system to supply water was developed for the royalty.

   (C) They were generally more successful than the Mesopotamians' gardens.

   (D) They were popular among many Egyptians during the time.

(3) How did the Mesopotamians contribute to horticultural knowledge?

   (A) By discovering how to keep plants alive during a drought

   (B) By studying when different seeds should be planted for best results

   (C) By writing a book about the best plants to grow in Mesopotamia

   (D) By improving upon Egyptian advances in irrigation technology

VOCABULARY **passage** 경과 **likewise** 마찬가지로 **manipulation** 조종, 교묘한 처리 **aesthetic** 미적인 **horticulture** 원예(술) **cultivate** 경작하다, 재배하다 **almanac** 책력, 연감

Basic Drill 2 — Negative facts

Read the passages and answer the questions.

1 The number of immigrants that come to the U.S. each year varies, depending on many factors. Almost half of the population growth in the U.S. occurred because of immigration during the first decade of the 20th century while natural increase accounted for only about 1 percent of the population growth per year during that period. The reasons for this are numerous, but it was mainly due to liberal immigration policies. Percentage of U.S. population growth from immigration, however, steeply declined to only about 1.5 percent during the 1930s. The combination of the Great Depression and the beginning of the Second World War discouraged people from immigrating. By the end of the century, a strong economy and a surplus of jobs attracted many more immigrants, who accounted for more than 30 percent of the nation's population growth.

(1) Which of the following is NOT true?

(A) Immigration has increased after the Depression and WWII.
(B) Today, nearly half of the U.S. population growth is from net immigration.
(C) Percentage of migration was greatly effected by the economic factors in US.
(D) Immigration had the greatest effect on population growth during the preceding century.

(2) All of the following accounts for the steep decline in immigrants in the 1930s EXCEPT

(A) The global economy was bad, so there was no reason to migrate.
(B) War prevented the easy movement of people.
(C) There was a lot of anti-immigrant violence in the U.S.
(D) There were very few jobs available in the U.S.

VOCABULARY decade 10년간 numerous 무수한 liberal 자유주의의 surplus 과잉, 잉여

2 Identity theft or identity fraud is the deliberate assumption of another person's identity and is one of the fastest-growing crimes in the nation. This crime has been growing in scope and cost over the past decade.(Figure 1)

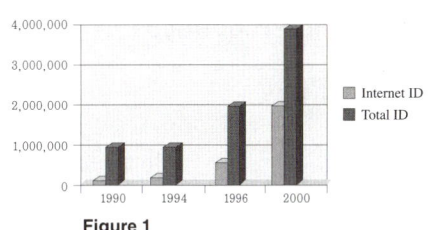
Figure 1

Although several reasons can be given for this, from the increased use of credit cards to purchase things on the Internet to the recent increase in workplace ID theft, one reason stands out. Quite simply, stealing one's identification over the Internet is impersonal. Even the most hardened criminals are known to have feelings of empathy toward their victims when they meet them face-to-face. But when the theft occurs in cyberspace, the victims are not known, or even seen. They're just names and numbers on a computer screen.

Techniques for obtaining identification information range from the crude, such as simply stealing mail or rummaging through rubbish, to the more sophisticated theft of personal information in computer databases, and infiltration of organizations that store large amounts of personal information.

(1) According to the graph, all of the following are true EXCEPT

(A) By the year 2000, the incidence of identity fraud had exploded.

(B) Between 1990 and 1995 there was little change in the overall number of identity crimes.

(C) In 1990, Internet identity fraud accounted for about 40 percent of identity theft cases.

(D) It more than doubled by 1996, with about a million-case increase in overall ID fraud.

(2) Which of the following is NOT an example of techniques of obtaining identity?

(A) Sneaking into a bank database

(B) Overhearing organizations

(C) Searching mailboxes

(D) Taking trash

VOCABULARY | identity theft 신분 위장 절도   fraud 사기   deliberate 계획적인   assumption 가장하기   scope 범위, 넓이   stand out 두드러지다   hardened 비정한, 냉담한   empathy 공감   obtain 손에 넣다   crude 조잡한   rummaging 샅샅이 뒤지기(찾기)   infiltration 침입

Vocabulary Preview for Exercise

Read and Pronounce

Exercise 1

hymn	[him]	*n.* a song of praise, usually religious
passionate	[pǽʃənit]	*adj.* showing or filled with energy, very eager
suspect	[səspékt]	*v.* to doubt the value or truth of something
well-meaning	[wélmíːniŋ]	*adj.* good intentions
rare	[rɛər]	*a.* extremely unusual or uncommon
strive	[straiv]	*v.* to make a great effort

Exercise 2

make up		to form as a whole, to create something
precious	[préʃəs]	*adj.* something of great value
devastating	[dévəstèitiŋ]	*adj.* completely destructive
scarce	[skɛərs]	*adj.* hard to find
absorb	[əbsɔ́ːrb]	*v.* to take or suck (especially liquids) in
cell	[sel]	*n.* a very small division of living matter, one of a number of small parts belonging to a larger structure
in turn		afterwards in an expected or correct order
adapt	[ədǽpt]	*v.* to make adjustments for new needs or different conditions

Exercise 3

proponent	[prəpóunənt]	*n.* a person who supports or argues in favor of something
reverse	[rivə́ːrs]	*v.* to change to the opposite direction
downturn	[dáuntə̀ːrn]	*n.* a lessening of business activity, production, etc.
work force		*n.* the group pf people who work in a factory or in industry
available	[əvéiləbəl]	*adj.* able to be had, used, seen, obtained, etc.
protest	[prətést]	*v.* to express disagreement, feeling of unfairness, annoyance, etc.
diminish	[dəmíniʃ]	*v.* to become or seem smaller
consequence	[kánsəkwèns]	*n.* the result of an action or set of conditions

| Check-up |

Fill in the blanks with an appropriate word or phrase. Change the form if needed.

| reverse | consequence | scarce | absorb |
| suspect | make up | adapt | devastating |

1 In the desert, water is _____ and costs a lot to buy.
2 Nina is a genius! She immediately _____ whatever she learns.
3 Friction between the two countries could bring _____ effects for those countries' economy.
4 I had to _____ to a new environment when my family moved to a different country.
5 He _____ Susan's motives and criticized her proposals.
6 The pitiable accident was the _____ of the driver's carelessness.
7 Tourism and trade _____ most of this country's industry.
8 They promised that they will not _____ their decision to support the research team.

Exercise 1

*i*BT Reading

Question 1 to 4

1. The word **diverse** in paragraph 1 is closest in meaning to
   - (A) complicated
   - (B) varied
   - (C) difficult
   - (D) effective

2. The word **employed** in paragraph 2 is closest in meaning to
   - (A) engaged
   - (B) entered
   - (C) applied
   - (D) recommended

3. Which of the following is NOT mentioned as a facility for her unique lyric style in paragraph 2?
   - (A) Different grammatical structure
   - (B) Uncommon vocabularies
   - (C) Musical hymn meter
   - (D) Imaginary illustrations

4. Which sentence below best expresses the essential information in the highlighted sentence in paragraph 3? *Incorrect* choices change the meaning in important ways or leave out essential information.
   - (A) After starting her career writing typically feminine poems, Dickinson changed course and wrote about things that interested her.
   - (B) Dickinson was able to create sentimental poems about philosophical topics that included a number of big ideas.
   - (C) Dickinson was more concerned with serious issues while other female poets were thought to write touching poems.
   - (D) Death, life, and love were what concerned Dickinson the most, while this was contrary to the society's conventional expectations of female poets.

Emily Dickinson and her Poetry

Though she had fewer than five poems published in her lifetime, Emily Dickinson is one of the United States' most famous poets. Her verse was wholly unlike other poems written during the mid-to-late 19th century. In part, this is because her influences were extremely diverse. She read books about science, politics, and philosophy, as well as literature. All of these subjects would appear in her poems, often in surprising ways.

Dickinson's poetry is often recognizable at a glance, and is unlike the work of any other poet. Her unique lyric style was created by combining extensive use of dashes and unconventional capitalization in her manuscripts, and her unusual vocabulary and imagery. In her poems, she also used "common meter," the musical rhyme structure employed by religious hymns that use four lines of length 8, 6, 8, 6. This shows that she thought the ordinary and everyday had a role to play in poetry.

Dickinson was not interested in publication for a number of reasons. Female poets at the time were expected to write sentimental verse about romantic love and family, but Dickinson was more interested in the philosophical problems of existence, including death, the meaning of life, and passionate love. Because she did not fit into the expected role of the female poet, she knew her work would not easily be accepted. She also suspected that well-meaning editors might try and change the work to make it more acceptable. This was not something Dickinson wanted for her work, so she only showed it to friends and family. It was only after she died that her family strove to get Dickinson's poetic accomplishment recognized. By the first half of the 20th century, though female poets were still relatively rare, Dickinson was widely regarded as a master.

Glossary

dash the symbol —, used in writing to separate two main parts which are closely connected in a sentence
common meter an iambic meter consisting of four lines of length 8, 6, 8, 6; used for ballads, and some hymns

Exercise 1

*i*BT Reading

Question 5 to 6

5. According to paragraph 3, which of the following is the reason Dickinson avoided publication?

   Ⓐ She was not confident of the quality of her work.
   Ⓑ She was concerned her original poems would be altered.
   Ⓒ She did not want to have her work read by strangers.
   Ⓓ She felt that her work was best appreciated by well-meaning editors only.

6. **Directions:** An introductory sentence for a brief summary of the passage is provided below. Complete the summary by selecting the THREE answer choices that express the most important ideas in the passage. Some sentences do not belong in the summary because they express ideas that are not presented in the passage or are minor ideas in the passage.

   Emily Dickinson is one of the America's most famous poets.

   Answer Choices

   Ⓐ Dickinson's poems are characterized by her unique writing style and many uncommon elements.
   Ⓑ Dickinson is a famous poet for her writing style and subjects of her poems which were very unusual for her time.
   Ⓒ Her unique lyric style can be found in her poems that have many unusual uses of words.
   Ⓓ Although Dickinson was one of the most famous poets, there are not many poems published because of her unusual style.
   Ⓔ Dickinson got more famous after death because her subjects and poems were not widely accepted during her lifetime.
   Ⓕ After Dickinson's death, her poems were published by accident by her friends, which resulted in her fame.

Emily Dickinson and her Poetry

Though she had fewer than five poems published in her lifetime, Emily Dickinson is one of the United States' most famous poets. Her verse was wholly unlike other poems written during the mid-to-late 19th century. In part, this is because her influences were extremely diverse. She read books about science, politics, and philosophy, as well as literature. All of these subjects would appear in her poems, often in surprising ways.

Dickinson's poetry is often recognizable at a glance, and is unlike the work of any other poet. Her unique lyric style was created by combining extensive use of dashes and unconventional capitalization in her manuscripts, and her unusual vocabulary and imagery. In her poems, she also used "common meter," the musical rhyme structure employed by religious hymns that use four lines of length 8, 6, 8, 6. This shows that she thought the ordinary and everyday had a role to play in poetry.

Dickinson was not interested in publication for a number of reasons. Female poets at the time were expected to write sentimental verse about romantic love and family, but Dickinson was more interested in the philosophical problems of existence, including death, the meaning of life, and passionate love. Because she did not fit into the expected role of the female poet, she knew her work would not easily be accepted. She also suspected that well-meaning editors might try and change the work to make it more acceptable. This was not something Dickinson wanted for her work, so she only showed it to friends and family. It was only after she died that her family strove to get Dickinson's poetic accomplishment recognized. By the first half of the 20th century, though female poets were still relatively rare, Dickinson was widely regarded as a master.

Exercise 2

*i*BT Reading

Question 1 to 4

1. The word **plagued** in paragraph 1 is closest in meaning to
   - Ⓐ ignored
   - Ⓑ tortured
   - Ⓒ blessed
   - Ⓓ influenced

2. According to paragraph 1, which of the following can likely be a consequence of insufficient water?
   - Ⓐ A severe shortage of food
   - Ⓑ Dried-up riverbeds, lakes and wells
   - Ⓒ An increase of unknown illnesses
   - Ⓓ Social instability in the effected region

3. The phrase **stave off** in paragraph 2 is closest in meaning to
   - Ⓐ withstand
   - Ⓑ destroy
   - Ⓒ decrease
   - Ⓓ prevent

4. The word **them** in paragraph 3 refers to
   - Ⓐ the resurrection plants
   - Ⓑ bad conditions
   - Ⓒ drought-tolerant plants
   - Ⓓ plants like corn

The Resurrection Plant

Making up 75% of the earth's surface, water is one of the most precious resources on earth. While some areas of the planet are plagued by too much water — rains, floods, and so on — other areas suffer through years-long droughts. The lack of water in these areas can be devastating. Famine is one likely result. In addition, major epidemics frequently occur. Thus, trying to find ways to help people who are without enough water to grow food is very important.

One possible way to achieve this is through science. By crossing the genes of drought-tolerant plants — plants that don't need a lot of water — with common food crops, it may be possible to create crops that can go long periods without water. This would help regions to continue to raise food and stave off hunger and disease, even when rain is scarce.

One plant in sub-Saharan Africa is extremely drought tolerant. The resurrection plant lives in the mountains, and can go months without water. When it does rain, this plant absorbs a great deal of water and stores it in its cells. This, in turn, helps the plant to survive extended periods of drought. Additionally, the resurrection plant is able to withstand high winds and great variations in temperature. This is in sharp contrast with corn, for example, which needs a steady supply of water each day. Corn does not use water very efficiently. It can't store it long. Plants like corn and other food crops have difficulty adapting to the cold or strong winds, making it very hard for them to survive.

Glossary

cross the genes to mix genes and get a combination of them
resurrection plant a plant with special qualities, which cause them to curl up when dry and to unfold when moist

Exercise 2

iBT Reading

Question 5 to 6

5. According to paragraph 3, which of the following best explains a resurrection plant?
   - Ⓐ It needs less sunlight but yields a lot more crops than corn.
   - Ⓑ It cannot stand strong wind and the cold.
   - Ⓒ It can store water in itself and can bear tough circumstances.
   - Ⓓ It thrives mainly in the desert and needs plentiful water supply.

6. **Directions:** Select the appropriate phrases from the answer choices and match them to the type of plant to which they relate. TWO of the answer choices will NOT be used.

   Answer Choices
   - Ⓐ Requires water only several times per year
   - Ⓑ Needs soil with many minerals to survive
   - Ⓒ Can live through various weather conditions
   - Ⓓ Can only store water for a short period of time
   - Ⓔ Will die if weather is too extreme
   - Ⓕ Needs to be watered steadily
   - Ⓖ Can produce good crops even without enough sunlight

   Typical Plant
   •
   •
   •

   Drought-tolerant Plant
   •
   •

The Resurrection Plant

Making up 75% of the earth's surface, water is one of the most precious resources on earth. While some areas of the planet are plagued by too much water — rains, floods, and so on — other areas suffer through years-long droughts. The lack of water in these areas can be devastating. Famine is one likely result. In addition, major epidemics frequently occur. Thus, trying to find ways to help people who are without enough water to grow food is very important.

One possible way to achieve this is through science. By crossing the genes of drought-tolerant plants — plants that don't need a lot of water — with common food crops, it may be possible to create crops that can go long periods without water. This would help regions to continue to raise food and stave off hunger and disease, even when rain is scarce.

One plant in sub-Saharan Africa is extremely drought tolerant. The resurrection plant lives in the mountains, and can go months without water. When it does rain, this plant absorbs a great deal of water and stores it in its cells. This, in turn, helps the plant to survive extended periods of drought. Additionally, the resurrection plant is able to withstand high winds and great variations in temperature. This is in sharp contrast with corn, for example, which needs a steady supply of water each day. Corn does not use water very efficiently. It can't store it long. Plants like corn and other food crops have difficulty adapting to the cold or strong winds, making it very hard for them to survive.

Exercise 3

iBT Reading

Question 1 to 4

1. The word **compensation** in paragraph 1 is closest in meaning to
   - Ⓐ schedules
   - Ⓑ payment
   - Ⓒ gains
   - Ⓓ battles

2. The word **this** in paragraph 1 refers to
   - Ⓐ overtime compensation
   - Ⓑ leisure time
   - Ⓒ the forty-hour, five-day workweek
   - Ⓓ working hour

3. The word **instituted** in paragraph 1 is closest in meaning to
   - Ⓐ enforced
   - Ⓑ started
   - Ⓒ ensured
   - Ⓓ permitted

4. According to paragraph 1, which of the following is mentioned as a change of working condition in the early 20th century?
   - Ⓐ Increased overall payment rates
   - Ⓑ Increased demands on training
   - Ⓒ Decreased working hours a week
   - Ⓓ Decreased needs for overtime work

The Reasons and Effects of Working Overtime

The early twentieth century marked a victory for proponents of a shorter workweek. The forty-hour, five-day workweek became standard for the majority of workers. Overtime compensation for those who worked beyond this was also instituted. However, over the last two decades, these gains in leisure time have been reversed, as more and more workers are spending longer hours at the office with little or no extra pay for that overtime.

This trend is the result of several factors. First is that the economic downturns in the late 1980s and late 1990s resulted in the reduction of the work force. Second, during the same period, demands for productivity remained the same or increased. Third, because of the scarcity of jobs in the market, employees were unable to reject the increased demands upon their time. So, there were fewer people available to do more work. In order to meet the demand, these remaining workers had to put in longer hours. And they were not in a position to protest these conditions.

While this trend has allowed for continually increasing productivity in the workplace, despite a diminished work force, there have been negative health consequences because of it. In fact, recent studies of workplace injury have shown that workers who work overtime were more than twice as likely to be injured or become ill than those who worked a 40-hour week. And workers who put in a 12-hour or more day were three times as likely to suffer negative health consequences.

Figure: Hours worked per week/ Injuries received on the job
— work day(hours)
— injury(per hundred)

Exercise 3

iBT Reading

Question 5 to 7

5. Based on the information in paragraph 2, which of the following is given as a reason for reduced number of workers in the late 1980s?
   - Ⓐ Declined productivity level
   - Ⓑ Demands on highly skilled workers
   - Ⓒ Depressed economic conditions
   - Ⓓ Automatization of production

6. Which sentence below best expresses the essential information in the highlighted sentence in paragraph 3? *Incorrect* choices change the meaning in important ways or leave out essential information.
   - Ⓐ Even though they are sick, the few workers that remain continue to produce more and more.
   - Ⓑ The overall increase in productivity can be seen as a positive consequence of worker health.
   - Ⓒ Despite health warnings, workers continue to work long hours and work many different jobs.
   - Ⓓ Workers are increasing their output without extra help, which resulted in increased illness and injury.

7. According to the graph, which of the following is NOT true?
   - Ⓐ The number of injuries has increased at a steady rate since the 1960s.
   - Ⓑ The number of injury had declined as the working hours was reduced during the first two decades.
   - Ⓒ As the number of work hours dropped below 40 per week, the number of injuries fell.
   - Ⓓ Although work hours leveled off in the 1920s, the numbers of injuries fell through the 1970s.

The Reasons and Effects of Working Overtime

The early twentieth century marked a victory for proponents of a shorter workweek. The forty-hour, five-day workweek became standard for the majority of workers. Overtime compensation for those who worked beyond this was also instituted. However, over the last two decades, these gains in leisure time have been reversed, as more and more workers are spending longer hours at the office with little or no extra pay for that overtime.

This trend is the result of several factors. First is that the economic downturns in the late 1980s and late 1990s resulted in the reduction of the work force. Second, during the same period, demands for productivity remained the same or increased. Third, because of the scarcity of jobs in the market, employees were unable to reject the increased demands upon their time. So, there were fewer people available to do more work. In order to meet the demand, these remaining workers had to put in longer hours. And they were not in a position to protest these conditions.

While this trend has allowed for continually increasing productivity in the workplace, despite a diminished work force, there have been negative health consequences because of it. In fact, recent studies of workplace injury have shown that workers who work overtime were more than twice as likely to be injured or become ill than those who worked a 40-hour week. And workers who put in a 12-hour or more day were three times as likely to suffer negative health consequences.

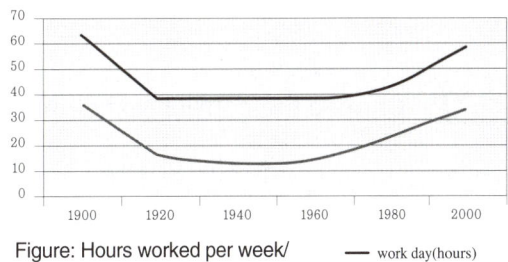

Figure: Hours worked per week/ Injuries received on the job
— work day(hours)
— injury(per hundred)

Exercise 3

*i*BT Reading

Question 8

8. **Directions:** An introductory sentence for a brief summary of the passage is provided below. Complete the summary by selecting the THREE answer choices that express the most important ideas in the passage. Some sentences do not belong in the summary because they express ideas that are not presented in the passage or are minor ideas in the passage.

In the early 20th century, employees' work hours began to fall.

Answer Choices

- (A) Even though a standard workweek has been set, workers tend to work more without much extra money for the overtime.
- (B) Because jobs were scarce in the 80s, employees were not in a favorable negotiating position.
- (C) Although work hours and work-related injuries at first declined in the 20th century, they later rose.
- (D) Economic factors caused a shrinking of the labor force in the 80s and 90s, which meant that those workers had to put in longer workdays.
- (E) Longer working hours has a direct effect on the increased incidence of on-the-job injuries.
- (F) Workers' unrest resulted in several changes, including the 40-hour workweek and payment for working overtime.

Text Outline Choose the correct text outline of the passage.

(A) P1 — The result of a fight for better working conditions
    P2 — Effects of the increased working hours
    P3 — Other consequences of the recent working conditions

(B) P1 — Introduction of a trend in recent working hours
    P2 — Causes of the trend
    P3 — Negative effects on health of the trend

The Reasons and Effects of Working Overtime

The early twentieth century marked a victory for proponents of a shorter workweek. The forty-hour, five-day workweek became standard for the majority of workers. Overtime compensation for those who worked beyond this was also instituted. However, over the last two decades, these gains in leisure time have been reversed, as more and more workers are spending longer hours at the office with little or no extra pay for that overtime.

This trend is the result of several factors. First is that the economic downturns in the late 1980s and late 1990s resulted in the reduction of the work force. Second, during the same period, demands for productivity remained the same or increased. Third, because of the scarcity of jobs in the market, employees were unable to reject the increased demands upon their time. So, there were fewer people available to do more work. In order to meet the demand, these remaining workers had to put in longer hours. And they were not in a position to protest these conditions.

While this trend has allowed for continually increasing productivity in the workplace, despite a diminished work force, there have been negative health consequences because of it. In fact, recent studies of workplace injury have shown that workers who work overtime were more than twice as likely to be injured or become ill than those who worked a 40-hour week. And workers who put in a 12-hour or more day were three times as likely to suffer negative health consequences.

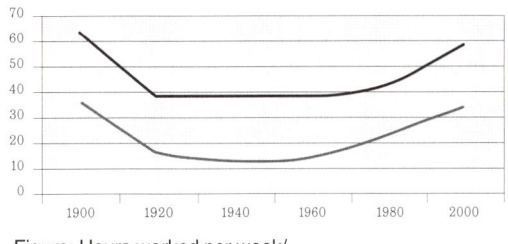

Figure: Hours worked per week/ Injuries received on the job
— work day(hours)
— injury(per hundred)

Vocabulary Test

Choose the closest meaning of each underlined word or phrase.

1. I am one of the proponents of equal rights for illegal aliens.
   (A) opponents   (B) counselors   (C) volunteers   (D) advocates

2. Scientists are investigating, by genetic manipulation, how to increase the productivity of crops.
   (A) treatment   (B) control   (C) means   (D) manners

3. My mother has a lot of precious jewelry, and some day she will give it to me.
   (A) great   (B) meaningful   (C) valuable   (D) initiated

4. The fear of terrorism has not diminished yet in America.
   (A) lessened   (B) Increased   (C) recognized   (D) eliminated

5. Our company suffers from a surplus of unqualified work force.
   (A) shortage   (B) excess   (C) supply   (D) demand

6. The world is changing rapidly, and we have to adapt ourselves accordingly.
   (A) adopt   (B) overcome   (C) agree   (D) adjust

7. Maggie owns a large field and she cultivates it herself.
   (A) farms   (B) appreciates   (C) revises   (D) calculates

8. Such opinions are not in the scope of this paper.
   (A) focus   (B) range   (C) capability   (D) point

9. Food becomes scarce after the severe drought.
   (A) abundant   (B) far   (C) infamous   (D) insufficient

10. She always strives to be ahead of others in her office.
    (A) claims   (B) debates   (C) disregards   (D) labors

11. There are numerous reasons to wake up early and exercise in the morning.
    (A) few   (B) proper   (C) countless   (D) unintended

PROGRESS TEST

READING SECTION DIRECTIONS

In this section you will read two passages and answer reading comprehension questions about each passage. Most questions are worth one point, but the last question in each set is worth more than one point. The directions indicate how many points you may receive.

You will have 30 minutes to read all of the passages and answer the questions. Some passages include a word or phrase that is underlined in blue. Click on the word or phrase to see a definition or an explanation.

When you want to move on to the next question, click on **Next**. You can skip questions and go back to them later as long as long as there is time remaining. If you want to return to previous questions, click on **Back**. You can click on **Review** at any time and the review screen will show you which questions you have answered and which you have not. From this review screen, you may go directly to any question you have already seen in the reading section.

When you are ready to continue, click on the Dismiss Directions icon.

Progress Test 3

*i*BT TOEFL Reading

Question 1 to 5

1. The word accumulation in paragraph 1 is closest in meaning to
   - Ⓐ evidence
   - Ⓑ addition
   - Ⓒ appearance
   - Ⓓ addiction

2. The word strikes in paragraph 1 is closest in meaning to
   - Ⓐ overlooks
   - Ⓑ worries
   - Ⓒ affects
   - Ⓓ exhausts

3. The word One in paragraph 2 refers to
   - Ⓐ Disease
   - Ⓑ Effect
   - Ⓒ Factor
   - Ⓓ Gene

4. All of the following are mentioned in paragraph 2 EXCEPT
   - Ⓐ Statistics show different rates of Alzheimer's in families.
   - Ⓑ Heredity plays a role in the development of the disease.
   - Ⓒ Alzheimer's can have serious effects on family members.
   - Ⓓ There are problems with attributing the disease to genes.

5. Which of the following best expresses the essential information in the highlighted sentence in paragraph 2? *Incorrect* answers change the information in important ways or leave out essential information.
   - Ⓐ People who have family members with the disease will probably develop it at some point.
   - Ⓑ The link between a family member's medical history and one's own is not yet clear.
   - Ⓒ People whose parents have Alzheimer's run a greatly increased risk of developing the disease.
   - Ⓓ Not everyone who has the disease in his family will get Alzheimer's, but the risk is higher.

Factors of Alzheimer's Disease

Alzheimer's disease is a brain disorder that, over a period of time, results in memory loss, dementia (the loss of control over senses and perceptions), and eventually death. It begins with an accumulation of protein on the parts of the brain that control memory. This increased protein progresses to affecting large areas of the brain by the end of its course. Alzheimer's primarily strikes older people, but it is not a normal part of the aging process. Though the process of the disease is well studied, its causes are not clear. There are, however, several theories about factors that may make some people more likely to get it than others.

One might be genetic. Studies have shown that people who have parents or brothers and sisters who have developed the disease have an increased risk of getting it themselves. In fact, the more members of a person's family that have Alzheimer's, the more the risk is increased. Though the risk is increased by family members' having the disease, it is not guaranteed that a person whose mother and brother had Alzheimer's will develop it, too. Instead, genes are merely one possible thing that makes a person more vulnerable.

Another factor that seems to increase the possibility of developing Alzheimer's is brain damage caused by stroke, high blood pressure, or head injury. In people who have experienced these problems, the risk of developing Alzheimer's later in life is slightly raised. Scientists suggest that the damage to the tissue makes it more susceptible to Alzheimer's. Again, however, there is no guarantee that brain damage will result in this brain disorder.

A third potential cause is environment. This theory is the most debatable of all proposed explanations of the disease. It also has the least support. Exposure to aluminum and other metals in the environment have been linked in some studies to the eventual development of the disease. Other studies, however, have found no such link. The evidence in favor of metals being a cause is limited at best, despite some people's opinions. Without further clinical research, those opinions should not be considered valid. There is not enough proof to claim that environmental factors cause this tragic disease.

Progress Test 3

*i*BT TOEFL Reading

Question 6 to 9

6. The phrase **susceptible to** in paragraph 3 is closest in meaning to
   - Ⓐ sick of
   - Ⓑ worried about
   - Ⓒ vulnerable to
   - Ⓓ hopeless about

7. According to paragraph 3, what is true about strokes?
   - Ⓐ People with Alzheimer's are more likely to develop strokes.
   - Ⓑ The brain damage caused by them may lead to the disease.
   - Ⓒ There is no treatment to cure strokes.
   - Ⓓ The damage caused by strokes and the disease is very similar.

8. The word **debatable** in paragraph 4 is closest in meaning to
   - Ⓐ controversial
   - Ⓑ influential
   - Ⓒ accepted
   - Ⓓ worrisome

9. What is the author's opinion on environmental causes of Alzheimer's?
   - Ⓐ She is convinced by the studies' conclusions.
   - Ⓑ She is concerned about the implications of the theory.
   - Ⓒ She is frightened about the studies' conclusions.
   - Ⓓ She is skeptical of the evidence provided.

Factors of Alzheimer's Disease

Alzheimer's disease is a brain disorder that, over a period of time, results in memory loss, dementia (the loss of control over senses and perceptions), and eventually death. It begins with an accumulation of protein on the parts of the brain that control memory. This increased protein progresses to affecting large areas of the brain by the end of its course. Alzheimer's primarily strikes older people, but it is not a normal part of the aging process. Though the process of the disease is well studied, its causes are not clear. There are, however, several theories about factors that may make some people more likely to get it than others.

One might be genetic. Studies have shown that people who have parents or brothers and sisters who have developed the disease have an increased risk of getting it themselves. In fact, the more members of a person's family that have Alzheimer's, the more the risk is increased. Though the risk is increased by family members' having the disease, it is not guaranteed that a person whose mother and brother had Alzheimer's will develop it, too. Instead, genes are merely one possible thing that makes a person more vulnerable.

Another factor that seems to increase the possibility of developing Alzheimer's is brain damage caused by stroke, high blood pressure, or head injury. In people who have experienced these problems, the risk of developing Alzheimer's later in life is slightly raised. Scientists suggest that the damage to the tissue makes it more susceptible to Alzheimer's. Again, however, there is no guarantee that brain damage will result in this brain disorder.

A third potential cause is environment. This theory is the most debatable of all proposed explanations of the disease. It also has the least support. Exposure to aluminum and other metals in the environment has been linked in some studies to the eventual development of the disease. Other studies, however, have found no such link. The evidence in favor of metals being a cause is limited at best, despite some people's opinions. Without further clinical research, those opinions should not be considered valid. There is not enough proof to claim that environmental factors cause this tragic disease.

Progress Test 3

*i*BT TOEFL Reading

Question 10

10. **Directions:** An introductory sentence for a brief summary of the passage is provided below. Complete the summary by selecting the THREE answer choices that express the most important ideas in the passage. Some sentences do not belong in the summary because they express ideas that are not presented in the passage or are minor ideas in the passage.

Though its causes are not well understood, there are several possible factors that may lead to Alzheimer's disease.

-
-
-

Answer Choices

(A) Older people are easier to develop Alzheimer's and the reasons have been studied.

(B) One's family medical history may play a role in developing the disease.

(C) Physical harm to the brain may also make you more likely to get Alzheimer's.

(D) The relationship between damage on brain and Alzheimer's are not yet proved.

(E) Some metals actually have some effects on brain and might cause Alzheimer's.

(F) Substances around us may also have some influence, but there is little proof.

Factors of Alzheimer's Disease

Alzheimer's disease is a brain disorder that, over a period of time, results in memory loss, dementia (the loss of control over senses and perceptions), and eventually death. It begins with an accumulation of protein on the parts of the brain that control memory. This increased protein progresses to affecting large areas of the brain by the end of its course. Alzheimer's primarily strikes older people, but it is not a normal part of the aging process. Though the process of the disease is well studied, its causes are not clear. There are, however, several theories about factors that may make some people more likely to get it than others.

One might be genetic. Studies have shown that people who have parents or brothers and sisters who have developed the disease have an increased risk of getting it themselves. In fact, the more members of a person's family that have Alzheimer's, the more the risk is increased. Though the risk is increased by family members' having the disease, it is not guaranteed that a person whose mother and brother had Alzheimer's will develop it, too. Instead, genes are merely one possible thing that makes a person more vulnerable.

Another factor that seems to increase the possibility of developing Alzheimer's is brain damage caused by stroke, high blood pressure, or head injury. In people who have experienced these problems, the risk of developing Alzheimer's later in life is slightly raised. Scientists suggest that the damage to the tissue makes it more susceptible to Alzheimer's. Again, however, there is no guarantee that brain damage will result in this brain disorder.

A third potential cause is environment. This theory is the most debatable of all proposed explanations of the disease. It also has the least support. Exposure to aluminum and other metals in the environment has been linked in some studies to the eventual development of the disease. Other studies, however, have found no such link. The evidence in favor of metals being a cause is limited at best, despite some people's opinions. Without further clinical research, those opinions should not be considered valid. There is not enough proof to claim that environmental factors cause this tragic disease.

Progress Test 4

iBT TOEFL Reading

Question 1 to 6

1. The word **irreparably** in paragraph 1 is closest in meaning to
   - Ⓐ partially
   - Ⓑ lastingly
   - Ⓒ temporarily
   - Ⓓ subtly

2. The word **displaced** in paragraph 2 is closest in meaning to
   - Ⓐ altered
   - Ⓑ forced out
   - Ⓒ escaped
   - Ⓓ transformed

3. The word **it** in paragraph 2 refers to
   - Ⓐ industry
   - Ⓑ protection
   - Ⓒ Caribbean
   - Ⓓ species

4. Based on the information in paragraph 2, which of the following does the author say about tourist resorts is true?
   - Ⓐ They benefit marine life by bringing in more conservation money.
   - Ⓑ They often provide beneficial habitats to endangered species.
   - Ⓒ They result in too many people on the beaches, harming animals.
   - Ⓓ They cause the destruction of the places where sea animals live.

5. What is the author's opinion of the tourist industry?
   - Ⓐ He is critical of its reliance on shoreline resorts.
   - Ⓑ He is positive about its contribution to the economy.
   - Ⓒ He is skeptical about its role in species extinction.
   - Ⓓ He is disapproving of its lack of responsibility.

6. The word **unintentional** in paragraph 3 is closest in meaning to
   - Ⓐ accidental
   - Ⓑ intelligent
   - Ⓒ experimental
   - Ⓓ minor

Reasons of the Extinction of Fish

Oceanographers predict that over the next decade, human beings will witness the extinction of a large number of ocean dwelling species. There are dozens of animals whose populations have been irreparably harmed — they will not likely be able to continue on. In fact, of the 21 known marine animals that have gone extinct in the past 300 years, 16 have died out since 1972. What accounts for these and the predicted die-outs? Human development on the coastline and overfishing are two of the biggest factors.

As the global tourist industry continues to grow, more and more resorts and hotels are built on the world's beaches. This provides wonderful opportunities for tourists to relax and enjoy the water, but it has a significant, and negative, impact for marine life inhabiting these shore areas. For example, lemon sharks, a rare species living in the Caribbean, are being displaced as mangrove trees, which grow in the water, are being ripped out to make way for shoreline development. The sharks live and feed among the mangrove roots. Without this protection, they will likely die out. There must be restrictions placed on the industry to make it more responsible to the environment. So far, it has not taken any steps on its own to stop the damage it has caused in the name of profit.

The fishing industry has been responsible for the majority of extinctions in fish species, also primarily in the name of profit. Large fishing boats, which are able to capture thousands of fish an hour, are estimated to be the cause of over half of the fish extinctions that have occurred over the last sixty years. Some of these extinctions were caused by a direct overfishing of a particular species, such as the Caribbean monk seal fish or the New Zealand grayling. In other words, despite the fact that the numbers of fish were decreasing rapidly, fishermen would continue to harvest a type of fish until it was gone. (See Figure 1). Other fishing related extinctions were unintentional — the fish that have died out just happened to get caught in the nets of the fishing boats frequently, so that they could not support a population.

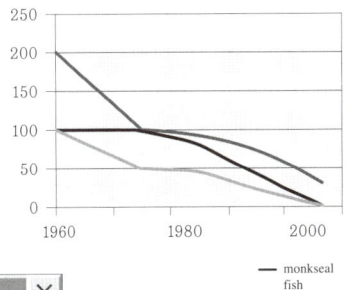

Glossary
Oceanographer a person who studies about sea currents, the fish and animals that live in the sea

iBT TOEFL Reading

Question 7 to 8

7. Which of the following best expresses the essential information in the highlighted sentence in paragraph 3? *Incorrect* answers change the information in important ways or leave out essential information.

   Ⓐ Fishing boats have become increasingly able to catch more fish over the last six decades.
   Ⓑ Big fishing vessels are responsible for about 50% of fish extinctions over the past 60 years.
   Ⓒ Thousands of fish have died because of the increase in numbers of fishing boats over the last 60 years.
   Ⓓ Fish extinctions have increased significantly over the past six decades.

8. According to the graph, which of the following is NOT true?

   Ⓐ Of the represented species, monk seal fish has experienced the greatest decline in actual numbers.
   Ⓑ In the 1990s, the number of lemon sharks was greater than that of graylings or monk seal fish.
   Ⓒ In 1960, the number of graylings and monk seal fish were roughly equivalent.
   Ⓓ The present figure given for lemon sharks is about 25% of the figure given for 1960.

Reasons of the Extinction of Fish

Oceanographers predict that over the next decade, human beings will witness the extinction of a large number of ocean dwelling species. There are dozens of animals whose populations have been irreparably harmed — they will not likely be able to continue on. In fact, of the 21 known marine animals that have gone extinct in the past 300 years, 16 have died out since 1972. What accounts for these and the predicted die-outs? Human development on the coastline and overfishing are two of the biggest factors.

As the global tourist industry continues to grow, more and more resorts and hotels are built on the world's beaches. This provides wonderful opportunities for tourists to relax and enjoy the water, but it has a significant, and negative, impact for marine life inhabiting these shore areas. For example, lemon sharks, a rare species living in the Caribbean, are being displaced as mangrove trees, which grow in the water, are being ripped out to make way for shoreline development. The sharks live and feed among the mangrove roots. Without this protection, they will likely die out. There must be restrictions placed on the industry to make it more responsible to the environment. So far, it has not taken any steps on its own to stop the damage it has caused in the name of profit.

The fishing industry has been responsible for the majority of extinctions in fish species, also primarily in the name of profit. Large fishing boats, which are able to capture thousands of fish an hour, are estimated to be the cause of over half of the fish extinctions that have occurred over the last sixty years. Some of these extinctions were caused by a direct overfishing of a particular species, such as the Caribbean monk seal fish or the New Zealand grayling. In other words, despite the fact that the numbers of fish were decreasing rapidly, fishermen would continue to harvest a type of fish until it was gone. (See Figure 1). Other fishing related extinctions were unintentional — the fish that have died out just happened to get caught in the nets of the fishing boats frequently, so that they could not support a population.

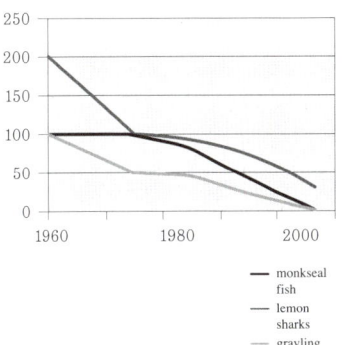

Progress Test 4

*i*BT TOEFL Reading

Question 9

9. **Directions:** Select the appropriate phrases from the answer choices and match them to the type of industry to which they relate. TWO of the answer choices will NOT be used.

Answer Choices

- (A) Makes changes on areas along the shore
- (B) Results in unintended animals being killed
- (C) Disregards laws concerning environmental protection
- (D) Releases pollutants into shoreline areas
- (E) Gives priority to construction over habitats
- (F) Affects habitats of certain sea creatures
- (G) Prevents animals from reproducing fast enough

Tourist Industry
-
-
-

Fishing Industry
-
-

Reasons of the Extinction of Fish

Oceanographers predict that over the next decade, human beings will witness the extinction of a large number of ocean dwelling species. There are dozens of animals whose populations have been irreparably harmed — they will not likely be able to continue on. In fact, of the 21 known marine animals that have gone extinct in the past 300 years, 16 have died out since 1972. What accounts for these and the predicted die-outs? Human development on the coastline and overfishing are two of the biggest factors.

As the global tourist industry continues to grow, more and more resorts and hotels are built on the world's beaches. This provides wonderful opportunities for tourists to relax and enjoy the water, but it has a significant, and negative, impact for marine life inhabiting these shore areas. For example, lemon sharks, a rare species living in the Caribbean, are being displaced as mangrove trees, which grow in the water, are being ripped out to make way for shoreline development. The sharks live and feed among the mangrove roots. Without this protection, they will likely die out. There must be restrictions placed on the industry to make it more responsible to the environment. So far, it has not taken any steps on its own to stop the damage it has caused in the name of profit.

The fishing industry has been responsible for the majority of extinctions in fish species, also primarily in the name of profit. Large fishing boats, which are able to capture thousands of fish an hour, are estimated to be the cause of over half of the fish extinctions that have occurred over the last sixty years. Some of these extinctions were caused by a direct overfishing of a particular species, such as the Caribbean monk seal fish or the New Zealand grayling. In other words, despite the fact that the numbers of fish were decreasing rapidly, fishermen would continue to harvest a type of fish until it was gone. (See Figure 1). Other fishing related extinctions were unintentional — the fish that have died out just happened to get caught in the nets of the fishing boats frequently, so that they could not support a population.

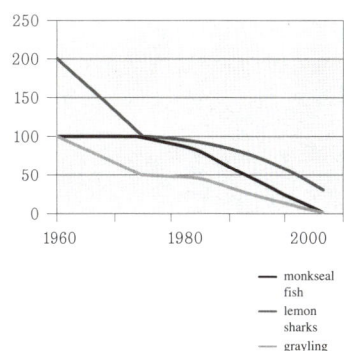

PART C
Inferencing Reading Questions

Chapter 07 **Rhetorical Purpose**
Chapter 08 **Insertion**
Chapter 09 **Inference**

Progress Test 5-6

Chapter 07
RHETORICAL PURPOSE

Chapter 7
Rhetorical Purpose

Sample Item Read the following passage and answer the questions.

*i*BT Reading

Question 1 to 2

1. Why does the author mention a beauty product?
   - Ⓐ To demonstrate an industry where a marketing campaign is commonly used
   - Ⓑ To give an example of a product that doesn't satisfy one of the positioning criteria
   - Ⓒ To explain the reason why proper positioning is important
   - Ⓓ To show that customers demand decent quality of a product

2. How does the author explain conditions for effective positioning?
   - Ⓐ By listing a number of things that are important for positioning
   - Ⓑ By comparing a product's uniqueness and its usefulness
   - Ⓒ By pointing out two main conditions that must be met
   - Ⓓ By arguing that its as necessary as uniqueness and usefulness

Product Positioning

Proper positioning is essential when creating a marketing campaign. Positioning is how your customers view your product in relation to the products of your competitors. Regarding this, two conditions must be met to achieve positioning success. First, your product must somehow be differentiated from other products on the market. In other words, it must be unique. Second, it must offer benefits to the consumer. So for instance, your company may sell a one-of-a-kind beauty product that is totally different from others. However, if your customers feel that your product doesn't work, or is less effective when compared with others, it will fail. This is because only one of the conditions for success has been met.

STUDY POINT
1. 지문에서 글쓴이가 beauty product를 언급한 이유는, 한 가지 조건을 충족하지 못하는 제품의 예를 들어 주려는 것이다.
2. 글쓴이는 effective positioning의 두 가지 condition들을 짚어 설명하고 있다.

Overview

Rhetorical Purpose

Rhetorical purpose 문제는 글쓴이의 요지를 효과적으로 전달하기 위해 사용된 표현들을 적절히 파악했는가를 평가하는 유형이다. 수사학(rhetoric)이란 글쓴이의 의도를 좀 더 효과적으로 나타내기 위해 사용하는 표현방법을 말한다. 이 유형에 대비하기 위해서는 주제와 보조내용들을 정확히 구분할 수 있어야 한다. 또한 세부사항이 나오면 그 내용을 왜 썼는지 의문을 가지고 읽고 세부사항에 숨어 있는 글쓴이의 의도를 파악할 수 있는 적극적 읽기를 해야 한다. 수사학적 의도 문제를 통해 우리는 글쓴이의 성격이나 학문의 깊이를 간접적으로 체험할 수도 있다. 수사학적 의도 파악 문제는 글을 전개하는 여러 방식을 알아 둠으로서 쉽게 해결할 수 있다.

▶ Frequent Rhetorics ◀

Define	소개하는 대상의 정의 및 나아가 기타 의미를 소개한다
Describe	대상의 모양새나 색깔 등을 묘사하거나 part를 설명한다
Illustrate	예를 들어 보여 준다
Compare/Contrast	다른 것에 비교하고 대조한다
Cause/Effect	원인과 그 결과를 설명한다
Explain/Justify/Persuade	요점을 주장하기 위해 여러가지를 설명하거나 증거를 제시해 정당화하거나 사실이나 이유들을 들어 저자의 주장을 설득한다

Question Type

– Why does the author mention X?
– How does the author explain X?

General Strategy

1. 특정 단어, 내용에 대한 저자의 의도를 파악하고, 그것이 글에서 어떤 역할을 하는지를 파악할 필요가 있다.
2. 글쓴이가 자신이 말하고자 하는 내용을 어떤 방식으로 전개하고 있는지, 요점을 어떻게 설명하고 있는지, 어떤 글의 전개방식을 사용하고 있는지를 파악한다.

Basic Drill 1 — Author's intent - Why?

Read the passages and find the author's intent.

1 Bipolar disorder is a type of mental illness that results in extreme changes in a person's mood, level of energy, and ability to function in daily life. Its symptoms are extreme variations in mood. A person will be what is called manic. He shows a lot of energy, sleeps very little, and behaves recklessly. Then, just as suddenly, he will become depressed. During these periods of depression, he sleeps excessively, feels guilty and worthless, and sometimes even ponders suicide.

Rhetoric of underlined: ☐ persuade ☐ define ☐ describe

Q. Why does the author mention manic?

(A) To give an example of symptoms that the illness has

(B) To show that the disorder is fatal in some cases

(C) To describe the symptoms of bipolar disorder

2 Art therapy is a type of psychotherapy that utilizes art-making and creativity to enhance emotional well-being. It enables those who suffer to express their feelings in images rather than through words. This can be extremely effective for people who have a difficult time talking about their problems. Children, for example, cannot easily describe their problems. They don't have sophisticated vocabularies. But they can use pictures to talk about how they feel.

Rhetoric of underlined: ☐ persuade ☐ illustrate ☐ describe

Q. Why does the author mention children?

(A) To give an example of people who can be helped through the therapy

(B) To contrast how it is used in children as opposed to adults

(C) To imply how difficult to treat people who can't express themselves

3 Psychologists have proven that coffee breaks are important. Coffee breaks promote physical well-being, as well. A break in one's daily routine gives employees the chance to relax and refresh a tired body and mind. <u>The researchers found that our internal biological clocks tell us that we need a break every hour and a half to two hours. After that time, one's heart rate and blood pressure actually increase, leading to feelings of restlessness and irritability.</u> But a well-timed break can reverse that occurrence.

Rhetoric of underlined: ☐ persuade ☐ illustrate ☐ compare/contrast

Q. Why does the author mention internal biological clocks?

(A) To show the effects that a proper coffee break has on workers
(B) To show what a coffee break might cause to a daily performance
(C) To prove that a coffee break helps one's physical condition

4 Some experts are criticizing the few schools in the United States that are now experimenting with gender-divided classrooms, in which boys and girls are taught completely separate of each other. They argue that the socialization process is slowed down because the boys and the girls don't learn how to interact. <u>Meanwhile, a number of university researchers claim that there is indeed evidence for differences in the brains of boys and girls, and that these differences cause boys and girls to learn in different ways. Therefore, boys and girls should be separated and taught in the most efficient way, based on their gender.</u>

Rhetoric of underlined: ☐ describe ☐ compare/contrast ☐ cause/effect

Q. Why does the author mention differences in the brains of boys and girls?

(A) To show how the differences in the brains affect their learning processes
(B) To argue that it might be helpful to separate based on their gender
(C) To point out the most serious problem of separating boys and girls

VOCABULARY　**bipolar disorder** 쌍극성 장애(조울증)　**variation** 변화, 변동　**manic** 조병 환자(정신병의 한 가지로, 주기적으로 기분이 상쾌했다가 우울해지는 현상이 반복됨)　**recklessly** 무모하게, 개의치 않고　**excessively** 과도하게　**ponder** 깊이 생각하다　**suicide** 자살　**enhance** 강화하다, 높이다　**promote** 촉진시키다　**internal** 내부의　**irritability** 화를 잘 냄　**socialization** 사회화　**meanwhile** 한편

Basic Drill 2

Author's intent - How?

Read the passages and find how the author organized the passages.

1 The first American automobiles with gasoline-powered internal combustion engines were completed in 1877 by George Selden. However, the automobile was not the first attempt at creating a self-propelled vehicle — one that didn't rely on horses or other things to move. Before that, there had been several attempts to make a vehicle that used other forms of power. <u>A steam-powered tractor was invented in 1769 by a French engineer named Cugnot. But it only went two and a half miles an hour and had to stop every 10 feet or so to build up steam. It wasn't as practical as gasoline-powered car that can provide high power to weight ratios together with excellent fuel energy-density.</u>

Rhetoric of underlined: ☐ cause/effect ☐ describe ☐ compare/contrast

Q. How does the author emphasize his point on the strength of automobiles?

(A) By explaining its parts that other early vehicle didn't have
(B) By comparing to an early vehicle used other energy sources
(C) By demonstrating how far it can travel without additional fuel

2 The World's Columbian Exposition, a fair celebrating the 400th anniversary of Columbus' journey to the new world, took place in Chicago in 1893. A massive effort went into <u>constructing the buildings and organizing the effort needed for this event. Forty thousand workers constructed almost 200 buildings at the fair grounds. In addition to the buildings a series of man-made lakes, ponds, and lagoons were built. These served as both routes for transportation — visitors could take paddle boats and water taxis to different areas of the expo —</u> and as a pleasant place to sit and rest while visiting.

Rhetoric of underlined: ☐ describe ☐ cause/effect ☐ illustrate

Q. How does the author emphasize his point on efforts to the expo?

(A) By providing the number of people involved in the expo
(B) By describing the construction that was done for the fair
(C) By detailing the skills needed by workers building the site

3

A type of advertising in which a character in a film or movie will use a specific brand of something is called product placement. Though the character does not call attention to the product, the label is easy to read, and the character is perceived to be promoting the product. This type of advertising, while subtle, is extremely effective. Companies pay millions of dollars per year to have their products featured in popular movies and films. One example of product placement can be seen in cigarette usage by movie or television actors.

Rhetoric of underlined: ☐ persuade ☐ define ☐ describe

Q. How does the author introduce the topic of the passage?

(A) By giving a definition of product placement
(B) By providing a background of product placement
(C) By giving an example that used product placement

4

Political cartoons are an extremely popular way to criticize and comment upon current political events and leaders. One of the famous people who used these cartoons was Martin Luther. He distributed broadsides or illustrated posters showing what he believed to be the problems and the corruption of the Church, such as priests taking money to forgive sins. These images proved to be incredibly effective, and Luther won the support of the people with them.

Rhetoric of underlined: ☐ describe ☐ compare/contrast ☐ illustrate

Q. How does the author explain political cartoons?

(A) By describing the use of political cartoons to reveal something
(B) By defining the appearance and function of political cartoons
(C) By giving an example of the cartoons used for political purposes

VOCABULARY

combustion 연소　**self-propelled** 자력 추진의　**vehicle** 탈 것, 차　**ratio** 비율　**density** 밀도　**fair** 박람회, 전시회　**massive** 무거운, 대규모의　**lagoon** 못, 늪　**product placement** 영화나 드라마에 상품을 사용하는 간접적인 광고　**perceive** 인식하다, 깨닫다　**subtle** 미묘한, 포착하기 어려운　**distribute** 배포하다　**broadside** 포스터와 같은 인쇄물　**corruption** 타락, 부정 행위

Vocabulary Preview for Exercise

| Read and Pronounce |

Exercise 1

mythology	[miθάlədʒi]	*n.* ancient stories and the beliefs
supernatural	[sùːpərnǽtʃərəl]	*adj.* something that is impossible to explain by natural laws; of or caused by the powers of spirits, gods, and magic
anonymous	[ənɑ́nəməs]	*adj.* name unknown; written or made by someone whose name is not known or stated
plain	[plein]	*adj.* simple; clear, easy to see, hear, or understand
complex	[kəmpléks]	*adj.* difficult to understand, explain, or deal with; not clear or simple, complicated or detailed
ornate	[ɔːrnéit]	*adj.* has a great deal of decoration; not simple
trait	[treit]	*n.* a particular quality or characteristic, especially of a person
mock	[mɑk]	*v.* to laugh at someone or something by copying it, or saying something funny about it
straightforward	[strèitfɔ́ːrwərd]	*adj.* simple, clear, and not difficult to understand

Exercise 2

distort	[distɔ́ːrt]	*v.* to change the way something sounds or looks that it becomes unclear or strange to recognize
procedure	[prəsíːdʒər]	*n.* a way of doing something, especially the correct or usual way
pioneer	[pàiəníər]	*v.* to do something important that is continued and developed later for the first time
examine	[igzǽmin]	*v.* to look at the body in order to check if a patient is healthy
underlying	[ʌ́ndərlàiiŋ]	*adj.* some features, ideas, causes that are the real ones but not directly stated

Exercise 3

supplier	[səpláiər]	*n.* a company, organization, or country that supplies or sells a product or service
shelter	[ʃéltər]	*n.* a building or roofed enclosure that gives cover or protection
dwelling	[dwéliŋ]	*n.* a house or building where people live
brick	[brik]	*n.* baked clay used in building construction
durable	[djúərəbəl]	*adj.* able to last

Check-up

Fill in the blanks with an appropriate word or phrase. Change the form if needed.

| anonymous | mythology | sink | durable |
| trait | mock | distort | examine |

1. Cindy majors in Greek and Roman _____ .
2. Charles is an atheist. He always _____ church and people's beliefs.
3. The ship hit a rock and _____ into the sea, causing the loss of a hundred lives.
4. Adam has _____ the shapes and forms of my painting!
5. This company's products are the best! They're _____ and don't break easily.
6. An _____ donor contributed $5000 to charity yesterday. Who could he be?
7. Frank's sense of humor is one of his most pleasing _____ .
8. My dentist told me that I had three new cavities after he _____ my teeth.

Exercise 1

*i*BT Reading

Question 1 to 4

1. The word **they** in paragraph 1 refers to
   - Ⓐ individuals and communities
   - Ⓑ historical events
   - Ⓒ the Icelandic Sagas
   - Ⓓ supernatural events

2. How does the author introduce the Icelandic Sagas in paragraph 1?
   - Ⓐ By giving examples of supernatural events in the 12th century epic poems
   - Ⓑ By comparing some shared qualities of epics from the time period
   - Ⓒ By referring to studies that doubt the dating of the Icelandic Sagas
   - Ⓓ By providing background on Icelandic civilization and culture

3. The word **admirable** in paragraph 2 is closest in meaning to
   - Ⓐ uncommon
   - Ⓑ normal
   - Ⓒ disrespectful
   - Ⓓ excellent

4. Why does the author mention other epics of the day in paragraph 2?
   - Ⓐ To indicate thematic similarities between them and the Sagas
   - Ⓑ To imply that the author of Beowulf also wrote some Sagas
   - Ⓒ To contrast with the differing styles of the Icelandic Sagas
   - Ⓓ To show some other types of epic that existed at the same time

The Icelandic Sagas

The Icelandic Sagas are epic tales written between the 12th and 13th centuries. Like many other epics composed or written during this time period, the stories tell the tales of important people and communities in the country's history and mythology. The stories are filled with the actions of heroes and important historical events and, like with other epics of the time, the Sagas detail the occurrences of supernatural events — gods interfering in order to help individuals or communities. However, while they are similar in some ways to other cultures' epics, the Icelandic Sagas are unique for a number of reasons.

The Icelandic Sagas, though written by different authors, most of them anonymous, all share in a plain, straightforward style. While other epics of the day, such as the Anglo-Saxon Beowulf, are extremely complex and ornate, the Icelandic Sagas seem to pride themselves on being very simple. That these characteristics are shared among the different authors of the Sagas seems to indicate that this was an admirable trait in Icelandic storytelling.

A second unique feature of the Sagas was their tone. While the stories were epic and heroic, telling the tales of brave men and women who were not afraid to die for their country, they were also often humorous. Because battle was usually the subject of the Sagas, this humor was frequently dark — that is, it made light of death and war. Other such epics took these matters very seriously, but the Icelandic point of view seemed to take the view that death was something to be mocked, not feared.

Glossary

saga a long story created in medieval times in Iceland or Norway
epic a long poem telling the story of the deeds of gods and great men and women, or the early history of a nation

Exercise 1

iBT Reading

Question 5 to 7

5. Which of the following best expresses the essential information in the highlighted sentence in paragraph 3? *Incorrect* choices change the meaning in important ways or leave out essential information.

   (A) The characters in the Sagas were courageous but funny at the same time.
   (B) The stories of Sagas were about brave men and women who weren't afraid to die.
   (C) The humorous characteristics of the heroes made the stories of Sagas light.
   (D) The humor used in the Sagas was another characteristic of the epic and heroic tales.

6. Why does the author mention humor in paragraph 3?

   (A) To show what kind of tone is used in other epics
   (B) To imply that the Sagas are read by many people
   (C) To give an example of tones used in the Sagas
   (D) To describe the Sagas' tone as a secondary feature

7. **Directions:** An introductory sentence for a brief summary of the passage is provided below. Complete the summary by selecting the THREE answer choices that express the most important ideas in the passage. Some sentences do not belong in the summary because they express ideas that are not presented in the passage or are minor ideas in the passage.

   The Sagas tell of the actions of heroes and historical and supernatural events.

   Answer Choices

   (A) The Icelandic Sagas' unique features come from their unique history and mythology.
   (B) Despite the similarities to other nations' epics, the Sagas have their own uniqueness.
   (C) The style of the Sagas is much simpler than that of other works at the time period.
   (D) The authors of the Sagas were not professional writers of ornate poetry.
   (E) The Sagas treated the subject of dying in a particularly unique and light way.
   (F) Death was not a subject that the writers of the Sagas were interested in.

The Icelandic Sagas

The Icelandic Sagas are epic tales written between the 12th and 13th centuries. Like many other epics composed or written during this time period, the stories tell the tales of important people and communities in the country's history and mythology. The stories are filled with the actions of heroes and important historical events and, like with other epics of the time, the Sagas detail the occurrences of supernatural events — gods interfering in order to help individuals or communities. However, while they are similar in some ways to other cultures' epics, the Icelandic Sagas are unique for a number of reasons.

The Icelandic Sagas, though written by different authors, most of them anonymous, all share in a plain, straightforward style. While other epics of the day, such as the Anglo-Saxon Beowulf, are extremely complex and ornate, the Icelandic Sagas seem to pride themselves on being very simple. That these characteristics are shared among the different authors of the Sagas seems to indicate that this was an admirable trait in Icelandic storytelling.

A second unique feature of the Sagas was their tone. While the stories were epic and heroic, telling the tales of brave men and women who were not afraid to die for their country, they were also often humorous. Because battle was usually the subject of the Sagas, this humor was frequently dark — that is, it made light of death and war. Other such epics took these matters very seriously, but the Icelandic point of view seemed to take the view that death was something to be mocked, not feared.

Exercise 2

*i*BT Reading

Question 1 to 4

1. The word opaque in paragraph 1 is closest in meaning to?
   - Ⓐ transparent
   - Ⓑ cloudy
   - Ⓒ black
   - Ⓓ thick

2. According to paragraph 1, which of the following is NOT a symptom of having cataracts?
   - Ⓐ Objects with particular colors cannot be distinguished.
   - Ⓑ Amount of light into eyes is decreased.
   - Ⓒ People undergo a slow vision loss.
   - Ⓓ A person's vision becomes distorted.

3. Why does the author mention halos in paragraph 1?
   - Ⓐ To give one of major causes of cataracts
   - Ⓑ To describe the blurry vision of people with cataracts
   - Ⓒ To show how cataracts can be detected
   - Ⓓ To emphasize the condition of cataracts

4. The phrase This technique in paragraph 2 refers to
   - Ⓐ Removing a clouded lens
   - Ⓑ Replacing a misty lens with new one
   - Ⓒ Surgical skills that are practiced in modern sugeries
   - Ⓓ Placing a patch on the eye

Cataract Surgery

Cataracts are a condition of the eye in which the clear lens becomes cloudy. Usually, this is a normal part of the aging process. Vision becomes slowly distorted, followed by a growing loss of vision. Halos appear around bright objects, such as car lights at night. Because almost no light can pass through an opaque lens, blindness may ultimately result. However, cataracts can form suddenly as the result of an injury.

Fortunately, this problem can be treated through a simple procedure of modern cataract surgery, pioneered by Sir Harold Ridley. After examining eyes, a surgeon can carefully remove the clouded lens and then replace it with an artificial one, an intra-ocular lens. A patch is then placed over the eye until the cut in the skin covering the outside of the eye heals. Vision is restored immediately. This technique is relatively free of complications and recovery time is minimal; however, the surgery cannot correct underlying medical problems already affecting the vision, such as glaucoma, an eye disease which can cause people to go gradually blind. In rare cases, an artificial lens can move out of its correct position and cause a surgical emergency or the loss of the eye.

But long before Ridley's method was employed, a far different surgical procedure existed. Documents show that cataract surgery was being performed as early as the 5th century B.C. in India. The first cataract surgeon, a man named Susruta, pioneered a technique that was still in use in some countries, up until the 20th century. This technique was called "couching" or "reclination." Rather than removing the clouded lens and replacing it with a clear one, the surgeon would push the cataract back into the eye. Though this improved vision, it did not perfectly restore a person's sight.

Glossary

cataract a layer over a person's eyes that prevent them from seeing properly
halo a circle of light around an object
intra-ocular relating to the inside of the eyes
patch a cover that is put on an injured eye
complication a medical problem that occurs as a result of another illness or disease

Exercise 2

iBT Reading
Question 5 to 6

5. How does the author explain Sir Harold Ridley's cataract surgery in paragraph 2?
   - Ⓐ By exemplifying the first cataract surgery by Dr. Ridley
   - Ⓑ By indicating side effects that can occur after a surgery
   - Ⓒ By explaining the major steps and the limitations of the cataract surgery
   - Ⓓ By listing the number of benefits of cataract surgery

6. **Directions:** Select the appropriate statements from the answer choices and match them to the type of surgery to which they relate. TWO of the answer choices will NOT be used.

   Answer Choices
   - Ⓐ It has a short recovery time.
   - Ⓑ Complications commonly occur.
   - Ⓒ More than two eye surgeries are required.
   - Ⓓ A surgeon pushes cataract back into the eye.
   - Ⓔ It was used up until the 20th century.
   - Ⓕ A patient's vision is restored right after surgery.
   - Ⓖ It was performed in India around 400 B.C.

   Ridley's Surgery
   •
   •

   Susruta's Surgery
   •
   •
   •

Cataract Surgery

Cataracts are a condition of the eye in which the clear lens becomes cloudy. Usually, this is a normal part of the aging process. Vision becomes slowly distorted, followed by a growing loss of vision. Halos appear around bright objects, such as car lights at night. Because almost no light can pass through an opaque lens, blindness may ultimately result. However, cataracts can form suddenly as the result of an injury.

Fortunately, this problem can be treated through a simple procedure of modern cataract surgery, pioneered by Sir Harold Ridley. After examining eyes, a surgeon can carefully remove the clouded lens and then replace it with an artificial one, an intra-ocular lens. A patch is then placed over the eye until the cut in the skin covering the outside of the eye heals. Vision is restored immediately. This technique is relatively free of complications and recovery time is minimal; however, the surgery cannot correct underlying medical problems already affecting the vision, such as glaucoma, an eye disease which can cause people to go gradually blind. In rare cases, an artificial lens can move out of its correct position and cause a surgical emergency or the loss of the eye.

But long before Ridley's method was employed, a far different surgical procedure existed. Documents show that cataract surgery was being performed as early as the 5th century B.C. in India. The first cataract surgeon, a man named Susruta, pioneered a technique that was still in use in some countries, up until the 20th century. This technique was called "couching" or "reclination." Rather than removing the clouded lens and replacing it with a clear one, the surgeon would push the cataract back into the eye. Though this improved vision, it did not perfectly restore a person's sight.

Exercise 3

*i*BT Reading

Question 1 to 4

1. The word prosper in paragraph 1 is closest in meaning to
   - Ⓐ build
   - Ⓑ succeed
   - Ⓒ discover
   - Ⓓ proceed

2. How does the author introduce the sod houses in paragraph 1?
   - Ⓐ By suggesting that the sod houses were well adapted to the environment
   - Ⓑ By implying that the pioneers didn't have experiences of construction
   - Ⓒ By showing how the sod houses are better than the ones in the east
   - Ⓓ By explaining the reasons why the pioneers had to build such a house

3. How does the author explain a sod house in paragraph 2?
   - Ⓐ By explaining the two major parts of the house and their function
   - Ⓑ By describing materials used to build major parts of the house
   - Ⓒ By describing the overall appearance of the house from the outside
   - Ⓓ By providing the reasons why the materials are used for the house

4. According to paragraph 2, grass roots
   - Ⓐ had to be shaken off the earth before being put on sod houses
   - Ⓑ were often wrapped around branches or twigs
   - Ⓒ were kept to hold the earth with them
   - Ⓓ prevented the houses from being easily moved

The Sod House

As pioneer families arrived from the eastern U.S. to the mid-western states, they had to use adaptive building techniques that had never been seen before on the East Coast. At first, the Midwest was a wide-open area inhabited here and there by Native Americans. So when the pioneers from the East arrived to begin their new lives on the prairie, there were no towns or suppliers where they could go and buy things to build a new home. It took time to mill the lumber needed to construct a home. Besides that, much of the Midwest is a giant grassland, lacking trees altogether. But finding shelter was important if they were to survive and prosper in their new homes. So many pioneer families built sod houses as their first homes on the prairie.

Sod houses, or "soddies," were small dwellings with walls built entirely of sod — a surface section of soil that has grass growing in it. The grass roots kept the sections of earth together, so that they could be used by the people as bricks in constructing the building. The roofs of sod houses were made by using whatever twigs, branches, and brush, which were then covered with more pieces of sod.

Though fairly simple, these homes were extremely warm and surprisingly durable. Families were able to live in them until they were able to construct something more permanent. They would move whatever furniture they had into the dwelling, as well as install a wood stove and chimney. Though there was very little wood on the prairies, anything found on the prairie such as animal dung and twigs provided fuel to get through the long winters.

Unfortunately, there weren't any windows in soddies, people frequently had many problems with the smoke from the wood fires, like if there were any problems with the chimney, the entire house could fill with smoke and everyone would have to leave until the air cleared.

Glossary

prairie a wide, treeless, grassy plain, especially found in North America
lumber rough pieces of wood, or trees cut down for wood
sod a piece of earth with grass and roots growing in it

Exercise 3

iBT Reading

Question 5 to 6

5. Why does the author mention branches and brush in paragraph 2?
   - Ⓐ To illustrate materials in housing construction
   - Ⓑ To imply that there were not many materials available
   - Ⓒ To emphasize that the houses were not well made
   - Ⓓ To suggest the pioneers should have used other materials

6. Which of the following best expresses the essential information in the highlighted sentence in paragraph 4? *Incorrect* choices change the meaning in important ways or leave out essential information.
   - Ⓐ Chimneys frequently caused problems because of the smoke from the wood fires inside the house.
   - Ⓑ Because there were no windows, the smoke from the wood fire would stay longer in the house.
   - Ⓒ People often suffered from wood fire smoke because there were no windows to release the smoke.
   - Ⓓ People had to open the door and leave the house because of the smoke from the wood fires.

The Sod House

As pioneer families arrived from the eastern U.S. to the mid-western states, they had to use adaptive building techniques that had never been seen before on the East Coast. At first, the Midwest was a wide-open area inhabited here and there by Native Americans. So when the pioneers from the East arrived to begin their new lives on the prairie, there were no towns or suppliers where they could go and buy things to build a new home. It took time to mill the lumber needed to construct a home. Besides that, much of the Midwest is a giant grassland, lacking trees altogether. But finding shelter was important if they were to survive and prosper in their new homes. So many pioneer families built sod houses as their first homes on the prairie.

Sod houses, or "soddies," were small dwellings with walls built entirely of sod — a surface section of soil that has grass growing in it. The grass roots kept the sections of earth together, so that they could be used by the people as bricks in constructing the building. The roofs of sod houses were made by using whatever twigs, branches, and brush, which were then covered with more pieces of sod.

Though fairly simple, these homes were extremely warm and surprisingly durable. Families were able to live in them until they were able to construct something more permanent. They would move whatever furniture they had into the dwelling, as well as install a wood stove and chimney. Though there was very little wood on the prairies, anything found on the prairie such as animal dung and twigs provided fuel to get through the long winters.

Unfortunately, there weren't any windows in soddies, people frequently had many problems with the smoke from the wood fires, like if there were any problems with the chimney, the entire house could fill with smoke and everyone would have to leave until the air cleared.

Exercise 3

iBT Reading

Question 7

7. Directions: An introductory sentence for a brief summary of the passage is provided below. Complete the summary by selecting the THREE answer choices that do not belong in the summary because the express ideas that are not presented in the passage or are minor ideas in the passage.

Pioneers coming to the American Midwest had to adapt their building technology to the region.

Answer Choices

- Ⓐ As the smoke could not exit the windows well, the houses often became quite smoky inside.
- Ⓑ Because there was always a lack of lumber and tools, it took time to mill trees for permanent housing.
- Ⓒ Smoke caused some problems but the strong prairie homes that they used before their permanent homes were warm and nice.
- Ⓓ The main material of the sod houses was sod, soil that has grass growing on it.
- Ⓔ They constructed their dwellings from brick made of soil and grass.
- Ⓕ Lacking traditional building materials, pioneers found that they had to use the materials they had at hand.

Text Outline Choose the correct text outline of the passage.

(A) P1 — Background of pioneer families' first homes: Sod houses
 P2 — Definition and general description of sod houses
 P3 — Explanation of some advantages of sod houses
 P4 — Explanation of the disadvantage of sod houses

(B) P1 — Historical background of new settlers in the western states
 P2 — Definition and description of sod houses
 P3 — Description and causes of sod houses
 P4 — Problems of sod houses

The Sod House

As pioneer families arrived from the eastern U.S. to the mid-western states, they had to use adaptive building techniques that had never been seen before on the East Coast. At first, the Midwest was a wide-open area inhabited here and there by Native Americans. So when the pioneers from the East arrived to begin their new lives on the prairie, there were no towns or suppliers where they could go and buy things to build a new home. It took time to mill the lumber needed to construct a home. Besides that, much of the Midwest is a giant grassland, lacking trees altogether. But finding shelter was important if they were to survive and prosper in their new homes. So many pioneer families built sod houses as their first homes on the prairie.

Sod houses, or "soddies," were small dwellings with walls built entirely of sod — a surface section of soil that has grass growing in it. The grass roots kept the sections of earth together, so that they could be used by the people as bricks in constructing the building. The roofs of sod houses were made by using whatever twigs, branches, and brush, which were then covered with more pieces of sod.

Though fairly simple, these homes were extremely warm and surprisingly durable. Families were able to live in them until they were able to construct something more permanent. They would move whatever furniture they had into the dwelling, as well as install a wood stove and chimney. Though there was very little wood on the prairies, anything found on the prairie such as animal dung and twigs provided fuel to get through the long winters.

Unfortunately, there weren't any windows in soddies, people frequently had many problems with the smoke from the wood fires, like if there were any problems with the chimney, the entire house could fill with smoke and everyone would have to leave until the air cleared.

Vocabulary Test

Choose the closest meaning of each underlined word or phrase.

1. The question is too complicated. Please give me a straightforward answer.
   (A) complex   (B) simple   (C) confusing   (D) unusual

2. Don't drive recklessly unless you want to die.
   (A) rudely   (B) fundamentally   (C) fast   (D) carelessly

3. I always ponder how to improve the efficiency in the workplace.
   (A) worry   (B) complain   (C) reflect on   (D) suggest

4. I didn't miss the subtle change in his face when he was blamed for the mistake.
   (A) consistent   (B) certain   (C) slight   (D) obvious

5. I hate Randy! He always mocks my way of walking.
   (A) laughs at   (B) judges   (C) blames   (D) praises

6. James became the CEO of a chemical company and now he is seeking a way to enhance his power.
   (A) distribute   (B) compromise   (C) increase   (D) reduce

7. The underlying problem causing the demonstrations is wage and racial discrimination.
   (A) fundamental   (B) first   (C) important   (D) remarkable

8. The tax reforms in the country was pioneered by a man named Bruce.
   (A) completed   (B) inherited   (C) developed   (D) interfered

9. Because of the excessively high prices in Korea, I decided to get one more part-time job at night.
   (A) temperately   (B) extremely   (C) exaggeratedly   (D) radically

10. Researchers perceive the phenomenon as dissolution.
    (A) solve   (B) claim   (C) warn   (D) recognize

11. I think angels are supernatural beings.
    (A) imaginary   (B) actual   (C) ghostly   (D) practical

12. An anonymous author wrote this letter to our magazine.
    (A) famous   (B) notorious   (C) naive   (D) nameless

Chapter 08
INSERTION

Chapter 8

Insertion

Sample Item **Read the following passage and answer the questions.**

*i*BT Reading

Question 1

1. Look at the four squares [■] that indicate where the following sentence could be added to the passage.

   Thus, they set up their own camp that was known as Ragtown.

   Where would the sentence best fit? Click on a square [■] to add the sentence to the passage.

   Ⓐ A
   Ⓑ B
   Ⓒ C
   Ⓓ D

The Hoover Dam Project

A When the U.S. government planned to build the Hoover Dam in the middle of the Mojave Desert during the Great Depression, it also planned to construct a town for workers to live in. B However, workers began arriving at the site where the dam would be constructed before the city could be built. C An impoverished settlement with no running water, sanitation, or electricity, this place served as home for hundreds of workers for many months into the Hoover Dam project. For a period, families there endured the desert heat and harsh living conditions, thankful that they had any work at all. But finally, the government, with the help of private enterprise, constructed Boulder City, a comfortable desert town still in existence today. D

STUDY POINT Thus란 부사와, they가 무엇을 받는지 살펴 주어진 문장을 대입해 보고, 연결이 가장 자연스러운 위치가 어디인지 파악한다.

Overview

Insertion

Insertion 문제는 전체 글 속의 문장들을 서로 일관성(coherence)있게 구성할 수 있는가를 평가하는 유형이다. 글쓴이는 주제를 효과적으로 전달하기 위해 일관성이란 요소를 사용하게 된다. 일관성이란 전체 글을 이루고 있는 문장들이 서로 긴밀하게 연결되어 있음을 말한다. 수험자가 글의 구체적인 내용과 논리적 흐름을 잘 파악하는 가를 측정하는데 주목적이 있다. 평소 글을 읽을 때 각 문장이 어떻게 긴밀하게 연결되어 있는지를 살피는 습관을 갖는 것이 중요하다.

Question Type

- Look at the four squares [■] that indicate where the following sentence could be added to the passage. Where would the sentence best fit? Click on a square [■] to add the sentence to the passage.

General Strategy

1. 주어진 문장의 뜻을 파악하고 square [■]가 있는 부분의 문장들을 이해하고 삽입되는 문장과 square [■]가 있는 부분의 clue들을 파악한다.
   - Addition: another, other, also, in addition to
   - Contrast: however/but, in contrast, though/although, while
   - Example: for example, for instance, such as, like, including
   - Cause/effect: because, thus, as the result, therefore
   - Reference: this, it, his, etc.
2. 문장과 문장은 어떤 연관성으로 이어져있다. 앞 문장의 예, 부연 설명, 결과 등과 같은 문장 간의 연관성을 생각하여 글의 흐름이 자연스럽도록 한다.

Basic Drill 1

Clues in the text

Indicate where the sentence best fits.

1 **Although traditional heating and air conditioning are used, it takes much less energy to cool or heat a "green" house.**

Wooden frames support most of the homes built in America. **A** This requires a huge amount of lumber, which of course comes from forests. **B** Houses built using green technology use roughly 60% less wood than traditional homes, due in large part to advanced engineering practices. **C** This is because the walls are thicker, which means more insulation can be used. **D** The highly insulated walls help keep the houses cool in summer and warm in the winter. And unlike traditional homes, all of the air that enters these houses is filtered.

(A) A (B) B (C) C (D) D

2 **For example, Ben Franklin, one of the most influential early Americans, claimed the turkey was a model of courage and far more respectable than the eagle.**

The bald eagle is the national symbol of the United States, but it had a strong competitor in the early days of the country. **A** At that time, the turkey, a large game bird found all over the country, was in fact nominated to serve as the national bird. Though today we think of the turkey as a fat, ungraceful, and slightly unintelligent animal, there were many who regarded it as an excellent choice. **B** The eagle, he felt, flew away when in danger. **C** On the other hand, he knew that a turkey would bravely defend its territory against attack. **D**

(A) A (B) B (C) C (D) D

3

> For instance, he is believed to have descended from the early kings of Athens, Greece on his father's side of the family.

Given his illustrious background, distinguished because of famous family members and wealth, Plato's intellectual achievement should be no surprise. **A** His mother's side of the family was noteworthy, as well. His mother, Perictione, was related to the 6th century B.C. lawmaker Solon, a man known both for his wisdom and his poetic abilities. **B** When Plato was still a child, his father died. **C** His mother then married a man named Pyrilampes, who was an associate of the renowned statesman Pericles. **D**

(A) A   (B) B   (C) C   (D) D

Basic Drill 2

Sequence signals

Arrange the following sentences in the correct order.

1
- **A** Home-buyers have become increasingly interested in environmental preservation.

- **B** Green building is defined as a building technology that uses natural materials sparingly and avoids the use of harmful chemical products.

- **C** In addition, the dwellings are specifically designed to use less electricity to heat and cool.

- **D** For this demands, construction engineers are now focusing more on "green building" practices.

_____ → _____ → _____ → _____

2
- **A** Therefore, even modern artists often use the old-fashioned process of making paint for themselves to get the vibrant colors they want.

- **B** These medieval tempera paints are much different than those sold in art supply stores today. The modern replacements are made with artificial pigments and a chemical base whose effects are nowhere near as clear and bright as their predecessors.

- **C** Different colored natural pigments extracted from stones and vegetables, were added to color the paint.

- **D** Tempera is a medium that is created from a mixture of egg and water. This medium dates back to the Middle Age and, over the years, it has been a favorite of many artists because of its extremely bright and vibrant colors.

_____ → _____ → _____ → _____

3

A Rather than building its own nest in a tree, like the larger owls, the burrowing owl lives in holes in the ground dug by prairie dogs or gophers, or even human beings.

B The burrowing owl is one of the smallest owls we know, growing only to about eight inches tall.

C Thus, the name "burrowing owl" is a very appropriate one for this bird.

D These creatures live in the desert and on the prairies, where they feed on a variety of prey, such as insects, rodents, and reptiles. One of the most interesting things about the burrowing owl is its nest.

_____ → _____ → _____ → _____

4

A Based on the comparison they made, the researchers suggest that the difference in spin rates can be attributed to the earth's magnetic fields.

B First, researchers charted the time it took for earthquake waves to travel through the core.

C While studying the rate of seismic waves from earthquakes, geologists recently made an interesting discovery: they found that the earth's core spins slightly faster than the rest of the planet.

D They then compared it to the time it took for the same waves to travel through different parts of the earth.

_____ → _____ → _____ → _____

VOCABULARY home-buyer 주택 구입자 preservation 보존, 유지 define ~을 정의하다, ~을 분명히 하다 sparingly 절약하여 old-fashioned 구식의, 옛날에 유행했던 vibrant (색 등이) 밝은, 빛나는 pigment 그림 물감 extract 뽑다, 추출하다 medium 제작 재료 date back (시기가) 거슬러 올라가다 prairie dog 프레리 도그(개 비슷한 울음 소리를 내는 북미 대초원의 marmot 일종) * marmot 땅을 파고 구멍에 사는 설치류 동물 gopher 땅다람쥐 rodent (쥐 등의) 설치류 reptile 파충류 attribute (원인을)~에 돌리다 magnetic field 자기장 chart 도표로 기록하다 core 핵 seismic wave 지진파

Vocabulary Preview for Exercise

Read and Pronounce

Exercise 1

dissatisfied (with)	[dissǽtisfàid] *adj.* feeling or showing displeasure
sloppy	[slápi] *adj.* done in a very careless way
dogmatic	[dɔ(:)gmǽtik] *adj.* usually holding one's beliefs very strongly and expecting other people to accept them without question
insistent	[insístənt] *adj.* saying very firmly that something should be done or that something is true
bring about	to make something happen, especially to cause changes in a situation
appreciation	[əprì:ʃiéiʃən] *n.* understanding of the worth of something; a positive judgment of the worth, quality or facts of something
hand down	to give or leave something to people who are younger or who will live after you
genuine	[dʒénjuin] *adj.* real; actually being what he/she/it seems to be
embrace	[imbréis] *v.* to include and accept something
sentiment	[séntəmənt] *n.* thought or judgment influenced by feeling

Exercise 2

take up	to fill or use, especially in an undesirable way
leach	[li:tʃ] *v.* to separate a substance from a material, or to remove substances in a material by passing water through it
bark	[bá:rk] *n.* the strong outer covering of a tree
sterile	[stéril] *adj.* being free from all harmful bacteria and other small living beings
emerge	[imə́:rdʒ] *v.* to come out from inside or from being hidden

| Check-up |

Fill in the blanks with an appropriate word or phrase. Change the form if needed.

| hand down | dogmatic | dissatisfied | embrace |
| sterile | genuine | bring about | leach |

1. This sword is a family treasure that was _____ by my great grandfather many years ago.
2. This liquid should be preserved as _____, with no bacteria.
3. The church that Alfred belongs to is considered to be very _____.
4. It's raining heavily. I think this rain will _____ pesticides the soil.
5. This bag is made from _____ alligator leather.
6. I deserve the better treatment. I'm _____ with your decision.
7. Her work traces developments in Ancient Greece and _____ the whole field of Ancient Greek Art.
8. New technology has _____ many social changes.

Exercise 1

*i*BT Reading

Question 1 to 4

1. The word cliched in paragraph 1 is closest in meaning to
   - Ⓐ interesting
   - Ⓑ surprising
   - Ⓒ boring
   - Ⓓ strange

2. Why does the author mention Raphael in paragraph 1?
   - Ⓐ To point out the similarities between him and the Pre-Raphaelite painters
   - Ⓑ To indicate where the group's name and philosophy originated
   - Ⓒ To contrast his theories of art with his disciples'
   - Ⓓ To imply that the Pre-Raphaelite painters were not as influential as him

3. Look at the four squares [■] that indicate where the following sentence could be added to the passage.

   In other words, they wanted paintings full of detail, color, and complicated compositions.

   Where would the sentence best fit? Click on a square [■] to add the sentence to the passage.
   - Ⓐ A   Ⓑ B   Ⓒ C   Ⓓ D

4. Which sentence below best expresses the essential information in the highlighted sentence in paragraph 2? *Incorrect* choices change the meaning in important ways or leave out essential information.
   - Ⓐ They were cautious of setting up their rules of painting that should be appreciated by artists.
   - Ⓑ Instead of insisting a certain way of paintings, they tried to respect individual painter's works.
   - Ⓒ There were specific ways of painting that they claimed individual artists should appreciate and follow.
   - Ⓓ They thought the individual painter who ignored the rules insisted by teachers should be respected.

The Pre-Raphaelite Brotherhood

The Pre-Raphaelite painters were a group of artists who were dissatisfied with the art of their time. **[A]** The Pre-Raphaelite Brotherhood was founded in 1848 by John Everett Millais, Dante Gabriel Rossetti and William Holman Hunt. **[B]** The group's intention was to protest what they saw as the wrong direction taken by painting following the influence of the painter Raphael. **[C]** Rather than follow sloppy technique that was a formulaic and cliched form of academic teaching of art, they sought to restore creativity and originality. **[D]**

These young painters were extremely idealistic and felt that they could change the nature of painting for the better. But they were also wary of being too dogmatic — that is, being too insistent of the rules of painting — saying that there were specific ways a good painter should follow, and they hoped to bring about an appreciation for the individual artist. Too many artists, they felt, were just following the models handed down to them by their teachers, rather than expressing their own ideas or emotions through the canvas.

Though they did not want to be too rigid or strict, the Pre-Raphaelites did have goals for their group. The first of which was to have genuine ideas to express. Artists, they felt, were just painting what was expected — portraits, landscapes, and so on — not what they were interested in. They also felt that painters should pay close attention to nature so as to be able to represent it effectively. Another important goal was to embrace sincerity. They felt that contemporary art was too cynical and unfeeling, while works from the past often contained true sentiment.

Glossary

formulaic not original and using a similar pattern that has been used many times before
portrait a painting, drawing, or photograph of a person
landscape a wide view of country scenery; a picture of such a scene

Exercise 1

iBT Reading

Question 5 to 6

5. The word rigid in paragraph 3 is closest in meaning to
   - Ⓐ inflexible
   - Ⓑ specific
   - Ⓒ expected
   - Ⓓ confusing

6. **Directions:** An introductory sentence for a brief summary of the passage is provided below. Complete the summary by selecting the THREE answer choices that express the most important ideas in the passage. Some sentences do not belong in the summary because they express ideas that are not presented in the passage or are minor ideas in the passage.

   The "Pre-Raphaelite brotherhood" was a new art movement born in the mid-19th century.

   Answer Choices

   - Ⓐ The Pre-Raphaelites were a group of artists who resisted following Raphael's painting style, aimed to create colorful, complicated works of art.
   - Ⓑ The Pre-Raphaelite painters generally followed Raphael's use of detail, color, and complicated compositions to painting.
   - Ⓒ These painters felt that the best art came from being individualistic, rather than following the rules.
   - Ⓓ Many of the artists at the time learned painting techniques following models provided by schools.
   - Ⓔ To improve portrait and landscape painting, they felt people needed to be more attentive to nature.
   - Ⓕ The group stressed sincerity, ideas, and attention to nature as the keys to good art.

The Pre-Raphaelite Brotherhood

The Pre-Raphaelite painters were a group of artists who were dissatisfied with the art of their time. [A] The Pre-Raphaelite Brotherhood was founded in 1848 by John Everett Millais, Dante Gabriel Rossetti and William Holman Hunt. [B] The group's intention was to protest what they saw as the wrong direction taken by painting following the influence of the painter Raphael. [C] Rather than follow sloppy technique that was a formulaic and cliched form of academic teaching of art, they sought to restore creativity and originality. [D]

These young painters were extremely idealistic and felt that they could change the nature of painting for the better. But they were also wary of being too dogmatic — that is, being too insistent of the rules of painting — saying that there were specific ways a good painter should follow, and they hoped to bring about an appreciation for the individual artist. Too many artists, they felt, were just following the models handed down to them by their teachers, rather than expressing their own ideas or emotions through the canvas.

Though they did not want to be too rigid or strict, the Pre-Raphaelites did have goals for their group. The first of which was to have genuine ideas to express. Artists, they felt, were just painting what was expected — portraits, landscapes, and so on — not what they were interested in. They also felt that painters should pay close attention to nature so as to be able to represent it effectively. Another important goal was to embrace sincerity. They felt that contemporary art was too cynical and unfeeling, while works from the past often contained true sentiment.

Exercise 2

iBT Reading
Question 1 to 4

1. Look at the four squares [■] that indicate where the following sentence could be added to paragraph 1.

   These can deprive the plant of nutrients as well as take up its space.

   Where would the sentence best fit? Click on a square [■] to add the sentence to the paragraph.

   Ⓐ A   Ⓑ B   Ⓒ C   Ⓓ D

2. The word rendering in paragraph 1 is closet in meaning to
   Ⓐ making
   Ⓑ buying
   Ⓒ producing
   Ⓓ controlling

3. How does the author emphasize the risks to plants in soil in paragraph 1?
   Ⓐ By indicating major insects and diseases in soil
   Ⓑ By giving examples of the problems that soil has
   Ⓒ By explaining problems that the weather causes
   Ⓓ By showing how beneficial nutrients are removed

4. The word conventionally in paragraph 2 is closest in meaning to
   Ⓐ traditionally
   Ⓑ carefully
   Ⓒ agriculturally
   Ⓓ methodically

202   Part C

Hydroponic Gardening

All plants need nutrients, light, and air to grow well. When seeds are planted in soil, they absorb nutrients in the soil through their roots. This soil, however, supports a number of potential risks to plant health as well. **A** Eggs and larvae of insects may be in the soil, for example, as well as soil-borne diseases and funguses. **B** Predatory plants or weeds may also be in the soil, creating problems. **C** Additionally, due to the weather or the environment, the soil can be robbed of its beneficial nutrients. **D** Even if fertilizers are added, rain and sun can leach the soil and remove the fertilizer, thereby rendering the added fertilizer worthless. Therefore, growing plants in the ground, while being the traditional horticulture method, still has risks and is not ideal.

Hydroponic gardening offers a solution to these problems. Essentially, this kind of gardening means to raise plants in water or another non-soil based medium. **E** For instance, a plant raised in peat moss or bark is considered a hydroponic-raised plant. **F** First of all, the medium is sterile, unlike soil, so pests and disease will not be able to attack the plant as it grows. **G** Weeds, too, will not emerge to compete with the plant. **H** Another benefit is that nutrients are added directly to the medium, and they cannot leach out. Hydroponic plants, because of these ideal conditions, are much stronger, bigger, and healthier than conventionally grown plants.

Glossary

larvae the worm-like young of an insect between leaving the egg and changing into a winged form
fungus a plant that has no flowers, leaves, or green coloring, such as a mushroom or a toadstool. Other types of fungus such as mould are extremely small and look like a fine powder
predatory especially a wild animal that kills and eats other animals
fertilizer a natural or chemical substance that is put on the land to make crops grow better
horticulture the study and practice of growing plants
medium a substance in which objects or living things exist

Exercise 2

iBT Reading

Question 5 to 7

5. Look at the four squares [■] that indicate where the following sentence could be added to paragraph 2.

   Whether in water or another non-soil medium, there are a number of advantages to hydroponics.

   Where would the sentence best fit? Click on a square [■] to add the sentence to the paragraph.

   (A)   (B)   (C)   (D) H

6. Why does the author mention plants raised in peat moss or bark in paragraph 2?
   (A) To imply that it is possible to grow plants in them
   (B) To provide major materials used for this type of gardening
   (C) To compare with plants raised in water
   (D) To give an example of non-soil based gardening

7. **Directions:** Select the appropriate statements from the answer choices and match them to the type of plants to which they relate. TWO of the answer choices will NOT be used.

   Answer Choices
   (A) Nutrients are at risk of being washed away.
   (B) Insects are not able to take nutrients.
   (C) Plants are able to grow very large.
   (D) Direct sunlight is not needed.
   (E) Invasive plants compete for space and nutrients.
   (F) Plants are immune to pesticides and other chemicals.
   (G) Plants are provided with sterilized conditions in which to grow.

   Traditional Plants
   •
   •

   Hydroponic Plants
   •
   •
   •

Hydroponic Gardening

All plants need nutrients, light, and air to grow well. When seeds are planted in soil, they absorb nutrients in the soil through their roots. This soil, however, supports a number of potential risks to plant health as well. [A] Eggs and larvae of insects may be in the soil, for example, as well as soil-borne diseases and funguses. [B] Predatory plants or weeds may also be in the soil, creating problems. [C] Additionally, due to the weather or the environment, the soil can be robbed of its beneficial nutrients. [D] Even if fertilizers are added, rain and sun can leach the soil and remove the fertilizer, thereby rendering the added fertilizer worthless. Therefore, growing plants in the ground, while being the traditional horticulture method, still has risks and is not ideal.

Hydroponic gardening offers a solution to these problems. Essentially, this kind of gardening means to raise plants in water or another non-soil based medium. [E] For instance, a plant raised in peat moss or bark is considered a hydroponic-raised plant. [F] First of all, the medium is sterile, unlike soil, so pests and disease will not be able to attack the plant as it grows. [G] Weeds, too, will not emerge to compete with the plant. [H] Another benefit is that nutrients are added directly to the medium, and they cannot leach out. Hydroponic plants, because of these ideal conditions, are much stronger, bigger, and healthier than conventionally grown plants.

Exercise 3

*i*BT Reading

Question 1 to 4

1. Which sentence below best expresses the essential information in the highlighted sentence in paragraph 1? *Incorrect* choices change the meaning in important ways or leave out essential information.
   - Ⓐ Though it is not often required, most people feel that early education is important, and the majority of American children attend kindergarten.
   - Ⓑ Regardless of the awareness of the importance of early childhood education, most of people generally send their kids since it is required by the state.
   - Ⓒ Though most American children attend kindergarten, many states don't actually require childhood education.
   - Ⓓ Because 5% of all American children fail to attend kindergarten, the individual state governments should implement policies that require attendance.

2. The word measurable in paragraph 1 is closest in meaning to
   - Ⓐ obscure
   - Ⓑ noticeable
   - Ⓒ useful
   - Ⓓ possible

3. The word resoundingly in paragraph 1 is closest in meaning to
   - Ⓐ possibly
   - Ⓑ hopefully
   - Ⓒ subtly
   - Ⓓ definitely

4. Why does the author mention underprivileged backgrounds in paragraph 1?
   - Ⓐ To note that more funding is needed to research the issue.
   - Ⓑ To imply that underprivileged children are not good at school
   - Ⓒ To emphasize that the results were true for all kinds of children
   - Ⓓ To suggest that underprivileged children don't need to enroll in kindergarten

Benefits of Early Childhood Education

Increasing awareness of the importance of early childhood education has resulted in almost 95 percent of all American children enrolling in kindergarten programs, though many states do not require that children attend kindergarten — only 13 of the 50 states actually require attendance. Enrollment in pre-school programs, which are available to children over three, is up significantly, as well. Is there a measurable benefit to having children enroll in educational programs so early in life? In fact, numerous studies have demonstrated that early school attendance has a resoundingly positive effect on children's later lives. This appears to be true even for children who come from underprivileged backgrounds.

According to the studies, children who enroll in school before the law requires receive several advantages. **A** First is in terms of their academic careers. **B** Children who went to kindergarten and pre-school are less likely to have to take remedial classes later on to improve their ability to read, write, or do mathematics, especially when they find these things difficult. **C** These students also have higher rates of graduation and better overall attitudes about school. **D**

Another type of advantage is in terms of careers. **E** This directly influences their earning potential and the types of jobs they can get. **F** These children, as they become adults, have lower rates of unemployment than those who did not enroll in early schooling. **G** Therefore, the effects of early childhood education can be seen to be beneficial both in the short and long-term. **H**

Glossary

underprivileged not having the advantages of an average person's life; poor living in bad housing, having low-quality education etc.
remedial curing, helping

Exercise 3

iBT Reading
Question 5 to 7

5. Look at the four squares [■] that indicate where the following sentence could be added to paragraph 2.

   Additionally, they are less likely to fail classes or score low grades during their school careers.

   Where would the sentence best fit? Click on a square [■] to add the sentence to the paragraph.

   Ⓐ A   Ⓑ B   Ⓒ C   Ⓓ D

6. How does the author emphasize the impact of early schooling on academic success in paragraph 2 and 3?
   Ⓐ By providing statistics about test scores
   Ⓑ By listing the many benefits it gives to children
   Ⓒ By noting teacher research on the issue
   Ⓓ By comparing pre-school graduates to non pre-school graduates

7. Look at the four squares [■] that indicate where the following sentence could be added to paragraph 3.

   Pre-school and kindergarten graduates are more likely to not only graduate high school, but to go on to college.

   Where would the sentence best fit? Click on a square [■] to add the sentence to the paragraph.

   Ⓐ E   Ⓑ F   Ⓒ G   Ⓓ H

Benefits of Early Childhood Education

Increasing awareness of the importance of early childhood education has resulted in almost 95 percent of all American children enrolling in kindergarten programs, though many states do not require that children attend kindergarten — only 13 of the 50 states actually require attendance. Enrollment in pre-school programs, which are available to children over three, is up significantly, as well. Is there a measurable benefit to having children enroll in educational programs so early in life? In fact, numerous studies have demonstrated that early school attendance has a resoundingly positive effect on children's later lives. This appears to be true even for children who come from underprivileged backgrounds.

According to the studies, children who enroll in school before the law requires receive several advantages. **A** First is in terms of their academic careers. **B** Children who went to kindergarten and pre-school are less likely to have to take remedial classes later on to improve their ability to read, write, or do mathematics, especially when they find these things difficult. **C** These students also have higher rates of graduation and better overall attitudes about school. **D**

Another type of advantage is in terms of careers. **E** This directly influences their earning potential and the types of jobs they can get. **F** These children, as they become adults, have lower rates of unemployment than those who did not enroll in early schooling. **G** Therefore, the effects of early childhood education can be seen to be beneficial both in the short and long-term. **H**

Exercise 3

iBT Reading

Question 8

8. **Directions:** An introductory sentence for a brief summary of the passage is provided below. Complete the summary by selecting the THREE answer choices that do not belong in the summary because they express ideas that are not presented in the passage or are minor ideas in the passage.

Preschool and kindergarten attendance is quite high countrywide.

Answer Choices

Ⓐ Many parents feel that early school programs play an important role in their children's lives both in school and later employment.

Ⓑ Not only wealthy parents, but parents who are not also send their kids to kindergarten and pre-school programs.

Ⓒ Students who begin school earlier tend to do better in their academic careers and also have a higher graduation rate.

Ⓓ Kids who start school early generally show better attendance in schools and this affects their success in college.

Ⓔ Early childhood education is popular in America and also seems to positively impact the adult lives of its attendees.

Ⓕ The fact that there are more children attending kindergartens has influenced the unemployment rate in the United States.

Text Outline Choose the correct text outline of the passage.

(A) P1 — Introduction of early enrollment and the reason of its increase
    P2 — Benefits of early education
    P3 — Other benefits of early education

(B) P1 — Introduction of the increase of enrollment in early education
    P2 — Positive effects on academic career
    P3 — Positive effects on job career

Benefits of Early Childhood Education

Increasing awareness of the importance of early childhood education has resulted in almost 95 percent of all American children enrolling in kindergarten programs, though many states do not require that children attend kindergarten — only 13 of the 50 states actually require attendance. Enrollment in pre-school programs, which are available to children over three, is up significantly, as well. Is there a measurable benefit to having children enroll in educational programs so early in life? In fact, numerous studies have demonstrated that early school attendance has a resoundingly positive effect on children's later lives. This appears to be true even for children who come from underprivileged backgrounds.

According to the studies, children who enroll in school before the law requires receive several advantages. [A] First is in terms of their academic careers. [B] Children who went to kindergarten and pre-school are less likely to have to take remedial classes later on to improve their ability to read, write, or do mathematics, especially when they find these things difficult. [C] These students also have higher rates of graduation and better overall attitudes about school. [D]

Another type of advantage is in terms of careers. [E] This directly influences their earning potential and the types of jobs they can get. [F] These children, as they become adults, have lower rates of unemployment than those who did not enroll in early schooling. [G] Therefore, the effects of early childhood education can be seen to be beneficial both in the short and long-term. [H]

Vocabulary Test

Choose the closest meaning of each underlined word or phrase.

1. The most noteworthy feature of the boy is that he can skillfully use his both feet when he plays soccer.
   (A) notorious (B) patient (C) earnest (D) notable

2. Shelley attributed her success to her honesty and hard work.
   (A) judged (B) denied (C) assented (D) ascribed

3. To write a great love-letter to my wife, I extracted some romantic passages from lots of poems.
   (A) discovered (B) described (C) took out (D) removed

4. The program has so many errors as to render it useless.
   (A) make (B) consider (C) complete (D) found

5. He was nominated as 'Most Valuable Player' by soccer fans.
   (A) implied (B) promised (C) misled (D) appointed

6. Green, orange, and yellow are three of the vibrant colors in his painting.
   (A) silent (B) dart (C) brilliant (D) loud

7. Drink the wine sparingly, there's not much left.
   (A) thriftily (B) willingly (C) precisely (D) loosely

8. Lee Sun Shin is one of the most illustrious Koreans in the world.
   (A) favorite (B) diligent (C) distinguished (D) scary

9. She has little patience for sloppy performance from her colleagues.
   (A) compassionate (B) funny (C) eminent (D) careless

Chapter 09
INFERENCE

Chapter 9
Inference

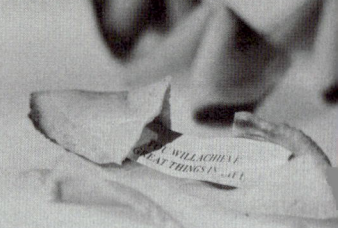

Sample Item Read the following passage and answer the question.

*i*BT Reading

Question 1

1. What can be inferred about erratics?

   Ⓐ They are mostly found in many valleys in Norfolk.
   Ⓑ They damaged many valleys in Great Britain.
   Ⓒ They are distinguished from original rocks in Norfolk.
   Ⓓ They are primarily responsible for carring the valley floors.

Erratics

During the many ice ages that the earth has undergone, large bodies of ice, called glaciers, have moved slowly south, away from northern areas. As they move, they carve out smooth valleys along the way. Sometimes they pick up huge rocks in their paths and transport them, often hundreds of miles. These rocks are called "erratics," and they are deposited on the ground after the glacier melts. Erratics found in Norfolk, Great Britain once baffled geologists. They could not imagine why the nonnative rocks existed in such large numbers in the valleys. The mystery was solved, however, when geologists learned more about glaciers and their movements. The geologists discovered that the mysterious rocks could be truly classified as erratics.

STUDY POINT nonnative rocks는 native rocks와 구별이 가능하다는 점을 유추할 수 있다.

Overview

Inference

Inference 문제는 전체 글, 문장, 단어 등에 숨어있는 의미를 정확히 파악했는가를 평가하는 유형이다. 수험자가 글 속에 숨겨진 의미나 결론 또는 다음 내용을 추론할 수 있는 가를 측정하는 것이 이 유형의 주목적이다. TOEFL 독해에서 가장 난이도가 높은 부분에 해당된다. 추론이란 근거가 있다는 점에서 추측과는 다르다. 추론의 근거를 정확히 파악하는 것이 가장 중요하며 주관적인 생각은 배제하여야 한다. 학습자는 평소 문제풀이를 할 때 오답은 오답이 되는 이유를 꼼꼼히 살피는 습관을 가져야 한다.

Question Type

- It can be inferred from paragraph X that …
- Which of the following can be inferred about X?

General Strategy

1. Inference of specific detail

특정 정보에서 추론할 수 있는 것을 파악한다. 대표적인 오답의 경우는 다음과 같다.

- 지문의 내용을 다르게 말하는 보기 (not true)
- 사실에 근거했다고 말하기 어려운 보기 (not based on fact)

2. Inference of main point

글쓴이는 자신의 point를 직접 말하기도 하지만, 다른 방법들을 통해 암시하기도 한다. 따라서 사실의 열거, 비교/대조, 상반되는 의견, 연구 결과 등의 내용을 통해 글쓴이의 point를 추론하도록 한다.

Basic Drill 1

Inference of specific detail

Read the passages and put the marks below for answer choices.

- **NT** – 지문의 내용을 다르게 말하는 보기 (not true)
- **NBF** – 사실에 근거했다고 말하기 어려운 보기 (not based on fact)
- **RI** – 타당한 추론 (right inference)

---

1 Bats native to the American Southwest often sleep during the day but leave their completely darkened cave homes at night to hunt for food.

(A) Bats in the American Southwest are vulnerable to daylight. ____
(B) Bats have special ability to sense and catch a prey even in the dark. ____
(C) Most bats leave the cave whenever they are hungry. ____

---

2 Researchers look into tree rings to give information about climate changes in the Chihuahuan Desert. The thin rings, which indicate extremely dry periods, seem to occur every 50-60 years.

(A) Some trees in the Chihuahuan Desert survive through extremely dry periods. ____
(B) Most of the trees in other regions provide climate information on the regions. ____
(C) The tree rings in the Chihuahuan Desert are often made every 50 to 60 years. ____

---

3 Giotto di Bondone, better known as simply Giotto, was the first major painter of the Italian Renaissance. His bold and interesting colors gave his paintings a life that was highly influential in the art world of the time. He explored religious subjects and themes in his work, bringing a force and realism to painting, which previously had not been seen in Medieval art.

(A) Giotto was a famous painter who was trained in a Medieval art school. ____
(B) Most of Medieval art works were not very strong, colorful, or realistic. ____
(C) Giotto had done a lot of research on religion and had much knowledge of it. ____

4 American bullfrogs were introduced to England several decades ago when people began selling them there as pets. However, they have been found to spread a disease in the wild, which resulted in some English frog species going extinct.

(A) The disease spread by bullfrogs was fatal to many English frogs. ____
(B) Some of infected English frogs transmitted the diseases to other species. ____
(C) Most species of English frogs disappeared many years ago. ____

5 In 1946, most people still used fountain pens or lead pencils to write with. Fountain pens were especially messy, prone to leaking. They also required constant refilling with ink. Within a few years, however, an invention from Argentina, the ballpoint pen, would revolutionize the way most people thought about writing instruments.

(A) Many people in 1946 didn't recognize the uniqueness of ball-point pens. ____
(B) Ball-point pens are more affordable than fountain pens or lead pencils. ____
(C) Most of the previous writing instruments were replaced by ball-point pens. ____

6 Though commonly used in modern skin-care products, as well as serving as the basis for aspirin, salicylic acid has been known for its useful properties throughout much of history. Derived from the bark of the willow tree, salicylic acid was traditionally used by many ancient peoples, including the Egyptians and the Native Americans as a pain reliever. It was also used in facial rinses by Middle Easterners and the Chinese to relieve the swelling and irritation caused by acne.

(A) Ancient people directly fed bark of willow trees to treat people with pain. ____
(B) The willow tree was one of the most valuable trees in ancient times. ____
(C) The effects of salicylic acid have been proven since long ago. ____

VOCABULARY **bold** 뚜렷한 **bullfrog** 황소개구리 **species** 종 **extinct** 멸종된 **messy** 흐트러진, 산란한 **leak** 새다 **revolutionize** 대변혁을 일으키다 **salicylic acid** 살리실산 **property** 특성, 특질 **derived (from)** ~에서 유래된, 파생된 **willow tree** 버드나무 **relieve** (고통 등을) 덜다 **swelling** 부은 데, 혹 **acne** 여드름

Basic Drill 2

Inference of the main point

Read the passages and put the marks below for answer choices.

- **NT** – 지문의 내용을 다르게 말하는 보기 (not true)
- **NBF** – 사실에 근거했다고 말하기 어려운 보기 (not based on fact)
- **RI** – 타당한 추론 (right inference)

1   Quebec is the largest province in Canada geographically, and the second most populous, after Ontario, with a population of 7.5 million. This represents about 24% of the Canadian population. Most Canadians are descendants of English settlers, and speak English as their first language. Quebec, on the other hand, is much more connected to France, linguistically as well as in terms of culture. Actually, Quebec is the only Canadian province where English is not an official language. In fact, Quebec has had several periods in its history where many of its residents wanted to form a new country, or break away from Canada.

(A) Quebec has different customs and is distinct from other parts of Canada. ____

(B) Most people in Quebec are proud to distinguish themselves from other Canadians. ____

(C) Language is the only difference between Quebec and other provinces in Canada. ____

2   From 1826 to 1843, for 17 years, on every clear day, Heinrich Schwabe scanned the sun and recorded its spots, dark parts on the sun's surface. During this period, he noticed a variation in the number of sunspots. He made the suggestion that the sunspot pattern was following a cycle over a ten year period. Johann Rudolf Wolf was greatly impressed by the discovery of the sunspot cycle by Heinrich Schwabe and he not only carried out his own observations, but collected all the available data on sunspot activity back as far as 1610 and calculated the period of the cycle as 11.1 years.

(A) It has been proven that the number of sunspots changes regularly. ____
(B) The number of the sunspots is constantly increasing during 11.1 years. ____
(C) Discovery of the sunspot changes has influenced many scientists. ____

3 Libraries have changed a great deal over the past few decades. Twenty years ago, each book in the library would have been listed on a separate card in a giant cabinet. So, sometimes, it could take hours to find a book. Today, libraries have come to rely heavily on computers to organize the information that used to be contained in the card catalog. It only takes a few seconds to find out if the book you're looking for is there. Additionally, many of the things that would have been found in paper journals and in books twenty years ago are now contained in on-line, computerized databases.

(A) Increased dependence on computers by libraries might increase other risks. ____
(B) Computer database system in libraries is more economical in the long term. ____
(C) The convenience of libraries has improved much within the past few decades. ____

4 Scientists recently changed the genes of a monkey, which is humankind's closest relative, to learn more about fighting diseases. They have known for years that certain "bad genes" can make a person more likely to have a terrible disease, like cancer or Alzheimer's. By putting these genes into a monkey, they will be able to learn valuable information regarding the nature of such diseases, and hopefully their treatment. But some experts argue that scientists have already spent a number of years changing the genes of mice with few results. They claim that it doesn't matter what kind of animal they experiment with, the results will be just as poor.

(A) The result of a study can vary greatly depending on the type of animals. ____
(B) It is hard to expect to have many results from the recent experiments on monkeys. ____
(C) The experiments on monkeys will take many more years before having valuable results. ____

VOCABULARY in terms of ~의 측면에서, ~의 점에서   province 주   populous 인구가 조밀한, 많은   descendant 후손
linguistically 언어의   sunspot 태양 흑점   carry out 수행하다, 집행하다

Vocabulary Preview for Exercise

Read and Pronounce

Exercise 1

infant	[ínfənt]	*n.* a newborn child
mimic	[mímik]	*v.* to copy someone's voice, facial expression, behavior, etc., usually for fun
register	[rédʒistər]	*v.* be aware of something; to remember something
affectionate	[əfékʃənət]	*adj.* showing gentle care and love
expose	[ikspóuz]	*v.* to leave something without protection

Exercise 2

playwright	[pléiràit]	*n.* someone who writes plays
fund	[fʌnd]	*v.* to provide money for an activity or organization
investor	[invéstər]	*n.* a person who puts money to a particular use in order to make profit
put on		to arrange for the performance of a play, show, etc.

Exercise 3

crucial	[krúːʃəl]	*adj.* of deciding importance
take in		to include something
assume	[əsjúːm]	*v.* to believe that something is true even though a person has not checked its accuracy or has no proof
atmosphere	[ǽtməsfìər]	*n.* the combination of gases that surrounds the Earth, star, etc.

| Check-up |

Fill in the blanks with an appropriate word or phrase. Change the form if needed.

| fund | affectionate | playwright | tragedy |
| register | take in | mimic | infant |

1 Angela can _____ my voice almost perfectly, and this has surprised my parents.
2 He is very _____ his adopted son.
3 Shakespeare is one of greatest _____ in the world.
4 I didn't remember her. She didn't _____ in my memory.
5 The book _____ the period between the rise of the Chosun Dynasty and Japanese invasion of Korea in 1592.
6 The young mother was putting her _____ to sleep.
7 The theater was privately _____ by the vice-president of our firm.
8 Jennifer is a famous actress who usually stars in _____ .

Exercise 1

*i*BT Reading

Question 1 to 4

1. The phrase **well documented** in paragraph 1 is closest in meaning to
   - Ⓐ very usual
   - Ⓑ well proven
   - Ⓒ frequently thought about
   - Ⓓ astonishing

2. The phrase **engaged in** in paragraph 2 is closest in meaning to
   - Ⓐ embarrassed by
   - Ⓑ surprised by
   - Ⓒ annoyed with
   - Ⓓ participated in

3. Which of the following can be inferred about depressed mothers?
   - Ⓐ Mothers with depression are shown to be less fond of their children.
   - Ⓑ They tend to be less involved and less caring with their babies.
   - Ⓒ Their emotions affect the size and weight of their babies as they grow.
   - Ⓓ They are likely to respond to their babies negatively and outrageously.

4. Why does the author mention womb in paragraph 4?
   - Ⓐ To note a physical reaction in babies of depressed mothers
   - Ⓑ To indicate another factor that affects infant development
   - Ⓒ To suggest that depression is caused by stress
   - Ⓓ To imply that all babies are under stress at birth

The Influences of Facial Expressions on Infants

The ability of infants to mimic the facial expressions of those around them is well documented through various studies. They learn happy expressions and sad expressions by imitating the people they see. It has been discovered that the content of those facial expressions may have a major impact on the overall well being and development of children.

A study of a group of three-month-old babies exemplifies this finding. Infants whose mothers were diagnosed with some form of depression were far more likely to make sad or angry faces than babies with non-depressed mothers. Additionally, these babies were not engaged in activities around them frequently.

Some researchers feel that the babies are simply mimicking their depressed mothers' facial expressions without registering the meaning of the expressions. But it doesn't mean that the babies wouldn't be affected by their mother's depression. These mothers did not respond enthusiastically to their infants, nor did they have affectionate conversations with them. This lack of positive interaction can have a negative effect on the child's developing mental and motor skills.

Interaction with depressed mothers is not the only possible explanation for these babies' delayed development. In the womb, the infants were also exposed to large amounts of stress hormones directly related to depression. These chemicals seem to result in children being less responsive, having fewer facial expressions, and being less active in general, from the moment they are born.

Glossary

womb the part inside a woman's body where a baby grows before its birth

Exercise 1

iBT Reading

Question 5 to 6

5. What can be inferred about the effect of facial expressions on babies?
    - Ⓐ Various facial expressions influence how babies develop as they grow.
    - Ⓑ Negative facial expressions can create high levels of stress hormones in babies.
    - Ⓒ Any emotional feeling that causes a certain facial expression can affect babies.
    - Ⓓ It was found that a mother's emotions are mostly irrelevant to her baby's health.

6. **Directions:** An introductory sentence for a brief summary of the passage is provided below. Complete the summary by selecting the THREE answer choices that express the most important ideas in the passage. Some sentences do not belong in the summary because they express ideas that are not presented in the passage or are minor ideas in the passage.

    A mother's depression can have a significant impact on how babies develop.

    Answer Choices
    - Ⓐ Many babies can smile soon after birth if their parents show them how.
    - Ⓑ The expression they see on their mother's face influences a newborn child's emotions.
    - Ⓒ Depressed mothers tend to have less interactions with their babies and this affects development of their babies.
    - Ⓓ Babies raised by depressed mothers are proven to have a high possibility of having difficulties in communicating.
    - Ⓔ Depression causes stress hormones that can affect babies' personalities.
    - Ⓕ Even before babies are born, their development is affected by their mothers' depression.

The Influences of Facial Expressions on Infants

The ability of infants to mimic the facial expressions of those around them is well documented through various studies. They learn happy expressions and sad expressions by imitating the people they see. It has been discovered that the content of those facial expressions may have a major impact on the overall well being and development of children.

A study of a group of three-month-old babies exemplifies this finding. Infants whose mothers were diagnosed with some form of depression were far more likely to make sad or angry faces than babies with non-depressed mothers. Additionally, these babies were not engaged in activities around them frequently.

Some researchers feel that the babies are simply mimicking their depressed mothers' facial expressions without registering the meaning of the expressions. But it doesn't mean that the babies wouldn't be affected by their mother's depression. These mothers did not respond enthusiastically to their infants, nor did they have affectionate conversations with them. This lack of positive interaction can have a negative effect on the child's developing mental and motor skills.

Interaction with depressed mothers is not the only possible explanation for these babies' delayed development. In the womb, the infants were also exposed to large amounts of stress hormones directly related to depression. These chemicals seem to result in children being less responsive, having fewer facial expressions, and being less active in general, from the moment they are born.

Exercise 2

iBT Reading

Question 1 to 4

1. Which of the following can be inferred about modern plays?
   - Ⓐ They usually spend much of the fund or various promotions.
   - Ⓑ They are mostly funded by governmental organizations.
   - Ⓒ Some of them cost tremendous amount of money.
   - Ⓓ Only popular ones are played in large theaters.

2. How does the author explains modern plays in paragraph 2?
   - Ⓐ By comparing to the plays in Ancient Greece
   - Ⓑ By pointing out the features of modern plays
   - Ⓒ By suggesting that modern plays are more entertaining
   - Ⓓ By explaining where modern plays are derived from

3. Which of the following is NOT a characteristic of modern plays?
   - Ⓐ They are performed many times.
   - Ⓑ They are mainly used to educate.
   - Ⓒ They have private money involved.
   - Ⓓ They use complex costumes.

4. Which of the following can be inferred about ancient Greek plays?
   - Ⓐ Different actors would perform in different plays.
   - Ⓑ The plays were generally performed during the spring planting time.
   - Ⓒ Audiences didn't need to buy tickets for the plays during the festivals.
   - Ⓓ The actors used extreme facial movement to emphasize emotions.

Drama, a Part of Ancient Greek Culture

Drama was an integral part of Ancient Greek culture. Viewing tragedies and comedies written by the day's most famous playwrights was an activity that most people hated to miss. However, the ancient Greek theater-going experience was somewhat different than going to see a play in modern times. There are important differences between ancient dramas and contemporary ones.

Today, plays are primarily entertainment events. Whether funny or serious, they are meant to provide an escape for the audience. Although local governments do sometimes promote the arts to a small degree, the money is almost always made through ticket sales. If a modern play proves to be popular, it could be played over and over again, even for years. Another feature of modern plays is the number of people who perform. Even though some require only a few actors, like those shown in small private theaters, many plays have a large cast and support crew. The crew organizes the costumes, makeup, and backgrounds. These are used to make the plays seem as realistic as possible.

The case in Ancient Greece was much different. Plays were funded by tax dollars alone and were put on as a part of religious festivals to honor the god of wine Dionysus. Usually, three plays were performed during the festival, and the people voted which they found to be the best, second best, and third best. **A** Additionally, the play, no matter how popular it was, would only be performed one time during the festival. **B** It might be performed again in a future festival, but most plays were only ever performed once. **C** The actors wore simple masks and would go backstage and change masks if they needed to perform another part. **D**

Glossary

tragedy a type of drama that is serious and sad, and often ends with the death of the main character

Exercise 2

iBT Reading

Question 5 to 6

5. Look at the four squares [■] that indicate where the following sentence could be added to paragraph 3.

   And Greek plays, no matter how many characters were written into the play, only had three actors.

   Where would the sentence best fit? Click on a square [■] to add the sentence to the paragraph.

   Ⓐ A   Ⓑ B   Ⓒ C   Ⓓ D

6. **Directions:** Select the appropriate statements from the answer choices and match them to the type of plays to which they relate. TWO of the answer choices will NOT be used.

   Answer Choices

   Ⓐ The popularity of a play allows it to be put on again and again.
   Ⓑ It is usually performed only once during the festivals.
   Ⓒ Many of the characters' lines are made up by actors.
   Ⓓ Actors sometimes need to memorize several different characters' lines.
   Ⓔ The playwright indicates what kinds of costumes actors wear.
   Ⓕ Profits can be made from a play.
   Ⓖ Many actors can be involved in a performance.

   Ancient Play
   •
   •

   Modern Play
   •
   •

Drama, a Part of Ancient Greek Culture

Drama was an integral part of Ancient Greek culture. Viewing tragedies and comedies written by the day's most famous playwrights was an activity that most people hated to miss. However, the ancient Greek theater-going experience was somewhat different than going to see a play in modern times. There are important differences between ancient dramas and contemporary ones.

Today, plays are primarily entertainment events. Whether funny or serious, they are meant to provide an escape for the audience. Although local governments do sometimes promote the arts to a small degree, the money is almost always made through ticket sales. If a modern play proves to be popular, it could be played over and over again, even for years. Another feature of modern plays is the number of people who perform. Even though some require only a few actors, like those shown in small private theaters, many plays have a large cast and support crew. The crew organizes the costumes, makeup, and backgrounds. These are used to make the plays seem as realistic as possible.

The case in Ancient Greece was much different. Plays were funded by tax dollars alone and were put on as a part of religious festivals to honor the god of wine Dionysus. Usually, three plays were performed during the festival, and the people voted which they found to be the best, second best, and third best. **A** Additionally, the play, no matter how popular it was, would only be performed one time during the festival. **B** It might be performed again in a future festival, but most plays were only ever performed once. **C** The actors wore simple masks and would go backstage and change masks if they needed to perform another part. **D**

Exercise 3

*i*BT Reading

Question 1 to 4

1. The word emit in paragraph 1 is closest in meaning to
   - Ⓐ release
   - Ⓑ repel
   - Ⓒ process
   - Ⓓ transform

2. According to paragraph 2, what can be be inferred about carbon dioxide?
   - Ⓐ Polluted air due to increased carbon dioxide is the main cause for a rise in temperature.
   - Ⓑ Scientists are concerned about the effects that an increased earth temperature can cause.
   - Ⓒ Trees and plants can produce more oxygen if they absorb an increased amount of CO_2.
   - Ⓓ Increased levels of CO_2 in the environment can make it hard for trees and plants to survive.

3. Why does the author mention the rise in the Earth's temperature in paragraph 2?
   - Ⓐ To imply that CO_2 can be a solution to it
   - Ⓑ To indicate that CO_2 is one of main causes of it
   - Ⓒ To suggest what CO_2 might cause in the future
   - Ⓓ To exemplify what CO_2 could turn into later

4. Based on the information in paragraph 2, which of the following can be inferred about the experiment?
   - Ⓐ Plants retain gases they do not need in their roots.
   - Ⓑ The forests were negatively impacted by too much carbon dioxide.
   - Ⓒ The rise in the Earth's temperature is a not a major cause for concern.
   - Ⓓ Researchers must discover another way to control global warming.

The Experiment for the Earth's Climate

Trees and plants are a crucial part of the global ecosystem because of their ability to absorb carbon dioxide and emit oxygen. The carbon dioxide is an important part of a tree's ability to photosynthesize, or produce the food it needs to survive.

Because of their ability to take in carbon dioxide and breathe out oxygen, many scientists assumed that trees would grow faster and stronger if there was more carbon dioxide in the atmosphere. Trees and plants then were seen as a possible solution to the increasing CO_2 levels in the environment, which has been blamed for a rise in the Earth's temperature. It was hoped that the trees would absorb any extra CO_2 from the atmosphere. However, the theory that plants would absorb the surplus CO_2 does not appear to be true.

To arrive at this conclusion, researchers studied the trees in a large forest. The researchers added extra carbon dioxide to the air around a section of the forest every day for four years. When compared with other trees in the forest, the carbon dioxide-supplemented trees exhibited no more growth, and were not different in size from the non-supplemented trees. Instead, these trees absorbed the carbon dioxide without processing it and released it into the soil through their roots. This means that increasing forests will not lessen the impact of greenhouse gases such as CO_2 on the Earth's climate.

Exercise 3

iBT Reading

Question 5 to 7

5. The phrase this conclusion in paragraph 3 refers to
   - A) CO_2 is not the direct cause of global warming.
   - B) CO_2 causes a rise in Earth's temperature.
   - C) Plants wouldn't usually release extra oxygen.
   - D) Plants don't take more CO_2 than they need.

6. How does the author explain the researchers' test whether trees grow faster in paragraph 3?
   - A) By explaining the study of trees in areas which are experiencing global warming
   - B) By detailing the test where they exposed trees to more carbon dioxide
   - C) By suggesting the amount of carbon dioxide trees released in the forest
   - D) By comparing the effects of oxygen and carbon dioxide from the trees in the forest

7. Which sentence below best expresses the essential information in the highlighted sentence in paragraph 3? *Incorrect* choices change the meaning in important ways or leave out essential information.
   - A) Trees with supplemented carbon dioxide didn't show any increase in their sizes.
   - B) Non-supplemented trees got much bigger than carbon dioxide supplemented trees.
   - C) Carbon dioxide supplemented trees only grow as much as other trees in the forest.
   - D) The sizes of the both carbon dioxide or non-supplemented trees were compared.

The Experiment for the Earth's Climate

Trees and plants are a crucial part of the global ecosystem because of their ability to absorb carbon dioxide and emit oxygen. The carbon dioxide is an important part of a tree's ability to photosynthesize, or produce the food it needs to survive.

Because of their ability to take in carbon dioxide and breathe out oxygen, many scientists assumed that trees would grow faster and stronger if there was more carbon dioxide in the atmosphere. Trees and plants then were seen as a possible solution to the increasing CO_2 levels in the environment, which has been blamed for a rise in the Earth's temperature. It was hoped that the trees would absorb any extra CO_2 from the atmosphere. However, the theory that plants would absorb the surplus CO_2 does not appear to be true.

To arrive at this conclusion, researchers studied the trees in a large forest. The researchers added extra carbon dioxide to the air around a section of the forest every day for four years. When compared with other trees in the forest, the carbon dioxide-supplemented trees exhibited no more growth, and were not different in size from the non-supplemented trees. Instead, these trees absorbed the carbon dioxide without processing it and released it into the soil through their roots. This means that increasing forests will not lessen the impact of greenhouse gases such as CO_2 on the Earth's climate.

Exercise 3

iBT Reading

Question 8

8. Directions: An introductory sentence for a brief summary of the passage is provided below. Complete the summary by selecting the THREE answer choices that do not belong in the summary because they express ideas that are not presented in the passage or are minor ideas in the passage.

Trees take in carbon dioxide and emit oxygen.

Answer Choices

Ⓐ Plants absorb carbon dioxide to create food and this ability is important for our world.

Ⓑ It was thought that plants would grow faster when they were exposed to higher levels of CO_2.

Ⓒ Most plants and trees in forests need carbon dioxide and oxygen for their reproduction and growth in the global ecosystem.

Ⓓ Scientists thought that trees might be able to process more CO_2 and this could be a solution to global warming.

Ⓔ The increased levels of CO_2 affected the trees in the forest but the effect was too little to recognize and the use of trees for lowering the global temperature is not realistic.

Ⓕ The trees that had been exposed to higher CO_2 levels did not grow more and this shows that planting more trees is not an effective solution to global warming.

Text Outline Choose the correct text outline of the passage.

(A) P1 — Introduction of the ability of plants
    P2 — Assumption and experiment based on the ability of plants
    P3 — Conclusion of the experiments and the reason

(B) P1 — Introduction of photosynthesis
    P2 — Description of the new theory and the experiment
    P3 — The result and possible implications

The Experiment for the Earth's Climate

Trees and plants are a crucial part of the global ecosystem because of their ability to absorb carbon dioxide and emit oxygen. The carbon dioxide is an important part of a tree's ability to photosynthesize, or produce the food it needs to survive.

Because of their ability to take in carbon dioxide and breathe out oxygen, many scientists assumed that trees would grow faster and stronger if there was more carbon dioxide in the atmosphere. Trees and plants then were seen as a possible solution to the increasing CO_2 levels in the environment, which has been blamed for a rise in the Earth's temperature. It was hoped that the trees would absorb any extra CO_2 from the atmosphere. However, the theory that plants would absorb the surplus CO_2 does not appear to be true.

To arrive at this conclusion, researchers studied the trees in a large forest. The researchers added extra carbon dioxide to the air around a section of the forest every day for four years. When compared with other trees in the forest, the carbon dioxide-supplemented trees exhibited no more growth, and were not different in size from the non-supplemented trees. Instead, these trees absorbed the carbon dioxide without processing it and released it into the soil through their roots. This means that increasing forests will not lessen the impact of greenhouse gases such as CO_2 on the Earth's climate.

Choose the closest meaning of the underlined word or phrase.

1. It was a crucial experiment that could prove his theory.
   (A) enormous   (B) vital   (C) intricate   (D) keen

2. I will carry out my goal at any cost.
   (A) endeavor   (B) manage   (C) bring on   (D) fulfill

3. He is a direct descendant of the company's founder.
   (A) steward   (B) relative   (C) offspring   (D) ancestor

4. The kitchen was so messy. It seemed like she hadn't cleaned her kitchen for a year!
   (A) untidy   (B) massive   (C) cozy   (D) subdued

5. My older sister is affectionate and cheerful.
   (A) cool   (B) loving   (C) gentle   (D) noble

6. There are hundreds of thousands of species of plants on this island.
   (A) scope   (B) goods   (C) variety   (D) class

7. She tried to relieve the pain of the patient.
   (A) soothe   (B) encourage   (C) overcome   (D) remember

8. Don't expose your skin to the sun for a long time.
   (A) hide   (B) uncover   (C) conceal   (D) defend

9. Let's assume that you will be promoted to management next year.
   (A) provoke   (B) make believe   (C) presume   (D) know

PROGRESS TEST

READING SECTION DIRECTIONS

In this section you will read two passages and answer reading comprehension questions about each passage. Most questions are worth one point, but the last question in each set is worth more than one point. The directions indicate how many points you may receive.

You will have 30 minutes to read all of the passages and answer the questions. Some passages include a word or phrase that is underlined in blue. Click on the word or phrase to see a definition or an explanation.

When you want to move on to the next question, click on **Next**. You can skip questions and go back to them later as long as long as there is time remaining. If you want to return to previous questions, click on **Back**. You can click on **Review** at any time and the review screen will show you which questions you have answered and which you have not. From this review screen, you may go directly to any question you have already seen in the reading section.

When you are ready to continue, click on the Dismiss Directions icon.

Progress Test 5

*i*BT Reading

Question 1 to 4

1. The word **insulate** in paragraph 1 is closest in meaning to
   - Ⓐ cool down
   - Ⓑ broaden
   - Ⓒ protect
   - Ⓓ darken

2. Why does the author mention structures using natural insulation in paragraph 1?
   - Ⓐ To show how natural insulation can help to lower the temperature
   - Ⓑ To compare previous technologies with those of modern refrigeration
   - Ⓒ To exemplify attempts made for cooler temperature in hot weather
   - Ⓓ To emphasize that invention of modern refrigeration

3. The word **This** in paragraph 2 refers to
   - Ⓐ A chamber
   - Ⓑ An experiment
   - Ⓒ Boiling ether
   - Ⓓ Refrigeration

4. Which of the following best expresses the essential information in the highlighted sentence in paragraph 2? *Incorrect* choices change the meaning in important ways or leave out essential information.
   - Ⓐ Since Scotland is cool, even during the summer, the professor did not notice the cooling effects that the experiment produced.
   - Ⓑ In spite of the surprising result of the experiment, it is said that living in cool place prevented Cullen from applying other practical uses of the discovery.
   - Ⓒ Cullen was interested in the experiment's results but he could not think of a practical way to produce refrigeration at such an early stage in its history.
   - Ⓓ Scotland is cool so it was an effective place to perform the experiments that ultimately shocked the professor, although he never considered the cooling effects could be useful.

Glossary
chamber a room designed and equipped for a particular purpose
molecule the smallest amount of a chemical substance which exist by itself

The Invention of Modern Refrigeration

Humankind had long looked for ways to stay cool in the summer heat prior to the invention of modern refrigeration. Some houses were designed to let the air blow freely through open windows or doors. Others used extremely thick walls made of soil to help insulate the inside of the structure and protect it against the heat. Also, in some desert areas, structures were actually dug into the ground to take advantage of its natural insulation value. But none of these created reliably cool indoor environments.

Then, in 1748, a man named William Cullen, a professor in Scotland, discovered the principles of refrigeration. Cullen did an experiment where he let a substance known as ether boil into a chamber. This caused a drastic and immediate cooling of the chamber. While reports of the event indicate that the professor was surprised at the reaction, he never considered its implications, and many believe this was because he was a native of Scotland, a generally cool place even in the summer. Indeed, it did not occur to Cullen that this experiment might be useful outside of the laboratory, so the age of refrigeration would have to wait longer.

It wasn't until 1842 that an American doctor named John Gorrie built a device to cool the air in hospital rooms. **A** The basic method involved compressing, or making smaller, air molecules. **B** Then the machine would blow those air molecules into the air outside of the machine, resulting in the temperature dropping. **C** This is more or less the same method that modern refrigerators use today. Within about a decade, this refrigeration technique was being used by the meat packing and brewing industries to increase their productivity and effectiveness. **D**

Another variation on this idea occurred in France in 1859 by a man named Ferdinand Carre. Unlike Gorrie's compression machine, which used air as a coolant, Carre's equipment used ammonia. The chemical properties of ammonia allow it to get much colder than the air Gorrie had used. But it was not as widely adopted as Gorrie's machine; however, Carre's refrigeration method was more successful. The reason behind this was because ammonia is extremely toxic and dangerous to use. Most people and businesses did not want to have machines that used this substance.

Progress Test 5

iBT TOEFL Reading

Question 5 to 8

5. Look at the four squares [■] that indicate where the following sentence could be added to the passage.

This reduction in the molecules' size cooled the surrounding air significantly.

Where would the sentence best fit? Click on a square [■] to add the sentence to the paragraph.

Ⓐ   Ⓑ   Ⓒ   Ⓓ

6. According to paragraph 3, what can be inferred about Gorrie's method?

   Ⓐ Many of techniques used in modern refrigeration were patented by Gorrie.
   Ⓑ It was widely accepted as one of the most effective ways of refrigeration.
   Ⓒ It was mainly used in hospitals because the machine took up much space.
   Ⓓ It used special air molecules that can be rapidly compressed in the machine.

7. The word **this** in paragraph 4 refers to

   Ⓐ effectively cooling
   Ⓑ using ammonia
   Ⓒ not being widely used
   Ⓓ the fact that ammonia gets much colder than the air

8. According to paragraph 4, ammonia

   Ⓐ was less effective at cooling than air.
   Ⓑ was not handled carefully by Carre.
   Ⓒ was more dangerous than air in cooling.
   Ⓓ is used today in industrial cooling.

The Invention of Modern Refrigeration

Humankind had long looked for ways to stay cool in the summer heat prior to the invention of modern refrigeration. Some houses were designed to let the air blow freely through open windows or doors. Others used extremely thick walls made of soil to help insulate the inside of the structure and protect it against the heat. Also, in some desert areas, structures were actually dug into the ground to take advantage of its natural insulation value. But none of these created reliably cool indoor environments.

Then, in 1748, a man named William Cullen, a professor in Scotland, discovered the principles of refrigeration. Cullen did an experiment where he let a substance known as ether boil into a chamber. This caused a drastic and immediate cooling of the chamber. While reports of the event indicate that the professor was surprised at the reaction, he never considered its implications, and many believe this was because he was a native of Scotland, a generally cool place even in the summer. Indeed, it did not occur to Cullen that this experiment might be useful outside of the laboratory, so the age of refrigeration would have to wait longer.

It wasn't until 1842 that an American doctor named John Gorrie built a device to cool the air in hospital rooms. **A** The basic method involved compressing, or making smaller, air molecules. **B** Then the machine would blow those air molecules into the air outside of the machine, resulting in the temperature dropping. **C** This is more or less the same method that modern refrigerators use today. Within about a decade, this refrigeration technique was being used by the meat packing and brewing industries to increase their productivity and effectiveness. **D**

Another variation on this idea occurred in France in 1859 by a man named Ferdinand Carre. Unlike Gorrie's compression machine, which used air as a coolant, Carre's equipment used ammonia. The chemical properties of ammonia allow it to get much colder than the air Gorrie had used. But it was not as widely adopted as Gorrie's machine; however, Carre's refrigeration method was more successful. The reason behind this was because ammonia is extremely toxic and dangerous to use. Most people and businesses did not want to have machines that used this substance.

Progress Test 5

iBT TOEFL Reading

Question 9

9. **Directions:** An introductory sentence for a brief summary of the passage is provided below. Complete the summary by selecting the THREE answer choices that express the most important ideas in the passage. Some sentences do not belong in the summary because they express ideas that are not presented in the passage or are minor ideas in the passage.

There were many developments that led to the development of modern refrigeration.

-
-
-

Answer choices

(A) Cullen discovered that boiling ether could cause rapid cooling in a chamber but it wasn't developed into a refrigeration.

(B) It was found that some substances cause a great temperature drop in a chamber and this was the beginning of refrigeration.

(C) The air compressor was invented to provide cool air to hospitals and the technology is being used in many hospitals today.

(D) The technology to cool air by compressing was invented and the principle continues to be used today.

(E) Carre's equipment using ammonia is being often compared to Gorrie's compression machine, which used air as a coolant.

(F) Another inventor realized that using ammonia was more effective than air but this wasn't widely used because it was too dangerous.

The Invention of Modern Refrigeration

Humankind had long looked for ways to stay cool in the summer heat prior to the invention of modern refrigeration. Some houses were designed to let the air blow freely through open windows or doors. Others used extremely thick walls made of soil to help insulate the inside of the structure and protect it against the heat. Also, in some desert areas, structures were actually dug into the ground to take advantage of its natural insulation value. But none of these created reliably cool indoor environments.

Then, in 1748, a man named William Cullen, a professor in Scotland, discovered the principles of refrigeration. Cullen did an experiment where he let a substance known as ether boil into a chamber. This caused a drastic and immediate cooling of the chamber. While reports of the event indicate that the professor was surprised at the reaction, he never considered its implications, and many believe this was because he was a native of Scotland, a generally cool place even in the summer. Indeed, it did not occur to Cullen that this experiment might be useful outside of the laboratory, so the age of refrigeration would have to wait longer.

It wasn't until 1842 that an American doctor named John Gorrie built a device to cool the air in hospital rooms. **A** The basic method involved compressing, or making smaller, air molecules. **B** Then the machine would blow those air molecules into the air outside of the machine, resulting in the temperature dropping. **C** This is more or less the same method that modern refrigerators use today. Within about a decade, this refrigeration technique was being used by the meat packing and brewing industries to increase their productivity and effectiveness. **D**

Another variation on this idea occurred in France in 1859 by a man named Ferdinand Carre. Unlike Gorrie's compression machine, which used air as a coolant, Carre's equipment used ammonia. The chemical properties of ammonia allow it to get much colder than the air Gorrie had used. But it was not as widely adopted as Gorrie's machine; however, Carre's refrigeration method was more successful. The reason behind this was because ammonia is extremely toxic and dangerous to use. Most people and businesses did not want to have machines that used this substance.

Progress Test 6

iBT TOEFL Reading

Question 1 to 5

1. The word **they** in paragraph 1 refers to
   - Ⓐ lasers
   - Ⓑ tiny cameras
   - Ⓒ recent developments
   - Ⓓ invasive surgery

2. Based on the information in paragraph 1, which of the following can be inferred about technology?
   - Ⓐ Alternatives to modern technology are somewhat controversial.
   - Ⓑ Doctors are now able to see diseased parts without opening the body.
   - Ⓒ The small cameras used by doctors are extremely costly.
   - Ⓓ Doctors should not rely so much on modern technology.

3. The word **they** in paragraph 2 refers to
   - Ⓐ doctors
   - Ⓑ bad blood
   - Ⓒ patients
   - Ⓓ leeches

4. Why does the author mention reattaching limbs in paragraph 2?
   - Ⓐ To exemplify the difficult medical situation caused by clotting
   - Ⓑ To show a medical treatment where leeches are the most effective
   - Ⓒ To indicate that modern medical practice has evolved from older medical practices
   - Ⓓ To suggest how modern technologies are useless compared to past medical practices

5. Based on the information in paragraph 2, what can be inferred about leeches?
   - Ⓐ They caused many people to die of blood loss.
   - Ⓑ They die shortly after they feed on the patients' blood.
   - Ⓒ They can provide blood that patients need to have their limbs treated.
   - Ⓓ Their abilities can be used to help the blood flow more easily.

Glossary

invasive surgery an operation where the body is cut open

gangrene the decay that can occur in a part of a person's body if the blood stops flowing to it, for example, as a result of illness or injury

Old-fashioned Medical Practice

Much of modern medicine revolves around new advances in technology. Lasers, nanotechnology, and tiny cameras used for exploration and diagnosis that can be used to avoid invasive surgery are all examples of recent developments in modern medicine. Doctors often rely on these without really considering whether they are the best option. Some doctors tend to assume that modern technology is always the best choice. But this isn't always the case. In fact, some doctors are now turning to much older medical wisdom to help them with their high-tech work.

One example of old-fashioned medical practices that has been renewed in modern times is the use of leeches. Leeches, worms that live in freshwater ponds and streams, are parasites that attach to the body and suck blood. Hundreds of years ago, doctors used them to drain a patient of what they called "bad blood," which they saw as being the cause of disease. While doctors no longer accept the medical diagnosis of "bad blood" as valid, leeches are being used again in surgery. Today they are used to help doctors reattach limbs and other body parts. When applied to the body, leeches deposit a chemical which prevents clotting, or the thickening of the blood, in the part that is being reattached. This allows the body time to restart the blood flow between the cut-off veins and the veins in the part being attached.

Another old-fashioned practice that has been revived in modern medicine is the use of maggots, the wormy larvae of the fly. **A** These creatures have been used for centuries by people in other cultures all over the world, from South America to Australia, to clean out dead flesh from wounds. **B** This can be extremely beneficial to people who have gotten gangrene, the decay or rot that can occur in a part of a person's body if the blood stops flowing to it. **C** Thus, they are another instance of an old-fashioned medical cure that has shown itself to be very useful in modern medical practice. **D**

iBT TOEFL Reading

Question 6 to 8

6. Why does the author mention maggots in paragraph 3?
    - (A) To imply that old fashioned practices are much better in most cases
    - (B) To give another example of practice that is used again in modern medicine
    - (C) To show that even a disgusting creature can be used in today's medicine
    - (D) To compare with the use and the effectiveness of medical leeches

7. Look at the four squares [■] that indicate where the following sentence could be added to the passage.

    Even in the most difficult-to-cure cases of gangrene, maggots have been effective at getting rid of the rot and leaving only healthy flesh.

    Where would the sentence best fit? Click on a square [■] to add the sentence to the paragraph.

    (A) A   (B) B   (C) C   (D) D

8. What is the author's opinion about traditional medical wisdom?
    - (A) She believes that its risks are generally greater than its benefits.
    - (B) She is skeptical about the use of older medical practices in modern times.
    - (C) She thinks that it can be used alongside modern practices effectively.
    - (D) She is neutral about using modern and older techniques together.

Old-fashioned Medical Practice

Much of modern medicine revolves around new advances in technology. Lasers, nanotechnology, and tiny cameras used for exploration and diagnosis that can be used to avoid invasive surgery are all examples of recent developments in modern medicine. Doctors often rely on these without really considering whether they are the best option. Some doctors tend to assume that modern technology is always the best choice. But this isn't always the case. In fact, some doctors are now turning to much older medical wisdom to help them with their high-tech work.

One example of old-fashioned medical practices that has been renewed in modern times is the use of leeches. Leeches, worms that live in freshwater ponds and streams, are parasites that attach to the body and suck blood. Hundreds of years ago, doctors used them to drain a patient of what they called "bad blood," which they saw as being the cause of disease. While doctors no longer accept the medical diagnosis of "bad blood" as valid, leeches are being used again in surgery. Today they are used to help doctors reattach limbs and other body parts. When applied to the body, leeches deposit a chemical which prevents clotting, or the thickening of the blood, in the part that is being reattached. This allows the body time to restart the blood flow between the cut-off veins and the veins in the part being attached.

Another old-fashioned practice that has been revived in modern medicine is the use of maggots, the wormy larvae of the fly. **A** These creatures have been used for centuries by people in other cultures all over the world, from South America to Australia, to clean out dead flesh from wounds. **B** This can be extremely beneficial to people who have gotten gangrene, the decay or rot that can occur in a part of a person's body if the blood stops flowing to it. **C** Thus, they are another instance of an old-fashioned medical cure that has shown itself to be very useful in modern medical practice. **D**

Progress Test 6

iBT TOEFL Reading

Question 9

9. **Directions:** Select the appropriate phrases from the answer choices and match them to the type of old-fashioned medical practices to which they relate. TWO of the answer choices will NOT be used.

Answer Choices

- Ⓐ Were believed to suck bad blood
- Ⓑ Have an ability to eat up rotten flesh
- Ⓒ Have been used to cure difficult wounds
- Ⓓ Help doctors reconnect body parts
- Ⓔ Increase the body's immune system
- Ⓕ Spread minor diseases when used in surgery
- Ⓖ Help to increase the flow of blood

Leeches
-
-
-

Maggots
-
-

Old-fashioned Medical Practice

Much of modern medicine revolves around new advances in technology. Lasers, nanotechnology, and tiny cameras used for exploration and diagnosis that can be used to avoid invasive surgery are all examples of recent developments in modern medicine. Doctors often rely on these without really considering whether they are the best option. Some doctors tend to assume that modern technology is always the best choice. But this isn't always the case. In fact, some doctors are now turning to much older medical wisdom to help them with their high-tech work.

One example of old-fashioned medical practices that has been renewed in modern times is the use of leeches. Leeches, worms that live in freshwater ponds and streams, are parasites that attach to the body and suck blood. Hundreds of years ago, doctors used them to drain a patient of what they called "bad blood," which they saw as being the cause of disease. While doctors no longer accept the medical diagnosis of "bad blood" as valid, leeches are being used again in surgery. Today they are used to help doctors reattach limbs and other body parts. When applied to the body, leeches deposit a chemical which prevents clotting, or the thickening of the blood, in the part that is being reattached. This allows the body time to restart the blood flow between the cut-off veins and the veins in the part being attached.

Another old-fashioned practice that has been revived in modern medicine is the use of maggots, the wormy larvae of the fly. **A** These creatures have been used for centuries by people in other cultures all over the world, from South America to Australia, to clean out dead flesh from wounds. **B** This can be extremely beneficial to people who have gotten gangrene, the decay or rot that can occur in a part of a person's body if the blood stops flowing to it. **C** Thus, they are another instance of an old-fashioned medical cure that has shown itself to be very useful in modern medical practice. **D**

FINAL TEST

READING SECTION DIRECTIONS

In this section you will read three passages and answer reading comprehension questions about each passage. Most questions are worth one point, but the last question in each set is worth more than one point. The directions indicate how many points you may receive.

You will have 45 minutes to read all of the passages and answer the questions. Some passages include a word or phrase that is underlined in blue. Click on the word or phrase to see a definition or an explanation.

When you want to move on to the next question, click on **Next**. You can skip questions and go back to them later as long as long as there is time remaining. If you want to return to previous questions, click on **Back**. You can click on **Review** at any time and the review screen will show you which questions you have answered and which you have not. From this review screen, you may go directly to any question you have already seen in the reading section.

When you are ready to continue, click on the Dismiss Directions icon.

FINAL TEST

*i*BT Reading

Reading 1

Question 1 to 4

1. According to paragraph 1, what is the cause of the feet changing?
   - Ⓐ Because people covered their feet to protect them.
   - Ⓑ Because people stepped on sharp objects on the ground.
   - Ⓒ Because the foot bones evolved to be weaker.
   - Ⓓ Because too much stress was often put on barefeet.

2. Look at the four squares [■] that indicate where the following sentence could be added to paragraph 2.

   This was a direct result of less stress being placed on the foot.

   Where would the sentence best fit? Click on a square [■] to add the sentence to the paragraph.
   - Ⓐ A Ⓑ B Ⓒ C Ⓓ D

3. Which of the following can be inferred from paragraph 2 about the feet of our ancestors?
   - Ⓐ The toes were more varied in size than they are now.
   - Ⓑ They were longer but narrower than today's feet.
   - Ⓒ Their bottom surfaces were much harder and thicker.
   - Ⓓ The bone structure of feet was much different.

4. Which of the following best expresses the essential information in the highlighted sentence in paragraph 3? *Incorrect* choices change the meaning in important ways or leave out essential information.
   - Ⓐ Shoes can prevent feet from getting injured by sharp things and cold weather, but shoes can not protect feet from getting injured while running.
   - Ⓑ Shoes can protect feet from sharp things and cold weather and they are very important for athletes' performance.
   - Ⓒ Wearing shoes can increase the chance to get injured while running but in general it protects feet from being very cold.
   - Ⓓ Though shoes provide protection to feet, running with shoes on might cause serious injury more often.

Glossary
incidence the number of cause of cases of an illness or a medical condition in a particular place, group, or situation

Shoes vs. Barefeet

Before the use of shoes became a common practice in human civilization, the human foot was extremely strong, flexible, and tough. However, about 40,000 years ago, as we began covering our feet with animal and plant materials to protect them from the cold and uneven walking surfaces, our feet began to change. Not only did the use of shoes change our feet, but surprisingly it may today be responsible for increased injury.

A It was during this time period that the four smaller toes on our ancestors' feet began to decrease in size. B Footprints or fossils proved that as humans began to cover their feet more, they had less need for strong toes that would grip the ground as they walked. C So today, human feet are more delicate than those of our ancestors. D An interesting aside is that this change is not an evolutionary one, as many scientists once thought. They discovered that the feet could be trained to become stronger, much as our ancestors' feet were.

While shoes clearly offer a great deal of safety to feet, protecting them from sharp objects on the ground and cold temperatures, sports physicists claim that wearing them while running actually increases the risk of injury that is fatal to athlete's performance. In South Africa and Australia, some of the top runners do not wear athletic shoes. Their feet are much closer in appearance to those of our ancient ancestors: they are bigger, tougher, and the foot muscles are more highly developed. Scientists feel that the increased muscle mass, combined with the increased toughness, tends to make their feet much less susceptible to injury than feet of today.

Footwear has been shown to increase the incidence of ankle sprains, the most common injury caused by running. The ankle is damaged when it twists or bends violently, due to the shoe raising the foot from the ground. Barefoot runners do not have this problem. Additionally, running in heavy shoes affects the way in which the foot hits the ground. In shoes, the feet are likely to land on the heels, which results in a harder landing. Repetition of this motion can result in knee injury. Barefoot runners tend to land more lightly, on the balls of their feet, again resulting in fewer injuries. Thus, athletic shoes, despite all of their advantages, may actually do more harm than good.

FINAL TEST

iBT Reading

Reading 1 Question 5 to 8

5. The word **they** in paragraph 3 refers to
   - Ⓐ South Africans' feet
   - Ⓑ ancestors' feet
   - Ⓒ runners' feet
   - Ⓓ scientists' feet

6. Why does the author mention some top runners in South Africa and Australia in paragraph 3?
   - Ⓐ To show that they can run better because they don't wear shoes
   - Ⓑ To exemplify barefoot runners are less likely to get injured
   - Ⓒ To explain why some top runners don't wear shoes while running
   - Ⓓ To compare with feet of other runners who wear athletic shoes

7. In paragraph 4, what does the author say about ankle sprains?
   - Ⓐ They were more common in barefoot runners.
   - Ⓑ They are one possible result of shoe use.
   - Ⓒ Ancient humans had very few ankle injuries.
   - Ⓓ They heal faster if shoes are not worn.

8. What is the author's opinion about shoes?
   - Ⓐ He feels that there should be more studies to clarify the effects of barefoot training.
   - Ⓑ He thinks that people should train themselves to walk or run without wearing shoes.
   - Ⓒ He is impressed by the advanced technology used in the athletic shoe design.
   - Ⓓ He is convinced that running with shoes on causes more injuries than running without them.

Shoes vs. Barefeet

Before the use of shoes became a common practice in human civilization, the human foot was extremely strong, flexible, and tough. However, about 40,000 years ago, as we began covering our feet with animal and plant materials to protect them from the cold and uneven walking surfaces, our feet began to change. Not only did the use of shoes change our feet, but surprisingly it may today be responsible for increased injury.

A It was during this time period that the four smaller toes on our ancestors' feet began to decrease in size. B Footprints or fossils proved that as humans began to cover their feet more, they had less need for strong toes that would grip the ground as they walked. C So today, human feet are more delicate than those of our ancestors. D An interesting aside is that this change is not an evolutionary one, as many scientists once thought. They discovered that the feet could be trained to become stronger, much as our ancestors' feet were.

While shoes clearly offer a great deal of safety to feet, protecting them from sharp objects on the ground and cold temperatures, sports physicists claim that wearing them while running actually increases the risk of injury that is fatal to athlete's performance. In South Africa and Australia, some of the top runners do not wear athletic shoes. Their feet are much closer in appearance to those of our ancient ancestors: they are bigger, tougher, and the foot muscles are more highly developed. Scientists feel that the increased muscle mass, combined with the increased toughness, tends to make their feet much less susceptible to injury than feet of today.

Footwear has been shown to increase the incidence of ankle sprains, the most common injury caused by running. The ankle is damaged when it twists or bends violently, due to the shoe raising the foot from the ground. Barefoot runners do not have this problem. Additionally, running in heavy shoes affects the way in which the foot hits the ground. In shoes, the feet are likely to land on the heels, which results in a harder landing. Repetition of this motion can result in knee injury. Barefoot runners tend to land more lightly, on the balls of their feet, again resulting in fewer injuries. Thus, athletic shoes, despite all of their advantages, may actually do more harm than good.

FINAL TEST

iBT Reading

Reading 1

Question 9

9. **Directions:** Select the appropriate phrases from the answer choices and match them to the type to which they relate. TWO of the answer choices will NOT be used.

Answer Choices

Ⓐ Keep feet from getting dry in harsh climates
Ⓑ Enable a runner to feel the position of their foot
Ⓒ Prevent a person from stepping on sharp things
Ⓓ Cause an increase in skin problems on the soles of the feet
Ⓔ Enable feet to stay warm during cold weather
Ⓕ Reduce the stress on a person's ankle while running
Ⓖ Result in softer landings on the balls of the feet

Shoes
•
•

Barefeet
•
•
•

Shoes vs. Barefeet

Before the use of shoes became a common practice in human civilization, the human foot was extremely strong, flexible, and tough. However, about 40,000 years ago, as we began covering our feet with animal and plant materials to protect them from the cold and uneven walking surfaces, our feet began to change. Not only did the use of shoes change our feet, but surprisingly it may today be responsible for increased injury.

[A] It was during this time period that the four smaller toes on our ancestors' feet began to decrease in size. [B] Footprints or fossils proved that as humans began to cover their feet more, they had less need for strong toes that would grip the ground as they walked. [C] So today, human feet are more delicate than those of our ancestors. [D] An interesting aside is that this change is not an evolutionary one, as many scientists once thought. They discovered that the feet could be trained to become stronger, much as our ancestors' feet were.

While shoes clearly offer a great deal of safety to feet, protecting them from sharp objects on the ground and cold temperatures, sports physicists claim that wearing them while running actually increases the risk of injury that is fatal to athlete's performance. In South Africa and Australia, some of the top runners do not wear athletic shoes. Their feet are much closer in appearance to those of our ancient ancestors: they are bigger, tougher, and the foot muscles are more highly developed. Scientists feel that the increased muscle mass, combined with the increased toughness, tends to make their feet much less susceptible to injury than feet of today.

Footwear has been shown to increase the incidence of ankle sprains, the most common injury caused by running. The ankle is damaged when it twists or bends violently, due to the shoe raising the foot from the ground. Barefoot runners do not have this problem. Additionally, running in heavy shoes affects the way in which the foot hits the ground. In shoes, the feet are likely to land on the heels, which results in a harder landing. Repetition of this motion can result in knee injury. Barefoot runners tend to land more lightly, on the balls of their feet, again resulting in fewer injuries. Thus, athletic shoes, despite all of their advantages, may actually do more harm than good.

FINAL TEST

iBT Reading

Reading 2 Question 10 to 14

10. The word **intact** in paragraph 2 is closest in meaning to
    Ⓐ safe
    Ⓑ growing
    Ⓒ peaceful
    Ⓓ unbroken

11. The word **this** in paragraph 2 refers to
    Ⓐ disagreement
    Ⓑ tension
    Ⓒ town
    Ⓓ accusation

12. According to paragraph 2, what caused the tension among the people in Salem?
    Ⓐ Disagreement on how the town should be separated as the town was growing with more people
    Ⓑ Distrust among the people in the town regarding the policies for the future made by the leaders
    Ⓒ Accusations between two politicians who had different opinions on the development of the town
    Ⓓ Argument on the better ways to develop the town as the town was getting bigger and bigger

13. Look at the four squares [■] that indicate where the following sentence could be added to paragraph 3.

    That's because as she played fortune-telling games with the girls, she naively thought she might have had the special talents of a witch.

    Where would the sentence best fit? Click on a square [■] to add the sentence to the paragraph.

    Ⓐ   Ⓑ   Ⓒ   Ⓓ

14. According to paragraph 3, which of the following is NOT true?
    Ⓐ One of three women who were claimed to be witches confessed.
    Ⓑ Three women who were named as witches were hanged.
    Ⓒ People didn't know what actually caused the illness that two girls had.
    Ⓓ The two girls actually knew all the names of witches who made them sick.

Glossary

hysteria a state of extreme or exaggerated emotion, like panic

sentence to state officially what someone's punishment will be

The Salem Witch Trials

In the year 1692 in the small town of Salem, Massachusetts, a state in the northeastern United States, an event occurred which is still well-known in American history: the Salem Witch Trials. 19 people were hanged after being charged and convicted of witchcraft, and over 100 others were sent to jail. There were several causes that led up to this tragedy.

The main cause was political tension in the town. Salem was growing, but there was disagreement between the townspeople on how this should occur. Some people in the town wanted to break off and reform their own town due to the increasing growth, while others preferred to keep Salem intact. This disagreement led to tension amongst the townspeople. And in turn, this made people be willing to betray one another. Many townspeople believed whatever accusations were made.

Therefore, when two young girls, Betty Parris and Abigail Williams, began acting strangely due to a mysterious illness — they would fall onto the floor and cry out — it was suspected that someone in the town was performing witchcraft. The girls were pressured to confess the name of the witch who had done this to them. **A** They named three women — a slave named Tituba, a homeless woman named Sarah Osborne, and an elderly woman who did not attend church, Sarah Goode. **B** When the women were brought to trial, only the slave woman confessed to the charges of witchcraft. **C** Regardless of the others' claim of innocence, all three women were sentenced to death by hanging. **D**

This was only the beginning, however. The first trial had resulted in another primary cause of the Witch Trials — hysteria. People in the town became convinced that Salem had been overrun and controlled by witches. Their superstitious beliefs made them unable to think clearly. When the girls' mysterious illness did not eventually improve, they were once more pressured to name more witches living in the town. They began to name more witches, often enemies of their family. And people who expressed doubt that Abigail and Betty were telling the truth were sent to jail as suspected witches. This fear among people in the town did not allow them to be critical of the girls. When the hysteria died down, 19 people were dead and many more were left in jail for years.

FINAL TEST

*i*BT Reading

Reading 2 — Question 15 to 18

15. The word overrun in paragraph 4 is closest in meaning to
    - Ⓐ visited
    - Ⓑ cursed
    - Ⓒ invaded
    - Ⓓ defeated

16. Why does the author mention fear in paragraph 4?
    - Ⓐ To suggest a reason for the townspeople's thoughts and actions
    - Ⓑ To explain why the girls created the story of the witches
    - Ⓒ To compare the major reasons for the Witch Hunts
    - Ⓓ To offer the conclusion the hysteria was the ultimate cause of the Witch Hunts

17. Which of the following can be inferred from paragraph 4 about the Witch Trials?
    - Ⓐ More girls who got sick during the trial periods were forced to name witches.
    - Ⓑ Two girls were blamed for not naming other witches after a couple of trials.
    - Ⓒ Witch trials frayed the souls of the Salem villagers.
    - Ⓓ People believed whoever the two girls said were witches throughout the trials.

18. What is the author's opinion about the people of Salem?
    - Ⓐ They had good reasons for their beliefs.
    - Ⓑ Development caused the conflict between them.
    - Ⓒ They were too involved in political issues.
    - Ⓓ They were not behaving rationally at the time.

The Salem Witch Trials

In the year 1692 in the small town of Salem, Massachusetts, a state in the northeastern United States, an event occurred which is still well-known in American history: the Salem Witch Trials. 19 people were hanged after being charged and convicted of witchcraft, and over 100 others were sent to jail. There were several causes that led up to this tragedy.

The main cause was political tension in the town. Salem was growing, but there was disagreement between the townspeople on how this should occur. Some people in the town wanted to break off and reform their own town due to the increasing growth, while others preferred to keep Salem intact. This disagreement led to tension amongst the townspeople. And in turn, this made people be willing to betray one another. Many townspeople believed whatever accusations were made.

Therefore, when two young girls, Betty Parris and Abigail Williams, began acting strangely due to a mysterious illness — they would fall onto the floor and cry out — it was suspected that someone in the town was performing witchcraft. The girls were pressured to confess the name of the witch who had done this to them. A They named three women — a slave named Tituba, a homeless woman named Sarah Osborne, and an elderly woman who did not attend church, Sarah Goode. B When the women were brought to trial, only the slave woman confessed to the charges of witchcraft. C Regardless of the others' claim of innocence, all three women were sentenced to death by hanging. D

This was only the beginning, however. The first trial had resulted in another primary cause of the Witch Trials — hysteria. People in the town became convinced that Salem had been overrun and controlled by witches. Their superstitious beliefs made them unable to think clearly. When the girls' mysterious illness did not eventually improve, they were once more pressured to name more witches living in the town. They began to name more witches, often enemies of their family. And people who expressed doubt that Abigail and Betty were telling the truth were sent to jail as suspected witches. This fear among people in the town did not allow them to be critical of the girls. When the hysteria died down, 19 people were dead and many more were left in jail for years.

FINAL TEST

*i*BT Reading

Reading 2

Question 19

19. Directions: An introductory sentence for a brief summary of the passage is provided below. Complete the summary by selecting the THREE answer choices that express the most important ideas in the passage. Some sentences do not belong in the summary because they express ideas that are not presented in the passage or are minor ideas in the passage.

There are a number of causes for the tragedy of the Salem Witch Hunts.

-
-
-

Answer Choices

(A) Tension from the disagreement over the town's potential growth was the root cause of the hunts.

(B) Those who disagreed with the two girls were considered to be witches and were thus sentenced to death.

(C) The trial of three women who were accused of being witches by two girls in the town initiated these hunts.

(D) Superstitious beliefs and uncontrollable fear that kept the people from rational thinking and behavior was another reason.

(E) Influenced by Salem, other towns near Salem began to start accusations and trials for witches in their towns.

(F) Some members of the town wanted to break away from Salem and start their own town since the population in the town was growing.

The Salem Witch Trials

In the year 1692 in the small town of Salem, Massachusetts, a state in the northeastern United States, an event occurred which is still well-known in American history: the Salem Witch Trials. 19 people were hanged after being charged and convicted of witchcraft, and over 100 others were sent to jail. There were several causes that led up to this tragedy.

The main cause was political tension in the town. Salem was growing, but there was disagreement between the townspeople on how this should occur. Some people in the town wanted to break off and reform their own town due to the increasing growth, while others preferred to keep Salem intact. This disagreement led to tension amongst the townspeople. And in turn, this made people be willing to betray one another. Many townspeople believed whatever accusations were made.

Therefore, when two young girls, Betty Parris and Abigail Williams, began acting strangely due to a mysterious illness — they would fall onto the floor and cry out — it was suspected that someone in the town was performing witchcraft. The girls were pressured to confess the name of the witch who had done this to them. **A** They named three women — a slave named Tituba, a homeless woman named Sarah Osborne, and an elderly woman who did not attend church, Sarah Goode. **B** When the women were brought to trial, only the slave woman confessed to the charges of witchcraft. **C** Regardless of the others' claim of innocence, all three women were sentenced to death by hanging. **D**

This was only the beginning, however. The first trial had resulted in another primary cause of the Witch Trials — hysteria. People in the town became convinced that Salem had been overrun and controlled by witches. Their superstitious beliefs made them unable to think clearly. When the girls' mysterious illness did not eventually improve, they were once more pressured to name more witches living in the town. They began to name more witches, often enemies of their family. And people who expressed doubt that Abigail and Betty were telling the truth were sent to jail as suspected witches. This fear among people in the town did not allow them to be critical of the girls. When the hysteria died down, 19 people were dead and many more were left in jail for years.

FINAL TEST

*i*BT Reading
Reading 3 — Question 20 to 25

20. The word **antiquity** in paragraph 1 is closest in meaning to
    - Ⓐ ancient past
    - Ⓑ near past
    - Ⓒ prehistoric times
    - Ⓓ middle ages

21. What is NOT mentioned as a result of polio?
    - Ⓐ Interference with breathing
    - Ⓑ Loss of ability to walk
    - Ⓒ Inability to remember
    - Ⓓ Loss of life

22. Why does the author mention Ancient Egypt in paragraph 1?
    - Ⓐ To imply that the Egyptians had successful treatments for polio
    - Ⓑ To suggest that the disease was first discovered in Egypt
    - Ⓒ To illustrate the claim that polio is an old disease
    - Ⓓ To indicate that polio had different effects in the past

23. The word **eradicated** in paragraph 2 is closest in meaning to
    - Ⓐ slowed down
    - Ⓑ restrained
    - Ⓒ wiped out
    - Ⓓ transformed

24. How does the author introduce the polio vaccine in paragraph 2 and 3?
    - Ⓐ By explaining how Salk created the first vaccine
    - Ⓑ By explaining the effect that decreases polio
    - Ⓒ By illustrating how the vaccine works on the body
    - Ⓓ By comparing polio to another problematic disease

25. Which of the following can be inferred from paragraph 3 about polio vaccinations?
    - Ⓐ The price of the vaccination has increased since there are less cases of polio reported.
    - Ⓑ A lot of funds were raised to provide enough vaccinations around the world in 1990s.
    - Ⓒ Many polio vaccines were invented to eliminate the polio virus from the world.
    - Ⓓ Some of the elements in the vaccine were not proven to be safe for adults.

Glossary

respirator a machine used in hospitals for helping people who cannot breathe on their own
cripple to make someone physically disabled, especially unable to walk
outbreak the sudden start of war, disease, violence, etc.

Eliminating Polio

The polio virus invades a person's nervous system. Not being able to walk, losing use of some limbs, being forced to live on a respirator, and even dying are some of the effects of polio. It has existed since antiquity — there are paintings of people who were crippled from polio in Ancient Egyptian times. The most recent outbreak in the western hemisphere occurred in the first half of the 20th century. In 1952, at the height of the epidemic, nearly 60,000 people were contracting polio each year and 3,000 were dying from it.

However, in 1955, the polio vaccine, which had been created by Jonas Salk, became widely available. In 1979, polio had been eliminated from the United States. By 1991, there were no naturally occurring polio cases in the western hemisphere. The disease had been eradicated, because of the vaccine. However, polio was still a common infection in the rest of the world. Thus, in 1988, global health agencies set the goal of completely eliminating polio from the planet.

This effort has been extremely successful. Each year, children all from over the world receive the polio vaccine. By 2004, cases of polio occurring worldwide were down almost 99% since the 1988 goal was set. However, there are still 20 countries on the planet that still report cases of polio each year even though the means for its eradication exists. Several obstacles such as wars and lack of funding make it difficult for medical personnel to get the vaccines to people in these countries and thereby reach the goal of eliminating the disease.

The first problem is political instability. It is one of the most common features in almost all of the 20 remaining countries with polio. The violence and disruption of war prevent goods and services from being easily distributed in these countries, especially to rural places with difficult access. This makes it almost impossible for doctors to give vaccinations in these places.

The second problem is money. **A** Everyone agrees that getting rid of polio is a positive goal. **B** However, it is difficult for global health organizations to raise the money needed to fund vaccination drives. **C** This is because polio has been eliminated from many places, so a lot of people don't think about it any more. **D** Thus raising public awareness becomes the main challenge to achieving the goal of polio eradication.

FINAL TEST

*i*BT Reading

Reading 3

Question 26 to 29

26. Which of the following best expresses the essential information in the highlighted sentence in paragraph 3? *Incorrect* answers change the information in important ways or leave out essential information.

Ⓐ Wars and lack of money make it difficult for people to deliver vaccine in these countries and to accomplish their goal.

Ⓑ The disease will not disappear because there are wars that make it hard to raise funds for the vaccine in these countries.

Ⓒ The goal to get rid of polio is not completed because of the difficulties that make it hard to distribute the vaccine in some countries.

Ⓓ It's difficult for medical personnel to get the vaccines in these countries because of several things that prevent raising money.

27. The word This in paragraph 4 refers to

Ⓐ Lack of stocks of vaccines
Ⓑ Violence and difficult access
Ⓒ Number of people needing vaccines
Ⓓ Lack of doctors available

28. Look at the four squares [■] that indicate where the following sentence could be added to paragraph 1.

And if people aren't thinking about it, they aren't very likely to donate funds and resources to help fight it.

Where would the sentence best fit? Click on a square [■] to add the sentence to the paragraph.

Ⓐ   Ⓑ   Ⓒ   Ⓓ

29. All of the following are mentioned as obstacles to eliminating polio EXCEPT

Ⓐ Lack of access to hard-to-reach places
Ⓑ Unwillingness by children to get vaccinated
Ⓒ The violence associated with war
Ⓓ Lack of money to fund vaccination

Eliminating Polio

The polio virus invades a person's nervous system. Not being able to walk, losing use of some limbs, being forced to live on a respirator, and even dying are some of the effects of polio. It has existed since antiquity — there are paintings of people who were crippled from polio in Ancient Egyptian times. The most recent outbreak in the western hemisphere occurred in the first half of the 20th century. In 1952, at the height of the epidemic, nearly 60,000 people were contracting polio each year and 3,000 were dying from it.

However, in 1955, the polio vaccine, which had been created by Jonas Salk, became widely available. In 1979, polio had been eliminated from the United States. By 1991, there were no naturally occurring polio cases in the western hemisphere. The disease had been eradicated, because of the vaccine. However, polio was still a common infection in the rest of the world. Thus, in 1988, global health agencies set the goal of completely eliminating polio from the planet.

This effort has been extremely successful. Each year, children all from over the world receive the polio vaccine. By 2004, cases of polio occurring worldwide were down almost 99% since the 1988 goal was set. However, there are still 20 countries on the planet that still report cases of polio each year even though the means for its eradication exists. Several obstacles such as wars and lack of funding make it difficult for medical personnel to get the vaccines to people in these countries and thereby reach the goal of eliminating the disease.

The first problem is political instability. It is one of the most common features in almost all of the 20 remaining countries with polio. The violence and disruption of war prevent goods and services from being easily distributed in these countries, especially to rural places with difficult access. This makes it almost impossible for doctors to give vaccinations in these places.

The second problem is money. A Everyone agrees that getting rid of polio is a positive goal. B However, it is difficult for global health organizations to raise the money needed to fund vaccination drives. C This is because polio has been eliminated from many places, so a lot of people don't think about it any more. D Thus raising public awareness becomes the main challenge to achieving the goal of polio eradication.

FINAL TEST

*i*BT Reading
Reading 3 — Question 30

30. Directions: An introductory sentence for a brief summary of the passage is provided below. Complete the summary by selecting the THREE answer choices that express the most important ideas in the passage. Some sentences do not belong in the summary because they express ideas that are not presented in the passage or are minor ideas in the passage.

After causing great harm to humans over the centuries, polio is nearly gone from the earth except in some countries.

-
-
-

Answer Choices

(A) The polio vaccine was created by Dr. Jonas Salk in the mid-20th century and it proved to be effective for children.

(B) The vaccine was created and it proved to be effective in the West, reducing new cases of polio.

(C) By the late 20th century, the disease had been erased from most parts of the world, but polio still remains a threat in some countries.

(D) There are some countries reporting the cases of polio because of lack of availability and affordability.

(E) Wars prevent doctors and supplies from reaching isolated communities and raising money to provide enough vaccines in those countries.

(F) Unstable conditions in countries and lack of money raised for the elimination of the disease prevents the complete elimination of polio.

Eliminating Polio

The polio virus invades a person's nervous system. Not being able to walk, losing use of some limbs, being forced to live on a respirator, and even dying are some of the effects of polio. It has existed since antiquity — there are paintings of people who were crippled from polio in Ancient Egyptian times. The most recent outbreak in the western hemisphere occurred in the first half of the 20th century. In 1952, at the height of the epidemic, nearly 60,000 people were contracting polio each year and 3,000 were dying from it.

However, in 1955, the polio vaccine, which had been created by Jonas Salk, became widely available. In 1979, polio had been eliminated from the United States. By 1991, there were no naturally occurring polio cases in the western hemisphere. The disease had been eradicated, because of the vaccine. However, polio was still a common infection in the rest of the world. Thus, in 1988, global health agencies set the goal of completely eliminating polio from the planet.

This effort has been extremely successful. Each year, children all from over the world receive the polio vaccine. By 2004, cases of polio occurring worldwide were down almost 99% since the 1988 goal was set. However, there are still 20 countries on the planet that still report cases of polio each year even though the means for its eradication exists. Several obstacles such as wars and lack of funding make it difficult for medical personnel to get the vaccines to people in these countries and thereby reach the goal of eliminating the disease.

The first problem is political instability. It is one of the most common features in almost all of the 20 remaining countries with polio. The violence and disruption of war prevent goods and services from being easily distributed in these countries, especially to rural places with difficult access. This makes it almost impossible for doctors to give vaccinations in these places.

The second problem is money. **A** Everyone agrees that getting rid of polio is a positive goal. **B** However, it is difficult for global health organizations to raise the money needed to fund vaccination drives. **C** This is because polio has been eliminated from many places, so a lot of people don't think about it any more. **D** Thus raising public awareness becomes the main challenge to achieving the goal of polio eradication.

NOTE

NOTE

NOTE

성공적인 학습을 위한 단계별 전략
NEXUS TOEFL iBT 시리즈

뉴 토플의 중요한 학습 포커스는 논술의 기초 능력 배양입니다.
정보의 요지 파악, 요약 정리 능력이 논술의 기초이기 때문입니다.

- Global understanding을 강조한 정보 통합, 요약 훈련 강조
- 다양한 테마별·수사학적 지문 구조 분석 강조
- 어휘력 확장, 나선형·반복형 학습 장치 강조
- 실전에 맞춘 단계별 연습문제 제공

	Starter	Level 1	Level 2	Level 3	iBT TOEFL
Reading	Vocab Workbook	Vocab Workbook	Vocab Workbook	Vocab Workbook	실전모의고사 1
Listening	Starter	Level 1	Level 2	Level 3	(LC / RC)
	Vocab Workbook	Vocab Workbook	Vocab Workbook	Vocab Workbook	
Writing		Starter	Level 1	Level 2	
Speaking		Starter	Level 1	Level 2	

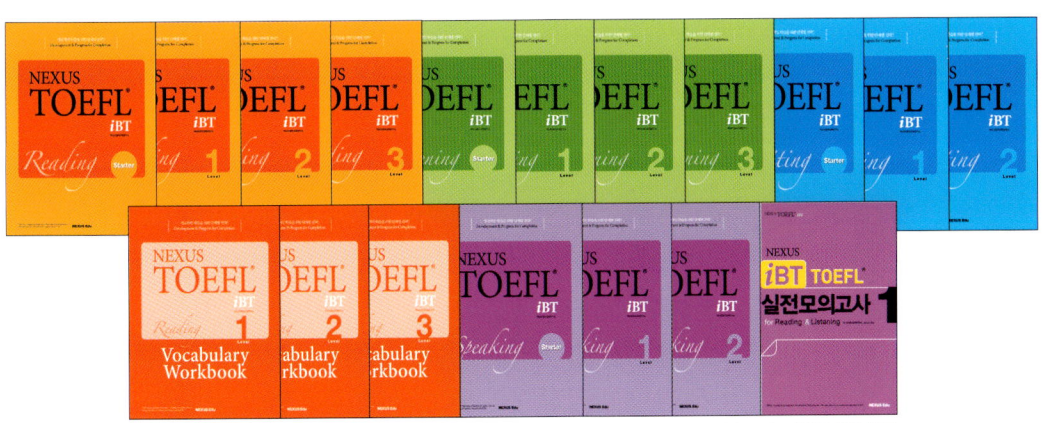

※ Listening MP3 별도 판매

넥서스 영어교육연구소 지음

Reading Starter - 13,500원
Reading Level 1 - 13,800원(CD 1개 포함)
Reading Level 2 - 14,000원
Reading Level 3 - 15,000원

Reading Starter Workbook - 3,500원
Reading Level 1 Workbook - 4,000원
Reading Level 2 Workbook - 4,000원
Reading Level 3 Workbook - 4,000원

Writing Starter - 13,800원(CD 1개 포함)
Writing Level 1 - 14,500원(CD 1개 포함)
Writing Level 2 - 14,500원(CD 1개 포함)

Listening Starter - 13,000원(MP3 별도: 4,900원)
Listening Level 1 - 13,800원(MP3 별도: 7,000원)
Listening Level 2 - 13,500원(MP3 별도: 7,000원)
Listening Level 3 - 13,800원(MP3 별도: 7,000원)

Listening Starter Workbook - 3,000원
Listening Level 1 Workbook - 3,000원
Listening Level 2 Workbook - 3,000원
Listening Level 3 Workbook - 3,000원

Speaking Starter - 13,500원(CD 1개 포함)
Speaking Level 1 - 15,000원(CD 2개 포함)
Speaking Level 2 - 15,000원(CD 2개 포함)

LEVEL CHART

NEXUS Edu

	초1	초2	초3	초4	초5	초6	중1	중2	중3	고1	고2	고3
VOCA	초등필수 영단어 1-2·3-4·5-6학년용											
					The VOCA + (플러스) 1~7							
			THIS IS VOCABULARY 입문·초급·중급					THIS IS VOCA 고급·어원·수능 완성·뉴텝스				
						WORD FOCUS 중등 종합 5000·고등 필수 5000·고등 종합 9500						
Grammar			초등필수 영문법 + 쓰기 1~2									
			OK Grammar 1~4									
			This Is Grammar Starter 1~3									
					This Is Grammar 초급~고급 (각 2권: 총 6권)							
						Grammar 공감 1~3						
						Grammar 101 1~3						
						Grammar Bridge 1~3						
						중학영문법 뽀개기 1~3						
					The Grammar Starter, 1~3							
							구사일생 (구문독해 Basic) 1~2					
								구문독해 204 1~2				
								그래머 캡처 1~2				
								[특급 단기 특강] 어법어휘 모의고사				

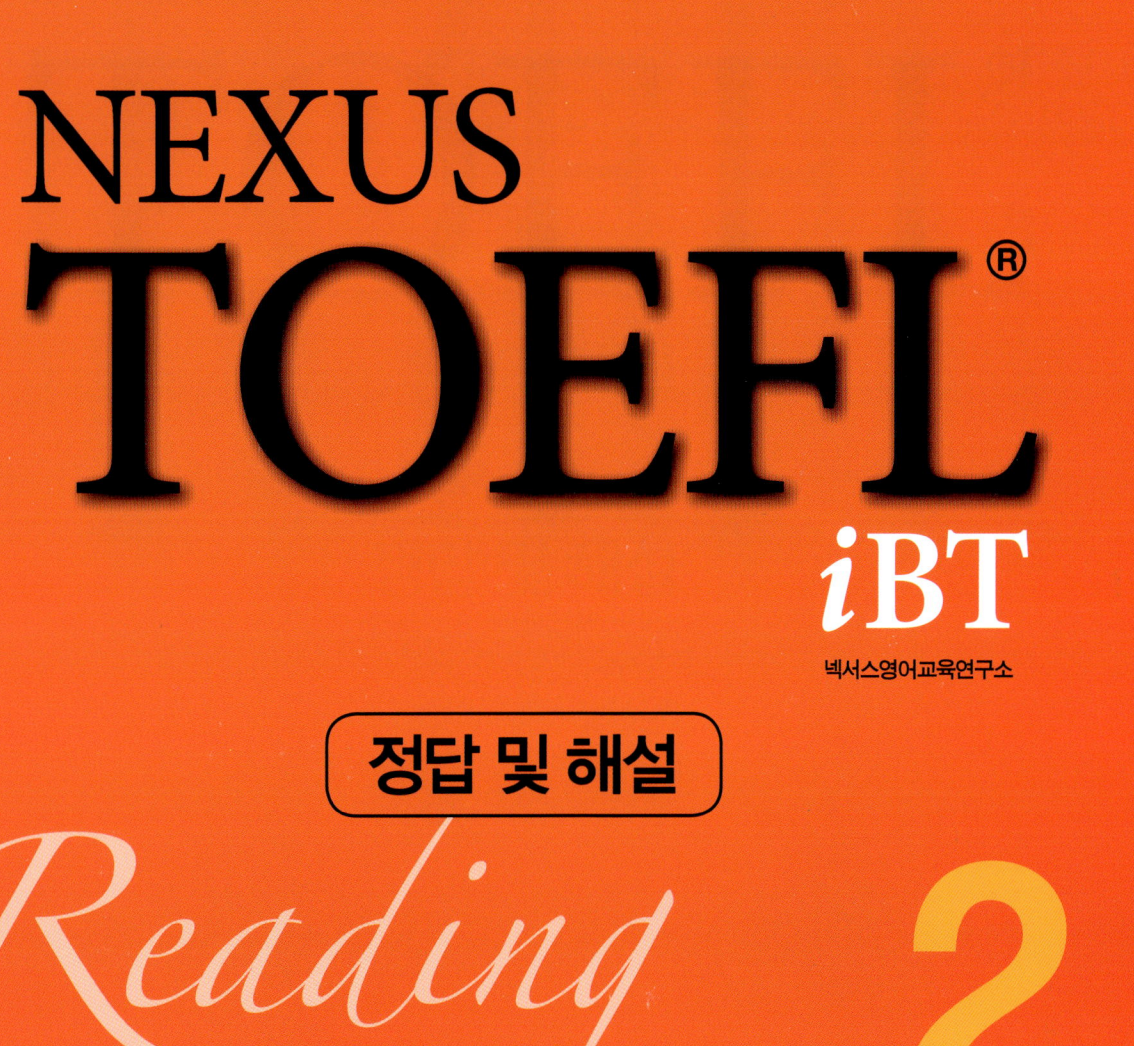

성공적인 학습을 위한 단계별 전략!
Development & Progress for Completion

NEXUS TOEFL® iBT

정답 및 해설

Reading

Level 2

NEXUS Edu

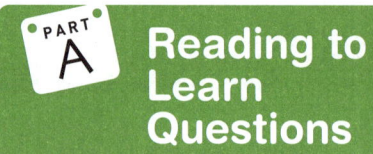

Chapter 1 Prose Summary p.14 - p.30

SAMPLE ITEM 정답 Ⓑ, Ⓔ, Ⓕ

해석 | 1622년, 유럽에서 온 최초의 식민지 개척자들은 북미에 꿀벌을 들여왔다. 이는 자신들이 수입한 많은 작물들이 꿀벌에 의지하여 수분을 하기 때문이었다. 많은 꿀벌은 도망쳤고 로키 산맥 동쪽으로 펼쳐진 넓은 대초원 지대의 가능한 모든 구석구석으로 재빨리 퍼져나갔다. 꿀벌이 자연적으로 로키 산맥을 넘은 것은 아니다. 그것들은 1850년대 초에 배로 캘리포니아로 옮겨졌다.

모든 곤충들 중에서 꿀벌이 가장 상업적으로 가치가 있는데, 이것은 꿀벌이 수분을 목적으로 이동할 수 있는 곤충이기 때문이다. 토양침식을 방지하는 데 도움이 되는 경작되지 않는 식물 뿐 아니라, 야채와 과일, 견과, 동물 먹이를 포함하는 약 50종의 작물이 이 수분 매개자에 의존한다.

꿀벌은 다른 많은 이유들로도 중요하게 여겨진다. 꿀벌이 만들어내는 꿀은 그 자체로도 맛있는 음식이면서 식품 산업에 다양한 용도로 사용된다. 밀랍이나 꽃가루, 봉랍과 로얄 젤리와 같은 꿀벌이 만들어내는 다른 제품들은 의약적 용도나 다른 목적으로 시장에서 팔린다. 예를 들면, 밀랍과 봉랍은 로션과 양초, 니스에 사용된다.

문제 | 지문에 대한 간단한 요약을 위한 도입 문장이 아래에 제시된다. 가장 중요한 내용을 표현한 3가지 대답을 선택하여 요약을 완성하시오. 몇몇 문장들은 단락에서 언급되지 않았거나 중요하지 않은 내용을 표현해서 요약에 들어갈 수 없다.

꿀벌은 농업에 중대한 역할을 수행하는, 상업적으로 중요한 곤충이다.

Ⓐ 꿀벌이 북미 지역 전역으로 퍼져나가는 데는 오랜 시간이 걸렸는데 이는 꿀벌들이 로키 산맥을 넘을 수 없었기 때문이다.

Ⓑ 최초의 꿀벌이 수분을 시키기 위해 북미로 들여져 온 이래, 꿀벌은 나라 전체에 급속하게 퍼졌다.

Ⓒ 꿀벌은 인간이 일상에서 소비하는 많은 종류의 작물을 수분시킬 수 있는 유일한 곤충이다.

Ⓓ 꿀벌이 만드는 로얄 젤리는 의학적으로나 다른 용도로 많이 쓰이기에 가장 쓸모 있는 제품이다.

Ⓔ 꿀벌의 제 1차적인 상업적 중요성은 50종의 작물을 수분시키는 데 그것들이 필요하다는 것이다.

Ⓕ 수분 외에, 꿀벌은 다른 유용한 제품들 중에서도 꿀과 밀랍을 생산한다.

해설 | Ⓐ는 로키 산맥을 넘지 못했다는 minor한 정보를 다루므로 오답이다. Ⓒ와 Ⓓ는 사실을 잘못 말하거나 자연적 또는 minor한 내용을 다루므로 오답이 된다.

Basic Drill

정답 1. P1- (C), P2- (A), P3- (C)
      2. P1- (B), P2- (A), P3- (B), P4- (A)

1. 해석 놀이 요법은 정신 건강에 대한 최신 분야이다. 이 요법은 정신 심리 요법, Rogerian 카운슬링, Axline 방법에 뿌리를 두고 있다. 이것은 연령과는 상관 없이 삶의 문제를 놀이를 통해 돕고자 시도한다. 이 요법은 특별히 언어를 통해 자신을 표현하는 데 어려움을 겪는 사람들에게 효과적이란 것이 입증되었다.

대부분의 사람들은 놀이 요법을 아이들과 관련 짓는데 이는 아이들이 자신의 생각을 제대로 표현하는 능력이 가장 낮고 이 요법을 통해 가장 많은 도움을 받기 때문이다. 놀이 요법은 숙련된 치료 전문가의 도움을 받아 아이들이 자신의 생각이나 느낌을 탐구할 수 있도록 한다. TV 쇼나 이야기에서 나온 행위들을 되풀이해 보는 것을 통해 놀이 치료 전문가는 아이들이 미리 자신을 압도하는 감정과 문제 등을 성공적으로 직시할 수 있게 도울 수 있다.

성공적인 치료의 핵심은 치료 전문가가 아이들의 신뢰를 얻어내는 능력에 달려 있는데, 이 신뢰를 통해 치료 전문가는 치료 기간 동안 아이들을 도울 수 있는 충분한 정보를 얻게 된다. 이러한 아이들은 두렵거나 부끄러워하기 때문에 문제를 드러내는 것을 내켜하지 않는다. 그렇게 되면 아이들은 치료 전문가에게 전혀 말을 하지 않게 된다. 놀이 치료를 하는 동안 현실은 중지되는 것처럼 보이고, 아이들이 안심하고 치료 전문가를 믿기 시작하면서 자신들의 개인적인 문제를 털어놓게 된다.

문제 | P1 (A) 놀이 요법은 삶에 문제를 가진 사람들을 위해 오랫동안 행해지고 있는 정신 건강 요법이다.

(B) 놀이 요법은 그 뿌리를 Rogerian 카운슬링과 Axline 방법에 두고 있는, 상당히 새로운 정신 건강 분야이다.

(C) 놀이 요법은 말로 자신을 표현하는 데 어려움을 겪는 사람들을 효과적으로 도울 수 있다.

해설 | 첫 번째 단락의 요지는 놀이 요법이 어떤 사람들에게, 어

떻게 도움이 되는지를 밝히는 단락 마지막 문장에 나와 있다.

문제 | P2 (A) 아이들은 보통 의사소통 기술이 떨어지기 때문에 놀이 요법으로 성공적인 도움을 받을 수 있는 대상들이다.
(B) 놀이 요법은 아이들이 치료 전문가의 생각과 느낌으로 실험하여 어떻게 자기들의 문제에 맞설지를 배울 수 있게 한다.
(C) 아이들은 놀이를 통해 어떻게 아이들의 느낌을 불러 일으켜야 하는지 잘 아는 숙련된 치료 전문가에게 도움을 받을 수 있다.

해설 | 두 번째 단락의 요지는 놀이 요법에 가장 적합한 대상이 누구인지, 또 어떻게 그 대상을 도와주는지이다.

문제 | P3 (A) 놀이 치료 전문가들은 아이들에 관한 정보를 얻기 위해 아이들을 신뢰해야 한다.
(B) 미래의 치료를 위해 중요한 정보는 아이들로부터 얻을 수 있다.
(C) 신뢰를 얻는 것은 아이들의 마음을 여는 것에 선행되는, 가장 중요한 요인이다.

해설 | 세 번째 단락의 요지는 아이들의 마음을 열게 하여 성공적인 치료가 이루어지기 위해서 치료 전문가가 아이들의 신뢰를 얻는 게 가장 중요한 일이란 점이다.

2. 해석   의학 연구자들은 식용 식물이 비타민과 미네랄을 포함해 생명 구조에 필요한 성분을 함유하고 있다는 것을 오랜 동안 알고 있었다. 하지만 그들은 최근에, 일련의 화학 합성물인 파이토케미컬은 식물에서만 찾을 수 있다는 사실을 발견했다. 몇 종류의 곡물과 견과에서도 찾을 수 있지만 파이토케미컬은 밝은 색의 과일과 야채에 특히 풍부하다. 이 화학물은 체리를 빨갛게, 브로콜리를 푸르게 만드는 성분이다. 그러나 이 물질은 식물을 예쁘게 보이도록 만드는 것 이상의 일을 한다. 사람들을 질병으로부터 보호해 주는 것이다.

임상 테스트를 통해 파이토케미컬이 질병을 예방한다는 것이 증명되었다. 산화 방지제라 불리는 어떤 파이토케미컬은 손상으로부터 세포를 보호하여 특정 종류의 암을 예방하는 데 도움을 준다고 알려져 있다. 양배추에 있는 다른 종류의 파이토케미컬은 에스트로젠이라고 하는, 여자들이 걸리는 유방암과 관련 있는 호르몬이 입히는 피해의 영향을 감소시킨다. 다른 파이토케미컬들은 고혈압, 당뇨, 심장 질환을 방지한다는 사실이 증명되었다. 이 물질들은 노화도 늦춘다고 밝혀졌다.

파이토케미컬이 건강에 미치는 모든 이익을 볼 때, 의사들이 더 많은 과일과 야채를 섭취하는 식단을 추천하는 것은 놀라운 일이 아니다. 가능한 많이 자연적으로 생기는 파이토케미컬의 혜택을 누리기 위해서는 다른 색상의 다양한 식물을 먹는 것이 가장 좋다. 노란색, 주황색, 붉은 색, 초록색, 푸른색, 보라색 과일과 야채는 함께 결합했을 때 잠재적으로 건강에 유익을 더하는 여러 다른 종류의 파이토케미컬을 가지고 있다.

파이토케미컬은 조리하는 과정에서 파괴되거나 없어진다고 여겨진다. 이 이유 때문에, 가공 처리된 식품은 그렇지 않은 식품에 비해 덜 유익하고, 더 적은 파이토케미컬을 함유하고 있다고 인식된다. 파이토케미컬의 부재 또는 결핍은 현대 사회에서 일어나는 질병의 발생률을 높이고 있다는 주장이 제기되고 있다.

문제 | P1 (A) 파이토케미컬은 과일과 야채에서도 발견할 수 있지만 견과류와 곡물에 가장 많다.
(B) 파이토케미컬은 사람들 건강에 이익을 줄 뿐만 아니라 식물에 색을 더해준다.
(C) 식용 식물에 있는 비타민과 미네랄 말고도 식물의 색을 만드는 화학물질이 발견되었다.

해설 | 첫 번째 단락은 파이토케미컬의 효능과 역할을 중점적으로 언급한다.

문제 | P2 (A) 파이토케미컬이 다양한 건강상의 문제를 예방한다는 것이 입증되었다.
(B) 여자들에게 발생하는 많은 암은 에스트로젠의 높은 수치와 밀접한 관련이 있다.
(C) 과일과 야채에 들어있는 유사한 파이토케미컬은 인체에도 존재한다는 것이 드러났다.

해설 | 두 번째 단락의 핵심적인 내용은 여러 종류의 파이토케미컬이 다양한 질병을 예방하는 데 효과가 있다는 것이다.

문제 | P3 (A) 파이토케미컬은 노란색, 주황색, 빨간색, 그리고 초록색을 포함하는 다양한 과일과 야채의 색을 만든다.
(B) 파이토케미컬의 영향으로 받은 이익을 극대화하기 위해서는 다양한 색의 과일과 야채를 섭취해야 한다.
(C) 다른 색상은 과일과 야채에 포함된 각기 다른 파이토케미컬을 나타낸다.

해설 | 세 번째 단락은 파이토케미컬이 야채와 과일의 색을 각각 다르게 만들고, 다양한 색상의 야채와 과일을 먹는 것이 건강에 도움이 된다는 내용을 말하고 있다.

문제 | P4 (A) 가공 처리되지 않은 식품은 조리 과정에서 파이토케미컬이 없어지지 않기 때문에 더 유익하다.
(B) 유익한 파이토케미컬은 열 때문에 식품 처리 과정을 거치면서 쉽게 파괴된다.
(C) 많은 인스턴트 음식에 파이토케미컬이 없는 것은 오늘날 발생하는 질병의 위험성을 증가시킬 것이다.

해설 | 네 번째 단락의 주요 내용은 가공 처리되지 않은 식품이 많은 파이토케미컬을 함유하고 있어서 우리 몸에 더 유익하다는 것이다.

VOCABULARY Preview

| Check-up |

1. primarily 2. denied 3. demonstrate
4. agricultural 5. crisis 6. altered
7. disruption 8. enthusiasm 9. exhausted
10. conversely 11. collapsed 12. tactic

다음 빈 칸에 들어갈 알맞은 말을 골라, 필요하면 고쳐 쓰시오.

1. 이 연극은 어린 아이들이 있는 가정이 <u>주요</u> 대상이다.
2. Paul은 특별 대우를 받게 될 것이란 소문을 여러 차례 <u>부정했다</u>.
3. 갈릴레오는 지구가 태양 주위를 돌고 있다는 것을 자신의 생전에 <u>증명할</u> 수 없었다.
4. 난 이 땅을 <u>농업적</u> 목적으로 사용하기 위해 샀지, 공업적 용도로 산 게 아니다.
5. 두 나라는 <u>위기를</u> 해결하기 위해 교섭을 벌였으나 실패했다.
6. Lisa는 대학을 졸업한 후에 성형수술로 얼굴을 <u>바꿨다</u>.
7. 항공사 파업은 수많은 사람들이 해외로 나가는 것을 <u>붕괴시킨</u> 주된 원인이다.
8. Henry의 음악에의 <u>열정은</u> 그의 생애를 통틀어 강하게 지속되었다.
9. 식량 공급이 <u>끊기자</u> 그 군대는 고국으로 귀환할 수 밖에 없었다.
10. 뭐, 우리 삶에서 벌어지는 상황들은 늘 나쁜 것도, <u>반대로</u> 항상 좋은 것도 아니지.
11. 계속되는 지진과 홍수로 인해 그 나라의 관광 산업은 <u>몰락했다</u>.
12. 직장을 그만두겠다고 위협한 그녀의 <u>작전은</u> 굉장히 효과적이었다.

Exercise 1

정답 1. Ⓒ 2. Ⓑ 3. Ⓑ, Ⓔ, Ⓕ

해석   노예 내러티브(이야기체 문학)는 오늘날까지 미국 문학에 지속적으로 영향을 미치고 있는 이야기의 한 종류이다. 1760년과 1860년 사이, 예전에 노예였던 이들에 의해 쓰여진 150개 정도의 내러티브가 노예제를 철폐하고자 일어난 운동인 노예제 폐지 운동을 지원하기 위한 일환으로 미국과 영국에서 출간되었다. 또한 이러한 내러티브들은 당시의 흑인들의 삶에 관해 많은 것을 알려준다.

이 장르의 가장 일차적인 역할은 작가의 인간성과 지성을 보여주는 것이었다. 자기 자신의 삶에 대한 이야기를 말하는 행위는 노예나 이전에 노예였던 사람들이 지적이었다는 것을 증명했을 뿐 아니라, 흑인도 다른 백인들과 유사한 감정을 가지고 산다는 것을 보여주었는데, 이는 노예제를 지지하는 사람들에 의해 부정되었던 사실이었다.

1820년대 중반 이후부터 이 장르는 노예제 폐지를 위한 투쟁을 더 열성적으로 일으키기 위해 의식적으로 더 자서전적 형식을 사용했다. 이 내러티브는 종종 각색한 대화를 도입함으로써 더욱 문학적인 형식을 갖추게 되었다. 1835년과 1865년 사이에, 그러한 형식을 갖춘 내러티브가 80권 넘게 출간되었다. 노예 경매와 가족의 해체, 그리고 빈번한 탈출이 이러한 내러티브에 나오는 일반적인 특징이었다.

문 1 | 첫 번째 단락에 따르면, 노예 내러티브가 쓰여진 이유는?
Ⓐ 미국 문학에 영향을 미치기 위해 구체적으로 집필되었다.
Ⓑ 이전에 노예였던 사람들에게 돈을 기부했다.
Ⓒ 노예제 종말에 기여하려는 목적을 갖고 있었다.
Ⓓ 그것들은 전(前) 노예 시대의 흑인들의 역사였다.

해설 | to help the Abolitionist Movement — the movement to end slavery. 부분에 narrative들이 쓰여진 이유에 대한 설명이 나온다.

문 2 | 첫 번째 단락에 따르면, 노예 내러티브에 관해 알려진 것은?
Ⓐ 노예 내러티브는 대부분 미국에서 출간되었다.
Ⓑ 노예들에 의해 쓰여진 대부분의 내러티브들은 그들의 삶에 관한 것이었다.
Ⓒ 노예 내러티브는 1760년에서 1860년까지 100년이 넘는 기간 동안, 매해 집필되었다.
Ⓓ 너무나 오래 전에 쓰여졌기 때문에, 그 이야기들은 현재 가치가 떨어진다.

해설 | 노예 내러티브는 아직까지 미국 문학에 영향을 미치고 있는 문학의 한 장르로서, 1760년부터 1860년까지 매년 집필된 것이 아니라 그 기간 동안 약 150편이 미국과 영국에서 출간되었으며 미국에서 더 많은 책이 출간되었다는 언급은 없다. 따라서 Ⓐ, Ⓒ, Ⓓ는 답이 아니다.

문 3 | 지문에 대한 간단한 요약을 위한 도입 문장이 아래에 제시된다. 가장 중요한 내용을 표현한 3가지 대답을 선택하여 요약을 완성하시오. 몇몇 문장들은 단락에서 언급되지 않았거나 중요하지 않은 내용을 표현해서 요약에 들어갈 수 없다.

노예 내러티브의 영구적인 기여 중 하나는 그것이 노예제를 폐지하는 데 도움을 주었다는 것이다.

Ⓐ 노예 내러티브는 미국에서 오늘날 계속해서 집필되고 있다.
Ⓑ 오늘날 미국 문학에 여전히 영향을 미치고 있는 가운데, 미국의 노예 내러티브는 노예의 삶을 묘사했고 노예제도를 폐지시키는 데 도움을 주었다.
Ⓒ 노예제 옹호론자들은 노예들이 지적인 존재라고 믿었다.
Ⓓ 노예 경매, 노예 가족의 해체, 그리고 탈출은 내러티브에 일반적으로 드러나는 특징이었다.
Ⓔ 작품의 목적은 사람들로 하여금 노예들이 지적이면서 그들처럼 감정을 지닌 사람이라고 여길 수 있도록 돕는 것이었다.
Ⓕ 1825년 즈음에 자서전적인 형식이 널리 퍼졌고, 각색된 내러티브가 노예폐지론자들의 주장을 증진시키기 위해 도입되었다.

해설 | Ⓐ는 지문에 나오지 않은 내용이고, Ⓒ는 지문의 내용과 반대되는 내용이고, Ⓓ는 세 번째 단락의 너무 지엽적인 내용이다.

Exercise 2

정답 1. Ⓑ   2. Ⓒ   3. Ⓑ, Ⓓ, Ⓔ

해석 몇 세기 동안 인류는 댐을 건설하여 강과 시내를 관리하고자 노력했다. 댐은 홍수를 방지하고, 관개에 필요한 물을 저장하며, 수력 전력을 생산하는 것으로 지역에 이익을 가져다 줄 수 있다. 그 결과, 대부분의 나라들은 댐을 건설하는 데 큰 액수의 돈과 인력을 투자한다. 그러나 댐 건설이 가져오는 이익과 그것이 가져오는 부정적인 영향을 필수적으로 저울질해야 한다. 댐 건설과 연결되는 환경 문제들은 종종 예측되지 않고, 이는 영구적인 피해를 일으킬 수 있다.

댐 주변의 땅은 여러 면에서 부정적인 영향을 받을 수 있다. 우선, 댐 뒤에 만들어진 저수지는 땅의 넓은 지역을 삼켜 골짜기와 농장, 그리고 숲을 물 밑에 잠기게 만들 수도 있다. 두 번째로, 강은 경로를 따라 흘러가면서 고운 입자의 흙과 모래인 퇴적물을 바다로 내보낸다. 하지만 댐은 씻겨나가는 퇴적물의 양을 바꾼다. 강의 많은 퇴적물은 댐 뒤에 모일 것이고 시간이 지남에 따라 저수지 안의 퇴적물은 여러 문제를 일으킬 것이다. 반대로, 댐 밑은 자연적으로 퇴적된 퇴적물이 부족하여 강둑을 따라 토양침식이 일어나고, 해안으로까지 침식이 확장될 것이다. 명백하게, 댐은 주변 땅에 영구적으로 부정적인 영향을 미칠 수 있다. 더욱이, 댐의 영향은 종종 식물과 동물의 서식지로까지 확대된다.

댐 건설은 서식지를 나눠 그 지역 내의 동식물들의 자연적인 이동을 막는다. 이것은 특히 번식을 위해 강을 거슬러 올라가야 하는 물고기에게 문제가 될 수 있다. 북미의 주요 댐들이 건설되면서, 여러 종의 연어가 멸종 위기에 처한 종 리스트에 들어가게 되었다. 또 다른 문제는 물의 흐름과 퇴적물이 바뀜에 따라 벌어진, 강가에 형성된 생태계의 붕괴이다. 대부분의 강의 생태계는 굉장히 깨지기 쉽고, 다양한 형태의 야생 생물을 부양한다. 이 서식지 없이는 전체 식물과 동물종이 멸종할 것이다.

문 1 | 첫번째 단락에 따르면, 다음 중 댐 건설의 이익으로 언급되지 않은 것은?
Ⓐ 수력 전기의 발생
Ⓑ 직장의 창출과 투자
Ⓒ 농가에 공급할 충분한 물
Ⓓ 장마철 동안의 강의 통제

해설 | preventing floods, storing water for irrigation and generating hydroelectric power. 에 Ⓐ, Ⓒ, Ⓓ가 언급되어 있다. Ⓑ의 직장의 창출이란 내용은 지문에 언급되어 있지 않다.

문 2 | 세 번째 단락의 reproduce와 가장 의미가 유사한 것은?
Ⓐ 먹이다
Ⓑ 죽다
Ⓒ 새끼를 낳다
Ⓓ 가정을 만들다

해설 | reproduce는 '번식하다'란 의미이다. 따라서 답은 Ⓒ이다.

문 3 | 지문에 대한 간단한 요약을 위한 도입 문장이 아래에 제시된다. 가장 중요한 내용을 표현한 3가지 대답을 선택하여 요약을 완성하시오. 몇몇 문장들은 단락에서 언급되지 않았거나 중요하지 않은 내용을 표현해서 요약에 들어갈 수 없다.

댐은 강과 시내를 관리하기 위해 오랫동안 사용되었다.

Ⓐ 댐과 관련된 환경적인 문제는 종종 수력 전기 발생의 결과이다.
Ⓑ 비록 유익하긴 하지만 댐은 영구적인 환경 문제를 야기할 수 있다.
Ⓒ 퇴적물이란 물의 흐름에 의해 이동되는 미세한 티끌이다.
Ⓓ 댐이 건설되고 난 후, 어떤 동물들에게는 그 지역에서 이동하는 것이 굉장히 어려워진다.
Ⓔ 댐 주변 지역은 퇴적물의 부족 또는 너무 많은 퇴적물로 인한 부정적인 영향을 받는다.
Ⓕ 북미에 있는 많은 연어 종은 현재 멸종 위기에 처해졌다.

해설 | Ⓐ는 지문과는 다른 내용을 말하고 있고, Ⓒ와 Ⓕ는 지엽적인 내용이다.

Exercise 3

정답 1. Ⓑ 2. Ⓒ 3. Ⓐ 4. Ⓒ 5. Ⓑ, Ⓒ, Ⓕ

Text Outline (A)

해석 Dust Bowl은 1930년대 미국 남중부 지역에서 일어났던 주로 사람에 의한 농업적 위기를 말한다. 이 지역이 오랫동안 아주 기름진 토양과 매우 비옥한 농지로 알려져 왔지만, 1930년대 들어 이 지역의 농업은 몰락했다.

그 지역의 농부들은 땅의 영양분이 소진되어 더 이상 식물을 부양할 수 없을 시점에 다다랐을 때까지 밭을 과도하게 사용했다. 토양은 매우 질이 나빠졌고, 영양분의 부족과 긴 가뭄이 합쳐져 많은 흙이 날아가 버렸다. 그 지역의 대다수의 주민들은 생계를 잃었고, 직장을 잡기 위해 어쩔 수 없이 다른 지역으로 이주할 수 밖에 없었다.

그 지역에 남은 농부들은 손상을 복구시키고 흙을 보충하기 위해 남았다. 그들은 여러 다른 종류의 지속 가능한 농업(sustainable agriculture)에 대해 배웠는데, 이것은 땅을 황폐하게 하지 않는 경작 방식이다. 그들이 택한 한 가지 수단은 윤작(crop rotation)이었다. 전통적인 농작에서는 농부들이 매해 밭에 같은 종류의 작물을 심곤 했다. 이 작물들은 토양에서 같은 영양분을 취했기에 다음 해의 식물 생장기 전까지 그 영양분들이 보충될 시간이 없었다. 그러나 윤작을 실시하여 농부들은 매해 다른 작물을 밭에 심게 되었다. 이 방식으로 자연은 식물 생장기 사이에 영양분을 보충할 수 있게 되었다.

농부들이 사용하기 시작한 다른 종류의 지속 가능한 농업 방식은 계단식 농작(terrace farming)이었다. 과거에 농부들은 밭을 가로질러 작물을 일직선으로 심었다. 이것 때문에 흙은 비바람에 쉽게 씻겨 내려갔다. 그러나 농부들은 작물을 원형으로 심거나 산허리에 심으면 침식 과정이 훨씬 덜 발생하게 된다는 것을 깨달았다.

문 1 첫 번째 단락의 fertile과 가장 의미가 유사한 것은?
Ⓐ 불모의
Ⓑ 비옥한
Ⓒ 무균의
Ⓓ 잡초투성이의

해설 fertile은 '땅이 기름진', '비옥한'이란 뜻이다. 뒤에 나오는 highly productive에서 힌트를 얻을 수 있다. Ⓒ의 rich는 '부유한'이란 의미 외에 '비옥한'이란 뜻이 있다.

문 2 두 번째 단락에 따르면, 다음 중 이 지역에 대해 올바르게 말하고 있는 것은?
Ⓐ 장기간 지속된 가뭄은 토양의 영양분을 황폐하게 만들었다.
Ⓑ 다른 종류의 직업을 가졌던 사람들은 이 지역에 남았다.
Ⓒ 더 이상 경작용으로 개발할 땅이 남아있지 않았다.
Ⓓ 농부들은 토양을 개선시키기 위한 시도로 비료를 뿌렸다.

해설 장기간의 가뭄이 토양의 영양분을 죽인 것은 아니므로 Ⓐ는 오답이고, Ⓑ와 Ⓓ의 다른 종류의 직업을 가진 사람들과 비료에 관한 이야기는 언급되지 않았다.

문 3 세 번째 단락의 tactic과 가장 의미가 유사한 것은?
Ⓐ 방법
Ⓑ 도구
Ⓒ 농지
Ⓓ 작물

해설 tactic은 '수단', '전술' 등의 의미를 지닌다. 문맥상 '방법', '방식'의 의미로 쓰였으므로 답은 Ⓐ이다.

문 4 네 번째 단락에 의하면, 비바람은
Ⓐ 큰 가뭄이 발생하면 농작할 때 생기는 유일한 걱정거리이다.
Ⓑ 농부들이 계단식 농작을 시작하도록 영감을 주었다.
Ⓒ 작물이 일직선으로 심겨지지 않는다면 흙을 덜 파괴할 것이다.
Ⓓ 원형의 계단식 형태로 심겨진 작물에 아무런 영향을 미치지 않는다.

해설 Ⓐ와 Ⓑ는 지문에서 언급되지 않은 내용이고, 비바람이 원형 계단식에 아무런 영향을 주지 않는다는 Ⓓ는 틀린 설명이다. 계단식 농작이 비바람에 의한 침식을 덜 발생시킨다는 설명을 하는 Ⓒ가 답이다.

문 5 지문에 대한 간단한 요약을 위한 도입의 문장이 아래에 제시된다. 가장 중요한 생각을 표현한 3가지 대답을 선택하여 요약을 완성하시오. 몇몇 문장들은 단락에서 언급되지 않았거나 중요하지 않은 생각을 표현해서 요약에 들어갈 수 없다.

Dust Bowl도 미국 농부들은 지속 가능한 농업에 대한 몇 가지 중요한 교훈을 배웠다.

Ⓐ 미국 남중부 지역의 토양과 농지의 질은 잘 알려져 있었다.
Ⓑ 땅의 과도한 사용과 장기간의 가뭄이 결합되어 토양이 척박해졌고, 많은 양이 날아가 버렸다.
Ⓒ 농부들은 매해 다른 종류의 농작물을 심는 것이 토양을 건강하게 유지시키는 데 도움을 준다는 것을 배웠다.
Ⓓ 농부들은 긴 가뭄이 영양가 없는 흙을 날아가버리게 할 수 있다는 것을 깨달았다.
Ⓔ 대부분의 농부들이 이 지역을 떠난 반면, 어떤 농무들은 손상을 복구하기 위해 남았다.
Ⓕ 농지를 유지시키기 위한 다른 방법은 농작물을 심는 방식을 변화시키고 있었다.

해설 Ⓐ는 첫 번째 단락의, Ⓔ는 두 번째 단락의 중요하지 않은 정보이다. Ⓓ는 지문의 내용과는 다른 내용이다. 지문에서 중요한 정보는 Dust Bowl에 대한 정의와 현상, 또 그 위기를 극복하기 위한 대안들이다.

VOCABULARY TEST

정답 1. (C)   2. (B)   3. (D)   4. (C)   5. (B)
      6. (D)   7. (D)   8. (A)   9. (B)   10. (C)
      11. (D) 12. (B)

밑줄 친 어휘나 구와 가장 유사한 의미를 지닌 것을 고르시오.

1. 그는 그 문제에 대해 더욱 조심스러운 접근을 채택하기로 결정했다.
   (A) 적응시키다   (B) 접촉하다
   (C) 채택하다   (D) 끄다

2. 숙제를 끝내기 위한 도움을 요청하는 것이 내키지 않았다.
   (A) 날카로운   (B) 마음 내키지 않는
   (C) 기묘한   (D) 준비된

3. 그 연극은 예술과 돈의 관계를 탐구한다.
   (A) 반영하다   (B) 묘사하다
   (C) 통합하다   (D) 엄밀히 조사하다

4. 빈혈은 몸에 철분이 부족할 때 생긴다.
   (A) 충족   (B) 여분
   (C) 결핍   (D) 결점

5. 이 일을 얻을 수 있는 사람은 넓은 범위의 학문 분야에 대한 지식을 갖고 있어야 한다.
   (A) 연구   (B) 학과
   (C) 조사   (D) 증명서

6. 파업의 결과로, 많은 고용인들이 해고되었다. 즉, 생계 수단을 잃어버렸다.
   (A) 결과   (B) 돈
   (C) 가정   (D) 직업

7. 어제 거기서 내가 만난 남자는 너무나 무례해서, 난 떠나고 싶다는 굉장한 열망을 느꼈다.
   (A) 민감한   (B) 충격적인
   (C) 두려운   (D) 강한

8. 그 나라는 석유와 관광 명소가 풍부하다.
   (A) 풍부한   (B) 불충분한
   (C) 예리한   (D) 불모의

9. 이 조각은 매우 깨지기 쉬우므로 조심스럽게 다루어야 한다.
   (A) 묵직한   (B) 불안정한
   (C) 되는 대로의   (D) 중요한

10. James는 이전에 파트타임으로 고용되었다.
    (A) 정밀하게   (B) 귀중하게
    (C) 이전에   (D) 적합하게

11. 기술의 진보로 이제는 진짜 꽃과 인공적으로 만든 것을 분간하기가 매우 어렵다.
    (A) 영구적인   (B) 훌륭한
    (C) 가공하지 않은 (D) 인공적인

12. 나이나 성별에 상관 없이 누구나 선거에 출마할 수 있습니다.
    (A) 일반적으로   (B) ~에 관계 없이
    (C) ~을 좋아하는 (D) ~에 따라

Chapter 2 Schematic Table   p.32 - p.46

SAMPLE ITEM   정답 Laboratory Meat - Ⓐ, Ⓔ, Ⓖ / Natural Meat - Ⓑ, Ⓕ

해석 유전 공학의 새로운 발전으로 과학자들은 실험실에서 상업적으로 고기를 키울 수 있게 될 것이다. 실험실에서 육류를 생산하는 데에는 현재 고기로 사용되고 있는 소나 다른 동물들의 근육 조직을 제거하는 일도 포함될 것이다. 이러한 조직은 배양되어 후에 "실제" 육류 조직을 만드는 데 사용될 것이다.

이것은 궁극적으로 소와 같은 동물들에 대한 육류 생산 의존도와 이로 인한 환경문제를 줄일 것이다. 예를 들면, 소떼는 과도하게 풀을 뜯어 먹고 대기 중으로 메탄가스를 방출하여 환경에 타격을 끼친다. 실험실에서 육류를 생산하는 것은 지구 온난화의 속도를 늦추고 목초지의 파괴가 심화되지 않도록 보호하는 데 도움이 될 것이다.

환경에 이익이 되는 것 외에, 고기를 먹는 사람들도 실험실에서 생산된 고기를 먹는 것을 통해 이익을 얻게 될 것이다. 과학자들은 건강에 좋지 않거나 도움이 되지 않는 지방을 건강에 더 좋은 요소로 대체시킴으로써 고기의 영양소를 조절할 수 있다. 이로써 고기를 생산하는 동물들에게 사용되고 있는 약물이나 항생제의 사용을 중지시킬 수 있고, 이것은 소비자 건강에 더 좋을 것이다.

그러나 실험실에서 키워지는 고기는 초기에는 개발 과정에서 발생하는 문제점들로 인해 가격이 더 비쌀 것이다. 육류 실험실을 세우고 운영하는 비용이 개발에 장애가 될 수 있다. 쇠고기 근육은 어류나 닭고기보다 키우는 게 더 어렵다. 왜냐하면 천연 육류와 거의 동일한 조직을 갖기 위해 쇠고기 근육을 운동시키고 늘릴 필요가 있기 때문이다. 다행히도, 생선과 닭고기 근육은 실험실에서 제법 잘 자랐다.

문제 | 적절한 보기를 골라 관련 있는 육류의 종류와 짝지으시오. 두 개의 보기는 제외됩니다.
Ⓐ 선택된 영양소에 의해 더 건강에 좋을 수도 있다.
Ⓑ 양질의 고기를 얻기 위해 항상제와 약을 사용한다.
Ⓒ 특정 문화에서는 문제를 일으킬 수 있다.
Ⓓ 발생 가능한 질병을 줄이거나 제거할 수 있다.
Ⓔ 생선과 닭고기에 대한 의존도를 줄일 수 있다.
Ⓕ 사람에게 불필요한 영양소를 포함하고 있을 수 있다.
Ⓖ 처음에 그것을 생산하는 데 많은 돈이 들 수 있다.

해설 | 선택된 영양소를 함유하고, 생선이나 닭고기와 같은 자연산 고기에 대한 의존도를 낮추며, 초기 생산에 많은 돈이 들어갈 수 있는 것은 실험실에서 배양된 고기이다. 반면, 항생제와 약을 투여하고, 지방과 같은 인체에 좋지 않은 영양소를 포함하는 것은 자연산 고기이다. Ⓒ와 Ⓓ는 언급되지 않은 내용이다.

Basic Drill

정답 | 1. ① Be at the tops of high mountains all over the world ② 50 days ③ 180 days ④ minus 30 degrees ⑤ 55 degrees ⑥ below freezing ⑦ Soil ⑧ poor drainage ⑨ ponds ⑩ bogs ⑪ Root ⑫ extremes of temperature

해석　툰드라 지역은 매우 추운 지역으로 나무가 없고, 비나 눈이 거의 안 오며, 동물의 종류가 다양하지 않고, 사는 식물의 생태가 단순한 것이 특징이다. 지구상에는 북극 툰드라와 고산(산악) 툰드라라는 두 종류의 툰드라 지역이 있다. 양 지역은 앞서 언급된 특징들을 공유하면서 동시에 각각 독특한 특색을 지닌다.

　북극 툰드라는 북극을 둘러서 남쪽으로 내려가 북유럽의 숲과 아시아까지 이르는 반면, 고산(산악) 툰드라 지역은 전 세계의 높은 산꼭대기에 있다. 북극 툰드라 지역에서 식물이 자랄 수 있는 기간은 너무나 짧다. 연간 약 50일 동안만 자랄 수 있고, 겨울 기온은 섭씨 영하 30도까지 내려간다. 그러나 여름 기온이 높게는 55도까지 올라가므로 이 지역은 생명을 유지시킬 수 있다. 고산(산악) 툰드라 지역의 (식물의) 성장 기간은 보다 긴 180여일 정도이지만, 밤 기온은 연중 어떤 때든 영하로 내려간다.

　북극 툰드라 지역에는 비나 눈이 거의 오지 않지만, 나쁜 배수 기능이 땅을 습하게 유지시킨다. 그래서 이 지역에는 작은 연못이나 늪지대가 많다. 이것이 그곳에서 자라는 식물들을 기른다. 비록 단순하지만, 이 식물들은 기후에 적응한다. 그 예로, 이 식물들은 영양분을 만들기 위해 많은 햇빛을 필요로 하지 않는다. 또한 얕은 뿌리에도 불구하고 강한 바람을 견딜 수 있다. 북극 툰드라와는 달리, 고산(산악) 툰드라의 토양은 배수 기능이 더 높다. 식물 또한 기후에 잘 적응한다. 북극 툰드라에 서식하는 식물과 마찬가지로, 양 툰드라의 지배적인 식물인 풀, 이끼, 지의와 같은 고산(산악) 툰드라의 식물은 살아남기 위해서 뿐만 아니라 다른 종의 식물들을 죽일 수 있는 혹독한 상황 속에서 잘 자랄 수 있게끔 진화해 왔다. 그리고 북극 툰드라뿐만 아니라 이곳의 식물도 뿌리가 얕고 극한의 기온을 견디는 능력을 가진다.

해설 | 비교 / 대조 또는 논쟁의 글에는 어떤 특징들이나 원칙들에 대한 양쪽의 차이점이나 비슷한 점을 설명하게 된다. 위 지문은 두 지역을 6가지 특징에 대하여 비교하는 전형적인 비교 / 대조의 글로 어떻게 서로 다르고 어떤 점들이 비슷한지를 파악하도록 한다.

VOCABULARY Preview

| Check-up |

1. passively   2. alternative   3. visible
4. figure   5. curious   6. characterize
7. standardized 8. immensity
9. screen   10. slogan

다음 빈 칸에 들어갈 알맞은 말을 골라, 필요하면 고쳐 쓰시오.

1. Ronald는 수업에 집중하지 않는다. 그저 <u>수동적으로</u> 칠판을 응시할 뿐이다.
2. 그 곳에 도착할 수 있는 <u>대안적</u> 방법이 있어야만 한다.
3. 그 간판은 매우 커서 상당히 먼 거리에서도 <u>보였다</u>.
4. 그는 금세기에 생물공학 분야에서 유력한 <u>인물</u>이었다.
5. Steve는 내 조국의 언어와 문화에 대해 <u>궁금해 한다</u>.
6. 자신의 <u>특징</u>을 어떻게 묘사하시겠습니까?
7. 나는 입학고사를 위해 <u>표준화된</u> 테스트를 만들어야 한다고 생각한다.
8. 밤에 볼 수 있는 별의 <u>광대함</u>은 놀랍다.
9. 이 새로운 검사는 암에 걸릴 위험이 있는 사람들을 <u>가려낼</u> 것이다.
10. 우리 회사의 새 광고 <u>슬로건</u>을 만드는 데 백만원이 들었다.

Exercise 1

정답 1. Ⓐ 2. Ⓒ 3. Ⓑ 4. Lunar Eclipse- Ⓐ, Ⓒ / Solar Eclipse- Ⓑ, Ⓔ, Ⓕ

해석   식(eclipse)은 태양, 지구 그리고 달이 정확히 일직선상에 위치하게 될 때마다 일어난다. 달이 지구의 그림자를 통과하는 보름달에 이 현상이 일어나면 이를 월식이라 한다. 보름달은 달이 태양으로부터 지구의 반대쪽에 놓일 때 발생하는 달의 (변화)단계이다. 보름달은 월식이 가능한 유일한 시기이다. 그 때 달은 지구가 드리운 그림자를 통과하여 이동한다. 그러나 지구 주위를 도는 달의 궤도는 5도 경사져있기 때문에, 달은 그림자의 위쪽 또는 아래쪽으로 통과한다. 그래서 월식은 보름달이 뜰 때 매번 일어나지는 않는다.

매년 적어도 두 번에 걸쳐 월식이 있다. 지구상에서 상대적으로 작은 특정 지역에서만 볼 수 있는 일식과는 달리, 월식은 밤이면 지구의 어느 지역에서든 볼 수 있다. 과학자들이 지구의 둥근 그림자가 달 표면을 지나가는 것을 안전하게 관찰하게 됨에 따라, 월식은 지구가 둥글다는 것을 증명하는 첫 번째 힌트였다.

일식은 달이 태양 앞을 지나며 태양을 완전히 혹은 부분적으로 가릴 때 일어난다. 일식은 월식만큼 넓은 지역에서 볼 수 없다. 일식은 달의 그림자가 지구 표면을 가로질러 이동할 때, 표면 위의 띠와 같은 경로에서 관찰할 수 있다. 일식이 진행되는 동안, 과학자들은 태양 표면의 폭발과 태양 흑점, 태양 코로나의 크기 및 구성과 같은 것들과 광선이 태양의 중력장에 접근할 때 어떻게 굴절되는지를 관찰한다.

문 1 | 첫 번째 단락의 inclined와 가장 의미가 유사한 것은?
Ⓐ 경사진
Ⓑ 위치한
Ⓒ 던져진
Ⓓ 낮춘

해설 | incline은 '기울이다', '경사지게 하다'란 의미로, 뒤에 above or below가 힌트가 된다.

문 2 | 두 번째 단락의 circular와 가장 의미가 유사한 것은?
Ⓐ 어두운
Ⓑ 이동하는
Ⓒ 둥근
Ⓓ 걸린

해설 | circular는 '원형의' 또는 '순환성의'란 뜻으로, 앞에 round가 단서가 된다.

문 3 | 두 번째 단락의 it이 가리키는 것은?
Ⓐ 태양
Ⓑ 달
Ⓒ 지구
Ⓓ 식(蝕)

해설 | 지구의 그림자가 it의 표면을 지나가고 있다는 곳에서 답을 찾을 수 있다. 월식에 대한 설명이므로 it이 가리키는 것이 달이라는 것을 알 수 있다.

문 4 | 적절한 보기를 골라 관련있는 식의 종류와 짝지으시오. 두 개의 보기는 제외됩니다.
Ⓐ 지구는 태양과 달 사이에 놓인다.
Ⓑ 달은 지구와 태양 사이에 놓인다.
Ⓒ 지구의 어느 위치에서도 관찰될 수 있다.
Ⓓ 달에서 빛을 반사해 태양으로 비춘다.
Ⓔ 굴절하는 광선을 관찰할 수 있는 기회를 제공한다.
Ⓕ 지구의 특정 지역에서만 볼 수 있다.
Ⓖ 달의 표면을 더 효과적으로 연구하는 데 도움을 준다.

해설 | Ⓓ와 Ⓖ는 지문에 언급되지 않은 내용이다.

Exercise 2

정답 1. Ⓒ 2. Ⓓ 3. Dewey's View- Ⓑ, Ⓓ, Ⓖ / Other Views- Ⓒ, Ⓕ

해석   20세기 미국 교육 분야에서 중요한 인물인 존 듀이는 교육 철학 전반에 중요한 영향을 미쳤다. 듀이는 학생이 적극적으로 참여할 때 최상의 학습이 이루어진다고 믿었다. 즉, 교사는 강의를 하고 학생은 수동적으로 앉아 있는 것은 효과적인 학습 방법이 아니라는 것이다. 그의 슬로건은, 학교가 학생이 "행함을 통한 학습"을 격려해야 한다는 것이었다. 그는 아동이 선천적으로 적극적이며 호기심이 많다는 것을 사람들이 깨닫기를 원했다. 많은 학생들은 학교의 실습 과정과 실제 체험 학습을 통해 학습과정에 보다 실질적으로 관련됨으로써 큰 도움을 받았다.

그의 사상이 상당히 인기가 있었고, 몇 가지 (이론적인) 가치와 용어가 널리 퍼지긴 했어도, 그의 사상은 미국 공립학교에 결코 광범위하고 깊게 통합되어 시행되지 못했다. 많은 학교와 교사들은 교사의 정확한 통제와 지도가 없으면 효과적인 교육이 이뤄질 수 없다고 생각해서, 그들은 제한되고 통제된 교수법을 유지했다. 창의성과 적극적이면서 실질적인 학생의 참여는 휴식 시간이나 글쓰기 활동과 같은 시간을 위해 남겨진 것이었다.

듀이는 교육의 역할이 학습경험을 확장시키는 것이라고 믿었다. 그의 철학에서 이러한 부분은 박물관과 도서관처럼, 그의 총체적인 교육 철학이 가장 잘 반영된 대안 학습장에 가장 큰 영향을 미쳤다. 이러한 학습장은 이곳을 방문하는 학생들을 교육시키는 방법에 변화를 줌으로써 듀이의 덜 형식적인 교육 방식을 적용해왔다.

불행히도, 박물관에서 학생 스스로 주도하는 학습 경험이 지나치게 확산될 경우, 경험하게 되는 데이터의 방대함 때문에 학습의 방향이 상실된다. 교사 없이 진행되는 경우, 학생들은 흥미롭고 중대한 자료를 찾게 될 수는 있겠지만, 그것이 학생들의 현재와 미래의 학업 성과에 도움이 되지 않을 수도 있다.

문 1 | 두 번째 단락의 hands-on과 가장 의미가 유사한 것은?
Ⓐ 유용한
Ⓑ 수동적인
Ⓒ 활동적인
Ⓓ 변형된

해설 | hands-on의 사전적 의미는 '실제로 참가하는', '실지의'란 뜻으로 앞에 practical involvement가 힌트가 될 수 있다.

문 2 | 첫 번째 단락에 따르면, 다음 중 듀이의 효과적 학습법에 관해 올바른 것은?
Ⓐ 학생은 교실에 학습할 자료를 가지고 와야 한다.
Ⓑ 교사는 자신이 만든 질문을 활용하여 학습 과정을 지도해야 한다.
Ⓒ 그것은 학생의 공부법에 관한 전통적인 관념을 바꿨다.
Ⓓ 학생은 수업 중 활동에 참여하는 것을 통해 가장 잘 학습한다.

해설 | 듀이는 학생들이 학습에 적극적으로 참여할 때 최상의 학습이 이루어진다고 믿었다.

문 3 | 적절한 보기를 골라 관련 있는 견해의 종류와 짝지으시오. 두 개의 보기는 제외됩니다.
Ⓐ 학생들은 방대한 지식으로부터 많은 이익을 얻을 수 있다.
Ⓑ 학생들은 실험에 참여함으로써 학습해야 한다.
Ⓒ 학생들은 어떤 정보가 중요한지 모를 수도 있다.
Ⓓ 교사는 아이들의 선천적인 특성을 제한해서는 안 된다.
Ⓔ 교사는 학생들의 연령대에 맞는 교육 자료를 책임진다.
Ⓕ 가이드 없이 너무 많은 정보가 주어질 때 유용하지 않을 수 있다.
Ⓖ 학생의 학습은 교실 내로 제한되어서는 안 된다.

해설 | Ⓐ는 방대한 정보가 가이드 없이는 의미가 없다는 내용을 틀리게 말하는 것이고, Ⓔ는 지문에 언급되지 않은 내용이다.

Exercise 3

정답 1. Ⓓ   2. Ⓒ   3. Ⓑ   4. Ⓒ
5. Projective Test - Ⓐ, Ⓕ /
   Inventory-type - Ⓑ, Ⓒ, Ⓓ

Text Outline   (B)

해석   심리학자와 정신과 의사들이 인간에 대해 더 많이 이해할 수 있게 돕는 많은 심리 테스트가 있다. 가장 대중적인 두 가지 투영검사는 로르샤흐검사(Rorschach Inkblot Test)와 주제통각검사(Thematic Apperception Test, TAT)이다. 로르샤흐검사는 10장의 연속된 얼룩을 보여주는 것이다. 참가자는 각각의 얼룩을 관찰한 후, 그 특징을 묘사하라고 요청받는다. TAT는 그 관계가 애매모호한 사람들이 그려진 31장의 그림이 제시된다. 참가자의 임무는 각각의 그림에 등장하는 사람들에 대한 생각과 느낌을 포함하여, 수반되는 각각의 그림을 하나의 이야기로 만들어 내는 것이다.

참가자가 한 묘사와 설명의 서로 다른 견해는 개인의 성격에 대한 평가를 산출해 내기 위해 점수화된다. 이런 검사들에 대한 해석에 도움을 주는 표준화된 응답이 존재하지 않는다. 더욱 최근에는 TAT가 조사 도구로 주로 활용되었다. 예를 들어, 꿈을 연구하고, 활용도는 낮지만 스트레스를 많이 받는 직무에 종사하는 직원을 가려내는 데에도 사용되었다.

두 번째 검사 유형은 목록 유형으로서, 질문에 대한 정해진 응답을 포함한다. 이러한 검사들은 일반적으로 투사법의 자유 응답을 허용하지 않는다. 그 고전적인 예가 미네소타 다면 인격 목록(Minnesota Multi-Phasic Personality Inventory-2, MMPI-2)이다. 이 검사는 다양한 진술문이 참가자에게 주어진다. 참가자의 임무는 각 질문에 "맞음," "틀림", 또는 "응답할 수 없음"으로 응답하는 것이다. 이 검사 또한 피검사자의 성격 특성을 산출해 낸다. 이 검사법은 보통 정신병과 같은 비정상적 성격을 진단하는 데 활용된다.

목록 유형의 심리검사의 다른 예로는, 매우 어려운 질문들을 통해 특정 분야에 대한 능력을 측정하는 파워 테스트와 응답하기 쉬운 질문들을 제한된 시간에 응답하는 스피드 테스트가 있다.

* projective test : 개인 성격의 특성을 발견하는 인성 검사법

문 1 | 첫 번째 단락에서 ambiguous와 가장 의미가 유사한 것은?
Ⓐ 명백한

Ⓑ 포부가 있는
　　Ⓒ 속이는
　　Ⓓ 명확하지 않은

해설 | ambiguous은 '모호한', '분명치 않은' 이라는 뜻이므로 답은 Ⓓ이다.

문 2 | 첫 번째 단락에 따르면, 로르샤흐검사에 관해 사실인 것은?
　　Ⓐ 그것은 다양한 이야기를 가진 10개의 다른 이미지들로 구성되어 있다.
　　Ⓑ 그것은 일련의 31개 얼룩 그림이다.
　　Ⓒ 그것은 그 내용이 명확하게 알려지지 않은 얼룩 이미지들을 사용한다.
　　Ⓓ 그것은 등장인물들의 생각과 감정을 포함하는 하나의 이야기를 요구한다.

해설 | 로드샤흐 검사는 참가자가 각각의 특성을 묘사해야 하는 10장의 얼룩 이미지를 사용한다. 그 얼룩의 내용은 정해져 있지 않다.

문 3 | 두 번째 단락의 yield와 가장 의미가 유사한 것은?
　　Ⓐ 저항하다
　　Ⓑ 산출하다
　　Ⓒ 사임하다
　　Ⓓ 포기하다

해설 | 문맥 상 지문에서 쓰인 yield는 '생산하다', '산출하다' 로 쓰였으므로 답은 Ⓑ이다.

문 4 | 세 번째 단락의 diagnose와 가장 의미가 유사한 것은?
　　Ⓐ 분리하다
　　Ⓑ 묘사하다
　　Ⓒ 결정하다
　　Ⓓ 구성하다

해설 | diagnose는 '진단하다' 란 의미이다. 문맥에서 그 사람에게 정신병 같은 성격적 결함이 있는지 없는지를 진단한다는 것은, 그 사람의 상태를 결정한다는 뜻이므로 답은 Ⓒ이다.

문 5 | 적절한 보기를 골라 관련 있는 시험의 종류와 짝지으시오. 두 개의 보기는 제외됩니다.
　　Ⓐ 이미지들은 참가자들에게 제시된다.
　　Ⓑ 주어진 진술에 근거하여 응답해야 한다.
　　Ⓒ 몇몇 참가자들은 검사에서 만점을 얻을 수 있다.
　　Ⓓ 수치화된 점수는 성격을 평가하는 데 사용될 수 있다.
　　Ⓔ 검사를 완료하는 데 소요된 시간이 점수에 반영된다.
　　Ⓕ 응답에 대한 해석이 차이가 날 수 있다.
　　Ⓖ 대부분의 피고용자들은 검사 중 하나를 하도록 요구받는다.

해설 | Ⓐ는 TAT에 대한 내용이다. Ⓔ는 객관식의 스피드 테스트에서 시간이 제한되는 것을 잘못 설명하고 있고, Ⓖ는 언급되지 않은 내용이다.

VOCABULARY TEST

정답　1. (B)　2. (B)　3. (A)　4. (C)　5. (B)
　　　6. (A)　7. (D)　8. (B)　9. (C)　10. (A)

밑줄 친 어휘나 구와 가장 유사한 의미를 지닌 것을 고르시오.

1. 겨울이 오면, 우리는 노르웨이의 혹독한 추위를 견뎌야 한다.
   (A) 온화한　　　　　(B) 맹렬한
   (C) 눈에 띄는　　　(D) 육중한

2. 12월에는 보통 이것보다는 훨씬 더 춥다.
   (A) 어지간히　　　　(B) 일반적으로
   (C) 절대적으로　　　(D) 아마도

3. 경고등이 분명하게 보였다.
   (A) 식별 가능한　　　(B) 밝은
   (C) 시각의　　　　　(D) 눈의

4. 그 건물은 뼈대 무게를 견디어내도록 설계되지 않았다.
   (A) 더하다　　　　　(B) 재다
   (C) 견디다　　　　　(D) 낮추다

5. 강한 햇빛과 풍부한 물 덕분에 우리 집 정원의 꽃들은 잘 자라고 있다.
   (A) 시들다　　　　　(B) 자라다
   (C) 지다　　　　　　(D) 열매를 맺다

6. 그들은 공지사항에 대해 수동적으로 반응하고 있었다.
   (A) 순종적으로　　　(B) 비정상적으로
   (C) 단호히　　　　　(D) 철저히

7. 그 소식에 대한 그녀의 반응이 궁금하다.
   (A) 무관심한　　　　(B) 걱정하는
   (C) 확신하는　　　　(D) 알고 싶어 하는

8. 학우관계에서의 변화가 흥분을 초래했다.
   (A) 끝냈다　　　　　(B) 생기게 했다
   (C) 되찾았다　　　　(D) 사라졌다

9. 나는 인간이 유인원으로부터 진화했다는 생각을 받아들일 수 없다.
   (A) 살아남았다　　　(B) 닮았다
   (C) 발달했다　　　　(D) 쇠퇴했다

10. 짙은 안개가 모든 것을 가려서 우리는 아무것도 볼 수 없었다.
    (A) 덮어 가렸다　　(B) 드러냈다
    (C) 밝게 했다　　　(D) 분명하게 했다

Progress Test 1

정답 1. ⓒ   2. ⓑ   3. ⓓ   4. ⓑ   5. ⓒ
　　 6. ⓒ   7. Ⓐ, ⓒ, Ⓔ

해석　19세기 말엽까지, 대부분의 도시의 지평선에는 몇몇 높은 빌딩들의 윤곽이 나타났었다. 그러나 이들 중 어느 것도 오늘날 우리가 알고 있는 마천루만큼 높지는 않았다. 그러나 1910년대 말에 이르자, 빌딩의 높이가 급격하게 올라가기 시작했다. 국가의 변화에 따른 필수적인 현상이었을 뿐 아니라, 기술의 진보가 마천루의 등장을 가능하게 했다.

　도시설계사들에게 마천루의 건설을 선택 가능한 것으로 만들었던, 기술적 발달의 첫 번째 요소는 저렴한 강철의 대량 생산이었다. 철을 변형하여 제조된 주철은 매우 강하다. 그러한 강도는 이런 거대한 구조물을 건설하는 데 결정적인 역할을 한다. 왜냐하면 마천루는 규모가 작은 건물과 같은 방식으로 무게를 지탱할 수 없기 때문이다. 4층 높이까지의 무게를 지탱하는 데에는 건물의 벽을 이용할 수 있는 반면, 그보다 높으면 붕괴되곤 했다. 따라서 기사들은 이러한 거대한 건물들에 적합한 강철 골격을 설계해야 했다. 그런 뒤에 벽들은 그 골격에 부착되었다.

　마천루를 건설하는데 필수적인 두 번째 기술적 발달은 엘리베이터의 발명이었다. 마천루가 세워지기 전, 도시에는 6, 7층 건물들이 몇 채 있었는데, 그 많은 층계의 계단을 올라가야 하는 것은 심각한 문제였다. 그러므로 건물들이 점점 높아진다면, 그러한 높이까지 사람과 물자를 운송할 수단이 필요했다. 건물에 설치된 최초의 승객용 엘리베이터는 1857년에 선보였다. 1898년까지 나라 전역에 걸쳐, 점점 늘어나는 고층 빌딩들에 이것들이 사용되었다.

　다수의 마천루가 세워진 세 번째 원인은 기술적인 것이 아니라 사회적인 것이었다. 20세기 초반, 미국의 주요 도시에는 가파른 인구 밀집도와 함께 제한적인 토지 공급이 나타나게 되었는데, 이것은 혁신적인 새로운 건물 양식이 필요함을 의미했다. 이러한 사실을 확실히 보여줄 수 있는 곳으로 뉴욕만한 곳이 없었다. 매일 그 곳으로 도착하는 수천 명의 새로운 사람들을 수용하고 부양하기를 기대한다면, 더 많은 건물들을 공급해야 했다. 따라서 밖으로 확장하기 보다 하늘을 향해 세우는 건축 경향이 되었다.

문 1 | 첫 번째 단락의 considerably와 가장 의미가 유사한 것은?
　　Ⓐ 온화하게
　　Ⓑ 중요하게
　　ⓒ 크게
　　ⓓ 유용하게

해설 | considerably는 '상당히', '꽤'란 의미를 지니고 있다. 따라서 답은 유의어인 ⓒ이다.

문 2 | 두 번째 단락의 viable과 가장 의미가 유사한 것은?
　　Ⓐ 추가적인
　　ⓑ 가능한
　　ⓒ 비현실적인
　　ⓓ 희망적인

해설 | viable은 '실행 가능한', '실용적인'이라는 뜻을 가지고 있다. 문맥상 ⓑ가 답이다.

문 3 | 두 번째 단락의 crucial과 가장 의미가 유사한 것은?
　　Ⓐ 값비싼
　　Ⓑ 겁을 주는
　　ⓒ 눈에 띄는
　　ⓓ 중요한

해설 | crucial은 '중요한', '결정적인'이라는 의미이다. 따라서 동의어인 ⓓ가 답이다.

문 4 | 두 번째 단락의 정보에 따르면, 고층 건축물과 기존의 건물은 어떤 점이 달랐는가?
　　Ⓐ 건물의 붕괴를 막기 위해 강철이 벽 속에 심겨졌다.
　　ⓑ 벽이 아니라, 골격이 건물의 무게를 지탱하는 데 사용되었다.
　　ⓒ 건물의 높이를 높이기 위해, 강철 골격은 4층에 덧붙여졌다.
　　ⓓ 낮은 건물들은 벽돌과 철로 건축되었다.

해설 | 4층 건물 이상의 건물들은 벽으로 무게를 지탱할 수 없어서 강철 골격을 이용한다.

문 5 | 세 번째 단락의 these가 가리키는 것은?
　　Ⓐ 승객
　　Ⓑ 건물
　　ⓒ 엘리베이터
　　ⓓ 계단

해설 | 앞 문장을 보면 첫 번째 승객용 엘리베이터가 1857년에 고층 건물에 설치되었다고 나온다. 따라서 그 뒤에 나오는 these는 앞의 엘리베이터이다.

문 6 | 네 번째 단락에 따르면, 다음 중 사실인 것은?
　　Ⓐ 도시에 있는 마천루의 역할은 새로운 도시 거주자들을 끌어들이는 것이다.
　　Ⓑ 많은 마천루를 건설하는 것은 나라의 경제력을 보여주는 한 가지 방법이다.
　　ⓒ 인구증가는 도시 계획과 건축에 중요한 영향을 미쳤다.
　　ⓓ 뉴욕시는 유명한 마천루로 인해 가장 인기 있는 도시이다.

해설 | 급격한 인구 성장으로 인해 새로운 건물 양식이 필요했다.

문 7 | 지문에 대한 간단한 요약을 위한 도입 문장이 아래에 제시된다. 가장 중요한 내용을 표현한 3가지 대답을 선택하여 요약을 완성하시오. 몇몇 문장들은 단락에서 언급되지 않았거나 중요하지 않은 내용을 표현해서 요약에 들어갈 수 없다.

몇 가지 이유로, 20세기 들어 도시들은 새로운 방식의 건물을 필요로 하게 되었다.

Ⓐ 견고함과 저렴한 생산비로 인해 강철은 마천루의 발달을 가져온 중요한 요인이었다.
Ⓑ 강철의 가격을 낮추기 위해, 강철을 다른 다양한 금속과 혼합해서 마천루에 사용되었다.
Ⓒ 인구 증가와 제한된 토지로 인해 주요 도시들은 마천루와 같은 고층 빌딩이 필요했다.
Ⓓ 대도시들은 도시 내에 일꾼들을 위해 고층 건물을 짓고 거주 지역을 확장시켜야 했다.
Ⓔ 엘리베이터의 진보는 마천루의 발달과 깊은 관계가 있다.
Ⓕ 마천루에 필요한 엘리베이터를 만드는 데 사용되는 기술은 이제 전 세계 대부분의 건물에 사용되고 있다.

해설 | Ⓑ는 본문에 언급되지 않은 내용이고, Ⓓ는 종적인 확장을 하게 되었다는 본문의 내용과 달리 횡적인 확장을 꾀했다고 나오므로 틀린 내용이다. Ⓕ는 주요한 내용이 아니므로 요약에 포함될 수 없다.

Progress Test 2

정답 1. Ⓓ 2. Ⓓ 3. Ⓒ 4. Ⓐ 5. Ⓐ
     6. Ⓒ 7. Merit-Based Award- Ⓑ, Ⓖ /
     Need-Based Award- Ⓒ, Ⓓ, Ⓕ

해석   미국에서 재정보조는 단과대나 종합대학 또는 사립학교 등록금이나 숙식비와 같은 제 비용을 학생들이 지불할 수 있도록 도움을 주려는 기금이다. 이 보조는 공교육을 위한 일반 정부 기금으로 간주되지 않는다. 재정보조는 특정한 개별 학생에게 수여되는 장학금을 일컫는다. 이 보조는 그것이 수여되는 기준에 근거해 분류될 수 있을 것이다. 대학생들에게 주어지는 재정보조에는 merit-based award와 need-based award가 있다.

merit-based award는 개별 단과대나 종합대학에 의해 주어지는 장학금과 외부 기관에 의해 수여되는 장학금을 포함한다. merit-based scholarship은 특기나 리더십 잠재력 또는 다른 특성으로 인해 수여될 수도 있지만, 이러한 장학금은 보통 높은 학업성취도에 대해 주어진다. merit-based scholarship은 종종 지원자의 경제적 어려움과는 상관없이 수여된다. 많은 대학들에서 모든 학생들은 merit-based scholarship의 수혜 대상으로 간주된다. 그러나 어떤 대학에서는 학생이 그러한 장학금에 지원해야 한다. 체육특기 장학금은 운동에 대한 특기를 하나의 특별한 기준으로 간주하는 merit-based scholarship의 한 형태이다.

Need-based award는 학생의 경제적 어려움에 근거하여 주어진다. 연방정부로부터 경제적 어려움에 근거하여 지급되는 재정보조금을 받으려면, 학생은 Free Application for Federal Student Aid(FAFSA)라는 특정 서류를 작성해야만 한다. 이 양식은 연방정부의 재정보조에 대한 자격요건을 갖추고 있는지를 결정하기 위해 매년 모든 미국 대학생들과 부모들에 의해 작성되어야 한다. 경제적 어려움에 근거하여 지급되는 재정보조는 양도나 융자 그리고 근로 장학금 프로그램의 형식으로 지급될 수 있다. 양도와 근로 장학금 프로그램은 상환될 필요가 없다. 일반적으로는 양도와 근로 장학금 프로그램이 단과대나 종합대학 교육비를 전부 충당할 수 없기 때문에, 많은 학생들은 정부와 사립 대출에 지원하기도 한다. 연방 교육 대출 프로그램은 대학교육을 재정적으로 지원하는 매력적인 방식인 낮은 이자율과 융통성 있는 상환 제도를 제공한다.

문 1 | 첫 번째 단락의 어휘 criteria와 가장 의미가 유사한 것은?
Ⓐ 치수
Ⓑ 비평
Ⓒ 역할
Ⓓ 기준

해설 | criteria는 '판단의 기준', 또는 '척도'를 말한다. 따라서 답은 동의어인 Ⓓ이다.

문 2 | 첫 번째 단락에 따르면, 다음 중 재정 보조에 대해 사실이 아닌 것은?
Ⓐ 재정 보조는 개별 학생에게 지급되는 장학금이다.
Ⓑ 재정 보조는 학생이 등록금 외 숙식비와 같은 고가의 교육비를 지불하는데 도움을 준다.
Ⓒ 재정 보조는 정부가 공교육에 자금을 대는 방안으로 간주되지 않는다.
Ⓓ 재정 보조는 수여하는 기관에 근거하여 분류된다.

해설 | 본문에서 언급된 재정 보조를 분류하는 기준은 수여 기관이 아니라, 수여 대상이다.

문 3 | 두 번째 단락의 어휘 potential과 가장 의미가 유사한 것은?
Ⓐ 성취
Ⓑ 요구
Ⓒ 가능성
Ⓓ 권력

해설 | potential이란 '가능성', '잠재력'을 뜻한다. 따라서 동의어인 Ⓒ가 답이다.

문 4 | 두 번째 단락에 따르면, merit-based scholarship에 대해 올바른 것은?
Ⓐ 장학생을 결정할 때 경제적인 어려움은 필요하지 않다.
Ⓑ 그것들은 need-based award로 간주된다.
Ⓒ 기관에서만 지급할 것이다.
Ⓓ 재정적 도움이 필요한 불우한 운동선수는 자격 요건을 갖추고 있지 않다.

해설 | 성적우수 장학금의 지급 기준은 학생의 재정적 필요가 아니라 학업 성취도이다.

문 5 | 세 번째 단락의 their parents가 가리키는 것은?
Ⓐ FAFSA라는 서류를 작성하는 학생들의 부모
Ⓑ 미국 학생들의 부모
Ⓒ 대학으로 돌아가길 원하는 부모님
Ⓓ 재정적 보조를 받을 자격을 갖춘 부모들

해설 | 재정보조를 받기 위해 특정 서류를 작성해야 하는 부모님을 가리킨다.

문 6 | 세 번째 단락에 따르면, 대학 기금에 있어서 FAFSA의 역할은 무엇인가?
Ⓐ FAFSA로 어떤 학생이 대학 내내 (장학금을) 지원받을 것인지 결정한다.
Ⓑ FAFSA 양식을 작성하지 않고는 그 어떤 미국 학생도 대학 교육을 받을 수 없다.
Ⓒ FAFSA는 federal student aid에 대한 기준에 충족하는 지를 결정한다.
Ⓓ FAFSA는 학생과 그들의 가족들이 성적우수 장학금을 지급하는 기관에 접근할 수 있도록 허락한다.

해설 | FAFSA는 재정보조를 받을 자격이 있는지를 결정할 수 있는 서류이다.

문 7 | 적절한 보기를 골라 관련 있는 장학금의 종류와 짝지으시오. 두 개의 보기는 제외됩니다.
Ⓐ 부모가 자식을 부양할 수 있도록 지급된다.
Ⓑ 특별한 재능이나 기술에 수여된다.
Ⓒ 재무제표에 근거하여 수여된다.
Ⓓ 몇 년 내로 상환될 필요가 없다.
Ⓔ 학생 스스로 학비를 충당하기 위한 시간제 일자리를 제공한다.
Ⓕ 낮은 이자율로 학생에게 대출된다.
Ⓖ 학생의 성취도에 달려있다.

해설 | Ⓐ와 Ⓔ는 지문에 나오지 않는 내용이다. Ⓑ와 Ⓖ는 Merit-based awards에 속하는 내용이고, Ⓒ, Ⓓ, Ⓕ는 Need-based awards에 대한 내용이다.

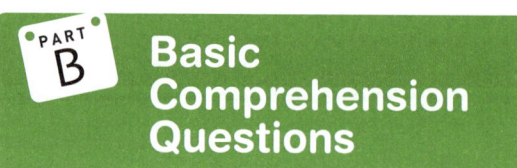

PART B Basic Comprehension Questions

Chapter 3 Sentence Simplification
p.60 - p.80

SAMPLE ITEM   정답 Ⓐ

해석   남아메리카의 한 부족인 Yanomamo는 열대우림 깊숙이 위치한 shabonos라고 부르는 원형 마을에 산다. shabono에서 남자들은 자신과 처자식들을 위해 기둥과 넝쿨로 오두막을 지어야할 책임이 있다. 이 구조물들 자체는 마을 주민을 위한 공동 구역으로 여겨지는 중앙 마당 주변에 배열된다. 흥미롭게도 오두막 사이의 공간은 덩굴로 덮여져 있는데, 이것은 건물들 사이로의 이동을 쉽게 만들어주어 사람들은 장마철에도 어려움 없이 다닐 수 있다. 보안 수단으로서, 뾰족하게 깎은 기둥으로 만들어진 벽은 마을 전체를 둘러싸고 있다.

문제 | 다음 중 지문의 하이라이트 된 문장의 핵심 내용을 가장 잘 표현한 것은? 틀린 보기는 본문의 내용을 심각하게 바꾸거나 핵심적인 내용을 누락시킨 것이다.
Ⓐ 집 주변의 덩굴 덕분에 사람들은 빗속에서도 오두막에서 오두막으로 쉽게 걸어 다닐 수 있다.
Ⓑ 건물이 넝쿨로 만들어졌기에 사람들은 장마철에 쉽게 이동하고 옮겨 다닐 수 있다.
Ⓒ 장마철 동안 이동의 편이성을 위해 사람들은 오두막 사이의 공간을 덩굴로 덮어놓는다.
Ⓓ 오두막 사이에 있는 덩굴을 움직이는 사람들은 빗속에서도 어려움 없이 건물들 사이를 쉽게 이동할 수 있다.

해설 | 하이라이트된 문장의 핵심 내용은, 오두막 사이를 넝쿨이 덮고 있어 장마철에도 (비에 젖지 않고) 이동이 자유롭다는 것이다.

Basic Dill 1

정답
1. that do not have a spine, such as lobsters that have tough outer shell systems that provide rigidity / (A)
2. such as cuckoos and cowbirds / (A)
3. an author and illustrator, *The Tale of Peter Rabbit* / (B)
4. keeping mice and rats away from grain stores / (B)

5. who are between the ages of 12 and 20 as teenagers / (B)
6. such as Superglue and Krazy Glue, are extremely strong /(B)

1. 해석 척추를 가지고 있지 않은 많은 무척추동물은, 가재가 견고함을 제공하는 단단한 외부 껍데기를 갖고 있는 것처럼 장기를 보호하는 바깥의 단단한 껍데기를 갖고 있다.

문제 | (A) 많은 무척추 동물은 단단한 외부 껍데기로 몸체를 보호한다.
(B) 많은 무척추 동물은 척추를 갖고 있지 않지만, 단단한 껍데기를 갖고 있다.

해설 | 무척추 동물에게는 척추가 없다는 것은 뜻 풀이를 해주는 것으로 같은 내용의 반복을 피하기 위해 삭제하고, 장기와 몸을 보호하는 단단한 외부 껍데기를 가지고 있다는 핵심만을 요약한다.

2. 해석 뻐꾸기와 찌르레기처럼 탁란 종류로 알려진 새들은 실제로 기생동물의 새끼를 키우게 될 다른 새들의 둥지에, 그들의 알을 넣는다.

*탁란 : 조류가 다른 조류의 둥지에 알을 맡기는 일

문제 | (A) 탁란 조류의 새끼들은 기생동물(어미)이 다른 새들의 둥지에 알을 떨어뜨린 후, 다른 새들에 의해 키워진다.
(B) 뻐꾸기와 찌르레기는 탁란 조류이기 때문에, 자기들의 알을 다른 새들의 둥지에 넣는다.

해설 | 뻐꾸기와 찌르레기는 brood parasite의 예일 뿐이다. 문장의 핵심적인 내용은, 탁란 조류는 대신 새끼를 키워줄 다른 새의 둥지에 자기들의 알을 넣는다는 것이다.

3. 해석 작가이자 삽화가인 Beatrix Potter는 그녀의 처녀작인 『피터 래빗 이야기』를 출간하도록 격려받았다. 그러나 그녀는 1902년까지 출판업자를 찾기 위해 분투했다.

문제 | (A) Beatrix Potter은 『피터 래빗 이야기』의 작가이자 동시에 삽화가였다.
(B) Beatrix Potter의 첫 작품은 1902년에 출판업자에 의해 받아들여졌다.

해설 | 문장의 핵심 내용은, Beatrix Potter가 자신의 처녀작인 『피터 래빗 이야기』를 출간해 줄 출판사를 1902년이 되어서야 찾게 되었다는 것이다.

4. 해석 최초의 길들여진 고양이는 5000년 전, 이집트에서 설치동물을 통제하는데 사용되었다. 이들은 생쥐와 쥐가 곡식창고로 들어오는 것을 막았다.

문제 | (A) 고양이는 설치동물을 죽이기 위해, 이집트인들에 의해 5000년 전에 이용되었다.
(B) 고양이가 생쥐와 쥐를 통제하는 데 도움이 되기에 이집트인들은 고양이를 애완동물로 만들었다.

해설 | control rodents를 부연하는 keeping mice and rats away는 요약할 때 중복하지 않고 삭제한다.

5. 해석 청소년들은 12세에서 20세 사이의 십대로서, 어린이의 세계에서 어른의 세계로 이동하는 사람들이다. (그 과정에서) 그들은 성숙한 성인으로 성장하는 법을 배우면서 종종 고생하며 나아간다.

문제 | (A) 많은 어려운 것들을 배워야 하기 때문에, 청춘기는 12세와 20세 사이의 십대들이 겪는 힘든 시기이다.
(B) 많은 청소년들은 유년 시절에서 성숙기로 넘어가면서, 어른의 역할을 배우고 적응하는 데 어려움을 겪는다.

해설 | 지문의 핵심 내용은 유년기에서 성인으로 넘어가는 중간 과정인 청소년기가 성인이 되어가기 위해 여러 가지를 힘겹게 배우는 시기라는 것이고, 사춘기를 정의하는 나이 부분은 삭제된다.

6. 해석 Superglue와 Krazy Glue와 같이 매우 강한 최신 접착제들은 수천 파운드에 달하는 무게를 지탱할 수 있기 때문에 현대 건설업에 있어 더욱 더 중요해지고 있다.

문제 | (A) Superglue와 Krazy Glue는 무거운 물체를 접착하기 위해 다양한 산업 분야에서 사용되는 최신 접착제이다.
(B) 접착제는 굉장히 무거운 무게를 지탱할 수 있는 기능 때문에 몇 가지 산업에서 매우 필수적인 요소가 되고 있다.

해설 | 지문의 핵심 내용은 현대의 접착제가 무거운 무게를 지탱할 수 있는 기능으로 인해 건설업과 같은 산업에 필수 요소가 되어가고 있다는 것이다. 예로 들어진 Superglue와 Krazy Glue는 요약에서 삭제된다.

Basic Drill 2

정답
1. (A) : 2   (B) : 답   (C) : 3
2. (A) : 3   (B) : 2   (C) : 답
3. (A) : 3   (B) : 답   (C) : 1
4. (A) : 답   (B) : 3   (C) : 1
5. (A) : 답   (B) : 3   (C) : 2
6. (A) : 1   (B) : 답   (C) : 3

1. 해석 1950년대 미국에서는 카드를 교환할 때 장미꽃

과 초콜릿과 같은 선물을 포함시키는 것으로 확장되었다.

문제 | (A) 20세기 미국에서는 장미꽃과 초콜릿이 카드와 함께 교환되었다.
(B) 20세기 미국에서는 사람들이 카드와 함께 선물을 주기 시작했다.
(C) 20세기 초에 미국에서는 모든 종류의 선물이 교환되기 시작했다.

해설 | 지문의 핵심 내용은, 1950년대 들어와서 선물과 함께 카드를 교환하게 되었다는 것이다. (A)의 장미꽃과 초콜릿은 선물의 예일 뿐이고, (C)는 20세기 초에 선물 교환이 시작된 것이 아니어서 주어진 문장과는 다른 정보를 말하고 있다.

2. 해설 중국의 전족은 아마도 성왕조 출신의 한 왕자의 아내가 특별한 춤을 추기 위해 자신의 발을 묶었던 때에서 그 기원을 찾을 수 있을 것이다.

문제 | (A) 성왕조 출신의 여성이 특별한 춤을 춘 이후에 자신의 발을 묶었다.
(B) 성왕조 출신의 한 왕자의 아내는 특별한 춤을 추곤 했다.
(C) 전족은 한 왕자의 아내가 발을 묶고 춤을 추었을 때 시작되었던 것 같다.

해설 | 전족의 기원은 어떤 왕자의 아내가 발을 묶고 춤을 춘 것이 그 시작이었을 것이라 내용이 지문의 핵심이다. (A)는 정보를 바꾸었고, (B)는 '발을 묶고 춤을 추었다' 는 핵심적 정보가 빠져 있다.

3. 해설 바로크의 세부 묘사는 흔히 섬뜩하고 추한 반면, 로코코의 세부 묘사는 자연에서 볼 수 있는 곡선을 그리는 잎사귀와 소용돌이치는 구름들, 그 외의 다른 곡선들을 보여준다.

문제 | (A) 로코코 스타일은 바로크 예술의 장식을 모방했지만, 괴물의 이미지를 활용하지 않았다.
(B) 바로크의 추한 세부 묘사와는 달리, 로코코는 자연에서 발견되는 곡선 형태를 보여준다.
(C) 로코코 예술은 일반적으로 자연에서 볼 수 있는 스타일로 장식되어 있다.

해설 | 바로크의 세부 묘사는 무시무시했던 반면, 로코코는 자연에서 흔히 볼 수 있는 곡선적인 선과 형태를 강조했다는 것이 지문의 핵심 내용이다. (A)는 문장과는 다른 내용을 말하고 있고, (C)는 '자연에서 발견되는 곡선미' 라는 핵심 정보가 빠져 있다.

4. 해설 각각의 식물이 (어떤) 곤충을 끌어들이거나 내치는 효과를 갖는지를 고려하여, 원예사들은 식물의 조합을 이용해 이로운 곤충을 끌어들이고 해가 되는 곤충은 쫓아버릴 수 있다.

문제 | (A) 원예사들은 원하는 곤충과 원하지 않는 곤충을 통제하기 위해 특정한 식물들을 사용할 수 있다.
(B) 다양한 종류의 식물들이 정원에 있는 곤충의 수효를 조절하기 위해 사용된다.
(C) 정원사들은 곤충을 쫓아내기 위해 특정 종류의 식물들을 사용할 수 있다.

해설 | 지문의 핵심 내용은, 원예사들이 식물의 조합을 통해 유익한 곤충을 끌어들이고 해가 되는 곤충은 퇴치할 수 있다는 것이다. (B)는 주어진 정보와는 다른 내용을 말하고 있고, (C)는 '유익한 곤충을 끌어들인다' 는 핵심적인 내용이 빠져 있다.

5. 해설 Old Faithful은 지하로부터 100피트 이상의 높이까지 뜨거운 물이 솟구쳐 나오는 가압 상태의 온천으로, 미국 내에서 가장 인기 있는 간헐천일 것이다.

문제 | (A) 아주 높이 솟아오르는 뜨거운 물로 인해 Old Faithful는 미국에서 가장 사랑받는 간헐천이다.
(B) Old Faithful은 지구상에서 많이 발견되는 100 피트 높이의 간헐천 중 하나로서, 가압된 증기로 뜨거운 물을 뿜어낸다.
(C) Old Faithful은 지면을 통해 뜨거운 온수가 100 피트 높이까지 솟아나오는 간헐천이다.

해설 | 지문의 핵심 내용은, Old Faithful이 100 피트 이상의 높이까지 뜨거운 물을 뿜어내 미국에서 가장 사랑받는 간헐천이라는 것이다. (B)의 100 피트 높이로 뜨거운 물을 뿜어내는 간헐천이 많다는 내용은 지문에 없다. (C)는 '미국에서 가장 사랑받는' 이란 핵심 내용이 빠져있다.

6. 해설 문어의 자기보호 메커니즘은 바위틈과 같은 작은 공간에 자신을 밀어 넣기도 하고, 포식자에게 눈을 멀게 하는 어두운 먹물을 뿜어내 포식자가 먹물만을 볼 수 있게 한다.

문제 | (A) 문어는 포식자가 출현할 때, 자신의 안전을 위해 물 밑에 있는 바위의 작은 틈새로 몸을 밀어 넣는 천성을 타고 났다.
(B) 문어는 좁은 틈으로 자신의 몸을 밀어 넣어 숨거나 어두운 먹물로 공격자의 눈을 멀게 하는 능력으로 자신을 보호할 수 있다.
(C) 문어는 바위틈으로 도망가기 위한 시간을 벌기 위해 먹물을 이용해 자신의 모습을 흐릿하게 만든다.

해설 | 지문의 핵심 내용은, 문어는 적이 나타났을 때 좁은 바위 틈새로 몸을 숨기거나 먹물을 내뿜어 적의 눈을 가리는 자기 보호 장치를 가지고 있다는 것이다. (A)는 '먹물을 뿜는다' 는 핵심 내용이 빠져 있고, (C)는 내용을 잘못 이야기 하고 있다.

VOCABULARY Preview

Check-up

1. barren
2. doomed
3. dislodge
4. induced
5. radical
6. trivial
7. sustain
8. risky
9. persists
10. underwent
11. sob
12. pasture

다음 빈 칸에 들어갈 알맞은 말을 골라, 필요하면 고쳐 쓰시오.

1. 그는 조부로부터 물려받은 <u>황량한</u> 대지를 경작하여 부유해졌다.
2. 두 국가 간의 영토 소유권에 관한 분쟁으로 그들의 동맹관계는 <u>종말을 향했고</u>, 지금은 깨졌다.
3. 다리에서 얼음을 <u>제거하는</u> 것은 불가능했다.
4. 이 병은 과도한 노동과 스트레스로 <u>야기된다</u>.
5. 저 애 옷 좀 봐! 평소의 청바지와 티셔츠 차림에서 벗어난 <u>과격한</u> 변화네.
6. 왜 그런 <u>사소한</u> 일로 그렇게 화를 내는 거야?
7. 과학자들은 화성이 생명체를 <u>부양할</u> 수 있는지 알고 싶어 한다.
8. 엔터테인먼트 산업에 투자하는 것은 다소 <u>위험이 따르</u>는 사업이다.
9. 우리 할머니는 매일 한복 입는 것을 <u>고집하신다</u>.
10. 아버지는 암에 대한 새로운 치료법으로 치료를 <u>받으시</u>고 회복되셨다.
11. 수학 점수를 확인하고 그녀는 <u>흐느껴 울기</u> 시작했다.
12. 젖소는 목초지 주위를 <u>배회하고</u> 있었다.

Exercise 1

정답 1. ⓑ 2. ⓓ 3. ⓐ 4. ⓑ 5. ⓑ, ⓒ, ⓕ

해석 뇌에 있는 혈관이 터지거나, 부유하는 혈병(피떡, 血餠) 또는 혈소판이라 일컬어지는 혈관 내의 제거된 조직에 의해 혈관이 갑자기 막힐 때 뇌졸중이 일어난다. 뇌졸중은 영향이 가벼울 수도 있지만, 대개의 경우, 움직이거나 말을 못 하게 만들고 심지어 생명까지 앗아가는 결과를 초래하는 끔찍한 신체적 사건이다. 의사들은 이 문제를 예방하기 위해, 건강에 좋은 식이요법과 운동을 포함한 다양한 방책을 제안한다. 그러나 지금까지 지지 요법과 위험한 수술을 제외하고는 일단 뇌졸중이 발생하면 환자들에게 할 수 있는 것이 거의 없었다.

그러나 뇌졸중 치료에 있어 최근의 개발은, 뇌졸중 희생자들이 고통을 덜 받게 하고 회복과 생존 가능성을 더 높일 것이다. 새로운 치료법에서 의사들은 뇌졸중이 발생한 3시간 이내에 저체온을 유도하는데, 저체온이란 사람의 신진대사 속도를 늦추는 굉장히 낮은 체온이다. 이 급진적이고 과격한 새로운 치료법으로 치료받은 환자들은 이 방법으로 치료받지 않은 사람들에 비해 두 배나 오래 살아남았다.

저체온 자체는, 치료받지 않은 상태로 내버려두면 사망을 초래할 수 있을 정도로 상당히 위험할 수 있다. 그러나 철저히 통제된 의료 환경에서 신진대사의 저하는 뇌 조직 파괴가 진행되는 속도를 늦출 수 있는 듯하다. 이것은 손상된 혈관을 회복시켜 주면서, 의사들에게 생명을 구할 수 있는 의학 치료를 할 수 있는 시간을 더 늘려주고, 뇌졸중 환자들도 또한 심각한 정신적·육체적 장애 없이 회복할 수 있는 비율이 높아진다.

문 1 | 첫 번째 단락의 devastating과 가장 의미가 유사한 것은?
ⓐ 마비된
ⓑ 해를 끼치는
ⓒ 일시적인
ⓓ 오래 가는

해설 | devastating의 사전적 의미는 '완전히 파괴적인' 으로 앞부분의 대조되는 문장에서 can be mild로부터 반대되는 뜻임을 유추한다.

문 2 | 첫 번째 단락의 this problem이 가리키는 것은?
ⓐ 다양한 방법
ⓑ 회복 시간
ⓒ 신체적 사건
ⓓ 뇌졸중

해설 | 앞부분에서 뇌졸중을 치료하기 위한 의사들의 치료법을 언급하고 있다.

문 3 | 첫 번째 단락에 따르면, 의사에 관한 내용 중 사실인 것은?
ⓐ 그들은 뇌졸중을 예방하기 위한 많은 제안을 가지고 있다.
ⓑ 그들은 뇌졸중을 치료하는 다양한 방법을 발견했다.
ⓒ 그들은 치료 중 식이요법과 운동을 제안한다.
ⓓ 그들은 많은 예외적인 수술로 뇌졸중을 치료한다.

해설 | Doctors suggest a variety of measures, including a healthy diet and exercise, to prevent this problem.을 보면 뇌졸중을 예방하기 위해 의사들이 많은 제안을 내놓는다는 사실을 알 수 있다.

문 4 | 다음 중 세 번째 단락의 하이라이트 된 문장의 핵심 내용을 가장 잘 표현한 것은? 틀린 보기는 본문의 내용을 심각하게 바꾸거나 핵심적인 내용을 누락시킨 것이다.
ⓐ 대부분의 새로운 치료법에서 이것은 의사들에게 수술할 수 있는 시간을 충분히 주기 때문에 효과적이다.
ⓑ 이것은 더 많은 수의 뇌졸중 환자를 구하고 심각한 장

애 없이 그들이 회복할 수 있는 가능성을 증대시킨다.
ⓒ 이것은 의사들에게는 손상된 혈관을 치료하는 시간을, 희생자들에게는 신체적 장애 없이 회복할 수 있는 시간을 절약해준다.
ⓓ 이것은 의사가 심각한 뇌졸중으로 고통 받는 환자를 더 많이 치료할 수 있는 가능성을 높인다.

해설 | 하이라이트된 문장의 핵심 내용은, 저체온을 활용한 치료법이 의사들이 뇌졸중 환자들을 치료할 수 있는 더 많은 기회를 주고, 심각한 장애없이 환자들이 회복할 수 있게 돕는다는 것이고, treatment를 부연하는 repairing damaged blood vessels는 생략한다.

문 5 | 지문에 대한 간단한 요약을 위한 도입 문장이 아래에 제시된다. 가장 중요한 내용을 표현한 3가지 대답을 선택하여 요약을 완성하시오. 몇몇 문장들은 단락에서 언급되지 않았거나 중요하지 않은 내용을 표현해서 요약에 들어갈 수 없다.

혈관이 막히거나 파열하면 끔찍한 뇌졸중이 유발된다.
ⓐ 의사들은, 흔히 움직이지 못하게 하거나 말을 못하게 하고 심지어 생명마저 앗아가는 뇌졸중을 앓고 있는 환자들에게 건강에 좋은 식이요법과 많은 운동을 제안한다.
ⓑ 비극적인 뇌졸중에는 지금까지 극히 소수의 치료법과 단 몇 가지의 예방책이 있다.
ⓒ 급진적이며 새로운 치료법 중, 신진대사의 속도저하를 유도하는 저체온법은 회복과 생존의 가능성을 증대시킨다.
ⓓ 저체온법은 인체의 신진대사를 활성화시켰고, 이로 인해 생존율이 두 배 높아졌다.
ⓔ 관리되지 않는 상황 속의 사람에게 저체온은 그 자체만으로도 상당히 위험할 수 상태일 수 있다.
ⓕ 저체온법을 사용하면, 두뇌 조직 파괴가 서서히 진행되기 때문에 치료할 수 있는 시간을 더 많이 벌게 되어, 심각한 장애 없이 뇌졸중을 치료할 수 있다.

해설 | ⓐ는 ⓑ에 대한 세부 내용이고, ⓔ도 저체온법에 대한 부연 설명이다. ⓓ는 저체온에 관해 잘못 말하고 있다.

Exercise 2

정답 1. ⓑ 2. ⓐ 3. ⓓ 4. ⓓ 5. Degatari - ⓐ, ⓔ / Geza - ⓓ, ⓕ, ⓖ

해석　카부키는 일본의 전통 연극 중 하나이다. 카부키의 시작은 16세기 후반으로 거슬러 올라간다. 예전만큼 번영하지는 않지만, 카부키 극은 사람들 사이에서 폭넓은 인기를 유지하고 있고 지금까지도 많은 관객들을 끌어모으고 있다. 카부키는 배우들의 정교한 의상과 무대 위 배우들의 움직임으로 가장 잘 알려져 있다. 사실적인 카부키 극에서 마저 가장 사소한 몸짓이 "연기"보다는 "춤"에 가까울 때가 많다. 이런 몸짓의 대부분이 음악을 동반하기 때문에 많은 음악가들이 상연에 참여한다. 그들 중 몇은 카부키가 상연되는 내내 무대 위에 출연하는 반면, 다른 사람들은 극이 끝날 때까지 무대 밖에 있다.

　무대 위의 악사들은 데카다리라고 불린다. 그들이 공연에서 가장 중요한 배우는 아닐지라도, 진행되는 이야기에 필수적인 존재들이다. 이 사람들은 무대에서 상연되는 이야기를 전개해 나가는 데 도움을 주기 위해 현악기를 주로 사용한다. 예를 들면, 배우 중 한 명이 울고 있다고 상상해 보라. 데카타리 악사들 중 한 명이 자신의 악기를 사용해 배우의 흐느낌을 따라하여, 이로 인해 연기는 더 극적이 되고 관객들은 더 쉽게 이해하게 될 것이다. 무대 위의 이 악사들은 또한 필요할 때면 관객들에게 극의 줄거리를 설명함으로써 이야기의 나레이터의 역할도 한다.

　가부키 극에서 무대 밖에 있는 악사들을 게자 악사라고 일컫는다. 그들은 보통 무대 오른편으로 떨어진 방에 앉는다. 그들은 극의 전개를 볼 수 있으나, 관객들은 그들을 볼 수 없다. 게자 악사들은 비나 바람 소리와 같은, 무대 위에서 벌어지는 연기에 맞춰 주로 타악기와 종을 사용하여 음향 효과를 낸다.

문 1 | 첫 번째 단락의 flourishing와 가장 의미가 유사한 것은?
ⓐ 발전하는
ⓑ 번영하는
ⓒ 퍼지는
ⓓ 변하는

해설 | flourishing은 '번창하는'이란 뜻으로 뒤에 비교되는 문장의 retains a wide popularity로부터 뜻을 유추한다.

문 2 | 두 번째 단락의 integral과 가장 의미가 유사한 것은?
ⓐ 필수적인
ⓑ 단독의
ⓒ 유익한
ⓓ 관련된

해설 | integral은 '없어서는 안 될'이라는 뜻이다. 앞에 나온 important를 clue로 쓸 수 있다.

문 3 | 두 번째 단락에 따르면, 데가타리 악사의 역할은
ⓐ 무대 위 공연자들의 연기를 관찰하는 것
ⓑ 무대 밖 악사들이 연주하는 음악을 지휘하는 것
ⓒ 무대 위에서 공연하는 배우를 안정시켜 주는 것
ⓓ 공연되는 이야기를 설명하고 질을 높이는 것

해설 | 데가타리의 역할은 배우의 연기에 맞춰 배우의 감정을 모방하는 음악을 연주함으로써 관객들이 극의 내용 전개를 더 잘 이해할 수 있게 돕는 것이라고 나와 있다. 또한, 필요할 때면 관객들에게 극의 줄거리를 설명해주기도 한다는 내용이 있으므로, 이 모든 것을 고려했을 때 답은

ⓓ이다.

문 4 | 다음 중 세 번째 단락의 하이라이트 된 문장의 핵심 내용을 가장 잘 표현한 것은? 틀린 보기는 본문의 내용을 심각하게 바꾸거나 핵심적인 내용을 누락시킨 것이다.
ⓐ 게자 악사들은 음향 효과 중에서도 비바람 소리만 낸다.
ⓑ 게자 악사들은 악기를 가지고 무대 위에서 공연한다.
ⓒ 게자 악사들은 비바람 소리를 내기 위해 타악기와 종을 연주한다.
ⓓ 게자 악사들은 연기에 맞춰 타악기와 종으로 음향 효과를 내는 역할을 한다.

해설 | 주어진 문장의 핵심은, 게자 악사들이 연기에 맞춰 타악기와 종으로 음향 효과를 낸다는 것으로 비나 바람 소리는 예이므로 제외한다.

문 5 | 적절한 보기를 골라 관련 있는 음악가의 종류와 짝지으시오. 두 개의 보기는 제외됩니다.
ⓐ 관객과 배우들이 볼 수 있다.
ⓑ 서너 해 동안 특별한 학교에서 훈련받는다.
ⓒ 날씨에 대한 심층적 지식을 가지고 있다.
ⓓ 배우들을 관찰할 수 있으나 다른 사람들은 볼 수 없다.
ⓔ 주로 현악기를 이용한다.
ⓕ 극이 진행되는 동안 날씨와 관련한 음향 효과를 낸다.
ⓖ 극 안에서 종과 타악기를 많이 사용한다.

해설 | ⓑ는 지문에서 언급되지 않은 내용이고, ⓒ는 잘못된 정보이다.

Exercise 3

정답 1. ⓒ 2. ⓒ 3. ⓑ 4. ⓒ 5. ⓐ, ⓓ, ⓔ
Text Outline (A)

해석 1000년 이상 전인 중세 온난기 동안, Eric the Red와 같은 선원들에 의해 이끌어진 바이킹은 북대서양의 섬들을 향해 항해하여 그 곳에 식민지를 설립했다. 초창기인 750년에 이미 이 섬의 정착자들은 성공적으로 양과 소와 같은 동물을 수입하여 사육했다. 그들은 낚시를 했고, 가능하면 언제라도, 밀과 보리 그리고 그 외의 다른 곡식들도 재배했다. 그러나 그들은 세제를 채택했고, 이와 더불어 소빙하 시대가 진행되자, 이 세제로 인해 마침내 아이슬란드와 그린란드와 같은 북대서양의 식민지들이 붕괴되었다.

초기에 대부분의 거주민들은 세금을 지불해야 하는 토지와 목초지에서 작업을 하는 토지소유주였다. 토지는 사람들의 필요를 채우기에 더할 나위 없이 적합했고, 유럽인들과의 무역으로 섬 외부로부터 수입도 창출되었다. 그러나 기후가 변했고, 기후의 변화는 곡물과 가축의 성장에 영향을 미치게 되었다. 그렇지만 정부는 기존에 거두어들였던 돈의 액수를 유지하기 위해, 세금을 올렸을 때의 결과는 생각하지도 않고, 감당할 수 없는 수준으로까지 세금을 인상했다. 사람들은 더 부유한 토지소유주에게 그들의 농장을 팔았고, 그러한 부유한 사람들은 세금을 지불하기 위해 일꾼들에게 생산량을 점점 더 높이도록 요구했다.

소작인의 입장에서 보면, 그들은 장기적인 영향을 거의 고려하지 않고 가능한 한 많은 양과 소를 사육했다. 불행하게도, 많은 농토가 과도한 방목과, 추위의 강도가 세지면서 서서히 황폐해졌다. 적응력의 결핍 또한 소작인들의 끔찍한 상황에 도움이 되지 못했다. 그들은 의류나 도구, 기타 유럽의 무역 품목에 대한 욕구에 집착했다. 또한 줄어든 수입원을 벌충하고자 세금을 올리는 정부의 정책도 계속 유지했다. 슬프게도, 1500년 무렵 그린란드의 식민지는 더 이상 존재하지 않게 되었다. 아이슬란드의 식민지는 계속 있었지만, 여러 세기에 걸쳐 이와 유사한 쇠퇴를 겪으며 고통 받았다.

문 1 | 첫 번째 단락의 constituted와 가장 의미가 유사한 것은?
ⓐ 위협했다
ⓑ 머물렀다
ⓒ 설립했다
ⓓ 파괴했다

해설 | constitute는 '제정하다', '설립하다' 란 의미를 가지고 있고, 앞에 항해로 North Atlantic에 갔다는 내용과 뒤에 settlers라는 부분에서 colonies를 세웠다고 유추한다.

문 2 | 다음 중 첫 번째 단락의 하이라이트 된 문장의 핵심 내용을 가장 잘 표현한 것은? 틀린 보기는 본문의 내용을 심각하게 바꾸거나 핵심적인 내용을 누락시킨 것이다.
ⓐ 북대서양 식민지들의 종말은 아이슬란드와 그린란드에서 세금의 부과로 시작되었다.
ⓑ 그들이 채택한 세제는 북대서양 식민지의 빙하기의 도래를 가져왔다.
ⓒ 세제의 채택과 추운 날씨는 북대서양 식민지들의 몰락을 초래했다.
ⓓ 소빙하 시대로 인한 추운 날씨는 북대서양 식민지들의 세제에 영향을 미쳤다.

해설 | 하이라이트된 문장의 핵심 내용은, 세제의 채택과 빙하기가 북대서양 식민지의 몰락을 가져왔다는 것이다.

문 3 | 두 번째 단락에 따르면, 다음 중 인상된 세금의 원인인 것은?
ⓐ 정부에 의해 책정된 높은 생산 수준
ⓑ 추운 날씨로 인한 수확물 산출량의 감소
ⓒ 환경 문제에 지불하기 위해 필요한 돈
ⓓ 정부의 확대된 권위

해설 | 세금 인상의 직접적인 원인은 날씨로 인한 수확물 산출량의 감소이다.

문 4 | 세 번째 단락에 따르면, 농지에 관한 내용 중 올바른 것은?
Ⓐ 밀은 소와 양을 사육하는 데 쓰여야만 했다.
Ⓑ 농지는 세금을 지불하기 위해 결국 정부에 팔렸다.
Ⓒ 소작인들은 농지를 과도하게 사용하면서 효율적으로 이용하는 데 실패했다.
Ⓓ 농지는 황폐해졌지만 여전히 동물들을 좀 사육할 수 있었다.

해설 | 소작인들이 가축을 과도하게 방목하여 길렀다는 내용이 나온다.

문 5 | 지문에 대한 간단한 요약을 위한 도입 문장이 아래에 제시된다. 가장 중요한 내용을 표현한 3가지 대답을 선택하여 요약을 완성하시오. 몇몇 문장들은 단락에서 언급되지 않았거나 중요하지 않은 내용을 표현해서 요약에 들어갈 수 없다.

북대서양의 식민지화 된 섬들은 초기에는 번영하였으나 몇 세기가 지나고 쇠락했다.

Ⓐ 북대서양 섬들의 초기 바이킹 정착자들은 불행하게도, 중세 온난기 이후 소빙하 시대에 부담스러운 세제를 선택했다.
Ⓑ 1000년 전 북대서양 섬 식민지의 창시자인 Eric the Red는 세재의 확립 또한 독려했다.
Ⓒ 과중한 세금을 낼 수 없는 사람들이 소유한 땅을 부유한 지주들이 빼앗고 생산량 수준을 올렸다.
Ⓓ 날씨 조건 때문에, 경제는 악화되었고, 이로 인해 정부는 토지소유주에게 부과하는 세금을 인상했다.
Ⓔ 추운 날씨 속에서 세금을 내고 생산량을 증대시키기 위해, 토지소유주들은 그들의 토지를 과도하게 사용하게 되었고, 변화하는 조건에 적응하는데 실패했다. 이로 인해 섬들은 멸망 즉, 쇠락하게 되었다.
Ⓕ 섬 지역의 많은 정착자들은 무역업자가 가져오는 유럽의 생산품과 다른 품목에 대한 그들의 욕구를 결코 잃지 않았다. 이로 인해 섬들을 궁극적으로 몰락했다.

해설 | Eric the Red가 세제의 도입을 독려한 주체인지 직접적으로 언급되지 않았으므로 Ⓑ는 답이 아니고, 부유한 대주주들이 땅을 뺏은 것이 아니므로 Ⓒ도 잘못된 보기이다. 유럽에서 수출하고자 하는 품목들로 인해서, 경제적 어려움에 봉착하게 된 것은 사실이지만, 이것이 쇠락의 궁극적인 요인은 아니므로 Ⓕ도 답이 될 수 없다.

VOCABULARY TEST

정답   1. (C)   2. (D)   3. (A)   4. (B)   5. (C)
      6. (D)   7. (B)   8. (C)   9. (D)   10. (A)
      11. (D) 12. (B)

밑줄 친 어휘나 구와 가장 유사한 의미를 지닌 것을 고르시오.

1. 갑자기 잠에서 깨어 창문에 있는 끔찍한 얼굴을 보았다.
   (A) 애처로운   (B) 진지한
   (C) 끔찍한   (D) 우울한

2. 군대는 어떠한 공격이라도 물리칠 준비를 갖추고 국경 근방에 있었다.
   (A) 싸우다   (B) 거절하다
   (C) 진출시키다   (D) 쫓아버리다

3. 어린애처럼 행동하지 마! 넌 성숙해져야 해!
   (A) 성숙한   (B) 순진한
   (C) 변민의   (D) 절제 있는

4. 그 가족은 가난을 극복하기 위해 몹시 애썼다.
   (A) 원했다   (B) 애썼다
   (C) ~에 반대했다   (D) 소유했다

5. 황폐한 땅을 개간하기 위해 그는 강에서 펌프로 물을 퍼 올려야 했다.
   (A) 비옥한   (B) 마른
   (C) 불모의   (D) 경사진

6. 많은 청소년들은 자신들이 관심 있는 것에 너무 민감하거나 너무 심각해지는 경향이 있다.
   (A) 어른들   (B) 소년들
   (C) 학생들   (D) 십대들

7. 논쟁으로 그들 사이의 계약이 실패로 돌아가게 되었다.
   (A) 해산시켰다   (B) ~할 운명이 되게 했다
   (C) 강화시켰다   (D) 쇠퇴했다

8. 개들은 초창기 인간의 역사에서부터 길들여진 동물이며, 현재 인류의 최고의 친구 중 하나이다.
   (A) 키운   (B) 교육된
   (C) 길든   (D) 야생의

9. 공장은 훈련된 일꾼들의 적절한 공급을 유지해야 한다.
   (A) 명백한   (B) 실제의
   (C) 복합적인   (D) 충분한

10. 이 나라는 조세 제도의 과격한 개혁이 필요하다.
    (A) 완전한   (B) 신중한
    (C) 점진적인   (D) 부득이한

11. 경제적인 불안은 궁극적으로 더 많은 실업을 초래하게 될 것이다.
    (A) 불필요하게   (B) 적당히
    (C) 따라서   (D) 결국

12. 그 계획을 완수하기 위해 세심한 노력이 기울여져야만 한다.
    (A) 유익한   (B) 상세한
    (C) 필사적인   (D) 굉장한

Chapter 4 Vocabulary   p.82 - p.102

SAMPLE ITEM   정답 1. Ⓑ   2. Ⓒ

해석   Magaret Mead는 원시적인 즉, 산업화 단계에 있지 않다고 인식되었던 사회에 대한 것에서부터 전쟁과 여성의 권리와 같은, 사람들에게 현대적이며 중요하게 여겨지는 이슈에 이르기까지 다양한 주제에 관해 글을 썼다. 전자에 대한 가장 중요한 예는 그녀의 첫 번째 주요 작품이었다. 그녀의 첫 번째 저작인 『Samoa의 다음 시대(Coming of Age in Samoa, 1928)』를 둘러싼 공방이 있었으나, 선구적인 인류학자로서의 그녀의 위치는 확고하다. 이 혁신적인 인류학의 역작은 대서양의 한 섬에서의 진행되는 사춘기의 성숙 과정을 묘사했다. 후자는 『Themes in French Culture』라는 책에서 예증된다. 그 책에서 그녀는 서구 사회에 관한 연구에 인류학을 적용하려고 시도했다.

문 1 | primitive와 가장 의미가 유사한 것은?
Ⓐ 주요한
Ⓑ 초기의
Ⓒ 자연의
Ⓓ 발달된

해설 | primitive는 '원시의', '초기의'란 뜻이다. 뒤에 나오는 or not at an industrial stage of development와 from ~ to modern issues에서 추측할 수 있다.

문 2 | groundbreaking과 가장 의미가 유사한 것은?
Ⓐ 유별난
Ⓑ 어려운
Ⓒ 새로운
Ⓓ 미성숙한

해설 | groundbreaking의 사전적 의미는 '창시의', '개척의'이다. 이것은 '새롭게 시작한다'라는 의미이므로 답은 Ⓒ이다.

Basic Drill 1

정답 1. naturally, in zoos, in the wild /(B)
2. enabled / (A)   3. weariness and sleepiness / (B)   4. start / (A)

1. 해석   갇혀져 사육되는 동물들은 종종 자연에서 발견되는 동물들과는 현저하게 다른 태도를 보여준다. 예를 들면, 동물원에서 사육될 때, 사자는 야생 환경에서 보편적으로 취하는 것과 다르게 하루에 4시간에서 5시간 이상 잠을 자는 경향이 있다.

문제 | (A) 자유롭게
(B) 우리 안에서

해설 | raised in zoos란 clue 등으로 보아 in captivity는 '사로잡혀', '감금되어'란 의미라는 것을 알 수 있다. 이는 '우리 안에 갇혀 있다'는 뜻이므로 답은 (B)이다.

2. 해석   현대 과학기술은 상당수의 놀라운 천문학적 발견을 가능케 했다. 예를 들면, 2003년에 최신 디지털 프로세서로 인해 과학자들은 태양계로부터 멀리 떨어져 태양의 궤도를 그리며 도는 명왕성의 1.5배의 크기를 지닌 천체를 태양계 내에서 발견했다.

문제 | (A) 가능한
(B) 가치 있는

해설 | feasible은 '실현 가능한', '가능성이 있는'이란 뜻으로, 예를 들어 설명하는 문장에서 enabled scientists to find가 clue가 된다.

3. 해석   일반적인 전염성 질병은 흔히 수 일 또는 심지어 수 주 동안 피로감을 야기한다. 예를 들면, 피로감과 졸음이 특징인 전염성 단구 증가증은 사춘기 청소년이나 젊은 층에 가장 흔히 나타나는 질병이다.

문제 | (A) 졸음
(B) 피로

해설 | 뒤에 피로감과 졸음을 동반하는 질병에 관한 예가 나오므로 fatigue는 '피로'라는 것을 알 수 있다.

4. 해석   성인식은 많은 아프리카 문화에서 중요한 부분이며, 흔히 추장에 의해 공식적으로 시작된다. 예를 들면, 성인식을 할 때, 추장은 공인된 방식으로 연설을 함으로써 이를 시작한다.

문제 | (A) 공식적으로 시작되는
(B) 일시적으로 멈추는
(C) 서열에 따라 등급이 매겨지는
(D) 책임에 따라 만들어지는

해설 | 뒤에 추장의 공식적 연설을 필두로 성인식이 시작(start)된다는 것이 예로 나오므로 formally initiated는 '공식적으로 시작이 된다'는 뜻임을 알 수 있다.

Basic Drill 2

정답 1. nothing today is so unique / (B)
2. light could pass through / (A)
3. ultimately took his life / (C)
4. reduce elevated temperatures / (A)

1. 해석 구텐베르크가 1450년 그의 첫 성경책을 인쇄할 때 사용한 종이의 질은 오늘날까지도 여전히 매우 뛰어나며 아주 튼튼하고 내구성이 있기 때문에, 오늘날 그 어떤 종이도 그렇게 우수하지 않다.

문제 | (A) 가장 오래된
(B) 최고인

해설 | 뒤에 나오는 nothing today is so unique가 clue가 되어 unsurpassed의 의미를 유추할 수 있다.

2. 해석 로마인들은 온실에 빛이 통과할 수 있는 (반)투명 바위를 사용했는데, 그 이유는 많은 열이 새어나가지 않으면서, 빛이 건물로 들어올 수 있기 때문이다.

문제 | (A) 속이 들여다보이는
(B) 얇은

해설 | 뒤에 나오는 light can pass through가 clue가 되어 답을 유추할 수 있다.

3. 해석 다른 이들에게 둘러싸인 채 소크라테스는 독약을 마셨고, 독약은 결국 그의 목숨을 앗아갔다.

문제 | (A) 죽음을 초래했다
(B) 최후를 맞이했다
(C) 독약을 마셨다
(D) 규율을 따랐다

해설 | 궁극적으로 소크라테스의 죽음을 앗아갔다는 뒤의 내용으로 보아, administered toxin은 (C)와 의미가 같음을 알 수 있다.

4. 해석 바이러스성 질병으로 인한 발열을 경험한 젊은 이들은 열을 억제하기 위해 아스피린을 복용할 수 있는데, 이 아스피린은 생명을 위협하는 레이증후군을 일으킬 수 있다. 그 증후군은 상승한 체온을 떨어뜨리고자 아스피린을 복용한 이후에 발병할 수 있다.

문제 | (A) 상승한 체온을 낮추다
(B) 바이러스를 제거하다
(C) 질병을 제거하다
(D) 질병을 억제하다

해설 | 뒤에 나오는 reduce elevated temperatures를 통해 control fever는 '열을 떨어뜨리는 것'이라는 의미임을 알 수 있다.

Basic Drill 3

정답 1. comes off / (B) 2. unending / (A)
3. suffering from severe joint pain / (C)
4. was released nationally / (A)

1. 해석 대부분의 사람들의 피부는 일반적으로 아주 작고 얇은 조각으로 떨어져 나간다. 그러나 흔히 fish scale disease라고 일컬어지는 병으로 고통 받는 사람들의 피부 세포는 물고기 비늘과 비슷한 정도의, 훨씬 더 큰 조각으로 떨어져 나간다.

문제 | (A) 남아있다
(B) 떨어져 나간다

해설 | 뒤에 나오는 comes off in much larger pieces로 보아, 문맥에서 shed는 '피부 세포가 떨어진다'라는 의미로 쓰였음을 알 수 있다.

2. 해석 많은 사람들은 핵에너지가 결코 소진되지 않는 에너지의 원천이라고 생각한다. 그러나 사실상, 이 에너지는 정말로 끝없이 사용할 수 있는 것은 아니다. 우라늄이나 플루토늄과 같은 방사능 원천이 바닥나면, 더 이상 핵에너지도 존재하지 않게 될 것이다.

문제 | (A) 영원한
(B) 일시적인

해설 | however 뒤에 this power source is not actually unending이 나오는 것을 보아, inexhaustible은 '무진장한', '없어지지 않는'이라는 의미임을 유추할 수 있다.

3. 해석 비록 많은 사람들이 관절염에 걸려 있지만, 심한 관절통의 고통을 멈추게 하는 효과적인 방법은 많이 개발되어 있지 않다.

문제 | (A) 이동하기를 거부하다
(B) 고통스런 질병을 견디다
(C) 관절염에 걸리다
(D) 이동하는 데 관절을 사용하다

해설 | suffering from severe joint pain으로부터 are faced with arthritis가 '관절염에 걸리다'라는 의미임을 유추할 수 있다.

4. 해석 뒤퐁 화학 회사는 최초의 합성소재 낙하산을 만들었고, 군사용으로 이를 생산할 것이라고 1939년에 발표했다. 그 뉴스는 그때까지는 비밀로 부쳐져 있었던 것이었으나, 2차 세계대전 이전에 국가적으로 보도되었고 많은 조종사들에게 환영받았다.

문제 | (A) 공표되었다
(B) 암시되었다
(C) 정의되었다
(D) 예견되었다

해설 | 인조 소재의 낙하산을 만들었다는 소식이 1939년까지는 비밀로 부쳐져 있었으나 2차 세계대전 전에 released nationally되었다는 것으로 보아, made public이 '공

표하다', '일반 대중에게 알리다'란 뜻이라는 것을 알 수 있다.

Basic Drill 4

정답 1. clear view / (A)   2. rather than alone, group / (B)   3. check and mend / (A)   4. limiting / (B)

1. 해석   'Messenger'라고 명명된 새로운 위성은 현재 수성의 궤도를 돌고 있다. 이것은 하루에 24시간 동안 그 행성을 인지할 수 있게 하여, 과학자들이 행성을 명확하게 관찰할 수 있게 해준다.

문제 | (A) 눈이 띄는
(B) 영속하는

해설 | 뒤에 나오는 allowing scientists a clear view of it이라는 부연 설명으로 보아, perceptible은 '인지할 수 있는'의 의미를 가지고 있음을 알 수 있다.

2. 해석   심리학자들은 사람들이 혼자 있을 때보다, 군중 속에 있을 때 상당히 다르게 행동한다는 사실을 발견했다. 그룹의 구성원은 종종 단체 행동이 해롭고 심지어 치명적인 것이라 해도, 자신의 욕구를 억제하고 다른 구성원들의 욕구를 따른다.

문제 | (A) 모임
(B) 군중

해설 | 뒤에 나오는 rather than alone과 members of a group을 보았을 때 clique는 '파벌', 또는 '당'과 같은 의미라는 것을 알 수 있고, 이것은 문맥상 '군중'이란 의미와 통한다.

3. 해석   허블 우주 망원경은 발사되었을 때부터 정기적으로 점검을 받았다. 일 년에 석 달마다, NASA는 망원경을 검사하고 수리하기 위해 엔지니어링 지원을 한다.

문제 | (A) 검사했다
(B) 교체했다

해설 | 뒤에 나오는 engineering support to check and mend the telescope란 부분을 보아, inspect는 '검사하다', '점검하다'란 의미가 있음을 알 수 있다.

4. 해석   과거에 결핵 환자들은 질병 확산에 대한 두려움 때문에 수년 동안 시설에 감금되었다. 사람들은 진행 중인 병을 보유한 환자들을 항 투베르쿨린 치료법을 효과적으로 시술할 수 있는 일정 지역에 가두어 둠으로써 계속되는 전염이 중단될 수 있다고 생각했다.

문제 | (A) 납치되었다
(B) 가두어졌다
(C) 보내졌다
(D) 보고되었다

해설 | 뒤에 limiting patients with active disease to an area 가 나오는 것을 보아, confine은 '가두다', '감금하다'란 의미가 있음을 알 수 있다.

VOCABULARY Preview

| Check-up |

1. converted   2. conscious   3. operation
4. optimistic   5. Apparently   6. uncover
7. upsetting   8. locomotion   9. self-destructive
10. solely

다음 빈 칸에 들어갈 알맞은 말을 골라, 필요하면 고쳐 쓰시오.

1. Mary는 성 베드로의 꿈을 꾼 이후, 카톨릭으로 <u>개종했다</u>.
2. 나는 Mike의 도착으로 분위기가 갑자기 바뀐 것을 <u>감지했다</u>.
3. 외과의사 선생님은 5시에 간단한 <u>수술</u>을 하기로 일정이 잡혀 있습니다.
4. 우리 아버지는 매우 긍정적인 분이셨으며 항상 자신의 미래에 대해 <u>낙관적</u>이었다.
5. <u>언뜻 보기에</u>, 그는 가업을 물려받으라는 부모님의 강요로 직업을 포기했다.
6. 경찰은 National Bank를 털려는 음모를 <u>폭로하는</u> 데 실패했다.
7. 당신이 사임한 것이 우리에게 얼마나 <u>곤란한</u> 일인지 모르시나요?
8. 새는 날개를 이용해 <u>이동</u>한다.
9. Paul의 비참한 유년기는 그를 빈정거리고 <u>자기 파괴적</u>인 인간이 되게 하였다.
10. 나는 <u>오로지</u> 우리 가족의 행복에 대해서만 염려한다.

Exercise 1

정답 1. ⓒ   2. ⓑ   3. ⓓ   4. ⓑ   5. ⓒ
6. ⓑ, ⓓ, ⓔ

해석   플라멩코 음악은 오늘날 스페인 민족 음악으로 잘 알려져 있다. 그 오랜 역사는 15세기까지 거슬러 올라간다. 그것은 유태인, 집시, 그리고 아랍 음악을 포함하여, 서로 다른 음악적 영향을 아주 다양하게 융합시켰다. 그 영향의 다양성은 스페인의 역사와 그 시대를 살았던 사람들에 의해 비롯된 결과이다.

중세와 초기 르네상스 시대에 여러 다른 민족들이 스페인에서 살았다. 북 아프리카 출신의 아랍인들 뿐 아니라, 중동에서 온 유태인들이 스페인에 영구적인 거주지를 마련했다. 인도에서 온 방랑인인 집시도 스페인에 거취를 마련했다. 그러나 1492년 스페인의 여왕인 이사벨라는 그 나라에 사는 사람은 누구든지 기독교로 개종을 하든가, 아니면 스페인을 떠나라고 명령하였다. 유태인과 아랍인들은 그들의 종교를 포기하려 하지 않았기에 어떤 사람들은 떠난 반면, 다른 사람들은 스페인의 산악 지역으로 이주했다.

유태인들과 아랍인들, 그리고 집시들이 서로에게 영향을 주게 된 장소는 바로 이 산악 지역이었다. 그들은 스페인에서 가장 보편적인 기독교적이며 종교적인 음악과 자신들의 문화가 스며있는 음악을 결합시켰다. 그 결과는 정말 유례없는 것이었다. 오늘날 우리가 플라멩코 음악을 들을 때 여전히 아랍 음악의 독특한 리듬과 인도 음악에서 공통적으로 나타나는 음과 단어의 반복을 들을 수 있다. 게다가, 많은 플라멩코 곡들은 전통적인 유대 말과 가락을 집어넣었다. 플라멩코 음악은 진정 서로 다른 많은 문화가 한데 어우러져 만들어진 결실이다.

문 1 | 첫 번째 단락의 integrated와 가장 의미가 유사한 것은?
Ⓐ 묘사했다
Ⓑ 창조했다
Ⓒ 혼합시켰다
Ⓓ 취했다

해설 | integrate은 '통합하다' 란 뜻을 가지고 있다. combining Jewish, Gypsy, and Arab music이라는 부분에서 뜻을 알 수 있다.

문 2 | 두 번째 단락에 따르면, 이사벨라 여왕에 관해 사실인 것은?
Ⓐ 그녀는 플라멩코를 스페인의 국민 음악이라 명명했다.
Ⓑ 그녀는 스페인에 있는 모든 사람들은 동일한 종교를 가져야 한다고 주장했다.
Ⓒ 그녀는 집시들에게 산악 지역으로 이동하도록 요구했다.
Ⓓ 그녀는 스페인에 있는 아랍민족과 유대민족을 믿지 않았다.

해설 | 이사벨라 여왕은 사람들에게 기독교로 개종하든지 아니면 나라를 떠나라고 했다.

문 3 | 세 번째 단락의 interacted와 가장 의미가 유사한 것은?
Ⓐ 약속했다
Ⓑ 응답했다
Ⓒ 만났다
Ⓓ 의사소통했다

해설 | interact는 '상호작용하다' 는 의미로, 가까이서 시간을 같이 보냈다는 말에서 단서를 찾을 수 있다.

문 4 | 세 번째 단락의 어휘 incorporate와 가장 의미가 유사한 것은?
Ⓐ 증가시키다
Ⓑ 포함하다
Ⓒ 모방하다
Ⓓ 나타내다

해설 | incorporate는 '집어넣다', '결합하다' 란 뜻이다. and contain tunes as well에서 단서를 찾는다.

문 5 | 다음 중 세 번째 단락의 하이라이트 된 문장의 핵심 내용을 가장 잘 표현한 것은? 틀린 보기는 본문의 내용을 심각하게 바꾸거나 핵심적인 내용을 누락시킨 것이다.
Ⓐ 종교 음악은 스페인과 다른 나라에서 가장 흔한 음악이었다.
Ⓑ 유태인들과 아랍인들, 그리고 집시는 스페인 음악에 가장 큰 영향을 미쳤다.
Ⓒ 그들은 자신들의 전통 음악과 보편적인 스페인 음악을 융합시켰다.
Ⓓ 스페인의 기독교 음악은 다른 많은 문화권의 음악에 영향을 미쳤다.

해설 | 하이라이트 된 문장의 핵심 내용은 유태인이나 아랍인, 그리고 집시들이 자신들의 고유한 문화가 반영된 음악에 보편적인 스페인 음악을 결합시켰다는 것이다.

문 6 | 지문에 대한 간단한 요약을 위한 도입 문장이 아래에 제시된다. 가장 중요한 내용을 표현한 3가지 대답을 선택하여 요약을 완성하시오. 몇몇 문장들은 단락에서 언급되지 않았거나 중요하지 않은 내용을 표현해서 요약에 들어갈 수 없다.

플라멩코 음악은 여러 다른 문화가 혼합된 산물이다.

Ⓐ 이사벨라 여왕은 스페인에 있는 모든 사람들이 기독교도가 되도록 강하게 요구했다.
Ⓑ 종교적인 억압의 결과로서 다른 음악적 영향들이 하나로 모였다.
Ⓒ 인도음악은 같은 음이 반복해서 연주되는 것을 통해 인지될 수 있다.
Ⓓ 세 가지의 독특하고 오래된 문화적인 음악 전통들을 오늘날 플라멩코의 음악에서 분명히 들을 수 있다.
Ⓔ 다른 문화들이 섞이면서, 각각의 문화는 독특한 음악 스타일을 만드는 데 기여했다.
Ⓕ 어떤 유대인들은 이사벨라 여왕의 결정에 반대하여 싸웠고 전쟁을 선포했다.

해설 | Ⓐ는 두 번째 단락의 핵심적이지 않은 내용이고, Ⓒ는 세 번째 단락의 부연 설명이다. Ⓕ는 지문과는 틀린, 언급되지 않은 내용이다.

Exercise 2

정답 1. Ⓐ 2. Ⓒ 3. Ⓐ 4. Ⓒ 5. Ⓒ
6. Cognitive-Behavioral Therapy - Ⓑ, Ⓔ /
Psychoanalysis - Ⓐ, Ⓓ, Ⓖ

해석 지난 수백년 동안, 다양한 심리적 장애를 앓는 사람들을 돕기 위한 많은 치료법이 개발되어 왔다. 오늘날 가장 흔하게 실행되는 치료법 중 두 가지는 인지행동요법과 정신분석요법이다.

인지행동요법은 어떤 사람이 가벼운 우울증이나 중독, 또는 두려움과 같은 문제를 겪게 된 이유는 이 문제를 초래하는 부정적인 생각에서 비롯된 것이라는 생각에서 시작한다. 따라서 치료사들은 이러한 생각들을 하지 않는 법을 배우도록 도와준다. 즉, 먼저 부정적인 생각과 그것이 끼치는 영향을 깨닫고, 그 다음에 이런 부정적인 생각을 긍정적인 것으로 대체하는 법을 배운다. 이 단 기간의 치료는 많은 사람들에게 성공적이었으며, 자기들의 행동을 급격하게 바꾸도록 이끌었다. 우울한 사람들은 긍정적이 되는 법 등을 배웠다. 이런 종류의 치료는 현재와 의식에 초점을 두고 있다.

정신분석요법은 이와는 상당히 다르다. 이것은 사람들이 내부 문제의 근원을 밝혀낼 수 있도록 도움을 줄 수 있는 방법을 찾고자 하는 좀 더 장기적인 전략이다. 이러한 치료는, 사람들의 문제가 잠재의식 깊은 곳에 존재하는 해결되지 않은 문제의 결과라는 생각에서부터 시작한다. 즉, 사람들은 이런 문제가 있는지조차 인식하지 못한다는 것이다. 그러나 이러한 문제들로 인해 사람들은 불행해지고, 자기 파괴적 행동을 하게 된다. 따라서 정신분석학자들은 이런 문제들을 밝혀내고 해결하기 위해 환자의 인생, 특히 유년 시절에 대해 심층적으로 이야기하도록 종종 요구할 것이다. 정신분석학자들은 성인의 많은 문제들이 유년기에 시작한다고 믿는다. 따라서 "그 때로 돌아가", 과거의 중요하고도 당황스러운 사건들을 기억하는 것을 통해 현재 더 건강하고 행복한 어른이 될 수 있다.

문 1 | 다음 중 두 번째 단락의 하이라이트 된 문장의 핵심 내용을 가장 잘 표현한 것은? 틀린 보기는 본문의 내용을 심각하게 바꾸거나 핵심적인 내용을 누락시킨 것이다.
Ⓐ 인지행동요법에 따르면 부정적인 생각이 문제의 근본 원인이다.
Ⓑ 인지행동 치료가들은 부정적인 생각을 초래하는 문제들을 연구하고자 노력한다.
Ⓒ 인지행동 치료가들은 나쁜 생각들이 가벼운 우울증이나 중독, 또는 두려움을 일으킨다고 주장한다.
Ⓓ 부정적인 생각을 치료받고자 하는 사람은 인지행동요법를 받아야 한다.

해설 | 하이라이트 된 문장의 핵심은, 인지행동요법에서는 부정적인 생각이 사람들의 심리적 문제를 일으킨다는 것으로, 우울증이나 중독, 두려움과 같은 예는 핵심 내용에 들어가지 않는다.

문 2 | 두 번째 단락의 undo와 가장 의미가 유사한 것은?
Ⓐ 듣다
Ⓑ 복종하다
Ⓒ 반대로 하다
Ⓓ 향상시키다

해설 | undo는 '취소하다'란 의미가 있는데, 문맥에서는 '부정적인 생각을 하지 않게 하다'라는 의미로 쓰였다. Ⓒ의 reverse는 '반대로 하다'란 뜻이므로 답이 된다.

문 3 | 두 번째 단락의 drastically와 가장 의미가 유사한 것은?
Ⓐ 상당히
Ⓑ 약간
Ⓒ 희망을 걸고
Ⓓ 임시로

해설 | drastically는 '철저하게'란 뜻을 가지고 있다. short term therapy가 successful했다는 내용이 단서가 될 수 있다.

문 4 | 세 번째 단락의 unresolved와 가장 의미가 유사한 것은?
Ⓐ 알려지지 않은
Ⓑ 예기치 않은
Ⓒ 해결되지 않은
Ⓓ 불친절한

해설 | unresolved는 '해결되지 않은'이란 뜻으로, seeks to help people uncover ~ problems에서 뜻을 유추할 수 있다.

문 5 | 글쓴이는 두 가지 이론을 무엇에 근거하여 비교하는가?
Ⓐ 각각의 치료법의 성공률
Ⓑ 각 종류의 치료법의 기원
Ⓒ 각각의 치료법의 지속 시간과 초점
Ⓓ 각 치료법으로 가장 치료가 잘 되는 환자의 유형

해설 | 인지행동치료법과 정신분석학이라는 두 가지 대표적 신경 질환 치료법에 대해, 치료에 소요되는 시간과 치료의 초점을 중심으로 비교하고 있다.

문 6 | 적절한 보기를 골라 관련 있는 치료법의 종류와 짝지으시오. 두 개의 보기는 제외됩니다.
Ⓐ 환자를 치료하는 데 꽤 오랜 기간이 소요된다.
Ⓑ 지금 현재에 초점을 맞춘다.
Ⓒ 자살하고 싶은 충동이 있는 사람들에게 가장 효과적이다.
Ⓓ 현재에 관한 답을 찾기 위해 과거를 살핀다.
Ⓔ 다르게 생각하는 방식을 배우도록 재교육을 하고자 한다.
Ⓕ 젊은 층에 더욱 효과적이다.
Ⓖ 삶 속에서 미해결 문제를 찾는다.

해설 | ⓒ와 ⓕ는 본문에 언급되지 않은 내용이다. 정신분석요법은 장기간에 걸친 치료법이라는 내용과, 삶 속의 해결되지 않은 문제들이 심리적 장애를 일으키는 데, 특별히 유년 시절이 중요하다는 것이 핵심적인 내용이다. 이에 따라 Ⓐ, Ⓓ, Ⓖ가 정신분석요법의 내용에 해당된다.

Exercise 3

정답 1. ⓒ 2. Ⓓ 3. Ⓐ 4. Ⓑ 5. Ⓑ, ⓒ, ⓕ
Text Outline (B)

해석   심해에서 발견되는 가장 신비하고 포착하기 힘든 생물 중에 하나는 대왕 오징어이다. 이 생물은 살아있는 상태로 과학자들에게 목격된 적이 없고 그 수생의 습관에 대해 알려진 것이 거의 없다. 한 때 선원들의 상상의 산물이라고 생각되었지만, 오늘날 우리는 두 가지 이유로 인해 그것들이 실재한다는 것을 알고 있다. 한 가지는 선원들과 어부들이 오랜 기간 동안 그 생물의 사진 증거를 제공해 왔기 때문이다. 다른 한 가지 증거는 더욱 명백하다. 세계 곳곳에서 몇몇의 대왕 오징어가 해변으로 밀려온 것이다.

이 생물에 대해 정확히 알려진 것은 무엇인가? 첫째로, 그들은 부드러운 몸과 몸을 보호하는 껍질을 가지고 있는 연체동물이다. 대합조개와 달팽이가 연체동물의 예이다. 오징어 또한 껍질을 가지고 있으나 그 껍질은 몸 안에 있다. 게다가 그들은 팔이 여덟 개인데, 그 중 두 개는 음식을 모으는데 사용된다. 반면, 여섯 개는 전적으로 바다를 가로지르는 이동을 보조하기 위해 사용된다. 대왕 오징어에 관한 또 하나의 흥미로운 특징은 눈이 그 어떤 다른 동물들보다 크다는 것이다. 눈의 지름이 18인치에 이를 정도로 크다. 그러나 눈만 큰 게 아니다. 이름이 암시하듯이, 대왕 오징어는 몸집이 거대하다. 길이가 20피트 이상 되는 것들이 발견되기도 했다.

사실상 이 생물들은 너무 커서 바다 속의 또 다른 거대 생물인 고래와 자주 싸움이 붙기도 한다. 어느 누구도 고래와 싸우는 대왕 오징어를 목격한 적은 없지만, 보기에 막상막하로 대결한 수중 싸움에 관한 증거가 존재한다. 때때로 대왕 오징어의 촉수가 죽은 고래 몸을 감싼 채 발견되기도 한다. 또 어떤 때는 대왕 오징어의 일부가 고래 위속에서 발견되기도 한다.

문 1 | 첫 번째 단락의 elusive와 가장 의미가 유사한 것은?
Ⓐ 환영의
Ⓑ 미신적인
ⓒ 드문
Ⓓ 진화적인

해설 | elusive는 '파악하기 어려운', '잡기 어려운'의 의미를 가지고 있다. 앞의 mysterious와 뒤의 This creature has never been seen alive by scientists and very little is known about its aquatic habits.에서 힌트를 얻을 수 있다.

문 2 | 첫 번째 단락의 tangible과 가장 의미가 유사한 것은?
Ⓐ 애매한
Ⓑ 의심스러운
ⓒ 설득력 있는
Ⓓ 유형의, 실제의

해설 | tangible은 '만져서 알 수 있는', '실체가 있는', '명백한'의 뜻이다. 뒤에 나오는 real giant squid가 힌트이다.

문 3 | 세 번째 단락의 witnessed와 가장 의미가 유사한 것은?
Ⓐ 보여진
Ⓑ 입증된
ⓒ 살아남은
Ⓓ 묘사된

해설 | witnessed는 '목격되다'란 뜻이다. 대조되는 내용에서 증거(evidence)를 통해 그 뜻을 유추할 수 있다.

문 4 | 세 번째 단락에 따르면, 오징어와 고래가 싸운다는 것을 주장하기 위해 글쓴이가 제시하는 근거는?
Ⓐ 싸우는 사진이 선원들에 의해 찍혔다.
Ⓑ 오징어의 잔해가 고래 안에서 발견되었다.
ⓒ 고래의 일부분이 오징어의 위에서 발견되었다.
Ⓓ 고래가 그들 주위를 둘러싸고 있는 오징어들과 함께 발견되었다.

해설 | 두 생물의 싸움의 증거로 글쓴이는 죽은 고래 몸을 감싼 채 발견된 오징어의 촉수와 고래 위속에 발견된 오징어의 일부를 들고 있다.

문 5 | 지문에 대한 간단한 요약을 위한 도입 문장이 아래에 제시된다. 가장 중요한 내용을 표현한 3가지 대답을 선택하여 요약을 완성하시오. 몇몇 문장들은 단락에서 언급되지 않았거나 중요하지 않은 내용을 표현해서 요약에 들어갈 수 없다.

심해에 사는 대왕 오징어는 자연에서 가장 신비한 생물 중 하나이다.

Ⓐ 어부들은 수년 동안 대왕 오징어가 존재한다고 주장했고 몇 장의 사진을 찍었다.
Ⓑ 한 때는 완전히 허구라고 생각되었으나, 대왕 오징어는 이제 실제로 존재하는 해양 동물로 알려져 있다.
ⓒ 대왕 오징어와 고래 사이의 싸움에 대한 증거는 대왕 오징어의 존재를 입증하는 또 하나의 증거이다.
Ⓓ 대왕 오징어는 특정 종류의 물고기가 급속도로 감소하도록 초래한 원인 중 하나이다.
Ⓔ 대왕 오징어가 실제로 존재한다는 것이 입증되었지만, 오늘날 많은 사람들은 여전히 그 존재를 의심한다.
ⓕ 발견된 증거를 토대로, 대왕 오징어가 연체동물이며, 상당히 큰 눈과 몸체를 갖고 있다고 알려졌다.

해설 | Ⓐ는 대왕 오징어의 존재를 입증할 수 있는 증거 중 하나에 대한 언급이므로 첫 번째 단락의 핵심 내용이라고는 볼 수 없고, Ⓑ는 본문에 언급되지 않은 내용이며, Ⓒ는 본문에서 말한 내용과는 다른 내용이다.

VOCABULARY TEST

정답 1. (B)   2. (D)   3. (A)   4. (C)   5. (D)
      6. (C)   7. (B)   8. (D)   9. (D)   10. (C)
      11. (B) 12. (A)

밑줄 친 어휘나 구와 가장 유사한 의미를 지닌 것을 고르시오.

1. 그 연구는 마침내 뼈의 구성 성분을 밝혀냈다.
   (A) 해결했다   (B) 밝혔다
   (C) 제안했다   (D) 이해했다

2. 길거리 이곳저곳을 돌아다니며 사진을 찍는 것이 내 취미 중 하나이다.
   (A) 달리며   (B) 시들며
   (C) 그림을 그리며   (D) 돌아다니며

3. 이 옷은 합성섬유로 만들어졌으나 세탁기로 세탁할 수 있다.
   (A) 합성의   (B) 나일론
   (C) 가공하지 않은   (D) 분석적인

4. 의사들은 질병의 전염을 막기 위해 최선을 다하고 있다.
   (A) 통제   (B) 변화
   (C) 확산   (D) 발생

5. Jennifer는 보기에 노래하는 것과 춤추는 데 소질이 있는 것 같다.
   (A) 걸출하게   (B) 어색하게
   (C) 진정으로   (D) 겉으로는

6. 당신의 감정을 억누르지 마시오. 솔직하고 진실해 지세요.
   (A) 놓아주다   (B) 위조하다
   (C) 억누르다   (D) 압박하다

7. 마케팅 계획을 세울 때 통계자료는 정기적으로 사용된다.
   (A) 좀처럼 ~하지 않다   (B) 일반적으로
   (C) 실질적으로   (D) 직접적으로

8. 우리 아버지는 도박 중독에 저항하여 싸우고 있다.
   (A) 태도   (B) 용기
   (C) 의지   (D) 강박관념

9. 그 와인을 마시지 마세요! 잔에 치명적인 독약이 들어 있어요.
   (A) 끔찍한   (B) 사악한
   (C) 파괴적인   (D) 치명적인

10. 나는 그가 그 계획의 실패를 전적으로 책임져야 하는 사람이라고 확신한다.
    (A) 확실히   (B) 지혜롭게
    (C) 전적으로   (D) 놀랍게

11. 소련은 지구의 주위를 도는 최초의 인공위성을 발사시킨 나라였다.
    (A) 발굴하다   (B) 선회하다
    (C) 보호하다   (D) 감시하다

12. 25살이 되던 해, Mike는 기독교로 개종했다.
    (A) 개심했다   (B) 옮겼다
    (C) 공유했다   (D) 즐겼다

Chapter 5 Reference   p.104 - p.124

SAMPLE ITEM   정답 Ⓒ

해석   문명의 많은 부분을 파괴했던 고대 홍수에 관한 신화는 다른 여러 문화에서 공통적으로 나타난다. 이러한 신화는 사실에 근거한 것일 수도 있다. 신화에서 흔히 묘사되듯이 갑작스러운 사건이라기보다 홍수는 지난 빙하 시대의 말기에 해수면이 상승된 결과로 발생한 것일 가능성이 있다. 상승한 해수가 지표면 뿐 아니라 심지어 도시들을 침수시켰을 거라는 주장도 존재한다. 쿠바 해변의 침수된 고대 마을에 대한 최근의 발견은 이러한 이론을 뒷받침하는 증거를 제시할 것이다.

문제 | 지문의 these가 가리키는 것은?
   Ⓐ 문화
   Ⓑ 홍수
   Ⓒ 신화
   Ⓓ 문명

해설 | these 앞의 어휘나 구를 대입했을 때, 문맥상 뜻이 통하는 것은 '신화' 이다.

Basic Drill 1

정답   1. (B)   2. (B)   3. (A)   4. (A)   5. (A)
       6. (C)

1. **해석**   어떤 개구리는 크기도 다양하고 풍선처럼 늘어나기도 하는 성낭(vocal pouch)를 갖고 있다. 이것이 소

리가 크게 울리게 하고 이런 식으로 개구리는 짝짓기를 위한 부름과 노래를 만들어 낼 수 있다.

문제 | (A) 풍선
(B) 주머니
(C) 개구리

해설 | these가 지칭할 수 있는 복수 명사는 frogs, vocal pouches, balloons가 있는데, balloons는 비유되어진 것으로 적절치 않고 내용상 vacal pouches가 올바르다.

2. 해설   취학 남아의 낮은 성취도가 심화되는 추세는 여러 관점으로 다뤄질 수 있다. 그 중 하나는 이러한 문제를 해결하기 위해서 역할 모델로 기여할 수 있는 남자 교사를 충원하는 것이다.

문제 | (A) 경향
(B) 각도(관점)
(C) 문제점

해설 | 문맥상 one은 취학 남아의 부진한 성취도에 대한 여러 가지 관점(angle) 중 하나를 의미한다.

3. 해설   가정 내 폭력을 줄이려는 의도로 제정되었음에도 불구하고, 금주법은 결과적으로 범죄를 증가시키는 주요원인이 되었다. 실제로 술(알코올)이 가정 내 폭력을 부추기지만, 이를 금하는 것이 그 문제를 명백하게 해결하는 방안이 아니었다.

문제 | (A) 가정 내 폭력
(B) 범죄의 증가
(C) 금주법

해설 | 알코올로 인해 심화된 it은 문맥상 domestic violence를 의미한다.

4. 해설   밀이 메소포타미아 지역과 유프라테스 강 계곡에서 처음으로 재배되었다는 것을 보여주는 증거가 존재한다. 그 당시 밀은 원래 야생 식물이었으나 이 곡물의 가능성을 처음으로 깨달았던 지역은 전자였다.

문제 | (A) 메소포타미아
(B) 유프라테스 강 계곡
(C) 증거

해설 | the former는 열거된 것 중 가장 처음에 등장하는 것을 가리킨다.

5. 해설   바람, 습도, 기압, 이 세 요소가 몬순을 형성하기 위해 충돌한다. 그러나 현대의 기상위성과 정교한 컴퓨터가 발달하기 이전에는, 기상 과학자들은 이러한 힘들이 실제로 어떻게 하여 그토록 강력한 기상 현상을 형성해내

는지에 대한 기초적인 지식만을 가지고 있었다.

문제 | (A) 바람, 습도, 기압
(B) 인공위성과 컴퓨터
(C) 기상 과학자

해설 | 기상 현상을 형성하는 these forces는 첫 문장에서 등장한 wind, moisture, pressure를 가리킨다.

6. 해설   20세기 전반기에는 이주자에 대한 반감이 증가했다. 동유럽출신의 이민자들 뿐 아니라 일본인 이민자들의 유입(쇄도)에 대한 분노는, 특별히 후자가 국가에 가져온 경제적인 이익은 무시하고, 많은 미국인에게 이민의 중단 또는 감소를 요청하게끔 만들었다.

문제 | (A) 일본인 이주민
(B) 미국인
(C) 동유럽 이주민

해설 | 후자(the latter)는 the influx of Japanese immigrants as well as those from Eastern Europe에서 나중에 열거된 Eastern European immigrants를 지칭한다.

Basic Drill 2

정답   1. ① listen to music without needing live musicians ② purchased jukeboxes to play recorded music
2. ① out-of-print book ② buying copyrights of out-of-print books and making relatively inexpensive copies
3. ① lye ② the lye mixed with animal fat
4. ① poisonous bite or large teeth ② fool predators into thinking they are more dangerous than they really are

1. 해설   음악 산업에 미친 기술의 영향은 과소평가될 수 없다. 전축 덕분에 사람들은 직접 연주하는 음악가들 없이 음악을 들을 수 있게 되었다. 이것은 레스토랑이나 술집이 녹음된 음악을 듣기 위해 주크박스를 구입하는 것과 마찬가지의 일이 되었다. 이런 현상은 아마도 소비자나 사업가에게는 이익이 되었겠지만, 일하기를 원했던 음악가에게는 부정적인 영향을 미쳤다.

해설 | The same: the same은 앞 문장의, '음악을 직접 연주하는 연주가 없이도 음악을 감상할 수 있게 되었다' 는 사

실을 받는다.
this: 앞 문장의 '레스토랑과 술집이 (연주자를 고용하지 않고) 주크박스로 대체하는 현상'을 가리킨다.

2. 해석 과거에 소비자들은 절판된 책을 구하기 위해서 수개월 동안 헌책방을 찾아야 했을 것이다. 이러한 책을 교재로 채택하기 원했던 교사들에게는 운이 나쁜 일이었다. 그러나 이제는 print-on-demand publisher(절판된 책을 다시 인쇄하여 펴내는 출판업자)가 절판된 책의 저작권을 사서, 필요한 비용보다 상대적으로 저렴하게 책을 인쇄한다. 이러한 방식으로 대량 인쇄뿐만 아니라, 판매를 위해 보관되는 재고 모두 필요하지 않게 되었다.

해설 | one: 앞 문장의 out-of-print book를 의미한다.
This way: 절판된 책의 저작권을 구입하여 비교적 저렴하게 사본을 만드는 것을 가리킨다.

3. 해석 과거에 사람들은 몸을 씻기 위한 비누를 가게에서 살 수 없었다. 그러므로 그들은 집에서 그것을 만들어야 했다. 비누를 제조하는 것은 두 단계의 과정이 있다. 첫째, 나무의 재를 모아 잿물을 만드는 과정을 거쳐야 했다. 그것(잿물)은 몸에서 때를 씻어 없애는 화학물질이다. 그런 다음, 잿물은 그것을 응고시키는 동물성 지방과 혼합된다. 이 물질은 고체 상태가 되도록 놓아지고, 곧 하나의 비누가 만들어졌다.

해설 | It: It은 몸을 깨끗하게 하는 화학물질이라는 설명을 보아, 앞에 나오는 lye를 받음을 알 수 있다.
This substance: 응고시켜 완성된 비누가 된다는 설명에서 동물성 지방과 섞인 잿물을 가리킨다는 것을 알 수 있다.

4. 해석 물 때 독성이 있거나 커다란 이빨이 있으면 동물의 생존을 보장해주는 데 도움을 줄 수 있다. 그러나 이러한 특성이 없어도 많은 동물들은 자신들을 실제보다 더욱 두려운 존재로 여기도록 천적을 속일 수 있는 특성이 있다. 이런 것은 등에 큰 눈처럼 보이는 무늬를 갖도록 진화된 모충류에서 확인할 수 있는데, 이 무늬는 그것을 실제보다 더 위협적으로 보이게끔 만든다. 다른 곤충들은 실제로는 침이 없을지라도 쏘는 말벌을 닮게끔 진화되었다.

해설 | these features: 바로 앞의 문장에 나타난 poisonous bite or large teeth를 가리킨다.
This: 모충류를 예로 들어 구체적으로 논지를 전개하는 것으로 미루어, this fool predators into thinking they are more dangerous than they really are를 가리킨다.

VOCABULARY Preview

| Check-up |

1. incredibly   2. spun   3. sticky
4. prey   5. prone   6. ensnared
7. lawn   8. tidy   9. trim
10. varied   11. along with 12. reflect

다음 빈 칸에 들어갈 알맞은 말을 골라, 필요하면 고쳐 쓰시오.

1. 첫 번의 시도에 합격하기에는 그 시험은 굉장히 어려웠다.
2. 그녀는 고속도로 한 가운데서 갑자기 핸들을 돌렸다.
3. 내 여동생은 딸기잼을 너무나 좋아하고 언제나 손가락이 잼으로 끈적거린다.
4. 거미는 거미줄을 쳐서 먹이를 잡는다.
5. 일본에는 지진이 일어나기 일쑤이다.
6. 그 남자는 가엾은 Jane이 가진 모든 돈을 그에게 주도록 함정에 빠뜨렸다.
7. 나는 이웃의 잔디를 깎아주고 용돈을 번다.
8. 우리 어머니는 항상 나더러 단정하라고 잔소리를 하신다.
9. 우리 아버지는 이번 주말 정원에 있는 나무를 다듬으실 것이다.
10. 그 콘서트홀에서는 일 년 내내 다양한 공연 프로그램이 열렸다.
11. 감기가 심하게 걸려서 학교에 갈 수 없었는데, 영어선생님께서 급우 두 명과 함께 우리 집을 방문하셨다.
12. 이 박사는 그 보고서가 자신의 의견을 반영하지 않았다고 주장했다.

Exercise 1

정답 1. Ⓐ 2. Ⓑ 3. Ⓓ 4. Ⓒ 5. Ⓐ
6. Ⓐ, Ⓓ, Ⓕ

해석 과거 텔레비전 프로그램 편성이 국가에 의해 결정되었던 나라들이 이제는 위성 방송 네트워크에 접근할 수 있게 되었다. 이 덕분에 서구의 텔레비전 프로그램이 서방 세계의 경계를 넘어서 (그 영향력이) 확대되고 있다.

서구 미디어의 영향력을 볼 수 있는 한 곳은 인도이다. 1990년대 초까지만 하더라도 인도 텔레비전은 자국의 프로그램으로만 편성되어 있었다. 뉴스, 인도 영화, 정부 방송이 인도 텔레비전의 주된 프로그램이었다. 그러나 경제 정책의 변화로 서구의 위성 방송국들이 방송을 시작할 수 있도록 허용되었다. 그리하여 곧 인도의 자국 방송 프로들은 더 인기 있는 것들로 대체되었다.

처음에 방영된 유일한 프로그램은 서구의 뉴스였다. 그러나 스포츠 방송, 음악 방송, 미국과 영국의 TV 쇼를 내세우는 오락 방송이 그 뒤를 이었다. 이러한 방송들은 엄청나게 인도의 시청자들에게 인기를 얻게 되었고, 곧 서구 음악과 방송들은 인도 젊은이들의 문화에서 큰 부분을 차지하게 되었다. 1990년대 말에는 2,000만이 넘는 인도의 가구들이 위성 방송 채널을 시청하게 되었다.

이와 같은 방송 프로그램의 변화와 함께 문화적 가치관에 변화가 초래되었다. 오늘날의 인도 젊은이들은, 결혼에 대한 태도나 남녀의 역할, 가족과 일에 대한 중요성과 같은 고유한 문화 규범에 의해 주로 형성된 기성 시대의 가치관과는 다른 가치관을 표방하기 시작했다. 이런 중요한 가치관이 서구의 영향을 반영하기 시작한 것이다. 패션 또한 서구의 영향을 받고 있다. 예를 들면, 인도의 십대 소녀들은 어머니 세대의 전통 의상보다는 서양의 록 스타들의 패션을 따라하고 있다. 분명히 서구 방송의 영향이 이러한 변화의 한 부분을 담당하고 있는 것이다.

문 1 | 두 번째 단락의 One이 가리키는 것은?
Ⓐ 나라
Ⓑ 네트워크
Ⓒ 정부
Ⓓ 위성

해설 | 서구의 방송 프로그램의 영향력을 볼 수 있는 곳으로 문장 끝에 India란 나라 명이 나온 것을 보아 One은 '국가'를 가리킨다는 것을 알 수 있다.

문 2 | 두 번째 단락의 dominated와 가장 의미가 유사한 것은?
Ⓐ 연결되는
Ⓑ 점유되는
Ⓒ 공유되는
Ⓓ 소유되는

해설 | dominate의 의미는 '지배하다', '억제하다'이다. '자국의 방송 프로그램에 지배받고 있었다'라는 것은 '자국의 방송 프로그램이 점유하고 있었다'와 같은 의미라고 볼 수 있다. 뒤에 News programs, Indian movies, and government programming were the main things on Indian TV.라는 부연 설명을 통해서도 답을 유추할 수 있다.

문 3 | 두 번째 단락의 these가 가리키는 것은?
Ⓐ 서구 위성 방송국들
Ⓑ 경제 정책
Ⓒ 인도의 TV 방송국들
Ⓓ 인도의 방송 프로그램

해설 | these가 '보다 인기 있는 (서구) 프로그램들로 대체되었다'라고 말하는 것으로 보아, these는 기존 인도의 방송임을 알 수 있다.

문 4 | 다음 중 네 번째 단락의 하이라이트 된 문장의 핵심 내용을 가장 잘 표현한 것은? 틀린 보기는 본문의 내용을 심각하게 바꾸거나 핵심적인 내용을 누락시킨 것이다.
Ⓐ 여성의 역할이 많이 바뀌고 있고 인도 여성들은 결혼보다 자신의 일을 더 중요하게 생각하기 시작했다.
Ⓑ 인도 부모들은 자기 아이들의 가치관을 받아들이기 시작했다.
Ⓒ 인도 젊은이들의 원칙이 바뀌고 있고, 이제 그들의 가치관은 부모들의 가치관과는 매우 다르다.
Ⓓ 오늘날의 인도 젊은이들은 그들의 부모들이 그러했듯이 전통과 현대가 혼합된 가치관을 가지고 있다.

해설 | 하이라이트 된 문장의 핵심은, 인도 젊은이들의 가치관이 부모들이 가졌던 전통적인 가치관과는 많이 달라졌다는 것이다.

문 5 | 인도와 관련하여 지문에서 언급되지 않은 내용은?
Ⓐ 위성 방송을 보는 인도인 인구
Ⓑ 서구 프로그램을 수용하기 전에 방영된 인도의 TV 프로그램들의 주요 컨텐츠
Ⓒ 인도 젊은 층에 미친 서구 프로그램의 영향
Ⓓ 인도에서 볼 수 있는 서구 프로그램의 종류

해설 | 위성 방송을 보는 인구수에 대한 내용은 나와 있지 않다.

문 6 | 지문에 대한 간단한 요약을 위한 도입의 문장이 아래에 제시된다. 가장 중요한 생각을 표현한 3가지 대답을 선택하여 요약을 완성하시오. 몇몇 문장들은 단락에서 언급되지 않았거나 중요하지 않은 생각을 표현해서 요약에 들어갈 수 없다.

서구 방송이 전 세계에 영향을 미치고 있다.

Ⓐ 인도는 서구 방송의 영향을 받은 나라의 좋은 예이다.
Ⓑ 1990년대까지 인도는 서구 방송을 그들 문화에 좋게 여겼지만 수용하지 않았다.
Ⓒ 서구의 오락 프로 방영의 확대가 인도 음악에 큰 영향을 미쳤다.
Ⓓ 방영되는 서구 프로그램의 수와 종류가 1990년대에 크게 확대되었다.
Ⓔ 인도 젊은이들의 방송 프로그램에 대한 가치관은 그들 부모 세대와는 확연히 다르다.
Ⓕ 서구 방송의 결과로 인도의 젊은 세대와 기성 세대 간에 관점의 차이가 발생하고 있다.

해설 | 인도를 예로 들어 서구 방송이 전 세계에 미치는 영향에 관해 쓴 글이다. 언제, 어떤 경로로 서구 방송이 인도에 방영되었는지, 어떤 영향을 끼쳤고 그 결과가 무엇인지에 대한 보기를 고른다. Ⓑ와 Ⓒ는 핵심적이지 않은 내용이고, Ⓔ는 지문의 내용과는 일치하지 않는다.

Exercise 2

정답   1. Ⓑ   2. Ⓐ   3. ⓒ   4. Ⓑ   5. Ⓓ
6. ⓒ   7. Typical Spider - Ⓑ, Ⓔ, Ⓖ /
Fisher Spider - Ⓐ, ⓒ

해석   우리가 거미를 떠올릴 때는 주로 먹잇감인 곤충을 잡기 위해 거미줄을 잣고 있는, 작고 다리가 여덟 개인 생물을 연상하기 쉽다. 그러나 이것이 모든 종류의 거미들에게 들어맞지는 않는다. 다른 거미들과는 여러 면에서 확연히 다른 하나는 fisher spider이다.

일반적인 거미줄은 거미의 복부에서 생산되는 끈적끈적한 비단실로 만들어진다. 의심 없는 곤충들이 거미줄로 걸어오거나 날아와 도망칠 수 없게 된다. 그러면 거미가 와서 먹기 위해 걸린 곤충을 더 많은 비단과 같은 거미줄로 감싼다. fisher spider는 비록 거미줄을 잣긴 하지만 먹이를 잡기 위해서가 아니라 관찰을 하기 위해 거미줄을 이용한다. 자신의 잠재적 먹잇감이 끈끈한 실에 걸려드는 것에 의존하는 대신, 자신이 주식으로 삼는 작은 물고기를 관찰할 수 있는 물 위에 거미줄을 짓고 성공 가능성이 충분할 때만 공격한다. 그리고 엄청난 속도로 먹이를 잡아 죽인다.

fisher spider와 다른 거미들의 또 하나의 차이점은 생식 능력에 있다. 보통 거미는 수천 개의 알을 낳아, 보호하기 위해 끈끈한 비단실로 감싼다. 거미는 이 알 자루를 안전한 장소에 놓아 그 어떤 다른 방해를 받지 않고 부화할 수 있도록 한다. 새끼 거미들은 태어난 즉시 세상 밖으로 나간다. 그러나 fisher spider는 알이 부화하기 바로 며칠 전까지 알 자루를 몸에 지니고 다닌다. 그런 다음에 알 자루를 근처의 잎이나 가지에 부착해 놓는다. 새끼 거미들이 태어나면 그들은 떠나기 몇 주 전까지 어미 곁에 머무른다.

문 1 | 첫 번째 단락의 One이 가리키는 것은?
Ⓐ 거미줄
Ⓑ 거미
ⓒ 곤충
Ⓓ 음식

해설 | one은 is the fisher spider와 동격으로 all spiders 중에 하나의 spider를 지칭한다.

문 2 | 두 번째 단락의 Unsuspecting과 가장 의미가 유사한 것은?
Ⓐ 의식하지 못하고 있는
Ⓑ 믿을 수 없는
ⓒ 알려지지 않은
Ⓓ 준비되지 않은

해설 | unsuspecting은 '의심하지 않는'이라는 뜻이다. 부정 접두의 un-과 어원인 suspect에서 그 뜻을 유추한다.

문 3 | 두 번째 단락의 them이 가리키는 것은?
Ⓐ 곤충
Ⓑ 거미
ⓒ 거미줄
Ⓓ 비단실

해설 | fisher spider가 '먹이를 관찰할 수 있는 장소로 그것을 이용한다'는 내용을 보아 them은 거미줄임을 알 수 있다.

문 4 | 세 번째 단락의 hatch와 가장 의미가 유사한 것은?
Ⓐ 안전한 상태로 있다
Ⓑ 밖으로 나오다
ⓒ 먹이를 주다
Ⓓ 보호하다

해설 | hatch는 알에서 '부화시키다'의 뜻이다. 문맥상 '(안에서) 밖으로 나오다'는 의미의 come out이 적절하다.

문 5 | 세 번째 단락에 따르면, 보통 거미들은 알 자루를 어떻게 하는가?
Ⓐ 알 자루를 나뭇가지나 잎 아래에 놓아둔다.
Ⓑ 알 자루를 거미줄 한 쪽 구석에 부착해 둔다.
ⓒ 알이 부화할 무렵까지 지니고 다닌다.
Ⓓ 위험으로부터 보호받는 장소에 알 자루를 둔다.

해설 | 거미는 알 자루를 안전한 장소에 놓아 누구의 방해없이 부화하도록 돕는다.

문 6 | 다음 중 두 번째 단락의 하이라이트 된 문장의 핵심 내용을 가장 잘 표현한 것은? 틀린 보기는 본문의 내용을 심각하게 바꾸거나 핵심적인 내용을 누락시킨 것이다.
Ⓐ fisher spider는 거미줄을 사용하여 작은 물고기와 보통 물에 서식하는 다른 먹잇감을 잡는다.
Ⓑ fisher spider는 주로 물 위에 쳐 놓은 거미줄로 작은 수생 생물을 잡는다.
ⓒ fisher spider는 거미줄을 먹이를 잡기 위한 도구가 아니라 먹이를 관찰하고 적당한 시기에 공격할 수 있는 장소로 사용한다.
Ⓓ fisher spider는 먹이가 서식하고 물가에 살기 위해 거미줄을 치고 이에 따라 먹이의 포획 가능성이 높다.

해설 | 하이라이트 된 문장의 핵심 내용은, fisher spider가 물고기를 관찰하기 위해 거미줄을 치고, 성공할 확률이 높을 때 공격한다라는 내용이다.

문 7 | 적절한 보기를 골라 관련 있는 거미의 종류와 짝지으시오. 두개의 보기는 제외됩니다.
Ⓐ 매우 빠른 속도로 먹이를 포획한다.
Ⓑ 먹이를 거미줄 안에 넣어 잡는다.
ⓒ 출생 후 새끼 거미 곁에서 몇 주 머문다.
Ⓓ 먹이사냥을 하지 않을 때에는 주로 지하에서 산다.
Ⓔ 일단 태어난 뒤에는 새끼들을 돌보지 않는다.
Ⓕ 먹잇감으로 설치류나 다른 종류의 거미들을 사냥한다.
Ⓖ 알 자루를 위험으로부터 떨어진 곳에 놓는다.

해설 | Ⓓ와 Ⓕ는 지문에 언급되지 않은 내용이다.

Exercise 3

정답 1. Ⓐ 2. Ⓒ 3. Ⓑ 4. Ⓒ 5. Ⓑ, Ⓒ, Ⓔ

Text Outline (B)

해석　하얀 말뚝 울타리와 굴뚝 그리고 주위를 뛰어다니는 행복한 개와 같이, 푸른 잔디는 전형적인 미국 가정의 이미지의 일부이다. 그러나 18세기까지만 해도 대부분의 미국 가정은, 지금은 대부분의 지역에서 일반화된 이러한 특징들을 갖고 있지 않았다. 그 때까지 푸른 잔디는 막대한 부의 상징으로 간주되었다. 그러한 잔디를 관리하기 위해 관리인을 고용할 수 있는 경제적 여유가 가정에 있어야 했다. 따라서 대부분의 (평범한) 미국인 집밖은 (푸른 잔디 대신) 흙 땅이나 채소밭이었다.

푸른 잔디밭을 유지하는 데 필요한 부 외에도 미국에는 관리하기 용이한 잔디가 없었다. 북미의 토종 잔디는 영국의 잔디만큼 부드럽고 모양새가 좋진 않았다. 대신, 토종 잔디는 질기고 통제하기 힘들 정도로 빨리 자랐다. 그러나 잔디 키우기에 대한 미국인들의 관심이 증가하자, 미국 농림부는 부드럽고 정돈된 영국식 잔디에 대한 미국인들의 열망에 부합하면서 다양한 미국 기후에서도 잘 자랄 수 있는 품종을 찾기 시작했다. 1915년 무렵, Kentucky Bluegrass라는 품종이 이에 대한 해결책으로 떠올랐고, 곧 토종의 잔디와 지피(地被)가 결합된 Kentucky Bluegrass가 수백만 미국 가정의 뜰을 뒤덮었다.

미국 가정의 외관을 바꾸는 것 외에도 잔디는 기술과 경제에도 중요한 영향을 끼쳤다. 심지어 무더운 여름에도 잔디에 물을 잘 주어야 했기 때문에 잔디에 물을 공급하는 가정 관개 기술이 향상되었다. 게다가 잔디를 다듬어야 할 필요성은 잔디 깎기 기계의 발전도 초래했다. 오늘날 잔디 관리 산업은 한 해 200억 달러 이상의 수익을 창출한다.

문 1 | 첫 번째 단락의 this feature가 가리키는 것은?
　Ⓐ 푸른 잔디밭
　Ⓑ 행복한 개
　Ⓒ 하얀 말뚝 울타리
　Ⓓ 굴뚝

해설 | 첫 번째 단락의 첫째 문장에서 하얀 말뚝, 굴뚝, 뛰어다니는 행복한 개와 더불어 미국 가정의 일반적인 이미지 중 하나로 꼽히는 것이 green grass lawn이라고 지문의 주제를 소개하고 있다. 보기를 대입해 보고, 뒤에 이어지는 내용들을 봤을 때 답은 Ⓐ가 된다.

문 2 | 첫 번째 단락에 따르면, 다음 중 사실과 다른 것은?
　Ⓐ 17세기에는 오직 부유층만 잔디 뜰을 가꿀 수 있었다.
　Ⓑ 잔디가 보편화되기 이전에 미국인들은 흙 마당을 갖고 있었다.
　Ⓒ 잔디 뜰은 오늘날 종종 지위의 상징으로 여겨진다.
　Ⓓ 전형적인 미국인 가정의 이미지를 완성하기 위해서는, 집에 하얀 울타리가 있어야 한다.

해설 | 예전에는 부의 상징으로 여겨졌으나 오늘날에는 전형적인 미국 가정의 이미지로 떠올려진다는 사실을 상기하면 답은 Ⓒ이다.

문 3 | 두 번째 단락의 tended to와 가장 의미가 유사한 것은?
　Ⓐ 심는
　Ⓑ 돌보는
　Ⓒ 물주는
　Ⓓ 수리하는

해설 | tend에는 (식물 등을) '기르다', '재배하다' 란 의미가 있다. 문맥에서 가장 맞는 것은 Ⓑ이다. 뒤의 부연설명으로 나오는 '질기고, 통제하기 힘들다' 는 것에서 뜻을 유추한다.

문 4 | 두 번째 단락의 they가 가리키는 것은?
　Ⓐ 미국인들
　Ⓑ 영국인들
　Ⓒ 토종 잔디
　Ⓓ 영국 잔디

해설 | 앞의 문장이 native North American grasses에 대해 언급하고 있다.

문 5 | 지문에 대한 간단한 요약을 위한 도입 문장이 아래에 제시된다. 가장 중요한 내용을 표현한 3가지 대답을 선택하여 요약을 완성하시오. 몇몇 문장들은 단락에서 언급되지 않았거나 중요하지 않은 내용을 표현해서 요약에 들어갈 수 없다.

대다수의 미국인들이 오늘날 잔디밭을 소유하고 있을지라도, 그것이 항상 전형적인 미국 뜰의 일부는 아니었다.

　Ⓐ 18세기까지 미국 부유층의 다수가 잘 관리된 뜰을 소유하고 있었다.
　Ⓑ 잔디를 가꾸는데 드는 비용 때문에 많은 사람들이 집 마당에 잔디를 어려웠다.
　Ⓒ 미국의 잔디 뜰에 대한 소유욕 증가가 잔디의 질을 개선시키는 결과를 낳았다.
　Ⓓ Kentucky Bluegrass가 없었다면 잔디 깎는 기계는 개발되지 않았을 것이다.
　Ⓔ 기르기 쉬운 잔디의 개량종의 개발은 많은 관련 사업들에 영향을 미쳤다.
　Ⓕ 잔디 품종이 형편없어서 미국인들은 잔디를 관리하기가 어려웠다.

해설 | 잔디가 보편적인 것이 아니라 특권층을 전유물이었으나, 집 마당에 잔디를 깔고 싶어 하는 다수의 욕구를 통해 미국 상황에 알맞은 품종의 잔디가 만들어졌고, 잔디가 관련 산업의 육성과 발전을 가져왔다는 것이 지문의 핵심 내용이다. Ⓐ와 Ⓕ는 minor한 내용이고, Ⓓ는 잘못 언급된 내용이다.

VOCABULARY TEST

정답 1. (C)   2. (A)   3. (B)   4. (D)   5. (B)
      6. (C)   7. (C)   8. (D)   9. (A)   10. (B)
      11. (C) 12. (D)

밑줄 친 어휘나 구와 가장 유사한 의미를 지닌 것을 고르시오.

1. 서양의 TV 프로그램은 중국 토착민의 전통적 가치관을 변화시키고 있다.
   (A) 근면한   (B) 총명한
   (C) 토착의   (D) 편견을 가진

2. 나는 누군가 나를 과소평가할 때 화가 난다. 누구든지 간에 나는 그들을 용서하지 않을 것이다.
   (A) (명예를) 손상시키다   (B) 비웃다
   (C) 동의하지 않다   (D) 비판하다

3. 나는 정부가 건물 안에서의 흡연을 금지시키기를 원한다.
   (A) 낙담시키다   (B) 막다
   (C) 부수다   (D) 파괴하다

4. 똑같은 외모를 가진 사람들은 없다. 성격 또한 다양하다.
   (A) 동일한   (B) 풍성한
   (C) 유창한   (D) 다른

5. Johnson 교수님의 강의는 끔찍했다. 특히 그의 발음이 웃겼다.
   (A) 부가적인   (B) 특히
   (C) 극심히   (D) 놀랍게도

6. 피부 선탠을 즐기는 사람들은 피부암에 걸리기 쉽다.
   (A) 어려운   (B) 민감한
   (C) 걸리기 쉬운   (D) 희망적인

7. 나이가 들어감에 따라 나는 어머니의 외모를 닮아간다.
   (A) 후회하다   (B) 적합하다
   (C) ~와 닮다   (D) 얻다

8. 꿀벌의 의사소통 체계는 매우 정교하다.
   (A) 영리한   (B) 단순한
   (C) 최고의   (D) 진보된

9. 폭동은 도시 안의 소수 민족의 비통함을 반영했다.
   (A) 보여주었다   (B) 갑절로 했다
   (C) 증명했다   (D) 해결했다

10. 피난민들의 유입으로 인해 많은 사회 문제들이 증가하고 있다.
    (A) 쇠퇴   (B) 급격한 증진
    (C) 출발   (D) 수입

11. 이 사본은 원본과 다소 차이가 있다.
    (A) 제조하다   (B) 유사하다
    (C) 차이가 나다   (D) 인용하다

12. 그녀는 회의에서 연설할 때 두려움을 해결하는 방법을 찾아내야만 했다.
    (A) 확인하다   (B) 협박하다
    (C) 몹시 놀라게 하다 (D) 다루다

Chapter 6 Details   p.126 - p.148

SAMPLE ITEM   정답 Ⓐ

해석 1950년대 미국은 현실적인 묘사보다 형태와 형상의 사용이 특징인 추상주의의 황금시대였다. 왜 이런 일이 벌어졌을까? 1950년대 이전 미국인들은 유럽의 사실주의 학파의 영향을 강하게 받고 있었다. 그러나, 50년대 미국의 예술가들은 그들만의 고유하고 독특한 미술 학파를 창조하길 갈망했다. 게다가 추상주의는 정치적이고 이념적인 이유 때문에도 매우 중요하게 여겨졌다. 50년대는 공산주의와 자본주의 간의 이데올로기적(이념적인) 전쟁이 절정에 달한 시기였다. 공산주의 사회들은 미술에 있어 인지 가능한 형태로 표현되는 현실주의 예술을 장려하였다. 그러자 추상주의는 자본주의 미술가들이 그들 스스로를 표현해야 했던 자유를 대표하게 되었다.

문제 | 다음 중 미국에서 추상주의가 발전한 이유로 언급되지 않은 것은?
Ⓐ 유럽 미술 학파의 영향
Ⓑ 공산주의와 자본주의 사이의 갈등
Ⓒ 독특한 예술 학파를 발달시키고자 하는 욕구
Ⓓ 자유를 표현하고자 하는 시도

해설 | 미국에서 추상주의가 발달하게 된 원인 중 하나는 기존 유럽의 사실주의 학파의 영향에서 벗어나고자 했던 욕구 때문이다.

Basic Drill 1

정답 1. (1)-(B), (2)-(D), (3)-(A)
      2. (1)-(A), (2)-(B), (3)-(B)

1. **해석** 전파 망원경과 위성 같은 현대 기술적인 진보는 현대인이 우주에 대해 더 잘 이해할 수 있게 도움을 주었

다. 그러나, 인간은 수 천년 동안 하늘에서 일어나는 변화와 사건들을 이해하기 위해 도구들을 사용해 왔다. 이런 하나의 예는 달력이다. 어떤 달력은 달에서 일어나는 변화를 관찰함으로써 만들어졌다. 다른 것들은 태양과 별의 움직임을 사용해 시간의 경과를 기록했다. 이러한 고대 달력의 증거는 몇 군데 다른 대륙에서 여전히 발견되고 있다. 영국에 있는 거대한 환상열석인 스톤헨지는 달력의 일종이라고 여겨진다. 어떤 사람들은 그것이 태양에 의한 시간의 경과를 측정했다고 생각한다. 마찬가지로, 고대의 북미 원주민들은 달의 변화를 기록하기 위해 환상열석을 사용하였다.

문 1 | 우주를 연구하기 위한 고대 도구의 증거가 되는 것은?
(A) 달의 변화를 기록하기 위한 돌 지대
(B) 시간 경과를 기록하기 위해 사용된 원형 구성물
(C) (태양의) 지점을 표시하기 위해 사용된 피라미드 구조물
(D) 별들의 위치를 적은 종이 조각

해설 | (B)의 '원형의 형태'라는 것이 본문에 나오는 stone circle, 즉 stonehenge라는 것을 알 수 있다.

문 2 | 도구에 관한 내용 중 사실인 것은?
(A) 현대 기술은 고대 달력들이 정확하지 않다는 것을 밝혀냈다.
(B) 하늘을 연구하기 위해 사용된 고대 도구들은 (현대 도구들에 비해) 더 발달되어 있었다.
(C) 고대에 별들 사이의 거리를 판단하는 것이 가능했다.
(D) 우주를 이해하기 위한 고대 도구들은 많은 장소에서 발견되어진다.

해설 | 몇몇 대륙에서 증거들이 발견됐다는 내용으로 보아, 여러 곳에서 고대 도구들이 발견되었다는 것을 알 수 있다.

문 3 | 환상열석은 어디에 사용되었는가?
(A) 태양이나 달의 움직임을 관찰하기 위하여
(B) 태양의 변화를 기록하기 위하여
(C) 지구 가까이 있는 행성들을 이해하기 위하여
(D) 시간을 기록하기 위하여

해설 | 환상열석은 태양의 움직임에 의한 시간의 경과를 기록하고, 달의 변화를 기록하는 데 사용되었다.

2. 해석 식량 생산과 (외관상) 미적인 부분을 향상시키기 위해 식물이나 종자를 고의적으로 조작하는 것을 원예라고 부른다. 인류는 식물의 최종 산물이라 할 수 있는 과일과 야채, 또는 꽃을 더 잘 얻기 위해 야생 식물의 씨를 저장하고 경작하면서 최소 만 천년 동안 원예를 실시해왔다. 이것은 재배에 대한 지식을 증가시켰을 뿐 아니라 (원예에 있어) 주요한 기술적인 혁신을 가져왔다. 예를 들어, 기원전 2800년까지 이집트인들은 파라오의 정원을 위해 광범위하고 복잡한 관개 시스템을 설계했다. 그리고 기원전 1700년까지 메소포타미아인들은 가장 좋은 파종 시기와 방법에 대한 정보를 담고 있는 연감을 완성했다.

문 1 | 원예의 목적은 무엇인가?
(A) 식물 발달의 최종 산물에 영향을 미치기 위하여
(B) 새로운 기술을 정당화하기 위하여
(C) 새로운 종의 꽃을 발명하기 위하여
(D) 가능한 많은 식량을 생산하기 위하여

해설 | 지문의 첫째 문장을 보면 원예가 식량 생산량을 높이거나, 외관상 미적인 측면에서 더 매력적으로 보이도록 만들기 위해 발달했다는 것을 알 수 있다.

문 2 | 이집트 정원에 대한 내용 중 올바른 것은?
(A) 고대 시대에 원예 기술로 가꾸어진 최초의 예(정원)이다.
(B) 물을 공급하는 시스템은 왕족을 위해 발달했다.
(C) 일반적으로 메소포타미아에 있는 정원들보다 더 훌륭했다.
(D) 그 당시 많은 이집트인들에게 인기가 있었다.

해설 | 왕의 정원을 가꾸기 위해 광범위하고 복잡한 관개 시스템이 설계되었다는 내용이 나온다.

문 3 | 메소포타미아인들은 원예 지식에 어떻게 기여했는가?
(A) 가뭄 동안 식물을 생존시킬 수 있는 방법을 발견함으로써
(B) 가장 좋은 수확을 거두기 위해 각각의 다른 종자들이 언제 심겨져야 하는지를 연구함으로써
(C) 메소포타미아에서 재배하기에 가장 좋은 식물들에 관한 책을 씀으로써
(D) 이집트의 진보된 관개 기술을 향상시킴으로써

해설 | 마지막 문장에 보면 메소포타미아인들이 각 식물의 최고의 파종시기와 방법을 담은 내용의 연감을 완성했다고 나와 있다.

Basic Drill 2

정답 1. (1) - (B), (2) - (C)   2. (1) - (C), (2) - (B)

1. 해석 미국으로 들어오는 이민자의 수는 많은 요인에 의해 매년 다르다. 20세기 초반 10년 동안의 이민은 그 시기의 미국의 인구 증가의 거의 반을 차지한다. 반면, 그 시기 동안의 자연적 증가는 매해 겨우 약 1퍼센트의 인구 성정에 그쳤다. 이것에 대한 이유는 무수히 많지만 자유 이민 정책이 가장 큰 원인이었다. 그러나 이민에 의한 미국의 인구 성장 퍼센트는 1930년대 동안 가파르게 감소하여 그 기간 동안의 인구 증가의 겨우 1.5퍼센트를 차지한다. 대공황과 2차 세계대전의 시작이 사람들의 이민을 막았다. 20세기 말까지, 부강한 경제와 넘쳐나는 직업이 더 많은 이민자를 끌어들였고, 그들은 국가 인구 성장의 30퍼센트를 차지

했다.

문 1 | 다음 중 사실이 아닌 것은?
(A) 대공황과 2차 세계대전 후 이민은 증가했다.
(B) 오늘날 미국 인구 성장의 거의 반은 이민에 의한 것이다.
(C) 미국 이민의 비율은 경제적 요인에 의해 크게 영향을 받았다.
(D) 바로 앞 세기 동안 이민은 인구 성장에 가장 큰 영향을 미쳤다.

해설 | 이민이 미국 인구 증가의 반을 차지한 것은 1910년대이다.

문 2 | 하나를 제외한 나머지는 1930년대의 급격한 이민의 감소를 설명한다.
(A) 세계 경제가 좋지 않아서 이민을 갈 이유가 없었다.
(B) 전쟁으로 사람들이 쉽게 이동할 수 없었다.
(C) 미국 내에 이민을 반대하는 많은 폭력이 있었다.
(D) 미국에서 거의 직업을 구할 수 없었다.

해설 | 그 시기는 세계적으로 경제 대공황의 상태였고, 이로 인해 미국 내에서도 일자리를 얻기가 어려웠으며 2차 세계대전이 발발하면서 이민율이 더 감소했다는 내용이 나와 있다.

2. 해석   신원 위장 절도나 사기는 고의적으로 다른 사람의 신분으로 가장하는 것이며, 나라에서 가장 빠르게 성장하고 있는 범죄 중 하나이다. 이 범죄는 범위나 비용에 있어 지난 10년 동안 성장하고 있다.

인터넷으로 물건을 구매하기 위한 신용카드 사용의 증가에서부터 최근 증가하는 직장내 ID 절도까지, 이런 류의 범죄가 발생하는 데는 여러 이유가 있지만 그 중 한 원인이 두드러진다. 단순히, 누군가의 ID를 인터넷상에서 훔치는 것은 개인과 관계가 없는 일이라는 점이다. 심지어 가장 비정한 범죄자들도 그들이 희생자와 얼굴을 마주 대하고 만날 때에는 공감의 감정을 느낀다고 알려져 있다. 그러나 사이버 공간에서 절도를 할 때, 희생자들은 자기들이 알지도, 본 적도 없는 사람들이다. 그들은 그저 컴퓨터 화면 상에서 이름과 숫자일 뿐이다.

신원 정보를 손에 넣는 기술은 단순히 메일을 훔치거나 쓰레기를 뒤지는 것과 같은 조잡한 것에서부터 컴퓨터의 데이터베이스에 있는 개인 정보를 훔쳐내는 것이나 대량의 개인 정보를 저장하고 있는 조직이나 기관에 침투하는 것과 같은 보다 정교한 절도에까지 이른다.

문 1 | 그래프에 의하면 하나를 제외한 나머지는 올바른 내용이다.
(A) 2000년까지 신원 사기의 발생은 폭발적으로 증가했다.
(B) 1990년부터 1995년 사이 신원 관련 범죄의 총체적 수치는 거의 변화가 없었다.
(C) 1990년에 인터넷 신원 사기는 전체 신원 사기 사건의 40 퍼센트를 차지한다.
(D) 전체적인 신원 사기 사건이 약 백만 건 이상 증가하면서, 1996년까지 두 배 이상 늘어났다.

해설 | 인터넷 신원 사기는 전체 신원 사기의 약 20% 정도의 수치를 나타내고 있다.

문 2 | 다음 중 신원을 손에 넣는 기술의 예가 아닌 것은?
(A) 은행 데이트베이스에 몰래 들어가기
(B) 기관을 도청하기
(C) 메일함 뒤지기
(D) 쓰레기에서 찾기

해설 | 도청 또는 엿듣는 것은 언급되지 않았다.

VOCABULARY Preview

Check-up

1. scarce   2. absorbs   3. devastating
4. adapt   5. suspected   6. consequence
7. make up   8. reverse

다음 빈 칸에 들어갈 알맞은 말을 골라, 필요하면 고쳐 쓰시오.

1. 사막에서는 물이 <u>부족하고</u> 사는 데 비용이 많이 든다.
2. Nina는 천재야! 그녀는 무엇이든지 배우는 족족 <u>흡수해</u>.
3. 두 나라 사이의 마찰은 이들 나라의 경제에 <u>엄청나게 파괴적인</u> 결과를 가져다 줄 수 있었다.
4. 우리 가족이 다른 나라로 이주했을 때 나는 새로운 환경에 <u>적응해야</u> 했다.
5. 그는 Susan의 동기를 <u>의심했고</u> 그녀의 제안을 비판했다.
6. 그 비참한 사고는 운전자의 부주의의 <u>결과</u>였다.
7. 관광업과 무역이 이 나라 산업의 대부분을 <u>구성한다</u>.
8. 그들은 연구팀을 지원하겠다는 그들의 결정을 <u>뒤집지</u> 않을 것이라고 약속했다.

Exercise 1

정답   1. ⓑ   2. ⓒ   3. ⓓ   4. ⓒ   5. ⓑ
        6. ⓐ, ⓑ, ⓔ

해석   비록 일생 동안 출판된 시는 5편도 안 되지만 에밀리 디킨슨은 미국에서 가장 유명한 시인 중 한 명이다.

그녀의 시는 19세기 중 후반 동안 쓰여진 다른 시들과 완전히 다르다. 부분적으로 이것은 그녀가 받은 영향이 매우 다양하기 때문이다. 그녀는 문학 뿐 아니라 과학, 정치학, 철학에 관한 책들을 읽었다. 이런 주제들이 그녀의 시에 종종 놀라운 방법으로 표현된다.

디킨슨의 시는 종종 첫눈에 알아볼 수 있고, 다른 시인의 작품과는 다르다. 그녀의 독특한 서정적 문체는 원고안에서 대시의 광범위한 사용과 관습을 깬 대문자 쓰기, 그리고 독특한 어휘와 수사적 표현의 조합으로 창조된다. 또한 그녀는 자기 시에 8, 6, 8, 6 길이의 네 줄로 이루어진 종교적인 찬송가 율격인 보통률(common meter)을 사용했다. 이는 평범하고 일상적인 것이 시에서 어떤 역할을 한다고 생각하는 그녀의 생각을 보여준다.

디킨슨은 몇 가지 이유로 (시집을) 출판하는 데 흥미를 느끼지 않았다. 그 당시의 여류 시인들은 낭만적인 사랑과 가족에 대한 감성적인 시를 쓰도록 요구되어졌는데, 디킨슨은 죽음과 인생의 의미, 열정적인 사랑을 포함하는 존재에 관한 철학적인 문제들에 더 관심이 있었다. 그녀가 여류 시인들에게 기대되는 역할에 들어맞지 않았기 때문에 그녀는 자신의 작품이 세상에 쉽게 받아들여지지 않으리란 사실을 알았다. 또한 그녀는 편집자들이 좋은 의도로 세상이 받아들일 수 있도록 자기의 작품을 손을 봐서 바꿀지도 모른다고 생각했다. 이것은 자신의 작품에게 벌어지길 원하는 것이 아니었기 때문에 디킨슨은 오직 친구들과 가족에게만 자신의 작품을 보여주었다. 그녀가 죽은 후에야 가족들은 디킨슨의 시적인 업적을 인정받기 위해 노력할 수 있었다. 20세기의 처음 반세기(1950년대)에 들어서, 비록 여류 시인들이 여전히 비교적 드물었지만, 디킨슨은 거장으로 널리 간주되었다.

문 1 | 첫 번째 단락의 diverse와 가장 의미가 유사한 것은?
Ⓐ 복잡한
Ⓑ 다양한
Ⓒ 어려운
Ⓓ 효과적인

해설 | diverse는 '다양한' 이라는 의미이다. 뒤에 부연되는 다양한 분야의 책들을 통해 그 뜻을 유추한다.

문 2 | 두 번째 단락의 employed와 가장 의미가 유사한 것은?
Ⓐ 약속된
Ⓑ 입장한
Ⓒ 적용된
Ⓓ 추천된

해설 | 본문에서 사용된 employ는 '고용하다' 가 아닌 '~에 쓰다' 라는 의미로, hymns에 대한 설명에서 나오는 use가 힌트가 된다.

문 3 | 두 번째 단락에서 디킨슨의 독특한 서정시 스타일에 대한 솜씨로 언급되지 않은 것은?
Ⓐ 다른 문법적 구조
Ⓑ 일상적이지 않은 어휘
Ⓒ 음악적인 찬송가 운율
Ⓓ 상상적인 삽화

해설 | 디킨슨의 시는 일반적인 문법의 파괴와 독특한 수사적 표현, 특이한 어휘의 사용, 그리고 찬송가에 많이 쓰이는 음악적 운율의 사용이 특징이다.

문 4 | 다음 중 세 번째 단락의 하이라이트 된 문장의 핵심 내용을 가장 잘 표현한 것은? 틀린 보기는 본문의 내용을 심각하게 바꾸거나 핵심적인 내용을 누락시킨 것이다.
Ⓐ 전형적인 여성 시로 시인의 직업을 시작한 이후, 디킨슨은 방향을 바꾸어 자신이 관심을 가진 것들에 대해 썼다.
Ⓑ 디킨슨은 다수의 큰 개념을 포함한 철학적인 주제에 대한 감상적인 시를 쓸 수 있었다.
Ⓒ 다른 여류 시인들은 감성적인 시를 쓸 것이라고 여겨졌지만 디킨슨은 진지한 문제들에 더 관심이 있었다.
Ⓓ 죽음과 삶, 그리고 사랑은 디킨슨이 가장 관심을 가졌던 것들인데, 이는 사회가 여류 시인들에게 가졌던 관습적인 기대와는 반대되는 것이었다.

해설 | 하이라이트 된 문장의 핵심 내용은 일반적으로 사회에서 기대했던 여류 시인들의 시의 주제는 낭만적인 사랑이나 가족과 같은 감성적인 것이었던 것에 반해 디킨슨은 보다 진지한 철학적인 주제들을 다루었다는 것이다.

문 5 | 세 번째 단락에 따르면, 디킨슨이 출판을 꺼린 이유는 무엇인가?
Ⓐ 작품의 질에 대한 자신이 없었다.
Ⓑ 시 원본이 바뀔 것을 걱정했다.
Ⓒ 타인이 자신의 작품을 읽기를 원치 않았다.
Ⓓ 좋은 의도를 가진 편집자들만이 자신의 작품을 가장 잘 감상할 수 있을 것이라고 생각했다.

해설 | 디킨슨은 자신의 시가 시대의 요구에 맞게 고쳐질 것을 두려워했다.

문 6 | 지문에 대한 간단한 요약을 위한 도입 문장이 아래에 제시된다. 가장 중요한 내용을 표현한 3가지 대답을 선택하여 요약을 완성하시오. 몇몇 문장들은 단락에서 언급되지 않았거나 중요하지 않은 내용을 표현해서 요약에 들어갈 수 없다.

에밀리 디킨슨은 미국의 가장 유명한 시인 중 한 명이다.

Ⓐ 디킨슨의 시는 그녀의 독특한 문체와 많은 특이한 요소들이 특징이다.
Ⓑ 디킨슨은 그 문체와 그 당시로는 독특했던 시의 주제들로 유명한 시인이다.
Ⓒ 디킨슨의 독특한 서정적 문체는 시 속에 독특하게 사용된 많은 어휘를 통해 알 수 있다.
Ⓓ 디킨슨은 가장 유명한 시인 중 한 명이었지만, 그녀의 독특한 문체 때문에 많은 시가 출판되지 않았다.
Ⓔ 디킨슨이 다루는 주제나 시는 그 당시에는 널리 받아들

여지지 않았기 때문에, 사후에 훨씬 유명해졌다.
Ⓕ 디킨슨 죽고난 후, 그녀의 시들은 친구들에 의해 우연히 출판되었고, 이것을 통해 그녀는 명성을 얻게 되었다.

해설 | Ⓒ의 내용은 Ⓐ에 대한 부연 설명이라 할 수 있고, Ⓓ와 Ⓕ는 틀린 내용을 언급하고 있다.

Exercise 2

정답 1. Ⓑ 2. Ⓐ 3. Ⓓ 4. Ⓓ 5. Ⓒ
      6. Typical Plant: Ⓓ, Ⓔ, Ⓕ /
         Drought-tolerant Plant: Ⓐ, Ⓒ

해석 지구 표면의 75%를 구성하는 물은 지구상에서 가장 귀중한 자원 중 하나이다. 지구상 어떤 지역들은 비나 홍수 등 너무 많은 물로 인해 고통을 받는 반면, 다른 지역은 몇 해에 걸친 긴 가뭄으로 고통을 겪는다. 이런 지역의 물 부족은 완전히 파괴적일 수 있다. 기근은 하나의 결과이다. 게다가 주요 전염병이 자주 발생한다. 그러므로 충분하지 않은 물로도 식물을 재배할 수 있게 사람들을 도울 수 있는 방법을 찾는 것이 매우 중요하다.

이것을 이룰 수 있는 한가지 방법은 과학을 통해서이다. 많은 물이 필요 없는 가뭄에 강한 식물과 일반 작물의 유전자 교배를 통해 오랜 기간 물 없이도 살 수 있는 작물을 만들게 될 것이다. 이것은 이 지역들에서 계속 작물을 재배하고, 비가 부족할 때일지라도 굶주림과 질병을 막을 수 있게 도움을 줄 것이다.

아프리카의 사하라 사막 아래 지역에 서식하는 한 식물은 가뭄을 매우 잘 견딘다. 이 부활초(resurrection plant)는 산에 서식하고 물 없이도 몇 달을 버틸 수 있다. 비가 오면, 이 식물은 다량의 물을 흡수하고 이 물을 세포에 저장한다. 이곳에 저장된 물이 가뭄이 계속될 동안 식물이 살아남을 수 있게 돕는다. 게다가, 부활초는 강한 바람과 큰 기온 변화에도 잘 견딘다. 이것은, 매일 지속적인 물의 공급이 필요한 옥수수와 같은 식물과는 아주 대조적이다. 옥수수는 물을 효율적으로 사용하지 않는다. 물을 오랫동안 저장할 수도 없다. 옥수수나 다른 식용 작물은 추운 날씨와 강한 바람에 적응하는 데 어려움이 있고 (이런 상황에서) 생존하기 힘들다.

문 1 | 첫 번째 단락의 plagued와 가장 의미가 유사한 것은?
Ⓐ 무시당하는
Ⓑ 고통 당하는
Ⓒ 축복 받는
Ⓓ 영향 받는

해설 | be plagued는 '괴롭힘을 당하다'라는 뜻으로 too much water와 비교되는 뒷문장의 suffer에서 힌트를 얻을 수 있다.

문 2 | 첫 번째 단락에 따르면, 다음 중 물 부족 결과로 일어날 수 있는 것은?
Ⓐ 혹독한 식량 부족
Ⓑ 마른 강바닥, 호수, 우물
Ⓒ 알려지지 않은 질병의 증가
Ⓓ 물이 부족한 지역의 사회적 불안정

해설 | Ⓑ와 Ⓓ는 언급되지 않은 내용이고, 세상에 알려지지 않은 질병이 증가하는 것이 아니라 주요 질병들이 창궐한다는 내용이 나와 있으므로 Ⓒ는 틀린 보기이다.

문 3 | 두 번째 단락의 stave off와 가장 의미가 유사한 것은?
Ⓐ 견디다
Ⓑ 파괴하다
Ⓒ 줄이다
Ⓓ 막다

해설 | stave off는 '막다', '피하다'란 의미이다. 문맥상 식량을 재배해 굶주림과 질병을 막는다는 뜻임을 파악할 수 있다.

문 4 | 세 번째 단락의 them이 가리키는 것은?
Ⓐ 부활초
Ⓑ 나쁜 상황
Ⓒ 가뭄에 강한 식물
Ⓓ 옥수수 같은 식물

해설 | them은 drought-tolerant plants와 비교되고 있는 다른 식물들이다.

문 5 | 세 번째 단락에 따르면, 다음 중 부활초에 관해 가장 잘 설명하는 것은?
Ⓐ 햇빛은 더 적게 필요로 해도 옥수수보다 훨씬 더 많은 수확을 낸다.
Ⓑ 강한 바람과 추위를 못 견딘다.
Ⓒ 자기 몸 안에 물을 저장할 수 있고 척박한 환경도 견뎌낼 수 있다.
Ⓓ 주로 사막에서 잘 자라고 풍부한 물 공급이 필요하다.

해설 | Ⓐ는 지문에 언급되지 않은 내용이다. Ⓑ는 옥수수와 같은 식물의 특성 중 하나이고, Ⓓ도 잘못된 내용이다.

문 6 | 적절한 보기를 골라 관련있는 식물 종류와 짝지으시오. 두 개의 보기는 제외됩니다.
Ⓐ 매해 단 몇 번만 물을 필요로 한다.
Ⓑ 생존하기 위해 많은 미네랄을 가진 토양이 필요하다.
Ⓒ 날씨가 다양해도 살 수 있다.
Ⓓ 단기간만 물을 저장할 수 있다.
Ⓔ 날씨가 극단적이면 죽을 것이다.
Ⓕ 지속적인 물의 공급이 필요하다.
Ⓖ 충분한 햇빛 없이도 좋은 수확을 낼 수 있다.

해설 | Ⓑ와 Ⓖ는 지문에 언급되지 않은 내용이다.

Exercise 3

정답 1. ⓑ 2. ⓒ 3. ⓑ 4. ⓒ 5. ⓒ 6. ⓓ
    7. ⓓ 8. ⓐ, ⓓ, ⓔ

Text Outline (B)

해석 20세기 초는 짧은 주당 근무시간을 지지하는 사람들의 승리로 기록되었다. 40시간, 주5일 근무가 대다수 근로자의 표준 근무 시간이 되었다. 이 시간을 초과해서 일하는 자들을 위한 초과 근무에 대한 보상 또한 마련되었다. 그러나 지난 이십 년 동안, 더 많은 근로자들이 초과 근무 수당을 거의 혹은 전혀 받지 못 하고 더 오랜 시간을 사무실에서 보내게 되면서 이러한 여가시간의 획득은 거꾸로 되었다.

　이런 경향은 몇 가지 요인에 의한 결과이다. 첫 번째는 노동 인구의 감소라는 결과를 초래하게 된 1980년대 후반과 90년대 후반에 걸친 경제 침체이다. 두 번째는 같은 기간 동안 생산성에 대한 요구는 같거나 높아졌다는 점이다. 세 번째는 시장에 직업이 부족하기에 고용인들이 작업 시간에 대한 요구의 증가를 거절할 수 없었다는 것이다. 그래서 더 많은 일을 할 수 있는 사람은 더 적어졌다. 요구에 부응하기 위해 남은 근로자들은 더 오랜 근무시간에 투입되어야 했다. 그리고 그들은 이런 상황에 항의할 수 있는 처지가 아니었다.

　감소된 노동력에도 불구하고, 이런 경향이 직장에서 생산성을 끊임없이 높이는 것을 용인하게 되면서, 이로 인해 건강상 부정적인 결과가 초래되었다. 실제로 최근의 직장 내 상해 관련 연구는 초과 근무를 하는 근로자는 주당 40시간 근무하는 노동자보다 부상을 입거나 병이 날 가능성이 2배 이상이라고 밝혔다. 그리고 하루에 12시간 또는 그 이상을 근무하는 근로자는 부정적인 건강 결과로 고통 당하게 될 확률이 3배에 달한다.

문 1 | 첫 번째 단락의 compensation과 가장 의미가 유사한 것은?
Ⓐ 스케줄
Ⓑ 보상
Ⓒ 획득
Ⓓ 전투

해설 | compensation은 '보상', '배상'의 의미이다. 뒤에 나오는 extra pay for that overtime에서 힌트를 얻을 수 있다.

문 2 | 첫 번째 단락의 this가 가리키는 것은?
Ⓐ 초과 근무 수당
Ⓑ 여가 시간
Ⓒ 40시간, 주 5일 근무
Ⓓ 근무 시간

해설 | this를 초과하여 근무하는 사람들에게 초과 근무 수당이 주어진다는 내용으로 보아, 40시간, 주 5일 근무 짧아진 근무 시간을 가리킨다는 것을 알 수 있다.

문 3 | 첫 번째 단락의 instituted와 가장 의미가 유사한 것은?
Ⓐ 강요된
Ⓑ 시작된
Ⓒ 보증한
Ⓓ 허용된

해설 | institute는 '규칙 등을 제정하다', '실시하다'란 의미로, also를 통해 앞에 나오는 became standard와 유사한 뜻임을 알 수 있다.

문 4 | 첫 번째 단락에 따르면, 20세기 초의 작업 조건의 변화로 언급된 것은?
Ⓐ 총체적인 (급여) 지불 금액의 인상
Ⓑ (근로자) 훈련에 대한 수요의 증가
Ⓒ 주당 근무 시간의 감소
Ⓓ 초과 근무에 대한 필요성 감소

해설 | 처음 두 문장에 단축된 근로 시간에 대한 언급이 나온다.

문 5 | 두 번째 단락에 따르면, 1980년대 말 노동인구의 감소에 대한 원인으로 제시된 것은?
Ⓐ 생산성 레벨의 감소
Ⓑ 고도로 숙련된 근로자들에 대한 수요
Ⓒ 경제 상황의 침체
Ⓓ 생산 과정의 자동화

해설 | Ⓐ의 생산성 수준에 대한 요구는 예전과 같거나 더 높아졌고, Ⓑ와 Ⓓ는 언급되지 않은 내용이다.

문 6 | 다음 중 세 번째 단락의 하이라이트 된 문장의 핵심 내용을 가장 잘 표현한 것은? 틀린 보기는 본문의 내용을 심각하게 바꾸거나 핵심적인 내용을 누락시킨 것이다.
Ⓐ 설령 아파도, 남아 있는 적은 수의 근로자들은 계속적으로 더 많이 생산을 하고 있다.
Ⓑ 생산성의 전반적인 향상을 노동자 건강의 긍정적인 결과로 볼 수 있다.
Ⓒ 건강에 대한 경고에도 불구하고 근로자들은 계속 오랜 시간 일하고 많은 다른 일을 한다.
Ⓓ 근로자들은 다른 도움 없이 생산을 늘리고 있는데, 이것이 질병과 상해를 증가시켰다.

해설 | 하이라이트 된 문장의 핵심 내용은, 노동 인력이 감소했는데도 작업 생산성에 대한 요구는 계속 증가하여 이것이 결과적으로 근로자들의 건강에 악영향을 초래했다는 것이다.

문 7 | 그래프에 따르면, 다음 중 사실이 아닌 것은?
Ⓐ 상해 건수는 1960대부터 끊임없이 증가하고 있다.
Ⓑ 상해 수치는 초반 20년간 근무 시간이 줄어들면서 내려갔다.
Ⓒ 근무 시간이 주당 40시간 이하로 내려감에 따라 상해 수치도 떨어졌다.
Ⓓ 비록 노동 시간은 1920년대에 평준화되었지만, 상해

수치는 1970년대가 지나 떨어졌다.

해설 | 1920년대에 근무 시간이 짧게 평준화되면서 상해 수치도 떨어졌다.

문 8 | 지문에 대한 간단한 요약을 위한 도입 문장이 아래에 제시된다. 가장 중요한 내용을 표현한 3가지 대답을 선택하여 요약을 완성하시오. 몇몇 문장들은 단락에서 언급되지 않았거나 중요하지 않은 내용을 표현해서 요약에 들어갈 수 없다.

20세기 초가 되어 근로자들의 근무 시간이 줄어들기 시작했다.

Ⓐ 비록 표준 주 근로 시간은 정해졌지만 근로자들은 초과 근무에 대한 특별 수당 없이도 더 일을 하는 경향이 있다.
Ⓑ 1980년대에는 일자리가 부족했기 때문에 근로자들은 유리한 협상 위치에 있지 않았다.
Ⓒ 근무 시간과 상해가 20세기에 들어서 처음에는 감소했지만, 나중에 다시 증가했다.
Ⓓ 경제적 요인들은 1980년대와 90년대에 노동력이 감소시켰고 이는 근로자들이 더 오래 근무해야 함을 의미했다.
Ⓔ 길어진 근무 시간은 직업적 상해 발생에 직접적인 영향을 미친다.
Ⓕ 근로자들의 불안은 주당 40시간의 근무 시간과 초과 근무에 대한 보상을 포함한 여러 변화를 초래했다.

해설 | Ⓑ와 Ⓒ는 핵심적이지 않은 내용이다. Ⓕ는 틀린 내용이다.

VOCABULARY TEST

정답 1. (D) 2. (B) 3. (C) 4. (A) 5. (B)
     6. (D) 7. (A) 8. (B) 9. (D) 10. (D)
     11. (C)

밑줄 친 어휘나 구와 가장 유사한 의미를 지닌 것을 고르시오.

1. 나는 불법 체재자에게 동등한 권리가 주어져야 한다는 것을 지지하는 사람 중 한 명이다.
   (A) 반대자   (B) 상담자
   (C) 자원자   (D) 지지자

2. 과학자들은 유전자 조작을 통해 작물의 생산성을 늘리는 것을 연구하고 있다.
   (A) 치료   (B) 조종
   (C) 수단   (D) 예절

3. 엄마는 귀중한 보석을 많이 갖고 계시고, 언젠가는 그것을 내게 물려주실 것이다.
   (A) 훌륭한   (B) 의미 있는
   (C) 값비싼   (D) 착수된

4. 테러에 대한 공포는 아직 미국 내에서 줄어들지 않았다.
   (A) 감소시켰다 (B) 증가했다
   (C) 인식했다   (D) 제거했다

5. 우리 회사는 부적합한 노동 인구의 과잉으로 고통을 겪고 있다.
   (A) 부족   (B) 과잉
   (C) 공급   (D) 수요

6. 세계는 빠르게 변화하고 있고, 우리는 그 변화에 따라 우리 스스로를 적응시켜야 한다.
   (A) 채택하다   (B) 극복하다
   (C) 동의하다   (D) 조절하다

7. Maggie는 넓은 밭을 소유하고 있고 홀로 그 밭을 경작한다.
   (A) 경작하다   (B) 감상하다
   (C) 수정하다   (D) 계산하다

8. 그런 의견은 이 논문의 범주에 들어가지 않는다.
   (A) 초점   (B) 범위
   (C) 능력   (D) 요점

9. 혹독한 가뭄이 지나면 식량이 부족하게 된다.
   (A) 풍부한   (B) 멀어지는
   (C) 악명 높은   (D) 불충분한

10. 그녀는 사무실에서 남들보다 앞서고자 항상 노력한다.
    (A) 주장하다   (B) 토론하다
    (C) 등한시하다 (D) 애쓰다

11. 아침에 일찍 일어나서 운동을 해야 할 무수히 많은 이유가 있다.
    (A) 거의 없는 (B) 적당한
    (C) 무수한   (D) 의도하지 않은

Progress Test 3

정답 1. Ⓑ 2. Ⓒ 3. Ⓒ 4. Ⓐ 5. Ⓓ
     6. Ⓒ 7. Ⓑ 8. Ⓐ 9. Ⓓ 10. Ⓑ, Ⓒ, Ⓕ

해석 알츠하이머병은 두뇌 질환으로, 오랜 시간에 걸쳐 기억력 상실과 치매(감각과 인지에 대한 통제력의 상실)를 가져오고 결국은 죽음에 이르게 한다. 이는 기억을 통제하는 두뇌 부위에 단백질이 축적되면서 시작된다. 이 늘어난 단백질은 끝에는 두뇌의 광범위한 부위에 영향을 미치는 데까지 발전하게 된다. 알츠하이머병은 주로 나이 든 사람에게 발병하지만, 정상적인 노화 과정의 일부는 아니다. 이 병의 진행과정에 대해서는 연구가 잘 이루어져 있지만 그 원인은 분명하지 않다. 그러나 어떤 사람들이 다른 사람들에 비해 더 쉽게 이 병에 걸리도록 할 수 있는 요인에 대해서는 몇 가지 이론이 있다.

그 중 한 가지는 유전적인 요인이다. 연구결과를 보면, 이 병에 걸린 부모나 형제자매가 있는 사람들은 이 병에 걸릴 위험이 높아진다. 사실, 가족들 중에 알츠하이머병을 앓고 있는 사람이 많을수록 그 위험성은 더욱 증가한다. 가족들이 이 병에 걸린 경우 발병 위험성이 높아지기는 하지만, 어머니와 형제가 알츠하이머병에 걸렸다고 하여 본인 또한 이 병에 걸린다고 장담할 수는 없다. 오히려 유전자는 그저 사람들이 이 병에 좀더 걸리기 쉽게 만들 수 있는 요인의 한 가지일 뿐이다.

알츠하이머병을 발병시킬 가능성을 높이는 것으로 보이는 또 다른 요인은 뇌졸중이나 고혈압, 머리 부상에 의해 발생한 두뇌 손상이다. 이러한 문제를 겪은 사람들은 나중에 알츠하이머병에 걸릴 위험성이 약간 높아진다. 과학자들은 세포 손상으로 알츠하이머병에 더 걸리기 쉽다고 언급한다. 그러나 다시 한 번 말하지만, 두뇌 손상이 이 두뇌 질환을 일으킬 것이라고 장담할 수 없다.

세 번째 잠재적인 원인은 환경이다. 이 이론은 이 병에 관해 거론한 모든 설명 가운데 가장 논란이 되는 것이며, 또한 가장 지지를 받지 못하고 있는 이론이다. 알루미늄과 기타 금속에 노출되는 환경이 궁극적으로 이 질병을 발생시킨다는 소수의 연구결과와 연관되어 있다. 그러나 이러한 연관성을 발견하지 못한 연구결과들도 있다. 몇 사람의 의견에도 불구하고, 금속이 발병의 원인이 된다는 것은 아무래도 한계가 있다. 더 많은 임상연구가 이루어지지 않는다면 그러한 의견은 타당성이 없다고 봐야 한다. 환경적인 요인들이 비극적인 질병을 일으킨다는 증거는 충분하지 않다.

문 1 | 첫 번째 단락의 accumulation과 가장 의미가 유사한 것은?
Ⓐ 증거
Ⓑ 추가
Ⓒ 출현
Ⓓ 중독

해설 | accumulation은 '누적', '퇴적'이라는 뜻이다. 뒤에 나오는 This increased protein에서 힌트를 얻을 수 있다.

문 2 | 첫 번째 단락의 strikes와 가장 의미가 유사한 것은?
Ⓐ 눈감아주다
Ⓑ 걱정하다
Ⓒ 영향을 미치다
Ⓓ 기진맥진하게 하다

해설 | strike는 '공격하다', '치다' 등의 의미를 지닌다. 본문에서 '나이든 사람들을 strike한다'는 것은 나이든 사람들이 그 병에 걸린다는 것이고, 뒤에 나오는 more likely to get it에서 힌트를 얻을 수 있다.

문 3 | 두 번째 단락의 one이 가리키는 것은?
Ⓐ 질병
Ⓑ 영향
Ⓒ 요인
Ⓓ 유전자

해설 | 바로 전 문장, ~ several theories about factors that may make some people more likely to get it than others.를 통해 one이 factor를 가리킨다는 것을 알 수 있다.

문 4 | 다음 중 두 번째 단락에서 언급되지 않은 것은?
Ⓐ 통계 자료는 가족들 내의 알츠하이머의 발병 비율이 다름을 보여준다.
Ⓑ 이 질병의 발병에는 유전이 한 원인이 된다.
Ⓒ 알츠하이머병은 가족들에게 심각한 영향을 미칠 수 있다.
Ⓓ 질병의 원인을 유전자로 보는 견해에는 문제점이 있다.

해설 | Ⓐ는 지문에 언급되지 않은 내용이다.

문 5 | 다음 중 두 번째 단락의 하이라이트 된 문장의 핵심 내용을 가장 잘 표현한 것은? 틀린 보기는 본문의 내용을 심각하게 바꾸거나 핵심적인 내용을 누락시킨 것이다.
Ⓐ 그 질환에 걸린 가족이 있는 사람들은 아마도 어느 시점에서 그 병을 얻게 될 것이다.
Ⓑ 가족 병력과 개인의 병력과의 연관성은 아직 명확하지 않다.
Ⓒ 알츠하이머병에 걸린 부모님이 계시면 질환이 발병할 위험도가 상당히 높아진다.
Ⓓ 가족 내에 그 질환을 가진 사람이 있는 사람들이 모두 알츠하이머병에 걸리는 것은 아니지만, 위험성이 높다.

해설 | 주어진 지문의 핵심 내용은, 가족 내에 알츠하이머병을 앓은 사람이 있으면 발병 확률이 높아지긴 하지만 반드시 그런 것은 아니라는 것이다.

문 6 | 세 번째 단락의 susceptible to와 가장 의미가 유사한 것은?
Ⓐ 싫증난
Ⓑ 걱정되는
Ⓒ 걸리기 쉬운
Ⓓ 희망이 없는

해설 | susceptible to는 '감염되기 쉬운', '영향받기 쉬운'이라는 뜻이다. 대조되는 뒤의 문장의 no guarantee ~ will result in ~에서 힌트를 얻을 수 있다.

문 7 | 세 번째 단락에 따르면, 뇌졸중에 관해 사실인 것은?
Ⓐ 알츠하이머병에 걸린 사람들은 훨씬 쉽게 뇌졸중을 앓는다.
Ⓑ 뇌졸중에 의해 발생한 두뇌 손상으로 인해 알츠하이머병에 걸릴 지도 모른다.
Ⓒ 뇌졸중을 치료할 수 있는 방법은 없다.
Ⓓ 뇌졸중에 의한 손상과 알츠하이머병은 매우 비슷하다.

해설 | 단락의 첫 문장, ~ increase the possibility of developing Alzheimer's is brain damage caused by stroke, high blood pressure, or head injury.에서부터 단락 전체에 걸쳐, 두뇌의 손상으로 인해 알츠하이머병이 일어날 수도 있음을 이야기하고 있다. Ⓐ, Ⓒ, Ⓓ는 언급되지 않은 내용이다.

문 8 | 네 번째 단락의 debatable과 가장 의미가 유사한 것은?
Ⓐ 논쟁의 여지가 있는
Ⓑ 영향력 있는
Ⓒ 허용된
Ⓓ 귀찮은

해설 | debatable은 '논란의 여지가 있는'의 의미이다. 어원인 debate와 '가능'을 나타내는 어미 -able로부터 뜻을 유추한다.

문 9 | 알츠하이머병을 일으킨다는 환경적 원인에 대한 글쓴이의 의견은?
Ⓐ 연구결과를 확신하고 있다.
Ⓑ 그 이론이 암시하는 바에 대해 걱정하고 있다.
Ⓒ 연구결과를 두려워하고 있다.
Ⓓ 제시된 증거에 대해 의문을 가지고 있다.

해설 | 네 번째 단락의 This theory is the most debatable, It also has the least support, have found no such link, There is not enough proof to claim that environmental reasons are the causes for this tragic disease. 등을 보아 글쓴이는 알츠하이머병을 일으킨다는 환경적 원인에 대해 확신이 없고, 의문을 가지고 있음을 알 수 있다.

문 10 | 지문에 대한 간단한 요약을 위한 도입 문장이 아래에 제시된다. 가장 중요한 내용을 표현한 3가지 대답을 선택하여 요약을 완성하시오. 몇몇 문장들은 단락에서 언급되지 않았거나 중요하지 않은 내용을 표현해서 요약에 들어갈 수 없다.

비록 알츠하이머병을 일으키는 원인이 제대로 밝혀지지는 않았지만, 그 병을 유발시킬 수 있는 몇 가지의 가능한 요인들은 존재한다.

Ⓐ 고령자들은 알츠하이머병에 더 걸리기 쉽고, 그 이유가 연구되고 있다.
Ⓑ 가족 병력이 질병을 발병시키는 원인일 수 있다.
Ⓒ 두뇌에 가해지는 물리적인 손상 또한 알츠하이머병에 걸리기 쉽게 만든다.
Ⓓ 뇌손상과 알츠하이머병의 관계는 아직 증명되지 않았다.
Ⓔ 몇 가지 금속들은 실제로 뇌에 영향을 미치고, 따라서 알츠하이머병을 유발시킬 수 있다.
Ⓕ 우리 주위에 있는 물질들이 어느 정도 영향을 미칠지도 모르지만, 이에 대한 증거는 거의 없다.

해설 | 알츠하이머병을 일으킬 수 있는 세 가지 요인들이 지문의 핵심 내용이다. Ⓔ는 지문의 내용을 잘못 말하고 있고, Ⓐ와 Ⓓ는 minor한 내용이다.

Progress Test 4

정답 1. Ⓑ   2. Ⓑ   3. Ⓐ   4. Ⓓ   5. Ⓓ
6. Ⓐ   7. Ⓑ   8. Ⓐ   9. Tourist Industry - Ⓐ, Ⓔ, Ⓕ / Fishing Industry - Ⓑ, Ⓖ

해석 해양학자들은 다음 십년 동안, 인류가 해양에 서식하는 수많은 생물들이 멸종하는 것을 목격하게 되리라고 예측한다. 그 수효에 있어서 돌이킬 수 없을 정도로 타격을 받고 있는 많은 동물들이 있으며, 그것들은 존속할 수 있을 것 같지 않다. 사실상, 지난 300년 동안 멸종되었다고 알려진 21 개종의 해양 동물들 중 16종이 1972년 이래 소멸했다. 무엇이 이러한 멸종과 앞으로 있을 (동물의) 멸종을 일으키는가? 인간의 의한 해변 개발과 과도한 어획 행위가 가장 큰 두 가지 요인이다.

전 세계적으로 관광산업이 계속적으로 성장함에 따라 더욱 더 많은 리조트와 호텔이 전 세계의 해변에 세워지고 있다. 이것은 관광객들이 휴식을 취하고 물을 즐길 수 있는 멋진 기회를 제공하지만, 이러한 해안 지역에서 서식하는 해양생물에게는 중요하면서도 부정적인 영향을 미치고 있다. 예를 들면, 물속에서 자라는 맹그로브 나무가 해안 개발로 뽑혀나감에 따라, 카리브 해에 서식하는 희귀종인 lemon shark는 쫓겨나가고 있다. 이 상어들은 맹그로브 뿌리 사이에서 살면서 먹이를 먹는다. 보호가 없다면 그들을 멸종될 것이다. 관광산업이 환경에 더욱 책임을 질 수 있도록 규제가 제정되어야 한다. 지금까지는 이익을 위해서라는 명목으로 산업이 끼친 피해를 막기 위해 어떠한 조취도 취해지지 않았다.

이익이라는 명목으로 어업 또한 다수의 물고기를 멸종시킨 책임이 있다. 한 시간에 수천마리의 물고기를 잡는 대규모의 어선들은 지난 60년 동안 발생한 절반 이상의 물고기 멸종에 대한 원인으로 평가된다. 이러한 멸종 중 어떤 것들은 카리브 해의 monk seal fish나 뉴질랜드

Grayling와 같은 특정한 종을 집중적으로 남획한 데서 비롯되었다. 다시 말해, 수효가 급격하게 감소하고 있음에도 불구하고, 어부들은 그 물고기가 멸종할 때까지 그것을 포획하곤 했다.(표1 참조) 멸종과 관련된 다른 어획은 의도적인 것은 아니었다. 멸종된 물고기들은 번번히 어선의 그물에 우연하게 걸려들어서 그 수를 유지할 수 없었다.

문 1 | 첫 번째 단락의 irreparably와 가장 의미가 유사한 것은?
Ⓐ 부분적으로
Ⓑ 영구적으로
Ⓒ 일시적으로
Ⓓ 미묘하게

해설 | irreparably는 '회복할 수 없는', '치료할 수 없는'의 의미이다. extinction 또는 not able to continue on이 clue가 된다. 또, repair와 '반대'의 접두사 ir-, '가능'의 -able을 통해 그 뜻을 유추할 수 있다.

문 2 | 두 번째 단락의 displaced와 가장 의미가 유사한 것은?
Ⓐ 바뀌는
Ⓑ 강제로 쫓겨나는
Ⓒ 도망치는
Ⓓ 변형되는

해설 | displace는 '쫓아내다', '기존의 자리에서 옮기다'란 뜻을 가지고 있다. 뒤에 '맹그로브'가 뽑혀나감에 따라'에서 뜻을 유추할 수 있다.

문 3 | 두 번째 단락의 it이 가리키는 것은?
Ⓐ 산업
Ⓑ 보호
Ⓒ 카리브 해
Ⓓ 종

해설 | 두 번째 단락에서는 멸종에 대한 원인으로 관광산업을 지적하고 있다. it이 가리키는 것은 앞 문장에 나온 the industry이다.

문 4 | 두 번째 단락에 따르면, 다음 중 관광 리조트에 관해 글쓴이가 이야기하는 바로 올바른 것은?
Ⓐ 해양생물 보호 기금을 들여옴으로써, 해양생물에게 이익을 준다.
Ⓑ 멸종 위기의 생물에게 이로운 서식지를 종종 제공한다.
Ⓒ 해변으로 너무 많은 사람들을 오게 하여, 동물들에게 해를 끼치게 된다.
Ⓓ 해양생물들의 서식지를 파괴한다.

해설 | Ⓐ와 Ⓒ는 지문에서 언급되지 않았다. 지문에는 리조트 건설로 인해, 많은 해양 생물들의 서식지가 파괴되고 있다는 내용이 나오므로 Ⓑ는 틀린 내용이다.

문 5 | 관광 산업에 대한 글쓴이의 의견은?
Ⓐ 관광산업이 해변 리조트에 의존하는 것에 대해 비판적이다.
Ⓑ 경제에 미치는 관광산업의 기여에 대해 긍정적이다.
Ⓒ 생물의 멸종에 끼친 관광산업의 역할에 대해 의문을 가지고 있다.
Ⓓ 관광산업이 책임감을 결핍하고 있는 데 대해 못마땅해 하고 있다.

해설 | 해안에 리조트와 호텔이 건설되는 것이 해양 생물에게 부정적인 영향을 미친다는 내용이나, 환경과 관련해 관광 산업에 규제를 둬야한다는 내용을 통해 글쓴이의 태도를 유추할 수 있다.

문 6 | 세 번째 단락의 unintentional과 가장 의미가 유사한 것은?
Ⓐ 우발적인
Ⓑ 지적인
Ⓒ 실험적인
Ⓓ 중요치 않은

해설 | unintentional은 '고의가 아닌'의 의미이다. 뒤에 나오는, just happened to get caught에서 힌트를 얻을 수 있다.

문 7 | 다음 중 세 번째 단락의 하이라이트 된 문장의 핵심 내용을 가장 잘 표현한 것은? 틀린 보기는 본문의 내용을 심각하게 바꾸거나 핵심적인 내용을 누락시킨 것이다.
Ⓐ 어선들은 지난 60년에 걸쳐 점점 더 많은 물고기를 잡을 수 있게 되었다.
Ⓑ 대형 어선들은 지난 60년 동안 발생한 물고기 멸종 중 대략 50%에 대한 책임이 있다.
Ⓒ 지난 60년 동안 수천마리의 물고기들이 어선들의 수적 증가로 인해 죽었다.
Ⓓ 물고기의 멸종은 지난 60년 동안 크게 계속 증가했다.

해설 | 지난 60년간 일어난 물고기 멸종의 50%는 대형 어선에 의한 것이라는 내용이 하이라이트 된 문장의 핵심이다.

문 8 | 그래프에 따르면, 다음 중 사실이 아닌 것은?
Ⓐ 제시된 종들 중, monk seal fish가 실제 수에 있어서 가장 많이 감소했다.
Ⓑ 1990년대에 lemon shark의 수는 grayling이나 monk seal fish의 수보다 많다.
Ⓒ 1960년의 grayling와 monk seal fish의 수는 대충 같다.
Ⓓ lemon shark의 현재 수치는 1960년대의 수치에서 대략 25% 정도이다.

해설 | 감소율을 나타내는 그래프의 기울기가 가장 가파른 것은 lemon sharks이다.

문 9 | 적절한 보기를 골라 관련 있는 산업 종류와 짝지으시오. 두 개의 보기는 제외됩니다.
Ⓐ 해변 지역을 변화시킨다.
Ⓑ 의도하지 않은 동물들을 죽음에 이르게 한다.
Ⓒ 환경보호에 대한 법률을 무시한다.
Ⓓ 해변지역으로 오염물질을 방출한다.
Ⓔ 서식지보다 공사를 우선한다.
Ⓕ 특정 바다생물의 서식지에 영향을 미친다.
Ⓖ 동물들이 충분히 빠르게 번식하는 것을 막는다.

해설 | Ⓒ와 Ⓓ는 언급되지 않은 내용이고 해변지역에 공사 등의 개발로 서식지를 변화시키는 것은(Ⓐ, Ⓔ, Ⓕ) Tourist industry에 속하는 설명이고, 의도하지 않은 생물의 죽음과 번식을 막는 것은 Fishing industry의 설명이다.

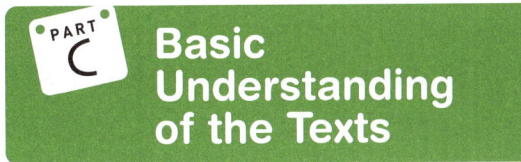

Basic Understanding of the Texts

Chapter 7 Rhetorical Purpose

SAMPLE ITEM　　정답 1. Ⓑ   2. Ⓒ　　p.166 - p.188

해석　제품의 적절한 포지셔닝은 마케팅 캠페인을 벌이고자 할 때 필수적인 것이다. 포지셔닝은 고객이 귀사의 제품을 경쟁사들의 제품과의 관계에서 어떻게 보는지이다. 이 점에서 성공적인 포지셔닝을 이루어내기 위해 두 가지 조건이 맞아야 한다. 첫째, 귀사의 제품이 시장에 있는 다른 제품들과는 차별점을 가지고 있어야 한다. 다시 말해, 독특해야 한다. 둘째, 귀사의 제품은 고객에게 이익을 제공해야 한다. 예를 들자면, 귀사는 다른 회사들과는 완전히 틀린 미용 제품을 팔아야 한다는 것이다. 그러나 만약 고객들이 귀사의 제품이 그다지 좋지 않거나, 타사 제품과 비교했을 때 그다지 효과적이지 않다고 느낀다면, 그 제품은 실패할 것이다. 이것은 두 가지 성공 조건 중 하나만이 충족되었기 때문이다.

문 1 ｜ 글쓴이가 미용 제품을 언급한 이유는?
Ⓐ 마케팅 캠페인이 일반적으로 이용되는 산업을 증명하기 위해
Ⓑ 포지셔닝 기준 중 하나를 만족시키지 않는 제품의 예를 들기 위해
Ⓒ 적절한 포지셔닝이 왜 중요한지 이유를 설명하기 위해
Ⓓ 고객들이 적절한 질의 제품을 요구한다는 것을 보여주기 위해

해설 ｜ 지문에서 글쓴이가 beauty product를 언급한 이유는, 한 가지 조건을 충족하지 못하는 제품의 예를 들어주려는 것이다.

문 2 ｜ 효과적인 포지셔닝을 위한 조건을 글쓴이는 어떻게 설명하고 있는가?
Ⓐ 포지셔닝에 중요한 몇 가지 조건들을 열거함으로써
Ⓑ 제품의 독창성과 유용성을 비교함으로써
Ⓒ 충족되어야 하는 두 가지의 주요 조건을 설명함으로써
Ⓓ 상품의 독창성과 유용성이 필요함을 주장함으로써

해설 ｜ 글쓴이는 effective positioning의 두 가지 condition들을 집어 설명하고 있다.

Basic Drill 1

정답　1. describe, (C)   2. illustrate, (A)
3. persuade, (C)   4. compare / contrast, (B)

1. 해석　쌍극성 장애(Bipolar disorder)란 사람의 기분과 힘의 수준, 그리고 매일의 활동할 수 있는 능력에 극단적인 변화를 가져오는 정신병의 일종이다. 이 병의 증상은 극단적인 기분의 변화이다. 이런 사람은 조병환자라 불리우게 된다. 이런 사람들은 에너지가 넘치고, 잠을 아주 적게 자고, 무모하게 행동한다. 그러다가 갑자기, 우울해진다. 이렇게 우울한 기간 동안은 지나치게 잠을 많이 자고, 죄책감과 무기력을 느끼며, 때로는 자살까지 생각하기도 한다.

문제 ｜ 밑줄 그은 부분의 레토릭: ▢ 설득 ▢ 정의 ■ 묘사

글쓴이가 조병환자를 언급한 이유는 무엇인가?
(A) 이 병이 가지는 증상의 예를 들기 위하여
(B) 이 장애가 어떤 경우에는 치명적이라는 것을 보여주기 위하여
(C) 쌍극성 장애의 증상을 묘사하기 위하여

해설 ｜ 단락의 3번째줄 They ~ suicide까지 질병에 대한 다양한 증상을 설명하므로 답은 (C)이다.

2. 해석　예술 요법은 감정적인 행복감을 높이기 위해 작품 만들기와 창의성을 이용하는 심리 치료의 한 가지 방법이다. 이것은 자신의 감정을 표현하는 데 어려움을 겪는 사람들이 말이 아닌 이미지를 통해 표현할 수 있게끔 한다. 이것은 자신의 문제를 이야기하기 어려워하는 사람들에게 매우 효과적일 수 있다. 예를 들면, 아이들은 그들의 문제를 쉽게 설명하지 못한다. 그들은 복잡한 어휘력을 가지지 못하지만 그림을 사용해서 자신이 어떻게 느끼는지를 표현할 수 있다.

문제 ｜ 밑줄 그은 부분의 레토릭: ▢ 설득 ■ 예증 ▢ 묘사

글쓴이가 아이들을 언급한 이유는 무엇인가?
(A) 이 치료를 통해 도움 받을 수 있는 사람의 예를 들어주기 위하여
(B) 어른과는 반대로 아이들에게 이 치료가 어떻게 사용되는지 대조하기 위하여
(C) 자신을 표현하지 못하는 사람들을 치료하기가 얼마나 어려운지 암시하기 위하여

해설 ｜ for example 이하는 이 치료법이 효과적인 대상을 예를 들어 설명하는 부분이다.

3. 해석   심리학자들은 커피 타임이 중요하다는 것을 (과학적으로) 증명했다. 커피 타임은 신체적인 건강 또한 증진시킨다. 매일의 일상적인 삶에서 휴식은 고용인들의 지친 몸과 마음에 휴식과 활력을 준다. 연구자들은 인체 내 생체 시계가 2시간마다 1시간 30분의 휴식을 필요로 한다고 우리에게 알려준다는 것을 알아냈다. 그 시간이 지나면, 심장 박동과 혈압이 높아져서 불안과 짜증을 유발시킨다고 한다. 하지만 적절한 시기에 갖는 휴식은 이 결과를 반대로 할 수 있다.

문제 | 밑줄 그은 부분의 레토릭: ■ 설득 □ 예증 □ 비교/대조

글쓴이가 인체 내 생체 시계를 언급한 이유는?
(A) 적절한 커피 타임이 근로자에게 미치는 영향을 보여주기 위하여
(B) 커피 타임이 매일의 활동에 어떤 결과를 야기시킬지 보여주기 위하여
(C) 커피 타임이 신체 컨디션(의 조절)을 도와준다는 것을 증명하기 위하여

해설 | 연구 결과를 언급함으로써 커피 타임이 미치는 긍정적 영향을 증명하고 있다.

4. 해석   어떤 전문가들은 교실에서 남학생과 여학생을 완전히 분리시키는, 남녀 분반 수업을 실험적으로 시행하고 있는 미국의 몇 학교들을 비판하고 있다. 그들은 남학생과 여학생이 서로 상호작용하는 것을 배우지 못하기 때문에 사회화 과정이 늦춰진다고 주장한다. 한편, 많은 대학의 연구자들은 남학생과 여학생의 뇌가 차이가 있다는 증거가 있고, 이 차이점 때문에 남학생과 여학생은 다른 방식으로 학습하게 된다고 주장한다. 따라서, 남학생과 여학생은 성별에 기초하여 따로 분리되어 가장 효율인 방식으로 배워야 한다.

문제 | 밑줄 그은 부분의 레토릭: □ 묘사 ■ 비교/대조 □ 원인/결과

글쓴이가 남학생과 여학생의 두뇌(구조)의 차이를 언급한 이유는 무엇인가?
(A) 두뇌 구조의 차이가 양쪽의 학습 과정에 어떻게 영향을 미치는지 보여주기 위해
(B) 성별을 바탕으로 (교실을) 분리시키는 것이 도움이 된다는 것을 주장하기 위해
(C) 남학생과 여학생을 분리시키는 것이 갖고 있는 가장 심각한 문제를 지적하기 위해

해설 | 이야기의 전환 또는 비교 / 대조를 하는 mean while 뒤에 나오는 내용을 통해 유추할 수 있다.

Basic Drill 2

정답   1. compare/contrast, (B) 2. describe, (B)
       3. define, (A) 4. illustrate, (C)

1. 해석   휘발유 내부 연소 엔진이 장착된 최초의 미국 자동차는 1877년 George Selden이 개발했다. 그러나 그 자동차가 자가 동력차, 즉 움직이는 데 말이나 다른 것에 의존하지 않는 자동차를 만들고자 했던 최초의 시도는 아니었다. 그 전에도 다른 형태의 동력을 이용한 차를 만들고자 한 여러가지 시도가 있었다. 증기 트랙터는 1769년에 Cugnot이란 이름의 프랑스 기사가 발명했다. 하지만 이것은 시간당 2.5마일만 갈 수 있었고, 증기를 축적시키기 위해 10피트 움직였을 때마다 멈춰야 했다. 이 운송수단은 연료의 놀라운 에너지 밀도와 무게 비율에 있어 높은 힘을 낼 수 있는 휘발유 동력차만큼 실용적이지 않았다.

문제 | 밑줄 그은 부분의 레토릭: □ 원인/결과 □ 묘사 ■ 비교/대조

글쓴이는 자동차의 강점에 대한 자신의 포인트를 어떻게 강조하고 있는가?
(A) 다른 초기 운송 수단이 가지지 않았던 부분을 설명함으로써
(B) 다른 에너지원을 사용하는 초기 운송 수단과 비교함으로써
(C) 추가 연료없이 얼마나 멀리 갈 수 있는지 증명함으로써

해설 | 휘발유를 이용하는 자동차 이전에 발명된 증기 트랙터와 비교하고 있으므로 답은 (B)이다.

2. 해석   Columbus의 신세계 향해 400주년을 기념하는 박람회인 World's Columbian Exposition이 1893년 시카고에서 열렸다. 이 행사에 필요한 건물들을 짓고 정비하는 데 엄청난 노력이 들어갔다. 4만명의 일꾼들이 박람회 부지에 거의 200채의 건물을 건축했다. 건물들 외에도 일련의 인공 호수와 연못, 그리고 석호가 만들어졌다. 이것들은 관람객들이 엑스포의 다른 지역으로 가기 위해 타는 패달식 보트나 수상 택시 같은 수송 루트의 기능을 수행한 동시에, 방문하는 동안 앉아 쉴 수 있는 쾌적한 공간으로서의 기능도 수행했다.

문제 | 밑줄 그은 부분의 레토릭: ■ 묘사 □ 원인/결과 □ 예증

글쓴이는 엑스포에 들어간 수소에 대한 그의 포인트를 어떻게 강조하고 있는가?
(A) 엑스포와 관계된 사람 수를 제시함으로써
(B) 박람회를 위해 행해진 건설 공사를 묘사함으로써
(C) 부지를 짓는 데 일꾼들에게 필요한 기술을 자세히 설명함으로써

해설 | 단락 4번째 줄 Forty thousand ~ grounds.에서 박람회를 위해 벌어진 건설 공사에 대해 묘사하며 설명하므로 답은 (B)이다.

3. **해석** 영화 속 등장인물이 특정 상표의 상품을 사용함으로써 상품을 광고하는 방법을 간접광고라고 부른다. 그 등장인물이 상품에 주의를 환기시키지 않아도 라벨은 쉽게 읽히고, 등장인물은 그 상품을 판촉하고 있는 것처럼 인식된다. 이런 종류의 광고는 미묘하긴 하지만 매우 효과적이다. 기업들은 자사 제품을 인기 있는 영화에 나오게 하기 위해 매년 수백만 달러를 지불한다. 간접광고의 한 예는 영화나 TV 배우들이 담배를 피우는 것에서 볼 수 있다.

문제 | 밑줄 그은 부분의 레토릭: □ 설득 ■ 정의 □ 묘사

글쓴이는 지문의 주제를 어떻게 소개하는가?
(A) 간접광고의 정의를 내림으로써
(B) 간접광고의 배경을 제공함으로써
(C) 간접광고가 쓰인 예를 듦으로써

해설 | A type of advertising in which a character in a film or movie will use a specific brand of something is called product placement.를 시작으로 주제에 대한 정의를 주고 있으므로 답은 (A)이다.

4. **해석** 정치풍자 만화는 현재의 정치적 사건이나 지도자들에 대해 논평하고 비판하는 아주 인기 있는 방법이다. 이런 만화를 이용한 유명인 중 한 명은 마틴 루터이다. 그는 신부가 죄를 용서해 주는 것에 대한 돈을 받는 것과 같은, 자신이 생각한 교회의 문제와 부패를 그린 포스터나 인쇄물을 배포했다. 이 삽화들은 믿기지 않을 만큼 효과가 있었고, Luther은 그 풍자 만화로 대중의 지지를 얻었다.

문제 | 밑줄 그은 부분의 레토릭: □ 묘사 □ 비교/대조 ■ 예증

글쓴이는 정치풍자 만화를 어떻게 설명하고 있는가?
(A) 어떤 것을 폭로하기 위해 정치풍자 만화를 사용한 것을 묘사함으로써
(B) 정치풍자 만화의 출현과 기능을 정의함으로써
(C) 정치적인 목적으로 사용된 풍자 만화의 예를 듦으로써

해설 | Political cartoon의 예를 보여주므로 답은 (C)이다.

VOCABULARY Preview

Check-up

1. mythology 2. mocks 3. sank
4. distorted 5. durable 6. anonymous
7. traits 8. examined

다음 빈 칸에 들어갈 알맞은 말을 골라, 필요하면 고쳐 쓰시오.

1. Cindy는 그리스와 로마 신화를 전공한다.
2. Charles는 무신론자이다. 그는 항상 교회와 신자의 믿음을 조롱한다.
3. 배가 암초에 부딪혀 바다에 가라앉아 수백명의 희생자가 발생했다.
4. Adam이 내 그림의 모양과 형태를 일그러뜨렸어!
5. 이 회사 제품은 최고야! 튼튼하고 거의 고장나지 않아.
6. 익명의 기증자가 어제 자선단체에 $5000를 기부했다. 그 사람은 대체 누구일까?
7. Frank의 유머 감각은 그의 가장 유쾌한 특성 중 하나이다.
8. 치과 의사는 내 이를 점검한 뒤 새로운 충치가 세 개 생겼다고 말했다.

Exercise 1

정답 1. ⓒ 2. ⓑ 3. ⓓ 4. ⓒ 5. ⓓ 6. ⓓ
7. ⓑ, ⓒ, ⓔ

해설 Icelandic Sagas(아이슬란드의 무용담)은 12세기와 13세기 사이에 쓰여진 서사시적 이야기다. 당대 쓰여진 다른 많은 서사시적 작품들처럼, 이 이야기들도 나라의 역사와 신화 속 중요한 인물과 집단에 대한 이야기이다. 그 시대의 다른 서사 작품들처럼, Saga도 영웅의 행적과 역사적으로 중요한 사건으로 가득차 있고, 신들이 개인이나 집단을 돕기 위해 끼어드는 초자연적인 사건들에 대해 상술한다. 그러나 아이슬란드의 서사 작품이 다른 문화의 서사 작품과 어떤 면에서 비슷하기는 하지만, 여러 이유들로 인해 독특하다.

Icelandic Sagas는 대부분 작자 미상의 다른 작가들이 썼지만 명료하고 직접적이며 단순한 표현법을 공유한다. 당대의 다른 영웅 서사시들이 앵글로 색슨족의 Beowulf처럼 아주 복잡하고 화려한 문체로 쓰인 것에 반해, Icelandic Saga는 간결함을 자랑으로 여기는 것처럼 보인다. 각각의 다른 작가들이 쓴 Saga에 이런 특징이 공통적으로 나타나는 것으로 보아, 이런 간결함(단순함)은 아이슬란드의 이야기 방식의 훌륭한 특색이었음을 나타내는 것으로 보인다.

Saga의 두번째 독특한 특징은 어조이다. 나라를 위해 죽음조차 두려워하지 않았던 용감한 남성과 여성에 대한 서

사적이고 영웅적인 이야기였던 반면에 또한 해학적이었다. Saga의 주제가 주로 전쟁이었기에 여기에 나오는 유머는 종종 어두웠다. 즉, 그 유머가 죽음과 전쟁의 무게를 가볍게 만들었다. 다른 영웅 서사시들이 이런 주제를 굉장히 진지하게 다룬 것에 비해 아이슬란드의 영웅 서사시는 죽음을 두려워할 대상이 아닌, 조롱의 대상이라는 시각을 취한 것으로 보인다.

문 1 | 첫번째 단락의 they가 가리키는 것은?
- Ⓐ 개인과 집단
- Ⓑ 역사상의 사건
- Ⓒ 아이슬란드의 무용담(Icelandic Sagas)
- Ⓓ 초자연적인 사건

해설 | 뒤에 they가 받는 주어, the Icelandic Sagas가 나온다.

문 2 | 글쓴이는 첫 번째 단락에서 Icelandic Sagas를 어떻게 소개하고 있는가?
- Ⓐ 12세기 영웅 서사시에서 노래한 초자연적인 사건들의 예를 제시함으로써
- Ⓑ 당대 서사 작품들과의 공통된 특징을 비교함으로써
- Ⓒ Icelandic Saga의 연대 시기에 대한 의문을 제시하는 연구를 참조함으로써
- Ⓓ 아이슬란드의 문명과 문화에 대한 배경을 제시함으로써

해설 | 당대의 다른 문화의 서사 작품들과의 공통점을 언급하며 Icelandic Saga를 소개하고 있다.

문 3 | 두번째 단락의 admirable와 가장 의미가 유사한 것은?
- Ⓐ 흔히 않은
- Ⓑ 보통의
- Ⓒ 무례한
- Ⓓ 훌륭한

해설 | admirable는 '훌륭한', '우수한'이라는 의미로, 앞에 shared among the different authors에서 그 뜻을 유추한다.

문 4 | 글쓴이가 두번째 단락에서 그 당시의 다른 서사시를 언급한 이유는 무엇인가?
- Ⓐ 그것들과 Saga와의 주제의 유사성을 나타내기 위하여
- Ⓑ Beowulf의 작가가 몇 편의 Saga를 썼다는 것을 암시하기 위하여
- Ⓒ Icelandic Saga와는 틀린 문체와 대조하기 위하여
- Ⓓ 그 시절 존재했던 다른 종류의 서사시를 보여주기 위하여

해설 | 두번째 단락 While other~ very simple.에서 두 작품의 문체 스타일을 대조하므로 답은 Ⓒ이다.

문 5 | 다음 중 세 번째 단락의 하이라이트 된 문장의 핵심 내용을 가장 잘 표현한 것은? 틀린 보기는 본문의 내용을 심각하게 바꾸거나 핵심적인 내용을 누락시킨 것이다.
- Ⓐ Saga의 등장인물들은 용감했고 동시에 웃겼다.
- Ⓑ Saga 이야기는 죽음을 두려워하지 않은 용감한 남성과 여성에 대한 것이었다.
- Ⓒ 영웅들의 유머러스한 특성은 Saga의 이야기를 가볍게 만들었다.
- Ⓓ Saga에 사용된 유머는 아이슬란드의 영웅 서사시와 영웅 설화의 또다른 특징이었다.

해설 | 하이라이트된 문장의 핵심 내용은, 비록 아이슬란드 Saga가 용감한 영웅들에 대한 이야기지만 이야기가 유머러스했다는 것이다. telling the tales ~ die for their country는 epic과 heroic의 부연으로 생략된다.

문 6 | 글쓴이가 세번째 단락에서 유머를 언급한 이유는 무엇인가?
- Ⓐ 다른 서사시에 어떤 종류의 어조가 사용되었는지를 보여주기 위하여
- Ⓑ 많은 사람들이 Saga를 읽었다는 것을 암시하기 위하여
- Ⓒ Saga에서 사용된 어조의 예를 들기 위하여
- Ⓓ Saga의 두번째 특징인 어조를 묘사하기 위하여

해설 | humor에 관한 것은 Saga의 두 번째 특징인 어조를 묘사하기 위함이다.

문 7 | 지문에 대한 간단한 요약을 위한 도입 문장이 아래에 제시된다. 가장 중요한 내용을 표현한 3가지 대답을 선택하여 요약을 완성하시오. 몇몇 문장들은 단락에서 언급되지 않았거나 중요하지 않은 내용을 표현해서 요약에 들어갈 수 없다.

Saga는 영웅들의 활약상과 역사적이고 초자연적인 사건들에 대해 이야기한다.

- Ⓐ Icelandic Saga의 독특한 특징은 그들의 특이한 역사와 신화에서 비롯된다.
- Ⓑ 다른 나라의 영웅 서사시와의 유사성에도 불구하고 Saga는 자신만의 고유한 독특함을 가지고 있다.
- Ⓒ Saga의 문체는 그 당시의 다른 나라 작품들에 비해 훨씬 단순하다.
- Ⓓ Saga의 작가들은 수사적인(화려한) 시를 쓸 수 있는 전문적인 작가들이 아니었다.
- Ⓔ Saga는 죽음이라는 주제를 특별히 독특하고 가볍게 다루었다.
- Ⓕ 죽음은 Saga 작가들이 흥미를 가진 주제가 아니었다.

해설 | Ⓐ와 Ⓓ에 대한 언급은 없고 Ⓕ는 지문의 내용과 틀리게 말한 것이다.

Exercise 2

정답 1. Ⓑ 2. Ⓐ 3. Ⓑ 4. Ⓑ 5. Ⓒ
6. Ridley's Surgery - Ⓐ, Ⓕ /
Susruta's Surgery - Ⓓ, Ⓔ, Ⓖ

해석 백내장은 맑은 수정체가 뿌옇게 흐려지는 눈의

상태이다. 이것은 보통 노화 과정의 정상적인 부분이다. 시력이 점점 떨어지면서 서서히 난시로 발전된다. 야간에 자동차 조명처럼 밝은 물체 주변에 후광이 나타난다. 불투명한 수정체를 통과할 수 있는 빛이 거의 없기 때문에, 궁극적으로는 시력을 잃게 된다. 그러나 백내장은 부상의 결과로 갑자기 형성될 수도 있다.

다행스럽게도, Harold Ridley에 의해 개척된 간단한 절차의 현대적 백내장 수술로 이 문제는 치료될 수 있다. 눈을 검사한 후, 의사는 조심스럽게 뿌옇게 된 수정체를 제거하고 intra-ocular라는 인공 수정체로 이를 대체할 수 있다. 그리고 눈의 외부를 덮고 있는 피부에 생긴 절단 부위가 회복될 때까지 안대가 눈 위에 덧대어진다. 시력은 즉시 회복된다. 이 기술은 상대적으로 합병증이 없으며, 회복 기간도 최소화된다. 그러나 이 수술은, 사람을 점차 맹인으로 만들 수 있는 눈의 질환인 녹내장처럼, 이미 시력에 영향을 미치고 있는 근원적인 의학적 문제점은 고칠 수는 없다. 드문 경우, 인공 수정체가 있어야 할 정확한 위치에서 이탈하여 수술을 요하는 긴급 사태 혹은 실명을 초래할 수 있다.

그러나 Ridley의 방법이 시술되기 오래전, 상당히 다른 수술 절차가 존재했다. 문서에 따르면, 백내장 수술은 인도에서 기원전 5세기에 이미 시술되고 있었다. 최초의 백내장 의사인 Susruta라는 한 남자가 20세기까지도 몇몇 나라에서 여전히 활용되고 있었던 기술을 개척했다. 이 기술은 "couching" 혹은 "reclination"이라고 불렸다. 뿌옇게 된 수정체를 제거하고 맑은 수정체로 교체하기보다, 의사는 백내장을 눈 속으로 다시 밀어넣었다. 비록 이것은 시력을 개선시키기는 했지만, 시력을 완벽하게 회복시키지는 못했다.

문 1 | 첫 번째 단락의 opaque와 가장 의미가 유사한 것은?
Ⓐ 투명한
Ⓑ 흐릿한
Ⓒ 흑색의
Ⓓ 진한

해설 | opaque는 '불투명한'의 의미이다. 지문의 첫 번째 줄, Cataracts are a condition of the eye in which the clear lens becomes cloudy.과 두 번째 단락의 After examining eyes, a surgeon can carefully remove the clouded lens ~.으로 보아 opaque가 cloudy와 동일한 의미로 쓰였음을 알 수 있다.

문 2 | 첫 번째 단락에 따르면, 다음 중 백내장의 증상이 될 수 없는 것은?
Ⓐ 특정 색깔의 물체를 구분할 수 없다.
Ⓑ 눈으로 들어오는 빛의 양이 줄어든다.
Ⓒ 서서히 시력을 상실하게 된다.
Ⓓ 난시가 진행된다.

해설 | Ⓐ는 나오지 않은 내용이다.

문 3 | 첫 번째 단락에서 글쓴이가 후광을 언급한 이유는?
Ⓐ 백내장의 주요한 원인 중 하나를 알려주기 위하여
Ⓑ 백내장을 가진 사람들의 흐릿한 시야를 묘사하기 위하여
Ⓒ 백내장이 어떻게 발견되는지 보여주기 위하여
Ⓓ 백내장의 상태를 강조하기 위하여

해설 | 지문의 내용을 보면, 백내장이 있는 사람들은 시야가 흐려져서 밝은 물체 주변에 후광이 생기는 현상을 겪게 된다고 하면서, 그 후광이 어떤 것과 비슷한지 묘사하고 있다.

문 4 | 두 번째 단락의 This technique이 가리키는 것은?
Ⓐ 탁한 수정체를 제거하는 것
Ⓑ 희미한 수정체를 새 수정체와 교체하는 것
Ⓒ 현대 수술에서 행해지는 수술 기술
Ⓓ 한쪽 눈에 안대를 대는 것

해설 | 앞에 나온, a surgeon can carefully remove the clouded lens and then replace it with an artificial one ~ 에서 This technique는 흐려진 수정체를 제거하고, 인공 수정체로 교체하는 것임을 알 수 있다. 안대를 대는 것은 그 수술이 끝난 뒤에 행해지는 치료 과정이다.

문 5 | 두 번째 단락에서 글쓴이는 Harold Ridley의 백내장 수술을 어떻게 설명하고 있는가?
Ⓐ Ridley 박사가 시술한 첫 번째 백내장 수술을 예로 듦으로써
Ⓑ 수술 이후 발생할 수 있는 부작용을 지적함으로써
Ⓒ 백내장 수술의 주요 단계와 그 한계를 설명함으로써
Ⓓ 백내장 수술의 유익을 나열함으로써

해설 | 두 번째 단락은 Harold Ridley 박사가 개척한 현대적인 백내장 수술의 과정과 그것이 가진 한계를 설명하고 있다.

문 6 | 적절한 보기를 골라 관련 있는 수술 종류와 짝지으시오. 두 개의 보기는 제외됩니다.
Ⓐ 회복 시간이 짧다.
Ⓑ 합병증이 흔하게 발생한다.
Ⓒ 두 번 이상에 걸친 눈 수술이 필요하다.
Ⓓ 의사는 눈 속으로 백내장을 밀어 넣는다.
Ⓔ 20세기까지 사용되었다.
Ⓕ 수술 직후 환자의 시력은 회복된다.
Ⓖ 400년대에 인도에서 시행되었다.

해설 | Ⓑ는 Ridley의 수술과 관련해 잘못 언급한 것이고, Ⓒ는 지문에 나오지 않은 내용이다.

Exercise 3

정답 1. Ⓑ 2. Ⓓ 3. Ⓑ 4. Ⓒ 5. Ⓐ 6. Ⓒ
7. Ⓒ, Ⓔ, Ⓕ

Text Outline (A)

해석 개척자 가족들이 미국 동부에서 중서부의 여러

주에 도착했을 때, 그들은 동부연안에서 보지 못했던 (환경에) 순응하는 건축기술을 사용해야만 했다. 초기에 중서부는 아메리카 원주민이 여기저기에 거주하는 넓게 트인 지역이었다. 따라서 동부에서 온 개척자들이 대초원에 도착해 자신들의 새로운 삶을 시작하고자 했을 때, 새로운 집을 지을 수 있는 재료를 파는 마을이나 공급지가 없었다. 집을 짓는 데 필요한 판재를 켜는 데는 시간이 걸렸다. 거기다가, 중서부 지역의 많은 부분은 거대한 초원지대라서 나무가 많이 부족했다. 하지만 그들이 새로운 보금자리에서 살아남고 번영하기 위해서는 집을 찾는 것이 매우 중요했다. 그래서 많은 개척자 가족들은 대초원 위의 최초의 집으로 뗏장집을 지었다.

　　잔디 집, 혹은 뗏장집은 벽이 완전히 뗏장으로 만들어진 작은 집이다. 뗏장은 표면에 잔디가 자라는 흙 조각이다. 잔디의 뿌리가 흙의 접합부분을 합쳐서 건물을 지을 때 벽돌로 사용될 수 있었다. 뗏장집 지붕은 잔가지, 나무 가지, 덤불로 (기본적으로) 만들어졌고, 그 위에 뗏장을 좀 더 덮었다.

　　매우 단순했지만 이런 집은 매우 따뜻했고 놀랍게 튼튼했다. 개척자 가족들은 보다 영속적인 집을 짓게될 때까지 거기서 살 수 있었다. 나무 스토브나 굴뚝을 설치했을 뿐 아니라 가진 모든 가구를 집 안에 들여놓았다. 초원에 나무는 거의 없었지만 동물 똥이나 잔가지처럼 초원에서 찾을 수 있는 것은 무엇이든지 긴 겨울을 이기기 위한 연료로 사용되었다.

　　불행하게도 뗏장집에는 창문이 없었기 때문에, 만약 굴뚝에 뭔가 문제가 있으면 집안 전체가 연기로 가득차서 공기가 깨끗해질 때까지 모든 사람들이 집밖으로 나가 있어야 했던 것과 같은, 장작불 연기로 인한 여러가지 문제를 종종 겪었다.

문 1 | 첫 번째 단락의 prosper와 가장 의미가 유사한 것은?
Ⓐ 짓다
Ⓑ 성공하다
Ⓒ 발견하다
Ⓓ 나아가다

해설 | prosper는 '번영하다', '성공하다'란 의미가 있다. 앞에 나온 survive가 clue가 될 수 있다.

문 2 | 글쓴이는 첫번째 단락에서 뗏장집을 어떻게 소개하고 있는가?
Ⓐ 뗏장집이 환경에 알맞은 것이었음을 시사함으로써
Ⓑ 개척자들에게 건축 경험이 없음을 암시함으로써
Ⓒ 동부지역의 집보다 뗏장집이 어떤 면에서 더 나은지를 보여줌으로써
Ⓓ 개척자들이 왜 그런 집을 지어야했는지 이유를 설명함으로써

해설 | 단락 전체에 걸쳐 뗏장집을 지을 수 밖에 없던 이유를 설명하고 있으므로 답은 Ⓓ이다.

문 3 | 글쓴이는 두번째 단락에서 뗏장집을 어떻게 설명하고 있는가?
Ⓐ 집의 중요한 두 부분과 그 부분들의 기능을 설명함으로써
Ⓑ 집의 주요 부분을 짓는 데 사용된 자료를 묘사함으로써
Ⓒ 외부에서 본 전체적인 집의 모습을 묘사함으로써
Ⓓ 어떤 재료가 집에 왜 사용되었는지 이유를 제시함으로써

해설 | 두 번째 단락은 뗏장집의 재료에 대해 구체적인 묘사를 하고 있다.

문 4 | 두 번째 단락에 따르면, 잔디 뿌리는
Ⓐ 뗏장집에 붙여지기 전에 뿌리에 붙은 흙을 털어내야 했다.
Ⓑ 가지나 잔가지로 감싸지곤 했다.
Ⓒ 흙을 한 덩어리로 묶이도록 했다.
Ⓓ 집이 쉽게 움직이는 것을 방지했다.

해설 | The grass roots kept the sections of earth together, so that they could be used by the people as bricks in constructing the building.참조.

문 5 | 글쓴이가 두번째 단락에서 가지와 덤불을 언급한 이유는 무엇인가?
Ⓐ 집 건축에 사용된 재료를 예시하기 위하여
Ⓑ 집을 짓는 데 사용가능한 재료가 별로 없었음을 암시하기 위하여
Ⓒ 집이 잘 지어지지 않았음을 강조하기 위하여
Ⓓ 개척자들이 다른 재료를 사용했어야 함을 암시하기 위하여

해설 | 뗏장 말고도 집을 짓는 데 어떤 재료들이 사용되었는지를 보여주고 있다.

문 6 | 다음 중 네 번째 단락의 하이라이트 된 문장의 핵심 내용을 가장 잘 표현한 것은? 틀린 보기는 본문의 내용을 심각하게 바꾸거나 핵심적인 내용을 누락시킨 것이다.
Ⓐ 집안 내부에서 지피는 장작불 연기 때문에 굴뚝은 빈번히 문제를 일으켰다.
Ⓑ 창문이 없었기 때문에 장작불 연기가 집안에 더 오래 남아 있곤 했다.
Ⓒ 연기를 빼내는 창문이 없었기 때문에 사람들은 장작불 연기로 종종 고생했다.
Ⓓ 장작을 뗄 때 나오는 연기 때문에 사람들은 문을 열고 집밖으로 나가야 했다.

해설 | 하이라이트 된 문장의 핵심 내용은 집에 창문이 없어 굴뚝이 막히면 집안에 연기가 가득차게 되어 사람들이 고생을 했다는 것이다. like of there were ~ 이하는 problem의 예를 들어 설명하는 것으로 생략된다.

문 7 | 지문에 대한 간단한 요약을 위한 도입 문장이 아래에 제시된다. 가장 중요한 내용을 표현한 3가지 대답을 선택하여 요약을 완성하시오. 몇몇 문장들은 단락에서 언급되지 않

았거나 중요하지 않은 내용을 표현해서 요약에 들어갈 수 없다.

미국 중서부로 온 개척자들은 건물 짓는 기술을 그 지역에 맞춰야 했다.

Ⓐ 연기가 창문 밖으로 제대로 빠져나갈 수 없어서 집안 내부는 종종 연기가 자욱했다.
Ⓑ 판자나 도구가 늘 부족했기 때문에 영구적인 집을 짓기 위해 나무를 켜는 데 시간이 걸렸다.
Ⓒ 연기가 몇 가지 문제를 야기시켰지만, 개척자들이 자신들의 영구적인 집을 짓기 이전에 이용한 튼튼한 초원의 집은 따뜻하고 좋았다.
Ⓓ 뗏장집의 주 재료는 뗏장이었는데, 이것은 풀이 자라는 흙조각이다.
Ⓔ 그들은 자기들의 집을 흙과 풀로 만들어진 벽돌로 지었다.
Ⓕ 전통적인 건축자재가 부족해서 개척자들은 가까이에 있는 재료를 사용해야 함을 깨달았다.

해설 | 뗏장집을 짓게 된 이유를 설명하는 Ⓕ와 초기 거주지의 재료를 설명하는 Ⓔ, 뗏장집의 장단점에 대한 설명인 Ⓒ가 요약에 필요한 핵심적인 내용이다.

VOCABULARY TEST

정답 1. (B)   2. (D)   3. (C)   4. (C)   5. (A)
      6. (C)   7. (A)   8. (C)   9. (B)   10. (D)
      11. (C) 12. (D)

밑줄 친 어휘나 구와 가장 유사한 의미를 지닌 것을 고르시오.

1. 이 질문은 너무 복잡해. 내게 <u>간단한</u> 답을 줘.
   (A) 복잡한   (B) 간단한
   (C) 혼란시키는   (D) 예외적인

2. 죽고 싶지 않다면 <u>무모하게</u> 운전하지마.
   (A) 무례하게   (B) 근본적으로
   (C) 빠르게   (D) 부주의하게

3. 나는 항상 직장에서 (근무) 효율성을 어떻게 높일까를 <u>곰곰이 생각한다</u>.
   (A) 걱정하다   (B) 불평하다
   (C) 숙고하다   (D) 암시하다

4. 나는 실수에 대한 책망을 받았을 때 그의 얼굴에 나타난 <u>미묘한</u> 변화를 놓치지 않았다.
   (A) 일관된   (B) 확실한
   (C) 약간의   (D) 명백한

5. 난 Randy가 싫어! 그 앤 항상 내 걸음걸이를 흉내내면서 <u>놀려</u>.
   (A) 비웃다   (B) 판단하다
   (C) 비난하다   (D) 칭찬하다

6. James는 화학 회사의 최고 경영자가 되었고, 현재는 자신의 힘을 <u>강화시킬</u> 수 있는 방법을 찾고 있다.
   (A) 분배하다   (B) 타협하다
   (C) 증대시키다   (D) 줄이다

7. 데모를 일으키는 <u>근원적인</u> 문제는 임금과 인종 차별이다.
   (A) 근본적인   (B) 첫째의
   (C) 중요한   (D) 주목할 만한

8. 이 나라의 세금 개혁은 Bruce란 이름의 사람을 통해 <u>개척되었다</u>.
   (A) 완성되었다   (B) 상속받았다
   (C) 발달되었다   (D) 방해받았다

9. 한국의 물가가 <u>지나치게</u> 높기 때문에, 나는 밤에 아르바이트를 하나 더 하기로 결정했다.
   (A) 적당하게   (B) 대단히
   (C) 과장되게   (D) 철저히

10. 연구자들은 그 현상을 용해라고 <u>인식한다</u>.
    (A) 해결하다   (B) 주장하다
    (C) 경고하다   (D) 인지하다

11. 나는 천사를 <u>초자연적인</u> 존재라고 생각한다.
    (A) 상상의   (B) 현실의
    (C) 유령 같은   (D) 실용적인

12. 한 <u>익명의</u> 작가가 우리 잡지에 이 편지를 썼다.
    (A) 유명한   (B) 악명 높은
    (C) 순진한   (D) 익명의

Chapter 8 Insertion   p.190 - p.212

SAMPLE ITEM   정답 Ⓒ

해석 미국 정부가 대공황 시기에 Mojave 사막 중앙에 후버 댐을 건설하기로 계획했을 때, 노동자들이 거주할 마을도 건설하기로 계획했다. 그러나 도시를 건설하기도 전에, 댐이 건설될 부지에 노동자들이 도착하기 시작했다. 이에 따라 그들은 스스로 Ragtown이라 알려진 캠프를 만들었다. 물과 공중위생시설, 전기 공급이 빈곤한 이 장소는 후버 댐 프로젝트를 위한 수백 명의 노동자들이 수개월동안 거주한 곳이었다. 이 기간 동안 그들은 어쨌든 무슨 일이든 있다는 것에 감사하며 사막의 더위와 극한 생활 상황들을 견뎌냈다. 그러나 마침내 정부는 사기업의 도움을 받아 오늘날에도 여전히 존재하는 안락한 사막 마을인 Boulder City를 지었다.

문제 | 지문에서 아래의 문장이 삽입될 수 있는 곳을 나타내는 네 개의 (■)를 보시오.

(Thus, they set up their own camp that was known as Ragtown.)

문장이 가장 잘 맞는 곳은 어디인가? (■)을 클릭해 지문에 문장을 삽입하시오.

해설 | Thus란 접속사에 주의한다. 노동자들 스스로가 자신들이 거주할 캠프를 만들어야 했다는 내용으로 보아, 이 상황을 일어나게끔 하는 원인이 되는 내용이 앞에 나와야 한다.

Basic Drill 1

정답 1. (C) 2. (B) 3. (A)

1. 해석   목재 골격은 미국에서 지어진 대부분의 주택들을 지탱하고 있다. 이것은 엄청난 양의 목재를 필요로 하는데, 물론 이 목재들은 숲에서 난 것이다. 환경친화적 기술을 활용하여 건축된 주택은 진보된 공학 덕분에, 전통적인 주택들보다 나무를 대략 60%정도 덜 사용한다. 전통적인 냉난방 시스템이 사용되더라도, 환경친화적인 주택을 시원하게 하고 따뜻하게 하는 데 에너지는 훨씬 적게 소모된다. 이것은 벽들이 더욱 두꺼워지기 때문이다. 이는 더 많은 단열재가 사용된다는 것을 의미한다. 단열 처리가 잘 된 벽은 여름에는 집을 서늘하게, 겨울에는 따뜻하게 한다. 그리고 전통적인 집과 달리, 집으로 통하는 모든 공기는 정화된다.

해설 | 전통적인 냉난방 시스템으로 지어도 환경친화적으로 지어진 집은 에너지를 더 적게 소비한다는 내용이므로, 그것의 이유가 되는 문장 앞에 들어가게 한다.

2. 해석   대머리 독수리는 미국의 상징이지만, 건국 초창기에는 강한 경쟁상대가 있었다. 당시에 나라 전역에서 볼 수 있었던 몸집이 큰 사냥새인 칠면조가 실제로 국조 후보로 지명되었다. 오늘날 우리는 칠면조를 뚱뚱하고, 품위 없고, 다소 우둔한 동물로 생각하지만, (그때는) 그것을 탁월한 선택이라 여기는 사람들이 많았다. 예를 들어 초기 미국인들 중 가장 영향력 있는 인사 중 한 명인 Ben Franklin은 칠면조가 용기를 상징하는 모델이고 독수리보다 훨씬 더 존중받을 만하다고 주장했다. 그는 독수리가 위험에 처하면 도망가는 동물이라 생각했다. 반면에 칠면조는 공격에 대항해서 용감하게 자신의 영역을 지킨다고 생각했다.

해설 | 주어진 문장은 독수리에 비해 칠면조가 용기 있고 존중받을 만한 동물이라고 생각한 사람을 구체적으로 밝혀서 이 문단의 주제를 논리적으로 뒷받침하고 있다. 대명사 he가 처음으로 등장한 문장 바로 앞에 Franklin을 언급한 선택지를 끼워 넣어야 자연스럽게 이어진다.

3. 해석   유명한 가족 구성원들과 부유함으로 인해 두드러진, 빛나는 배경 아래에서 플라톤의 지적 성취는 결코 놀랄만한 것이 아닐지도 모른다. 예를 들자면, 아버지 쪽의 가족과 관련하여, 그는 그리스 아테네의 초기 왕들의 자손이라고 여겨진다. 어머니 쪽의 혈통 또한 주목할 만했다. 어머니 Perictione도 기원전 6세기 지혜와 시적 재능 모두로 유명했던 인물인, 입법자 Solon과 친척이었다. 플라톤이 아직 어렸을 때, 그의 아버지가 세상을 떠났다. 그 후 그의 어머니는 Pyrilampes란 이름의 남자와 결혼했는데, 그 사람은 유명한 정치가 Pericles의 동료였다.

해설 | For instance로 시작되는 문장이 무엇에 대한 예를 드는 것인지 살펴본다. 문장의 내용이 플라톤의 화려한 가족 배경이므로 A 위치에 들어가야 적절하다.

Basic Drill 2

정답 1. A, D, B, C   2. D, C, B, A
      3. B, D, A, C   4. C, B, D, A

1. 해석   A 주택 구입자들의 환경보존에 대한 관심이 점점 더 높아지고 있다.

B 환경친화 건물(Green building)은 천연재료를 아껴서 사용하고 유해한 화학물질 사용을 피하는 건축 기술이다.

C 게다가 주택은 냉난방 시 전기를 덜 사용하도록 특별히 고안된다.

D 이러한 요구에 부응하기 위해, 건축 공학자들은 현재 환경친화 건물의 건축에 더욱 초점을 맞추고 있다.

해설 | A는 지문의 주제문이라 할 수 있기에 가장 먼저 나와야 하고, 주제문을 받쳐 본격적인 내용의 전개를 시작하는 D가 두 번째 나온다고 볼 수 있다. D에서 "green building"이 언급되므로, green building에 대한 소개 또는 정의를 내리는 B가 그 다음이라 볼 수 있다. C는 B에 부연되어 green building에 대한 설명이다.

2. 해석   A 그러므로 현대 미술가들도 자신들이 원하는 밝은 색깔을 얻기 위해 종종 구식 방법으로 물감을 만드는 방법을 사용한다.

B 중세 템페라 물감은 오늘날 화방에서 파는 물감과는 매우 다르다. 현대의 대체물은 인공 염료와 화학성분 염료를 사용하는데, 예전의 물감에 비해 맑고 밝지 않다.

C 돌과 식물에서 추출된 다른 색의 천연 염료는 물감에 색을 내기 위해 첨가되었다.

D 템페라 물감은 계란과 물의 혼합으로 만들어진 재료이다. 이 재료는 그 기원이 중세세대까지 거슬러 올라가며, 수년 동안 템페라 물감은 자체의 매우 밝고 빛나는 색깔로 인해 많은 예술가들의 선호 대상이었다.

해설 | 지문의 주제인 tempera paint를 소개하고 그것에 대한 정의를 내리는 D가 가장 먼저 나오는 지문이고, tempera paint의 원료에 대한 내용인 C가 다음에 나오기에 적절하다. A의 Therefore가 무엇에 대한 '그러므로'인지를 파악하는 것이 중요하다. A의 문장은 현대 미술가들이 자신들이 원하는 밝은 색의 물감을 얻기 위해 옛날 방식으로 물감을 만든다는 내용이므로, 그 결과를 발생시킨 내용이 앞에 나오는 것이 올바르다.

3. 해석 A burrowing owl는, 나무 내부에 자신의 둥지를 만드는 다른 큰 올빼미들과는 달리, 프레리 도그나 땅다람쥐, 혹은 사람이 땅에 파놓은 구멍 속에 산다.

B burrowing owl은 우리가 알고 있는 가장 작은 올빼미 중 하나로서, 겨우 8인치 정도에 이를 정도로만 성장한다.

C 따라서 "burrowing owl"이라는 이름은 이 새에게 아주 적절한 것이다.

D 이 올빼미는 사막이나 초원지대에 살며 그 곳에서 곤충, 설치류, 파충류 같이 다양한 먹이를 먹는다. burrowing owl에 관해 가장 흥미로운 점 중 하나는 그것의 둥지이다.

해설 | 지문의 주제를 소개하는 역할을 하는 B가 첫 번째로 나온다. A는 burrowing owl이 어디에 사는지 언급하는데, D는 둥지에 대한 내용이 나오도록 이야기를 이끄는 역할을 한다. 따라서 D-A 순으로 제시되고, A는 C의 근거가 된다.

4. 해석 A 그들이 한 비교에 근거하여, 연구자들은 회전률의 차이는 지구의 자기장 탓일 수도 있다고 말한다.

B 우선, 연구자들은 지진파가 지구의 핵을 통과하여 이동하는 데 소요되는 시간을 도표로 기록했다.

C 지진으로 인한 지진파의 속도를 연구하면서, 최근 지질학자들은 지구의 핵이 그 외의 나머지 부분보다 약간 빠르게 회전한다는 흥미로운 발견을 했다.

D 그리고 나서 그들은 같은 파장이 지구의 다른 부분들을 통과하는데 걸리는 시간을 이와 비교했다.

해설 | 지문의 주제를 제시해 주는 C가 가장 먼저 나오는 문장이다. D의 They then ~이 나오는 것으로 보아, D 이전에 연구자들이 한 어떤 실험 과정이 먼저 나올 것이라 추측할 수 있다. 따라서 B-D의 순서로 나오게 된다. B-D에서 한 실험의 결과를 비교해서 내린 결론에 대해 언급하는 A는 마지막 문장이 된다.

VOCABULARY Preview

| Check-up |

1. handed down 2. sterile 3. dogmatic
4. leach 5. genuine 6. dissatisfied
7. embraces 8. brought about

다음 빈 칸에 들어갈 알맞은 말을 골라, 필요하면 고쳐 쓰시오.

1. 이 검은 오래 전 우리 증조부 때부터 전해 내려오는 가보이다.
2. 이 액체는 박테리아 없이 무균상태로 보존되어야 한다.
3. Alfred가 속한 교회는 매우 독단적이라고 여겨진다.
4. 비가 많이 오네. 난 이 비가 토양에 있는 농약을 걸러낼 거라 생각해.
5. 이 가방은 진짜 악어가죽으로 만들어졌다.
6. 전 더 나은 대우를 받아야만 합니다. 당신의 결정이 불만스럽군요.
7. 그녀의 연구는 고대 그리스의 발전을 추적하고 고대 그리스 예술의 전 분야를 포함한다.
8. 새로운 기술은 여러 사회적 변화를 초래했다.

Exercise 1

정답 1. ⓒ 2. ⓑ 3. ⓓ 4. ⓑ 5. ⓐ
6. ⓐ, ⓒ, ⓕ

해석 라파엘 전파(Pre-Raphaelites, Pre-Raphaelite Brotherhood) 화가들은 당대 미술에 불만족스러워하던 예술가 집단이었다. 라파엘 전파는 1848년 John Everett Millais, Dante Gabriel Rossetti와 William Holman Hunt에 의해 창설되었다. 이 단체의 의도는, 화가 라파엘의 영향을 답습하는 회화에서 비롯된 왜곡된 화풍이라고 생각되는 것에 문제를 제기하는 것이었다. 그들은 공식에 매이고 진부한 예술 교육의 조잡한 기법을 따르기보다, 창조성과 독창성을 회복하기를 추구했다. 바꾸어 말하면, 그들은 세부묘사와 색상, 그리고 정교한 구조가 충분히 구현된 회화 작품을 원했다.

　이러한 젊은 화가들은 극도로 이상적이었고 회화 작품의 본질을 더 낫게 변화시킬 수 있다고 생각했다. 그러나 이와 더불어 그들은 지나치게 독단적이게 되는 것, 즉, 훌륭한 화가가 따라야 하는 특정한 방식들이 있다고 하면서 회화가의 규칙에 지나치게 고수하는 것을 경계했다. 그 대신 그들은 개개의 화가에 대한 존중을 불러일으키기를 원했다. 그들이 느끼기에는, 너무 많은 화가들이 자신들의 생각과 느낌을 캔버스에 담기보다 스승에게 전수받은 모범을 그저 답습하고 있었다.

　라파엘 전파 화가들은 완고하고 엄격하기를 원하지 않았지만, 집단의 목표는 확실했다. 첫 번째는 표현할 만한 진정한 생각을 갖고 있어야 한다는 것이다. 그들은 당대 화가들이 관심을 갖는 대상이 아닌 초상화나 풍경화 등 사회의 기대에 부응하는 것만을 그린다고 생각했다. 또한 화가들이 자연을 효과적으로 표현하기 위해 자연에 깊은 관심을 가져야 한다고 생각했다. 또 다른 중요한 목표는 진실성을 담아내는 것이었다. 그들은 그들과 동시대의 작품이 지나치게 냉소적이며 무정하지만, 과거 작품들(라파엘의 화풍이 유행하기 이전)은 흔히 진실한 정서를 담고 있다고 생각했다.

문 1 ｜ 첫 번째 단락의 cliched와 가장 의미가 유사한 것은?
　Ⓐ 흥미로운
　Ⓑ 놀라운
　Ⓒ 지루한
　Ⓓ 이상한

해설 ｜ cliched는 '케케묵은', '진부한'의 의미이다. 해당 문장의 formulaic하고 cliched한 형보다는 창조성과 독창성을 회복하고자 노력했다는 것에서 Ⓒ가 답이 됨을 알 수 있다.

문 2 ｜ 첫 번째 단락에서 글쓴이가 라파엘을 언급한 이유는?
　Ⓐ 라파엘과 라파엘 전파 화가들과의 유사점을 지적하기 위해
　Ⓑ 단체의 이름과 사상이 어디에서 유래되었는지 지적하기 위해
　Ⓒ 라파엘의 예술 이론과 그의 제자들의 예술 이론을 대조하기 위해
　Ⓓ 라파엘 전파 화가들이 라파엘만큼 영향력이 있지 않았다는 것을 암시하기 위해

해설 ｜ 라파엘 전파 화가들은 라파엘의 예술 이론과 테크닉 등을 그대로 답습하던 당대의 예술계에 반발하여 생긴 집단이라는 내용이 언급되어 있다.

문 3 ｜ 지문에서 아래의 문장이 삽입될 수 있는 곳을 나타내는 네 개의 〔■〕를 보시오.

　〔In other words, they wanted paintings full of detail, color, and complicated compositions.〕
문장이 가장 잘 맞는 곳은 어디인가? 〔■〕을 클릭해 지문에 문장을 삽입하시오.

해설 ｜ 부연 설명임을 나타내는 signal인 In other words에 주목한다. 뒤에 '세부묘사와 색상, 복잡한 구조가 충분히 구현된 회화를 원했다'는 내용을 보아, "그들이 구현하고자 했던 creativity and originality"에 대한 부연 설명임을 알 수 있다.

문 4 ｜ 다음 중 두 번째 단락의 하이라이트 된 문장의 핵심 내용을 가장 잘 표현한 것은? 틀린 보기는 본문의 내용을 심각하게 바꾸거나 핵심적인 내용을 누락시킨 것이다.
　Ⓐ 그들은 예술가들에 의해 인정받아야 하는 회화에 대한 그들의 규칙을 규정하는 데 주의를 기울였다.
　Ⓑ 특정한 화법을 고수하는 대신, 그들은 개별적인 화가의 작품을 존중하려 노력했다.
　Ⓒ 그들은 개개의 화가들이 인정하고 따라야 하는 회화의 특정한 방식이 있다고 주장했다.
　Ⓓ 그들은 교사들에 의해 고수되는 규칙을 피하는, 개별적인 화가가 존중받아야 한다고 생각했다.

해설 ｜ 하이라이트 된 문장의 핵심 내용은, 회화에 지켜야 하는 특정 규칙이 있다고 하면서 그 화풍을 독단적으로 고수하기 보다는 화가 개개인의 개성을 반영하고 투영하여 작품을 창조해야 한다는 것이다.

문 5 ｜ 세 번째 단락의 rigid와 가장 의미가 유사한 것은?
　Ⓐ 완고한
　Ⓑ 구체적인
　Ⓒ 예기된
　Ⓓ 혼란시키는

해설 ｜ rigid는 '완고한', '유연성이 없는'의 뜻이다. 문장에서 rigid와 동의어라 할 수 있는 strict가 나왔으므로 이를 참고하여 답을 고른다.

문 6 ｜ 지문에 대한 간단한 요약을 위한 도입 문장이 아래에 제시된다. 가장 중요한 내용을 표현한 3가지 대답을 선택하여 요약을 완성하시오. 몇몇 문장들은 단락에서 언급되지 않았거나 중요하지 않은 내용을 표현해서 요약에 들어갈 수 없다.

라파엘 전파는 19세기 중엽에 발흥한 새로운 예술 운동이었다.
　Ⓐ 라파엘 전파는 라파엘의 화풍을 답습하는 것에 저항하는 예술가 단체였으며, 다채롭고 정교한 예술 작품을 창조하려는 목표를 갖고 있었다.
　Ⓑ 라파엘 전파 화가들은 일반적으로 그림에 라파엘이 사용한 세부 묘사와 색상, 그리고 정교한 구성을 따라했다.
　Ⓒ 이 화가들은 최고의 예술은 규칙을 따라가기 보다는 개성을 살리는 것에서 창조된다고 생각했다.
　Ⓓ 당대의 대다수 화가들은 학교에서 가르침 받은 모범을 답습하는 회화 기법을 배웠다.
　Ⓔ 초상화와 풍경화를 발달시키기 위해, 그들은 사람들이 자연에 더 관심을 기울여야 한다고 생각했다.

Ⓕ 그 단체는 진실성, 아이디어, 세상에 대한 관심을 좋은 예술에 대한 핵심으로 강조했다.

해설 | Ⓑ의 내용은 라파엘 전파가 아닌 다른 화가들에 의해 자행되고 있었던 것이다. Ⓓ는 핵심 내용이 아닌 부차적인 내용이고, Ⓔ는 지문에 언급되지 않은 내용이다.

Exercise 2

정답 1. Ⓒ 2. Ⓐ 3. Ⓑ 4. Ⓐ 5. Ⓑ 6. Ⓓ
7. Traditional Plants - Ⓐ, Ⓔ /
Hydroponic Plants - Ⓑ, Ⓒ, Ⓖ

해석 모든 식물은 잘 자라기 위해 영양분과 빛, 그리고 공기가 필요하다. 씨가 흙에 심겨지면, 씨는 뿌리를 통해 흙에서 양분을 흡수한다. 그러나 흙에는 또한 식물성장을 저해시키는 많은 잠재적인 위험이 있다. 예를 들면, 흙에서 발생하는 질병이나 균류 뿐 아니라 곤충의 알이나 애벌레 등이 흙속에 있을 수 있다. 포식성인 식물이나 잡초 또한 흙속에 있어 문제를 일으킬 수 있다. 이런 것들은 식물이 자랄 공간을 차지할 뿐 아니라 양분도 빼앗아갈 수 있다. 게다가, 날씨와 환경으로 인해 흙은 그 유익한 영양분을 잃게 될 수도 있다. 비록 비료가 더해져도 비와 햇빛이 흙을 씻어 내려가게 하거나, 비료를 제거하기 때문에 더해진 비료를 무용지물로 만들어 버린다. 따라서 흙에 작물을 기르는 전통적인 원예방법이지만 여전히 위험하고 이상적인 것이 아니다.

수경 재배는 이런 문제들에 해결책을 제시한다. 본질적으로 이 재배 방법은 물이나 흙이 아닌 곳에서 식물을 재배하는 것이다. 예를 들자면, 이탄 이끼나 나무껍질에서 재배된 식물은 수경 재배 식물로 간주된다. 물속이든 다른 흙이 아닌 곳에서이든, 수경 재배법에는 여러 가지 이점이 있다. 우선 첫째로, 흙과는 달리 서식 장소가 무균 상태이기 때문에 해충이나 질병이 식물이 자라는 데 공격할 수 없다. 또한 잡초가 나타나 식물과 (영역을 확보하기 위하여) 경쟁하지도 않는다. 다른 이점은 영양분이 서식 장소에 직접 더해지고 제거되지 않는다는 점이다. 이와 같은 이상적인 조건들로 인해 수경 재배 식물은 전통적으로 재배된 식물들에 비해 더 튼튼하고, 크고, 건강하다.

문 1 | 첫 번째 단락에서 아래의 문장이 삽입될 수 있는 곳을 나타내는 네 개의 [■]를 보시오.

〔These can deprive the plant of nutrients as well as take up its space.〕

문장이 가장 잘 맞는 곳은 어디인가? [■]을 클릭해 해당 단락에 문장을 삽입하시오.

해설 | These가 무엇을 받는지 생각해 보고, 주어진 문장을 Ⓐ, Ⓑ, Ⓒ, Ⓓ에 대입해 본다. Ⓒ 뒤에 Additionally, ~ 내용이 나오는 것으로 보아, 주어진 문장이 들어가야 할 곳은 Ⓒ이다.

문 2 | 첫 번째 단락의 rendering와 가장 의미가 유사한 것은?
Ⓐ 만드는
Ⓑ 사는
Ⓒ 생산하는
Ⓓ 조절하는

해설 | render은 '(어떤 상태가) 되게 하다'란 의미를 지니고 있다. 문맥에서는 첨가된 비료를 쓸모없는 것으로 '만든다'라고 해석할 수 있으므로 답은 Ⓐ이다.

문 3 | 첫 번째 단락에서 글쓴이는 흙에서 자라는 식물들에게 가해지는 위험을 어떻게 강조했는가?
Ⓐ 흙속에 사는 주요한 곤충들과 질병을 나타냄으로써
Ⓑ 흙이 가지는 문제들의 예를 듦으로써
Ⓒ 날씨가 일으키는 문제들을 설명함으로써
Ⓓ 유익한 영양분이 어떻게 제거되는지를 보여줌으로써

해설 | This soil, however, supports a number of potential risks to plant health as well. 이후에는 모두 흙이 어떤 문제들을 일으킬 수 있는지가 나열되어 있다.

문 4 | 두 번째 단락의 conventionally와 가장 의미가 유사한 것은?
Ⓐ 전통적으로
Ⓑ 주의 깊게
Ⓒ 농업적으로
Ⓓ 조직적인

해설 | conventionally는 '전통적인', '관습적인'의 뜻이다. 또한, conventionally grown plants에 비해 새로운 재배 방식인 수경 재배 식물이 더 튼튼하고 강하고 건강하다는 내용으로 미루어보아, conventionally가 traditionally란 의미임을 알 수 있다.

문 5 | 두 번째 단락에서 아래의 문장이 삽입될 수 있는 곳을 나타내는 네 개의 [■]를 보시오.

〔Whether in water or another non-soil medium, there are a number of advantages to hydroponics.〕

문장이 가장 잘 맞는 곳은 어디인가? [■]을 클릭해 해당 단락에 문장을 삽입하시오.

해설 | Whether in water or other non-soil medium에 주목한다. in water or another non-soil medium이 언급된 뒤에 이 문장이 삽입되어야 하고, 수경 재배법의 이점에 대한 구체적인 언급이 나오기 전에 그것을 소개하는 역할을 할 수 있는 곳에 삽입해야 한다.

문 6 | 두 번째 단락에서 글쓴이가 이탄 이끼나 나무껍질에서 재배되는 식물을 언급한 이유는?
Ⓐ 거기서도 식물을 기를 수 있음을 암시하기 위해

Ⓑ 이 재배법에 사용되는 주요한 재료를 제시하기 위해
　　Ⓒ 물속에서 재배되는 식물과 비교하기 위해
　　Ⓓ 흙을 기반으로 하지 않는 다른 원예법의 예를 들기 위해

해설 | 수경 재배법은 식물을 키우기 위해 흙이 아닌 물이나 다른 곳을 이용한다. For instance, a plant can be raised in peat moss or bark, and be considered a hydroponic-raised plant.를 보면 이탄 이끼나 나무껍질에서 재배된 식물을 수경 재배법의 한 예로 들었음을 알 수 있다.

문 7 | 적절한 보기를 골라 관련 있는 식물 종류와 짝지으시오. 두개의 보기는 제외됩니다.
　　Ⓐ 영양분이 씻겨 나갈 위험이 있다.
　　Ⓑ 곤충이 영양분을 뺏을 수 없다.
　　Ⓒ 식물은 매우 크게 자랄 수 있다.
　　Ⓓ 햇빛이 직접적으로 필요하지는 않다.
　　Ⓔ (공간을) 침해하는 식물이 공간과 양분을 위해 얻기 위해 경쟁한다.
　　Ⓕ 식물은 농약과 다른 화학물질에 대한 면역이 있다.
　　Ⓖ 식물에게 자랄 수 있는 무균 환경이 주어진다.

해설 | 영양분이 씻겨 나갈 수 있고, 잡초처럼 공간을 확보하기 위한 경쟁을 벌이게 되는 위험이 있는 식물은 전통적인 방식으로 재배되는 식물들이다. 수경 재배법으로 자라는 식물은 곤충이나 흙에 의한 질병, 날씨 등으로 인해 영양분을 뺏길 염려가 없는 최상의 환경에서 자라기 때문에 크게 잘 자랄 수 있다.

Exercise 3

정답 1. Ⓐ   2. Ⓑ   3. Ⓓ   4. Ⓒ   5. Ⓒ
　　 6. Ⓑ   7. Ⓐ   8. Ⓐ, Ⓒ, Ⓔ

Text Outline　(A)

해석　미국의 50주 중 13개 주만 유치원 등록을 의무화하고 있지만, 초기 아동교육의 중요성에 대한 인식의 증가는 95%에 달하는 모든 미국 어린이들이 유치원에 입학하는 결과를 초래했다. 3세 이상의 어린이에게 가능한 취학전 교육 프로그램 입학도 크게 증가했다. 그렇게 일찍 아이들을 교육 프로그램에 보내는 것에 무시 못할 이익이 있는가? 사실, 무수히 많은 연구들은, 일찍 아이들을 교육 프로그램에 입학시키는 것이 아이들의 나중 인생에 대단히 긍정적인 영향을 미친다는 것을 증명했다. 이것은 (경제적, 사회적으로) 혜택 받지 못한 배경 출신의 아이들에게도 동일하다고 드러났다.

　조사에 따르면, 법이 요구하는 연령 전에 교육 기관에 입학한 아이들은 몇 가지 이점을 얻는다. 첫째는 학업적인 측면이다. 유치원이나 보육원에 다닌 아이들은, 특히 읽기와 쓰기, 그리고 산수가 어렵다는 것을 알게 되었을 때 이런 능력을 향상시키기 위해 나중에 보충 수업을 받아야 하는 경우의 수가 적다. 게다가, 그들은 학창 시절 동안 별로 낙제를 하거나 성적이 낮지 않다. 이런 학생들은 졸업 비율이 더 높고, 학교에 대해 전반적으로 더 나은 태도를 가진다.

　다른 이점은 직업적인 측면이다. 보육원이나 유치원을 졸업한 학생은 고등학교도 더 많이 졸업하지만, 대학에도 더 많이 진학한다. 이것은 그들이 얻을 수 있는 직업의 종류나 잠재적으로 벌게 될 수입에도 직접적인 영향을 미친다. 이런 아이들은 어린이 되면 취학 전 교육 프로그램에 등록하지 않은 아이들에 비해 실업률도 더 낮다. 그러므로 이른 유년기 교육의 영향은 단기적으로나 장기적으로 모두 이롭다.

문 1 | 다음 중 첫 번째 단락의 하이라이트 된 문장의 핵심 내용을 가장 잘 표현한 것은? 틀린 보기는 본문의 내용을 심각하게 바꾸거나 핵심적인 내용을 누락시킨 것이다.
　　Ⓐ 대개 의무화 되지 않지만 대부분의 사람들이 조기 교육을 중요하다고 생각해서 대부분의 미국 어린이들은 유지원에 입학한다.
　　Ⓑ 조기 어린이 교육의 중요성을 인식하고 있음에도 상관없이 대부분의 사람들은 주에서 의무적으로 정한 취학 연령이 되었을 때부터 자녀들을 교육 기관에 보낸다.
　　Ⓒ 대부분의 미국 어린이들이 유치원에 다니지만 많은 주에서는 실제로는 아동 교육을 의무화하지 않는다.
　　Ⓓ 미국 어린이들의 5%가 유치원에 입학하지 못하기 때문에, 각 주 정부는 아이들의 입학을 의무화하는 정책을 실행해야 한다.

해설 | 하이라이트 된 문장의 핵심 내용은, 주 정부에서 취학 전 아동 교육을 의무화하지 않아도 조기 교육의 중요성이 널리 퍼지고 있기 때문에 많은 미국 어린이들이 유치원에 입학한다는 것이다.

문 2 | 첫 번째 단락의 measurable과 가장 의미가 유사한 것은?
　　Ⓐ 불명료한
　　Ⓑ 두드러진
　　Ⓒ 유용한
　　Ⓓ 가능한

해설 | measurable은 '중요한', '무시 못할'의 의미를 가지고 있다. 지문에 benefit, positive effect 등의 표현이 나와 있는 것을 보아 답은 Ⓑ가 됨을 알 수 있다.

문 3 | 첫 번째 단락의 resoundingly와 가장 의미가 유사한 것은?
　　Ⓐ 가능하게
　　Ⓑ 유망하게
　　Ⓒ 미묘하게
　　Ⓓ 확실하게

해설 | resoundingly는 원래 '울려퍼지게', '철처히'란 의미이므로, 문맥에서 '대단히' 정도로 해석할 수 있다. 주어진

보기에서는 '부정하기 어려운', '명백한'의 의미인 definitely가 가장 가깝다.

문 4 | 첫 번째 단락에서 글쓴이가 혜택 받지 못한 배경을 언급한 이유는?
Ⓐ 이슈를 연구하기 위한 더 많은 자금이 필요하다는 것을 나타내기 위해
Ⓑ 혜택 받지 못한 아이들이 학교에서 잘 하지 못함을 암시하기 위해
Ⓒ (그) 결과가 모든 아이들에게 동일하게 적용됨을 강조하기 위해
Ⓓ 혜택 받지 못한 아이들은 유치원에 등록할 필요가 없음을 제안하기 위해

해설 | 조기 교육이 모든 아이들에게 이로운 영향을 준다는 것을 알리기 위해 혜택 받지 못한 아이를 언급하고 있다.

문 5 | 두 번째 단락에서 아래의 문장이 삽입될 수 있는 곳을 나타내는 네 개의 [■]를 보시오.

[Additionally, they are less likely to fail classes or score low grades during their school careers.]

문장이 가장 잘 맞는 곳은 어디인가? [■]을 클릭해 해당 단락에 문장을 삽입하시오.

해설 | Additionally란 signal이 붙는 것으로 보아 조기 교육 프로그램 입학에 제시된 이점으로 인한 두 번째 결과라는 것을 짐작할 수 있다. 그리고 내용 순서상, 졸업 비율이 더 높다는 언급 전에 학교에서 낙제를 하지 않는다는 내용이 와야 함을 알 수 있다.

문 6 | 두, 세 번째 단락에서 저자가 학업적인 성취 면에서 조기 학습의 영향을 어떻게 강조했는가?
Ⓐ 시험점수에 관한 통계자료를 제시하면서
Ⓑ 조기 교육이 아이들에게 주는 여러 장점들을 열거하면서
Ⓒ 그 논점에 관한 교사의 연구를 언급하면서
Ⓓ 프리 스쿨 졸업생과 비 프리 스쿨 졸업생을 대조하면서

해설 | 이른 입학이 학생들에게 미치는 이점을 열거하면서 조기 학습의 영향을 강조하고 있다.

문 7 | 세 번째 단락에서 아래의 문장이 삽입될 수 있는 곳을 나타내는 네 개의 [■]를 보시오.

[Pre-school and kindergarten graduates are more likely to not only graduate high school, but to go on to college.]

문장이 가장 잘 맞는 곳은 어디인가? [■]을 클릭해 해당 단락에 문장을 삽입하시오.

해설 | Another type of advantage is in terms of careers. 와 This directly influences their earning potential and the types of jobs they can get. 사이를 이어주는 내용이 없고, This를 받는 지시 대상이 앞에 나와야 할 필요가 있다.

문 8 | 지문에 대한 간단한 요약을 위한 도입 문장이 아래에 제시된다. 가장 중요한 내용을 표현한 3가지 대답을 선택하여 요약을 완성하시오. 몇몇 문장들은 단락에서 언급되지 않았거나 중요하지 않은 내용을 표현해서 요약에 들어갈 수 없다.

보육원과 유치원 출석률이 나라 전체적으로 높다.
Ⓐ 많은 부모들은 취학전 교육이 아이들의 학교생활과 후의 취업면에서 중요한 역할을 한다고 생각한다.
Ⓑ 부유한 학부모들뿐 아니라 그렇지 않은 학부모들도 자녀를 유치원이나 취학전 교육 프로그램에 등록시킨다.
Ⓒ 교육 기관에 더 일찍 입학하는 학생들은 학업 면에서 더 우수하고 졸업 비율이 더 높은 경향이 있다.
Ⓓ 교육 기관에 일찍 입학하는 아이들은 일반적으로 학교 출석률이 더 높고, 이것이 대학생활에서의 성공에 영향을 미친다.
Ⓔ 초기 아동 교육은 미국에서 인기가 있고 일찍이 이에 참여한 아이들의 성인이 되었을 때의 삶에 긍정적인 영향을 미치는 것으로 보인다.
Ⓕ 더 많은 아이들이 유치원에 다닌다는 사실이 미국의 실업률에 영향을 미치고 있다.

해설 | Ⓑ와 Ⓕ는 핵심적이지 않은 내용이고, Ⓓ의 '학교 출석률이 높다'는 것은 지문에 언급되지 않은 내용이다.

VOCABULARY TEST

정답 1. (D)   2. (D)   3. (C)   4. (A)   5. (D)
      6. (C)   7. (A)   8. (C)   9. (D)

밑줄 친 어휘나 구와 가장 유사한 의미를 가진 것을 고르시오.

1. 그 소년의 가장 주목할 만한 특징은, 축구할 때 양발을 사용할 수 있다는 것이다.
   (A) 악명 높은   (B) 참을성 있는
   (C) 성실한   (D) 주목할 만한

2. Shelley는 자신의 성공을 정직함과 근면함에 돌렸다.
   (A) 판단했다   (B) 부정했다
   (C) 동의했다   (D) ~에 돌렸다

3. 아내에게 멋진 러브레터를 쓰기 위해 나는 많은 시에서 낭만적인 문구들을 뽑아냈다.
   (A) 발견했다   (B) 묘사했다
   (C) 뽑아냈다   (D) 제거했다

4. 너무 많은 에러가 그 프로그램을 쓸모없는 것으로 만들었다.
   (A) 만들다   (B) 간주하다
   (C) 완성하다   (D) 창설하다

5. 그는 축구팬들에 의해 '경기 MVP'로 지명되었다.
   (A) 암시되었다   (B) 약속받았다
   (D) 오해받았다   (D) 임명되었다

6. 연두색과 주황색, 그리고 노란색이 그의 그림에서 볼 수 있는 세 개의 <u>밝은</u> 색상이다.
   - (A) 조용한
   - (B) 어두운
   - (C) 밝은
   - (D) 화려한

7. 그 와인은 <u>조금씩</u> 마셔라. 얼마 남아 있지도 않아.
   - (A) 절약하여
   - (B) 기꺼이
   - (C) 정확히
   - (D) 느슨하게

8. 이순신은 세계에서 가장 <u>유명한</u> 한국인 중 한 명이다.
   - (A) 아주 좋아하는
   - (B) 근면한
   - (C) 저명한
   - (D) 무서운

9. 그녀는 동료들의 <u>경솔한</u> 일처리를 거의 참지 못한다.
   - (A) 인정 많은
   - (B) 웃긴
   - (C) 우수한
   - (D) 경솔한

Chapter 9 Inference   p.214 - p.236

SAMPLE ITEM   정답 ⓒ

해석   지구가 경험한 여러 차례의 빙하시대 동안, 빙하라고 불리는 커다란 얼음 덩어리가 북쪽 지역에서 더 남쪽으로 서서히 이동한다. 그것들이 이동할 때, 그들은 그 경로를 따라서 매끄러운 계곡을 새겨놓는다. 때때로 그것들은 자기들이 가는 경로에 있는 거대한 바위를 들어 종종 수백만 마일을 옮기기도 한다. "표석"이라고 일컬어지는 그 바위들은 빙하가 녹은 후에, 지상에 놓인다. 영국의 Norfolk에서 발견된 표석은 한 때 지질학자들을 당황하게 만들었다. 그들은 왜 계곡에 토착 바위가 아닌 바위들이 그렇게나 많이 존재하는지 이유를 상상할 수 없었다. 그러나 지질학자들이 빙하와 빙하의 이동에 대해 더 많은 것을 알게 되자 수수께끼가 풀렸다. 지질학자들은 그 신비로운 바위들이 표석(標石)이라는 것을 발견했다.

문제 | 표석에 관해 추론할 수 있는 것은?
  Ⓐ 그것들은 Norfolk에 있는 많은 계곡에서 주로 발견된다.
  Ⓑ 그것들은 영국의 많은 계곡들을 훼손했다.
  Ⓒ 그것들은 Norfolk의 토착 바위들과 구별된다.
  Ⓓ 그것들은 주로 계곡 바닥을 옮기는 원인이었다.

해설 | They could not imagine why the nonnative rocks existed in such large numbers in the valleys에서 표석이 nonnative rocks이라면 그것들과 구별되는 native rocks가 있다는 것을 유추할 수 있다.

Basic Drill 1

정답
1. (A) - NBF / (B) - RI / (C) - NT
2. (A) - RI / (B) - NBF / (C) - NT
3. (A) - NT / (B) - RI / (C) - NBF
4. (A) - RI / (B) - NBF / (C) - NT
5. (A) - NT / (B) - NBF/ (C) - RI
6. (A) - NT / (B) - NBF/ (C) - RI

1. 해석   미 남서부의 토종 박쥐들은 흔히 낮 동안 자고, 야간에 먹이를 사냥하기 위해 완전히 어두워진 동굴 안식처를 떠난다.

문제 | (A) 미국 남서부의 박쥐들은 햇빛에 약하다.
  (B) 박쥐들은 어둠속에서 먹이를 감지하고 잡는 특수한 능력이 있다.
  (C) 대부분의 박쥐들은 배가 고플 때마다 동굴을 떠난다.

해설 | 야간에 먹이를 사냥한다는 것에서 박쥐가 어둠에서 먹이를 잡을 수 있는 능력이 있음을 알 수 있다. 박쥐가 햇빛에 약하다는 것은 사실에 근거하지 않은 내용이고, 박쥐가 배가 고플 때마다 동굴을 떠난다는 것은 지문의 내용을 잘못 말하는 것이다.

2. 해석   연구자들은 Chihuahuan Desert의 기후 변화에 대해 정보를 주기 위해 나무의 나이테를 조사한다. 이 가는 나이테들은 (이 기간 동안 기후가) 극도로 건조한 기간임을 나타내며 매 50년에서 60년 마다 (이런 나이테들이) 발생하는 것으로 보인다.

문제 | (A) Chihuahuan Desert의 어떤 나무들은 매우 건조한 기간 동안에도 살아남는다.
  (B) 다른 지역의 대부분의 나무들은 그 지역의 기후에 관한 정보를 제공해 준다.
  (C) Chihuahuan Desert에 있는 (나무의) 나이테들은 매 50년에서 60년마다 만들어진다.

해설 | Chihuahuan Desert에 자라는 나무들은 극심한 가뭄에도 견딘다는 것을 유추할 수 있다. (B)의 내용은 지문에 주어진 사실을 통해 유추하기는 어려운 보기라 할 수 있고, (C)의 내용은 지문의 내용과는 다른 것을 언급하고 있다.

3. 해석   지오토라고 더 잘 알려진 Giotto di Bondone는 이탈리아 르네상스 시대의 최초의 주요 화가였다. 그는 뚜렷하고 흥미로운 색상을 사용함으로써 그의 회화에 생기를 불어넣었다. 이로 인해 당대의 미술 세계에 상당한 영향을 미쳤다. 그가 작품에서 종교적 주제와 테마를 계속해서 탐구했고, 지오토는 중세 시대의 회화에서 보여지지 않았던 힘과 사실주의를 부여했다.

문제 | (A) 지오토는 중세의 예술 학교에서 교육받은 유명한 화가였다.
(B) 대부분의 중세 시대의 회화 작품은 힘이 넘치거나, 색채가 풍부하거나, 사실적이지 않았다.
(C) 지오토는 종교에 관한 많은 조사를 해서 충분한 지식을 가지고 있었다.

해설 | 지문의 내용으로 보아 중세 시대의 회화 작품들이 지오토의 작품들처럼 색채가 다양하거나 사실적이지 않았다는 것을 유추할 수 있다. (A)는 내용은 지문의 내용을 다르게 말하는 보기이고, (C)에서는 종교에 대한 지식이 많다는 것을 추론하기 힘들다.

4. 해석 미국 황소개구리가 잉글랜드에 소개되었을 때 사람들은 그것을 애완동물로서 팔기 시작했다. 그러나 황소개구리는 야생 상태에서 질병을 퍼뜨렸다. 이것은 다수의 영국 개구리 종들이 멸종하게 했다.

문제 | (A) 황소개구리가 퍼뜨리는 질병은 많은 영국 개구리에게는 치명적이었다.
(B) 일부 감염된 개구리는 다른 종들에게 질병을 전염시켰다.
(C) 대다수의 영국 개구리 종들은 오래 전에 멸종했다.

해설 | 지문의 내용으로 보아, 황소개구리로 인해 전염되는 질병이 영국 본토의 개구리들에게는 치명적이었다는 것을 유추할 수 있다. (B)는 황소개구리가 질병을 전염시켰고 감염된 개구리에 대한 설명이 없으며, (C)는 지문의 내용을 다르게 말하고 있다.

5. 해석 1946년에 대다수의 사람들은 여전히 만년필이나 연필을 필기도구로 사용했다. 만년필은 새는 경향이 있어서 특히 지저분했다. 게다가 잉크를 계속해서 리필해야 했다. 그러나 몇 년 안에 아르헨티나에서 만들어진 볼펜이라는 발명품이 대다수의 사람들이 필기구에 대해 생각하는 방식에 혁명을 불러일으켰다.

문제 | (A) 1946년의 많은 사람들은 볼펜의 독특함을 깨닫지 못했다.
(B) 볼펜은 만년필이나 연필보다 더 저렴하다.
(C) 기존에 있던 대부분의 필기구는 볼펜으로 대체되었다.

해설 | 지문의 내용으로 보아, 볼펜에 대한 인식이 확장되면서 기존에 쓰이던 대부분의 필기구가 볼펜으로 대체되었음을 유추할 수 있다. (A)는 1946년에는 볼펜이 개발되지 않은 상태로 사실이 아니다. (B)의 가격은 추론하기 힘들다.

6. 해석 아스피린의 기본 성분으로서 사용될 뿐 아니라, 현대의 피부 관리 제품에도 일반적으로 사용되지만, 살리신산은 그것의 유용한 속성으로 인해 역사상 유명했다. 버드나무 가지에서 추출된 살리신산은 전통적으로 이집트인과 미국 원주민을 포함한 많은 고대인들에 의해 진통제로 사용되었다. 그것은 또한 중동지역 사람들과 중국인들에 의해 여드름으로 인해 야기된 종기와 염증을 완화시키기 위한 세안 행굼제로 사용되었다.

문제 | (A) 고대인들은 진통을 느끼는 사람들을 치료하기 위해 버드나무 가지들을 그대로 먹었다.
(B) 버드나무는 고대에서 가장 귀중한 나무 중 하나였다.
(C) 살리신 산의 효과는 오래 전부터 입증되어 왔다.

해설 | 지문의 내용으로 보아, 살리신 산의 효과가 오래 전에 이미 입증되었다는 것을 유추할 수 있다. (A)의 내용은 지문의 내용과는 다르고, (B)에서는 귀중한 나무였다는 것은 추론하기 힘들다.

Basic Drill 2

정답 1. (A) - RI / (B) - NBF / (C) - NT
2. (A) - RI / (B) - NT / (C) - NBF
3. (A) - NT / (B) - NBF / (C) - RI
4. (A) - NT / (B) - RI / (C) - NBF

1. 해석 퀘벡은 지리적으로 캐나다에서 가장 넓은 지방이다. 그리고 인구 7백 오십만 명의 온타리오에 이어 두 번째로 인구가 많다. 이것은 캐나다 인구의 대략 24%에 해당한다. 대부분의 캐나다인들은 영국에서 온 이주자들의 후손이며 제 1언어로 영어를 사용한다. 반면, 퀘벡은 관습과 문화의 관점에서 뿐만 아니라, 언어에 있어서도 프랑스와 훨씬 더 깊이 관련된다. 실제로 퀘벡은 영어가 공식 언어가 아닌 캐나다 내의 유일한 주이다. 사실 퀘벡은 그곳의 많은 거주민들이 몇 십 년 동안 새로운 나라를 형성하고자 한, 즉 캐나다로부터 분리하고자 했다.

문제 | (A) 퀘벡은 관습이 다르고 캐나다 내의 다른 주들과 다르다.
(B) 퀘벡의 대부분의 거주민은 다른 (주의) 사람들과 구별되는 것에 대해 자부심을 갖고 있다.
(C) 퀘벡과 캐나다 내의 다른 주와의 유일한 차이점은 언어이다.

해설 | 글쓴이는 퀘벡에 대한 사실들을 열거함으로 다른 곳들과 다르다는 것을 암시하고 있다. 따라서 (A)의 내용을 추론할 수 있다. (B)의 내용은 사실에 근거하지 않았고, (C)의 내용은 지문의 내용을 다르게 말하고 있다.

2. 해석 1826년부터 1843년까지 17년 간, 맑은 날이면, Heinrich Schwabe는 태양을 조사하면서 그 표면에 있는 어두운 부분인 흑점들을 기록했다. 이 기간에 그는 태양흑점의 개수가 규칙적으로 변한다는 것을 깨달았다. 그는 태양 흑점의 주기가 10년으로 가정한다는 제안을 했다.

Johann Rudolf Wolf는 Heinrich Schwabe에 의해 제기된 태양흑점 주기의 발견에 깊은 감명을 받았다. 그는 자신의 관찰을 수행했을 뿐 아니라, 1610년까지 소급하여, 태양흑점의 활동에 관한 가능한 모든 데이터를 수집해서, 11.1년이라는 주기를 계산했다.

문제 │ (A) 태양흑점의 개수는 규칙적으로 변한다는 것이 증명되었다.
(B) 태양흑점의 개수는 11.1년 동안 지속적으로 증가한다.
(C) 태양흑점의 변화에 대한 발견은 많은 과학자들에게 영향을 끼쳤다.

해설 │ 글쓴이는 연구 결과 또는 발견을 통해 알게 된 사실을 통해 흑점의 변화가 규칙적이라는 것을 암시한다. 따라서 (A)를 추론할 수 있다. (B)의 내용은 지문과는 다른 내용이고, (C)의 내용은 사실에 근거하지 않은 내용이다.

3. 해석   도서관들은 과거 몇 십 년에 걸쳐 엄청나게 변화했다. 20년 전, 도서관에 있던 각각의 책들은 커다란 캐비넷 안에 개별 카드로 정리되었다. 그래서 때때로 책 한 권을 찾는데 몇 시간이 걸릴 수 있었다. 오늘날 도서관은 카드 카탈로그에 포함되어 있곤 했던 정보를 정리하는 데 컴퓨터에 상당 부분 의존하게 되었다. 찾고자 하는 책이 그 곳에 있다면 찾는 데는 단지 몇 초 밖에 걸리지 않는다. 게다가 종이 학술지나 책에서 찾을 수 있었던 많은 내용들이 이제는 온라인 즉, 컴퓨터의 데이터베이스에 포함되어 있다.

문제 │ (A) 도서관에서 컴퓨터에 대한 의존도의 증가는 다른 위험성을 증가시킬 수 있다.
(B) 도서관의 컴퓨터 데이터베이스 시스템은 장기적 안목으로 볼 때 더 경제적이다.
(C) 지난 몇 십 년 동안 도서관의 편리함은 많이 향상되었다.

해설 │ 글쓴이는 예전과 지금을 비교하면서 도서관이 훨씬 편리해 졌음을 암시하므로 (C)의 내용을 추론 가능하다. (A)의 내용은 지문의 내용을 다르게 말하고 있고, (B)는 사실에 근거하지는 않은 내용이다.

4. 해석   과학자들은 질병의 치료에 대해 더 많은 것을 알기 위해, 최근 인류와 가장 유사한 친척인 원숭이의 유전자를 변형시켰다. 그들은 수년 동안 특정 "불량한 유전자"가 암이나 알츠하이머 병과 같은 끔찍한 질병을 걸리게 할 확률을 높인다는 것을 인지하고 있었다. 이러한 유전자를 원숭이에게 주입함으로써, 질병의 속성에 대한 가치 있는 정보를 배울 수 있을 뿐 아니라, 바라건대 그 치료법 또한 알 수 있을 것이다. 그러나 어떤 과학자들은 거의 결과를 내지 못한 채 이미 쥐의 유전자를 바꾸는 데 수많은 세월을 보냈다고 주장한다. 그들은 자신들이 실험하고 있는 동물의 종류는 중요한 것이 아니고 그 결과는 마찬가지로 보잘 것 없을 거라고 주장한다.

문제 │ (A) 연구 결과는 (실험 대상인) 동물의 종류에 따라 크게 바뀔 수 있다.
(B) 원숭이에 대한 최근의 실험에서 많은 결과를 얻는 것을 기대하기에는 무리가 있다.
(C) 원숭이에 대한 실험으로부터 가치있는 결과를 얻기까지는 더 많은 시간이 걸릴 것이다.

해설 │ 글쓴이는 하나의 견해와, 그리고 상반된 또 하나의 견해를 소개하여 결과에 대한 회의적인 입장을 암시하고 있다. 따라서, (B)의 내용을 알 수 있다. (A)는 지문의 내용을 다르게 말하고 있고, (C)는 사실과는 다른 내용을 말하고 있다.

VOCABULARY Preview

| Check-up |

1. mimic   2. affectionate   3. playwrights
4. register   5. takes in   6. infant
7. funded   8. tragedies

다음 빈 칸에 들어갈 알맞은 말을 골라, 필요하면 고쳐 쓰시오.

1. Angela는 내 목소리를 거의 완벽하게 흉내 낼 수 있어서, 나의 부모님을 많이 놀라게 한다.
2. 그는 입양한 아들에게 절대적으로 애정을 쏟는 듯하다.
3. 셰익스피어는 세계에서 가장 위대한 극작가 중 한 명이다.
4. 나는 그녀를 기억하지 못했다. 그녀는 내 기억에 새겨져 있지 않았다.
5. 이 책은 조선 왕조의 개국과 대한 일본의 침략기였던 1592년 사이의 기간을 포함하고 있다.
6. 젊은 엄마는 아기가 잘 수 있도록 내려놓고 있었다.
7. 그 극장은 우리 회사 부사장이 개인적으로 투자하고 있는 곳이다.
8. Jennifer는 보통 비극에서 주역을 맡아 연기하는 유명한 여배우이다.

Exercise 1

정답 1. ⓑ 2. ⓓ 3. ⓑ 4. ⓑ 5. ⓒ
6. ⓑ, ⓒ, ⓕ

해설   자신의 주변에 있는 사람들의 얼굴 표정을 흉내 내는 유아의 능력은 다양한 연구들을 통해 충분히 입증되어 있다. 그들은 자기들이 보는 사람들을 모방하면서 행복한 표정과 슬픈 표정을 배운다. 그런 얼굴 표정에 담긴 내용이 아동의 전반적인 행복과 발달에 중요한 영향을 미칠 수도 있다는 것이 밝혀졌다.

3개월 된 한 유아 집단에 관한 연구가 이러한 발견을 예증한다. 모종의 우울증을 앓고 있다는 진단을 받은 엄마의 아기들은 우울증에 걸리지 않는 엄마의 아기들보다 슬프거나 화난 얼굴 표정을 지을 가능성이 높았다. 게다가, 이러한 아기들은 자신의 주변의 활동들에 종종 관여되지 않았다.

어떤 연구자들은 그 아기들이 표정의 의미를 이해하지도 못한 채, 단순히 우울증 걸린 자신의 엄마의 얼굴 표정을 흉내 내고 있다고 생각한다. 그러나 이것이 아기들이 엄마의 우울증에 영향을 받지 않는다는 것을 의미하지 않는다. 이러한 어머니들은 자기 아기들에게 열심히 반응하지도 않았고, 그들과 애정 깊은 대화도 나누지 않았다. 긍정적인 상호작용의 결핍은 아기들의 정신능력과 운동기술의 발달에 부정적인 영향을 미칠 수 있다.

우울증에 걸린 엄마와의 상호작용이 이러한 아기들의 발달 지체를 설명할 수 있는 유일한 것은 아니다. 자궁 내에서 이 아기들은 우울증과 직접적으로 관련된 상당량의 호르몬에 노출되었다. 이러한 화학물질은, 아기들이 출생한 순간부터 덜 반응하고, 얼굴 표정도 더 적으면서, 일반적으로 덜 활동적이 되는 결과를 낳는 것으로 보인다.

문 1 | 첫 번째 단락의 well documented와 가장 의미가 유사한 것은?
Ⓐ 매우 일상적인
Ⓑ 충분히 입증된
Ⓒ 빈번히 고려된
Ⓓ 놀라운

해설 | document는 '~을 증거로 입증하다'란 의미가 있다. 문맥상 '다양한 연구들을 통해 입증되었다'는 뜻을 유추한다.

문 2 | 두 번째 단락의 engaged in과 가장 의미가 유사한 것은?
Ⓐ 당황하는
Ⓑ 놀라는
Ⓒ 짜증이 난
Ⓓ 참여하는

해설 | engage in은 '~에 종사하다', '관여하다'란 의미이다. 문맥상 Ⓓ가 답이다.

문 3 | 우울증에 걸린 엄마에 관해 추론할 수 있는 것은?
Ⓐ 우울증을 앓는 엄마들은 자기 아이들을 덜 좋아하는 것으로 보인다.
Ⓑ 그들은 아기들과 함께하려 하지 않고 돌보지 않으려 하는 경향이 있다.
Ⓒ 그들의 감정은 아기들이 자라면서 아기들의 사이즈와 몸무게에 영향을 줄 수 있다.
Ⓓ 그들은 자기 아기들에게 부정적이고 난폭하게 반응하는 경향이 있다.

해설 | 두 번째 단락에 나온 내용을 보면, 우울증에 걸린 엄마들은 아기들과의 활동에 무관심한 경향을 보인다고 한다.

문 4 | 네 번째 단락에서 글쓴이가 자궁에 관해 언급한 이유는?
Ⓐ 우울증 걸린 엄마의 아기들의 신체적 반응을 언급하기 위해
Ⓑ 아기의 성장에 영향을 미치는 다른 요인을 나타내기 위해
Ⓒ 우울증이 스트레스로 인해 초래된다는 것을 제시하기 위해
Ⓓ 모든 아기들이 출생 시에 스트레스를 받는다는 것을 암시하기 위해

해설 | Interaction with depressed mothers is not the only possible explanation for these babies' delayed development.라는 첫 번째 문장을 시작으로 아이들에게 부정적인 영향을 미치는 또 다른 원인으로 엄마 자궁에서 받게 되는 스트레스를 설명하고 있다.

문 5 | 아기에게 영향을 미치는 얼굴 표정에 대해 추론할 수 있는 것은?
Ⓐ 다양한 얼굴 표정은 아기들이 자랄 때 어떻게 아기들이 성장할지에 영향을 줄 수 있다.
Ⓑ 부정적인 얼굴 표정은 아기들에게 높은 스트레스 호르몬 수치를 만들 수 있다.
Ⓒ 특정 얼굴 표정을 짓게 하는 감정이 아기들에게 영향을 미칠 수 있다.
Ⓓ 엄마의 감정은 아기의 건강과 보통은 관계가 없다는 것이 발견되었다.

해설 | 비록 얼굴 표정에 담긴 의미를 아이들이 제대로 이해하지 못할지라도 얼굴 표정의 내면에 있는 감정들은 아기에게 영향을 미친다는 것을 전반적인 내용을 통해 추론할 수 있다.

문 6 | 지문에 대한 간단한 요약을 위한 도입 문장이 아래에 제시된다. 가장 중요한 내용을 표현한 3가지 대답을 선택하여 요약을 완성하시오. 몇몇 문장은 단락에서 언급되지 않았거나 중요하지 않은 내용을 표현해서 요약에 들어갈 수 없다.

엄마의 우울증은 아기의 성장 방식에 중요한 영향을 미칠 수 있다.
Ⓐ 부모가 아기들에게 웃는 방법을 보여주게 되면 대다수의 아기들은 출생 이후 바로 웃을 수 있다.
Ⓑ 그들이 엄마의 얼굴에서 보는 표정이 아기의 감정에 영향을 미친다.
Ⓒ 우울증 걸린 엄마들은 아기와 상호작용을 잘 안 하는 경향이 있고, 이것이 아기들의 발달에 영향을 미친다.
Ⓓ 우울증 걸린 엄마들이 기른 아기들은 의사소통에 있어서 어려움을 직면할 가능성이 높다고 입증되었다.

　　　　Ⓔ 우울증은 아기의 인성에 영향을 미칠 수 있는 스트레스 호르몬을 상당량 유발할 수 있다.
　　　　Ⓕ 아기들이 태어나기 전부터, 그들의 성장은 엄마의 우울증에 영향을 받는다.

해설 | Ⓐ와 Ⓓ는 지문에 언급되지 않은 내용이고, Ⓔ는 지문의 내용과는 다르다.

Exercise 2

정답　1. Ⓒ　2. Ⓑ　3. Ⓑ　4. Ⓒ　5. Ⓒ
　　　6. Ancient Play - Ⓑ, Ⓓ /
　　　　Modern Play - Ⓐ, Ⓕ, Ⓖ

해석　연극은 고대 그리스 문화에서 필수적인 요소였다. 당대의 가장 유명한 극작가들이 집필한 비극과 희극을 보는 것은 대부분의 사람들이 빠뜨리지 않으려는 활동이었다. 그러나 고대 그리스 시대의 연극 관람은 현대에서의 연극 관람과는 다소 달랐다. 이러한 고대 연극과 오늘날의 연극 간에는 중요한 차이점들이 있다.

　오늘날, 연극은 주로 오락을 위한 행사이다. 재미있는 것이든 진지한 것이든지 그것들은 관객들에게 일종의 탈출구를 제공하려고 의도된 것이다. 비록 지방 정부가 일정 부분을 지원한다 해도, 수익은 거의 항상 티켓 판매를 통해 만들어진다. 현대극은 대중성이 있다고 인정되면, 수년 동안이라도 반복해서 공연될 수 있다. 현대극의 또 다른 하나의 특징은 공연하는 사람들의 수이다. 어떤 연극은 사설 소극장에서 공연되는 연극처럼 단지 서너 명의 배우만을 필요로 하지만, 대부분의 연극은 다수의 배우와 연출진이 있다. 연출진은 의상, 분장 그리고 무대장치들을 준비한다. 이것들은 연극이 가능한 한 사실적으로 보이도록 만들기 위해 이용된다.

　고대 그리스에서는 이와 달랐다. 왜냐하면 그 곳의 연극들은 세금으로만 투자를 받았고 주신(酒神)인 디오니소스에게 영광을 돌리기 위한 종교적 축제의 일환으로 공연되었다. 보통 세 편의 연극이 축제 기간에 공연되었고, 사람들은 최고로 우수한 작품, 두 번째로 우수한 작품, 그리고 세 번째로 우수한 작품을 가려내기 위한 투표를 했다. 게다가 얼마나 인기가 있느냐에 상관없이, 그 연극은 축제 기간 동안 단 1회만 공연되곤 했다. 다음 축제 기간에 재공연 될 수는 있었겠지만, 대부분의 연극들은 한 번만 공연되었다. 그리고 그리스 연극에는, 대본에 얼마나 많은 등장인물이 있든 간에, 딱 세 명의 배우만이 나왔다. 배우들은 간단한 가면을 썼고, 다른 역을 연기해야 할 필요가 있으면 무대 뒤쪽으로 가서 가면을 바꿔 썼다.

문 1 | 다음 중 현대 연극에 대해서 추론할 수 있는 것은?
　　　Ⓐ 그들은 보통 많은 자금을 쓰고 다양한 판촉을 한다.
　　　Ⓑ 그들은 정부의 기관에 의해 대부분 투자를 받는다.
　　　Ⓒ 몇몇의 현대 연극은 굉장히 많은 비용이 든다.
　　　Ⓓ 대중성이 있는 현대 연극만 큰 극장에서 공연이 된다.

해설 | 현대 연극은 다수의 연출진과 배우들 등 여타 다른 비용이 상당히 들어갈 거라는 추측이 가능하다.

문 2 | 두 번째 단락에서 글쓴이는 현대 연극을 어떠한 방식으로 설명하고 있나?
　　　Ⓐ 고대 그리스의 연극과 비교함으로써
　　　Ⓑ 현대 연극의 특징을 지적함으로써
　　　Ⓒ 현대 연극이 오락적 요소가 더욱 강하다는 것을 제시함으로써
　　　Ⓓ 현대 연극의 기원을 어디에서 찾을 수 있는지 설명함으로써

해설 | 두 번째 단락에서는 현대극의 특징을 서술하고 있다.

문 3 | 다음 중 현대 연극의 특징이 아닌 것은?
　　　Ⓐ 수차례 공연된다.
　　　Ⓑ 주로 교육에 활용된다.
　　　Ⓒ 개인의 자금과 관련되어 있다.
　　　Ⓓ 정교한 의상을 사용한다.

해설 | 인기에 따라 수차례 공연되고, 개인 투자를 받아 자금을 충당하고, 최대한 사실적인 의상을 입는 것은 현대극에 속하는 특징이다. Ⓑ의 내용은 지문에 언급되어 있지 않다.

문 4 | 다음 중 고대 그리스 연극에 대해 추론할 수 있는 것은?
　　　Ⓐ 다른 배우들이 다른 연극에서 공연할 것이다.
　　　Ⓑ 연극들은 일반적으로 봄에 씨뿌리는 기간 동안 공연되었다.
　　　Ⓒ 관객들은 축제 기간에 연극 티켓을 구매할 필요가 없었다.
　　　Ⓓ 배우들은 감정을 강조하기 위해 극단적인 얼굴 표정을 지었다.

해설 | This was not the case in Ancient Greece as plays there were funded by tax dollars alone ~을 참조한다. 세금으로만 자금을 충당했기 때문에 개인이 따로 티켓을 구매할 필요가 없었음을 추론할 수 있다.

문 5 | 세 번째 단락에서 아래의 문장이 삽입될 수 있는 곳을 나타내는 네 개의 [■]를 보시오.

　　　〔And Greek plays, no matter how many characters were written into the play, only had three actors.〕

　　　문장이 가장 잘 맞는 곳은 어디인가? [■]을 클릭해 해당 단락에 문장을 삽입하시오.

해설 | **Ⓒ** 다음의 내용이 '역할이 바뀔 때 배우가 가면을 바꿔 쓰고 연기했다'라는 것이므로 배우의 인원이 극에 등장하는 인원보다 적었다는 것을 유추할 수 있다. 따라서 이 내

용이 서술되기 전에 극본의 등장인물의 수와 실제 공연할 때의 배우의 수를 비교할 수 있는 정보를 언급한 주어진 문장이 **C** 에 들어가는 것이 적절하다.

문 6 | 적절한 보기를 골라 관련 있는 극 종류와 짝지으시오. 두 개의 보기는 제외됩니다.
Ⓐ 연극이 대중성이 있으면 반복해서 공연하게 된다.
Ⓑ 축제 기간 동안 딱 한 번만 공연된다.
Ⓒ 등장인물의 대다수의 대사가 배우에 의해 만들어진다.
Ⓓ 배우들은 다른 등장인물의 대사를 때때로 암기해야 한다.
Ⓔ 극작가는 배우가 어떤 종류의 의상을 입을지 기재한다.
Ⓕ 극을 통해 수익이 창출된다.
Ⓖ 많은 배우가 한 공연에 참여할 수 있다.

해설 | 극이 인기가 있으면 몇 번이고 반복해서 공연되는 것이나, 한 공연에 많은 배우들이 참여할 수 있는 것은 현대극의 특징이다. 종교적인 의식의 일부분이면서 축제 기간에만 볼 수 있고, 배우들이 여러 배역의 대사를 암기해야만 한 것은 고대 그리스의 연극이다.

Exercise 3

정답 1. Ⓐ 2. Ⓑ 3. Ⓑ 4. Ⓓ 5. Ⓓ
      6. Ⓑ 7. Ⓒ 8. Ⓐ, Ⓓ, Ⓕ

Text Outline (B)

해석   나무와 식물은 이산화탄소를 흡수하고 산소를 배출하는 능력 때문에, 전세계의 생태계에 전반적으로 중요한 부분을 차지한다. 이산화탄소는 나무의 광합성, 즉 나무가 생존하기 위해 필요한 식량을 생산하는 능력에 있어 중요한 부분이다.

이산화탄소를 빨아들이고 산소를 배출해내는 나무의 능력으로 인해, 많은 과학자들은 대기 중에 더 많은 이산화탄소가 있다면, 나무가 더 빠르고 더 건강하게 성장할 거라고 가정했다. 나무와 식물은 지구의 온도 상승에 대한 원인인 이산화탄소의 증가를 해결할 수 있는 가능성으로서 여겨졌다. 나무가 대기 중에 있는 여분의 이산화탄소를 흡수할 것이라 사람들은 예상했다. 그러나 식물들이 여분의 이산화탄소를 흡수한다는 이론은 사실인 것 같지 않다.

이러한 결론을 도출하기 위해, 연구자들은 커다란 숲에 있는 나무들을 연구했다. 연구자들은 4년 간 매일 그 숲의 특정 구역 주변에 여분의 이산화탄소를 추가했다. 숲의 다른 나무들과 비교했을 때, 이산화탄소가 추가된 나무들은 더 많은 성장을 보이지 않았다. 이산화탄소가 추가되지 않는 나무들과 크기에 있어서 별다른 차이가 없었던 것이다. 대신 이 나무들은 처리 과정을 거치지 않고 이산화탄소를 흡수하여 뿌리를 통해서 토양 속으로 방출했다. 이것은 숲이 많아진다고 지구의 기후에 대한 이산화탄소 같은 온실가스의 영향을 줄일 수 없다는 것을 의미한다.

문 1 | 첫 번째 단락의 emit와 가장 의미가 유사한 것은?
Ⓐ 방출하다
Ⓑ 반박하다
Ⓒ 처리하다
Ⓓ 변형시키다

해설 | emit은 '내뿜다' 는 의미이다. 문맥에서 '이산화탄소를 흡수하고 산소를 emit한다' 라는 내용을 보아 emit은 absorb의 반대 의미로 사용되었음을 알 수 있다.

문 2 | 두 번째 단락에서 이산화탄소에 대해 추론할 수 있는 것은?
Ⓐ 증가한 이산화탄소로 인해 오염된 공기가 (지구의) 온도 상승의 주요 원인이다.
Ⓑ 과학자들은 올라간 지구의 기온이 일으킬 수 있는 상황에 대해 염려한다.
Ⓒ 나무와 식물은 더 많은 양의 이산화탄소를 흡수하면 더 많은 산소를 만들어낼 수 있다.
Ⓓ 환경 중에 증가한 이산화탄소 레벨로 인해 지구에 나무와 식물이 살기 어렵다.

해설 | 과학자들이 지구의 온도를 상승시키는 이산화탄소의 증가를 해결할 수 있는 방법을 찾는다는 것은 지구 온도가 높아졌을 때 일어나는 상황들을 염려하기 때문이라고 추론할 수 있다.

문 3 | 두 번째 단락에서 글쓴이가 지구의 온도 상승을 언급한 이유는?
Ⓐ 이산화탄소가 그에 대한 해결책이라는 것을 암시하기 위해
Ⓑ 이산화탄소가 그의 주요 원인 중 하나라는 것을 나타내기 위해
Ⓒ 이산화탄소가 미래에 일으킬 수 있는 일을 제시하기 위해
Ⓓ 이산화탄소가 후에 무엇으로 변화할 수 있을지를 예증하기 위해

해설 | 이산화탄소로 인해 일어난 결과를 언급하려 하고 있다.

문 4 | 두 번째 단락에 따르면, 실험에 관해 추론할 수 있는 것은?
Ⓐ 식물은 뿌리 내에 필요하지 않은 가스를 보존한다.
Ⓑ 숲은 너무 많은 이산화탄소에 의해 부정적으로 영향을 받았다.
Ⓒ 지구의 온도 상승은 문제에 대한 주요 원인이 아니다.
Ⓓ 연구자들은 지구 온난화를 통제할 수 있는 또 다른 방법을 찾아야 한다.

해설 | 연구자들이 세운 가설은 잘못된 것이었기 때문에 지구 온난화를 위한 새로운 대안을 찾아야 함을 유추할 수 있다.

문 5 | 세 번째 단락의 this conclusion이 가리키는 것은?
Ⓐ 이산화탄소는 지구 온난화의 직접적인 원인이 아니다.

Ⓑ 이산화탄소는 지구의 온도를 상승시킨다.
　　Ⓒ 식물은 보통 여분의 산소를 방출하지 않는다.
　　Ⓓ 식물들은 그들이 필요한 것 이상의 이산화탄소를 흡수하지 않는다.

해설 | this conclusion은 실험을 통해 도출한 결론으로, '식물이 여분의 이산화탄소는 흡수하지 않는다' 는 것이다.

문 6 | 세 번째 단락에서 글쓴이는 나무가 더 빠르게 성장하는지 여부에 대한 연구자들의 실험을 어떠한 방식으로 설명하는가?
　　Ⓐ 지구 온난화를 겪고 있는 지역에 있는 나무들에 대한 연구를 설명함으로써
　　Ⓑ 더 많은 이산화탄소에 나무들을 노출시키는 실험을 설명함으로써
　　Ⓒ 나무가 숲에 방출한 이산화탄소의 양을 제시함으로써
　　Ⓓ 숲에 있는 나무들에서 방출한 산소와 이산화탄소의 영향을 비교함으로써

해설 | 세 번째 단락을 살펴보면, 과학자들이 더 많은 이산화탄소를 나무들에 노출시켜 자신들의 이론을 입증하고자 했음을 알 수 있다.

문 7 | 다음 중 세 번째 단락의 하이라이트 된 문장의 핵심 내용을 가장 잘 표현한 것은? 틀린 보기는 본문의 내용을 심각하게 바꾸거나 핵심적인 내용을 누락시킨 것이다.
　　Ⓐ 이산화탄소가 보충된 나무들은 크기에 있어서 그 어떤 성장도 보여주지 않았다.
　　Ⓑ 이산화탄소가 보충된 나무들은 보충되지 않은 나무들보다 훨씬 더 성장했다.
　　Ⓒ 이산화탄소가 보충된 나무들은 숲속의 다른 나무와 동일한 정도로 성장한다.
　　Ⓓ 이산화탄소가 보충된 나무들과 그렇지 않은 나무들 둘의 크기가 비교되었다.

해설 | 하이라이트 된 문장의 핵심 내용은, 여분의 이산화탄소를 공급받은 나무가 더 성장하지 않았다는 것이고, making not much~는 no growth에 대한 부연이므로 생략된다.

문 8 | 지문에 대한 간단한 요약을 위한 도입 문장이 아래에 제시된다. 가장 중요한 내용을 표현한 3가지 대답을 선택하여 요약을 완성하시오. 몇몇 문장들은 단락에서 언급되지 않았거나 중요하지 않은 내용을 표현해서 요약에 들어갈 수 없다.

나무는 이산화탄소를 흡수하고 산소를 배출한다.
　　Ⓐ 나무들은 영양분을 만들어내기 위해 이산화탄소를 흡수하고, 이 능력은 이 세상에서 중요하다.
　　Ⓑ 식물들은 그것들이 더 많은 양의 이산화탄소에 노출될 때, 더 빨리 성장할 것이라고 여겨졌다.
　　Ⓒ 숲속에 있는 대부분의 식물들과 나무들은 전 세계적 생태계에 있어서 번식과 성장을 위해 이산화탄소를 필요로 한다.
　　Ⓓ 과학자들은 나무들이 더 많은 이산화탄소를 처리할 수 있을 것이므로 지구 온난화에 대한 해결책이 될 수 있을 거라고 생각했다.
　　Ⓔ 증가한 이산화탄소의 레벨은 숲의 나무에 영향을 미쳤으나 그 영향이 너무 미미하여 괄목할 만하지 않았고, (지구) 온도를 낮추기 위해 나무를 이용한다는 것은 현실적이지 않다.
　　Ⓕ 더 많은 레벨의 이산화탄소에 노출되었던 나무들은 더 성장하지 않았고, 이것은 나무가 지구 온난화에 대한 효과적인 해결책이 될 수 없다는 것을 보여준다.

해설 | Ⓑ는 지문에서 설명되는 실험의 기본 전제이긴 하지만 글 전체에서는 핵심 내용이 아니고, Ⓒ도 핵심 내용이 아니며, Ⓔ는 지문과는 다른 내용이 들어있다.

VOCABULARY TEST

정답　1. (B)　2. (D)　3. (C)　4. (A)　5. (B)
　　　6. (D)　7. (A)　8. (B)　9. (C)

다음 빈 칸에 들어갈 알맞은 말을 골라, 필요하면 고쳐 쓰시오.

1. 그것은 그의 이론을 입증하는 중요한 실험이었다.
　(A) 막대한　　　(B) 중대한
　(C) 복잡한　　　(D) 예리한

2. 나는 그 어떤 대가를 치루더라도 나의 목적을 수행할 것이다.
　(A) 노력하다　　(B) 운영하다
　(C) 초래하다　　(D) 수행하다

3. 그는 회사 창립주의 직계 후손이다.
　(A) 집사　　　　(B) 친척
　(C) 자손　　　　(D) 조상

4. 부엌은 너무 지저분했다. 그녀는 1년 동안이나 부엌을 청소하지 않았던 것 같다.
　(A) 지저분한　　(B) 육중한
　(C) 아늑한　　　(D) 차분한

5. 우리 언니는 애정이 많고 쾌활하다.
　(A) 멋진　　　　(B) 애정이 있는
　(C) 부드러운　　(D) 고상한

6. 이 섬에는 수백, 수천만 종의 식물이 있다.
　(A) 범위　　　　(B) 상품
　(C) 다양성　　　(D) 종류

7. 그녀는 환자의 통증을 완화시키기 위해 노력했다.
　(A) 덜어주다　　(B) 격려하다
　(C) 극복하다　　(D) 기억하다

8. 오랜 시간 동안 태양에 피부를 노출시키지 마시오.
　(A) 숨기다　　　(B) 노출시키다
　(C) 감추다　　　(D) 막다

9. 내년에 당신이 경영진으로 승진하게 되리라고 가정해 보자.

(A) 약올리다 (B) ~인 체하다
(C) 추정하다 (D) 알다

Progress Test 5

정답 1. Ⓐ 2. Ⓒ 3. Ⓒ 4. Ⓑ 5. Ⓑ
      6. Ⓑ 7. Ⓒ 8. Ⓒ 9. Ⓐ,Ⓓ,Ⓕ

해석 인류는 현대적인 냉동을 개발되기 전에 여름의 열기 속에서도 서늘함을 유지할 수 있는 방안을 오랫동안 찾아 왔다. 어떤 주택은 창문과 문으로 공기가 자유롭게 드나들도록 할 수 있도록 설계되었다. 다른 주택들은 건물의 내부를 단열하고, 열에서 보호하는데 도움이 되도록, 토양으로 만들어진 두꺼운 벽을 사용했다. 또한 어떤 사막 지역에서는 자연 차단기능의 이점을 활용하기 위해 건물들이 실제로 땅속에 지어졌다. 그러나 이것 중 어느 것도 서늘한 실내 환경을 확실하게 조성하지 못했다.

이후에 1748년 스코틀랜드의 교수인 William Cullen은 냉동의 원리를 알아냈다. Cullen은 방안에서 에테르가 가열되도록 하는 실험을 했다. 이로 인해 방은 바로 급격히 서늘해졌다. 이 사건의 기록은 교수가 그 반응에 충격을 받았다는 것을 나타내지만, 그는 결코 이것이 시사하는 점을 알아채지 못했으며 많은 사람들은 이에 대한 원인을 그가 여름에도 일반적으로 서늘한 지방인 스코틀랜드에 사는 토착민이라는 점에 찾는다. 사실, Cullen은 이 실험이 실험실 밖에서도 유용하리라고 생각하지 못했다. 그래서 냉장의 시대는 좀 더 기다려야만 했던 것이다.

미국출신 의사인 John Gorrie는 1842년이 되어서야 병실에 공기를 식히는 장치를 설치했다. 그 기본적인 방법에는 압축한 즉, 더욱 작은 공기분자가 있어야 한다. 분자의 크기를 줄임으로써 이 주변 공기가 현저하게 냉각되었다. 그리고 그 기계는 그 공기분자를 기계 밖에 있는 대기 속에 방출하게 되면, 온도가 떨어지게 된다. 이것은 오늘날의 현대적 냉장고가 활용하는 방법과 다소 유사하다. 대략 십 년 내로 이 냉장 기술은 생산성과 효율성을 향상하기 위해 통조림 제조업과 양조업에 사용되어 졌다.

이 아이디어에 대해 또 하나의 변형은 1859년 프랑스에서 Ferdinand Carre라는 사람에 의해 나타났다. 공기를 냉각제로 사용했던 Gorrie의 압축 기계와 달리 Carre의 장치는 암모니아를 사용했다. 암모니아의 화학적 특성으로 인해 Gorrie가 사용했던 공기보다 훨씬 더 공기를 차가워진다. 그러나 Carre의 냉장 기술은 좀 더 성공적이었지만, Gorrie의 기계만큼 널리 보급되지는 않았다. 이면에 가려진 이유는 암모니아가 매우 독성이 강하고 사용하기에 위험이 따르기 때문이다. 대다수의 사람들과 기업들은 이 물질을 사용한 기계를 보유하기를 원하지 않았다.

문 1 | 첫 번째 단락의 insulate와 가장 의미가 유사한 것은?
Ⓐ 식다
Ⓑ 넓히다
Ⓒ 보호하다
Ⓓ 어둡게 하다

해설 | insulate는 '단열하다'의 의미로, and로 연결된 protect it against the heat에서 의미를 유추할 수 있다.

문 2 | 첫 번째 단락에서 글쓴이가 자연의 열 차단 기능을 활용하는 건물을 언급한 이유는 무엇인가?
Ⓐ 자연의 열 차단이 어떠한 방식으로 온도를 낮추는 데 도움이 되는지 보여주기 위해
Ⓑ 이전의 기술과 현대적인 냉동 기술을 비교하기 위해
Ⓒ 더운 날씨에 기온을 서늘하게 하려고 한 시도의 예를 들기 위해
Ⓓ 현대적인 냉동의 발명을 강조하기 위해

해설 | 인간이 현대적 냉동 기술을 발명하기 이전, 온도를 낮추기 위해 노력했다는 도입 문장에 대한 예를 들고 있다.

문 3 | 두 번째 단락의 this가 가리키는 것은?
Ⓐ 방
Ⓑ 실험
Ⓒ 끓어오르는 에테르
Ⓓ 냉동

해설 | this는 방을 서늘하게 한 원인이므로 '끓어오르는 에테르'를 가리킨다.

문 4 | 다음 중 두 번째 단락의 하이라이트 된 문장의 핵심 내용을 가장 잘 표현한 것은? 틀린 보기는 본문의 내용을 심각하게 바꾸거나 핵심적인 내용을 누락시킨 것이다.
Ⓐ 스코틀랜드는 여름에도 시원하기 때문에, 교수는 실험이 산출했던 냉각 효과를 눈치채지 못했다.
Ⓑ 놀라운 실험 결과에도, 서늘한 지역에 거주한 것으로 인해 Cullen이 그 발견을 다른 실용적 용도에 응용하지 못하게 했다고들 말한다.
Ⓒ Cullen은 실험의 결과는 관심이 있었지만 그는 그것의 역사의 초기 단계에서 냉동을 발생시키는 실용적 방법은 생각하지 못했다.
Ⓓ 비록 그는 결코 냉각 효과가 유용하다고 생각하지는 않았지만, 스코틀랜드는 서늘했으므로 결국 교수를 놀라게 한 실험을 수행할 효과적인 장소였다.

해설 | 교수는 냉각 효과 자체를 눈치채지 못한 것이 아니라 기후가 서늘했기 때문에 그것을 활용해야겠다는 동기가 유발되지 않았을 거라고 사람들은 추측한다. 따라서 Ⓐ는 답이

될 수 없고, ⓑ가 정답이 된다.

문5 | 주어진 문장이 지문에 들어갈 수 있는 4개의 네모(■)를 살펴보시오.

[This reduction in the molecules' size cooled the surrounding air significantly.]

문장이 들어갈 가장 적절한 곳은?
단락에 문장이 들어갈 한 개의 네모(■)를 클릭하시오.

해설 | 공기분자의 크기를 줄인다는 내용이 ⓑ의 앞에 있는 문장에서 언급된다. 선택지는 공기분자의 크기를 줄이는 효과에 대한 내용이므로 ⓑ에 놓여야 한다.

문6 | 세 번째 단락에 따르면, Gorrie의 방법에 대해 추론될 수 있는 것은?
Ⓐ 현대적인 냉동에 이동된 많은 기술들은 Gorrie에게 특허가 있었다.
Ⓑ 그것은 냉동의 가장 효과적인 방법들 중 하나로 널리 인정받았다.
Ⓒ 그것은 많은 공간을 차지하기 때문에 주로 병원에서 사용되었다.
Ⓓ 그것은 기계로 빠르게 압축될 수 있는 특별한 공기분자를 이용했다.

해설 | 현대적 냉장고가 사용하는 방법과 유사하다는 점에서 ⓑ를 유추할 수 있다.

문7 | 네 번째 단락의 this가 가리키는 것은?
Ⓐ 효과적으로 냉각화함
Ⓑ 암모니아를 사용함
Ⓒ 널리 활용되지 않음
Ⓓ 암모니아가 공기보다 훨씬 더 차갑게 한다는 사실

해설 | 바로 앞 문장에서 암모니아가 냉각효과에서 우수하더라도 널리 보급되지 않았다는 내용을 다루고 있다.

문8 | 네 번째 단락으로 보아 암모니아는
Ⓐ 공기보다 냉각 효과가 떨어졌다.
Ⓑ Carre에 의해 신중하게 다루어지지 않았다.
Ⓒ 냉각하는 데 있어서 공기보다 더 위험이 따른다.
Ⓓ 오늘날 산업적 용도로 활용되는 냉각에 사용된다.

해설 | 암모니아가 독성이 있고 사용하기에 위험하다는 내용을 확인한다.

문9 | 지문에 대한 간단한 요약을 위한 도입 문장이 아래에 제시된다. 가장 중요한 내용을 표현한 3가지 대답을 선택하여 요약을 완성하시오. 몇몇 문장들은 단락에서 언급되지 않았거나 중요하지 않은 내용을 표현해서 요약에 들어갈 수 없다.

현대적인 냉장 기술 발전을 이끈 많은 발명이 있었다.
Ⓐ Cullen은 가열된 에테르가 방 안에서 급속 냉각을 유발할 수 있다는 것을 발견했으나, 그것을 냉장 기술로 발달시키지 않았다.
Ⓑ 일부 성분이 방안의 기온을 엄청나게 떨어뜨렸다는 것이 발견되었고, 이것이 냉동 기술의 시초였다.
Ⓒ 공기 압축기는 병원에 차가운 공기를 제공하기 위해 발

명되었고 이 기술은 오늘날 많은 병원에서 사용되고 있다.
Ⓓ 압축해서 공기를 냉각하는 기술이 개발되었고, 그 원리는 오늘날에도 계속해서 사용된다.
Ⓔ 암모니아를 사용하는 Carre의 장치는 냉각제로 공기를 사용하는 Gorrie의 압축기와 종종 비교된다.
Ⓕ 또 다른 한 명의 발명가는 암모니아를 사용하는 것이 공기보다 더 효과적이라는 것을 깨달았지만 이것은 너무 위험하기 때문에 널리 사용되지 않았다.

해설 | 에테르를 가열시켜 냉동에 성공한 Cullen, 공기를 압축해서 냉동한 Gorrie, 암모니아를 이용해 냉동을 한 Carre의 냉동 기술의 발달을 바르게 요약한다.

Progress Test 6

정답 1. Ⓒ 2. Ⓑ 3. Ⓐ 4. Ⓑ 5. Ⓓ
6. Ⓑ 7. Ⓒ 8. Ⓒ 9. Leeches - Ⓐ, Ⓓ, Ⓖ / Maggots - Ⓑ, Ⓒ

해석 현대 의학의 상당 부분은 기술에서 새로운 진보를 중심으로 행해진다. 절개 수술을 피하기 위한 검사와 진단에 활용되는 레이저와 나노테크놀로지, 초소형 카메라 모두 현대 의학에서의 최근 발달의 실례이다. 의사들은 그것들이 최고의 선택인지 진지하게 고민하지도 않고 종종 이에 의존한다. 어떤 의사들은 현대 과학 기술이 항상 최고의 선택이라고 생각하는 경향이 있다. 그러나 이것이 항상 그런 것은 아니다. 사실 몇몇 의사들은 이제 그들의 최첨단 작업을 하는데 도움을 얻기 위해 훨씬 더 오래된 의학적 지혜에 의존을 하고 있다.

현대에 부활한 오래된 의술의 한 예는 거머리의 사용이다. 담수 못과 시냇물에서 사는 거머리는 몸에 붙어 혈액을 빨아 먹는 기생충이다. 수백 년 전에, 의사들은 질병의 원인으로 간주했던 "bad blood"라고 일컬어지는 것을 환자에게서 짜내기 위해 거머리를 사용했다. 의사들은 더 이상 "bad blood"의 의료 진단을 유효한 것으로 받아들이지 않지만, 거머리들이 다시 수술에 사용되고 있다. 오늘날 그것은 의사들이 팔다리와 다른 인체의 부위들을 재 접합하는데 도움을 주기 위해 이용되었다. 인체에 시술되었을 때, 거머리들은 재 접합 된 부위에 혈액이 응고하는 것 즉 농축되는 것을 막는 화학물질을 주입한다. 이로 인해 생체시계는 절단된 혈관과 접합 된 부위에 있는 혈관 사이의 혈액의 흐름이 다시 시작되도록 한다.

현대 의학에서 부활한 또 하나의 구식 의술은 파리의 벌레 같은 유충인 구더기의 활용이다. 이 생물은 상처에서 죽은 피부를 잘라내기 위해, 수 세기 동안, 남미에서 호주에 이르기까지 전 세계적으로 다른 문화권 사람들에 의해 활용되어 왔다. 이것은 괴저를 앓는 사람들에게 상당히 도움이 될 수 있다. 괴저는 인체의 기관에 혈액이 흐르는 것이 멈추게 될 때 발생하는 썩거나 소모하는 질환이다. 치료하기 가장 어려운 괴저의 경우조차도 구더기들은 소모성 질환을 제거하고 건강한 피부만을 남겨놓는 데 가장 효과적이었다. 그러므로 그것들은 그 자체가 현대 의술에 상당히 유용하다는 것을 보여주는 구식 의학 치료법의 한 예이다.

문 1 | 첫 번째 단락의 they가 가리키는 것은?
ⓐ 레이저
ⓑ 작은 카메라
ⓒ 최근의 발달
ⓓ 절개 수술

해설 | 현대 의사들은 최근의 발달한 의학 기술들을 사용한다.

문 2 | 첫 번째 단락에서 기술에 대해 유추할 수 있는 것은?
ⓐ 현대 과학기술에 대한 대안이 다소 논쟁적이다.
ⓑ 의사들은 이제 인체를 절개하지 않고 질환이 있는 부위를 볼 수 있다.
ⓒ 의사들이 사용하는 소형 카메라는 상당히 가격이 비싸다.
ⓓ 의사들은 현대 과학기술에 그렇게 많이 의존해서는 안 된다.

해설 | 절개 수술(invasive surgery)을 피하려고 최신 기술을 이용한다고 했으므로 의사들은 최신 기술을 이용하면 절개 수술을 하지 않고도 질병을 진단할 수 있다고 추론할 수 있다.

문 3 | 두 번째 단락에서 they가 가리키는 것은?
ⓐ 의사들
ⓑ 나쁜 피
ⓒ 환자
ⓓ 거머리

해설 | they는 bad blood를 질병의 원인으로 간주하지 않는 주체로 이 문장의 주어인 "doctors"이다.

문 4 | 두 번째 단락에서 재접합하는 수족을 글쓴이가 언급한 이유는?
ⓐ 응고하면서 일어나는 힘든 의료 상황을 예시하려고
ⓑ 거머리가 가장 효과적인 치료법임을 제시하기 위해
ⓒ 현대 의술이 예전의 의술에서 발전하였다는 것을 지적하기 위해
ⓓ 현대 과학기술이 과거의 의술과 비교하여 어떻게 쓸모가 없는지를 제시하기 위해

해설 | 오늘날 의사들이 거머리를 팔다리 재부착에 활용하는 내용은 의술이 고도로 발달한 시대에도 역시 거머리의 효과적인 치료효과를 언급하고자 하기 때문이다.

문 5 | 두 번째 단락에서 거머리에 대해 유추할 수 있는 것은?
ⓐ 그것들은 혈액을 상실하게 해서 많은 사람들을 죽게 했다.
ⓑ 그것들은 환자의 피를 빨아 먹은 직후에 죽는다.
ⓒ 그것들은 환자의 수족을 치료하기 위해 필요한 피를 공급할 수 있다.
ⓓ 그들의 능력은 충분한 피가 쉽게 흐르도록 하는데 사용될 수 있다.

해설 | 거머리는 피가 응고하는 것을 막고 혈액의 흐름을 원활하게 한다.

문 6 | 세 번째 단락에서 필자가 구더기를 언급한 이유는 무엇인가?
ⓐ 구식 치료법이 대부분은 훨씬 낫다는 것을 암시하기 위해
ⓑ 현대 의학에서 다시 사용되는 의술의 또 하나의 예를 들어주기 위해
ⓒ 오늘날의 의학에서는 혐오스러운 생물조차 활용될 수 있다는 것을 보여주기 위해
ⓓ 의학용 거머리의 활용과 효과를 비교하기 위해

해설 | 본문에서는 구식 의학이 현대의 첨단 의학에 재도입되어 활용되는 예로 거머리와 구더기를 예로 들어 설명하고 있다.

문 7 | 주어진 문장이 단락에 들어갈 수 있는 4개의 네모(■)를 살펴보시오.

[Even in the most difficult-to-cure cases of gangrene, maggots have been effective at getting rid of the rot and leaving only healthy flesh.]

문장이 들어갈 가장 적절한 곳은?
단락에 문장이 들어갈 한 개의 네모(■)를 클릭하시오.

해설 | ⓒ 다음 문장에 있는 Thus는 결론을 이끄는 접속사로 구더기가 유용하다는 결론을 내리고 있으므로 그 근거가 되는 주어진 문장은 Thus 앞인 ⓒ에 와야 한다.

문 8 | 전통적인 의학 지혜에 관한 글쓴이의 의견은?
ⓐ 필자는 일반적으로 그 혜택보다는 위험이 더 크다고 믿는다.
ⓑ 필자는 현대에 전통 의술을 활용하는 데 대해 회의적이다.
ⓒ 필자는 현대 의술에 효과적으로 통합되어 활용될 수 있다고 생각한다.
ⓓ 필자는 현대의술과 과거의 의술을 함께 사용하는데 중립적인 태도를 보인다.

해설 | 이 글의 주제는 현대 의술에 과거의 의술이 어떻게 효과적으로 활용되는지를 다루고 있으므로, 정답은 ⓒ이다.

문 9 | 보기에서 적절한 구를 선택하여 관계 있는 오랜 의술 사용의 유형에 분류하시오. 두 개의 보기는 제외됩니다.
ⓐ 나쁜 피를 빨아 먹는다고 생각된다.
ⓑ 부패한 살을 먹는 능력을 갖추고 있다.
ⓒ 치료하기 힘든 상처를 치료하는데 사용되어 왔다.
ⓓ 신체의 부위들을 다시 부착하도록 의사들을 돕는다.

ⓔ 신체의 면역체계를 강화한다.
ⓕ 수술에 사용될 때 가벼운 질병을 퍼뜨린다.
ⓖ 혈액의 흐름을 원활하게 하는 것을 돕는다.

해설 | 거머리는 나쁜 피를 빨아내고 혈액의 흐름을 원활히 하므로 신체의 부위를 접착하는데 유용할 수 있다. (ⓐ, ⓓ, ⓖ) 반면, 구더기는 죽은 피부를 제거하는 역할을 하므로 치료하기 힘든 상처에 도움이 될 수 있다. (ⓑ, ⓒ)

Final Test

정답
1. ⓐ 2. ⓒ 3. ⓒ 4. ⓓ 5. ⓒ
6. ⓑ 7. ⓑ 8. ⓓ 9. Shoes - ⓒ, ⓔ / Barefeet - ⓑ, ⓕ, ⓖ 10. ⓓ
11. ⓑ 12. ⓓ 13. ⓒ 14. ⓓ 15. ⓒ
16. ⓐ 17. ⓒ 18. ⓓ 19. ⓐ, ⓒ, ⓓ
20. ⓐ 21. ⓒ 22. ⓒ 23. ⓒ 24. ⓑ
25. ⓑ 26. ⓒ 27. ⓑ 28. ⓓ 29. ⓑ
30. ⓑ, ⓒ, ⓕ

[1~9]

인간 문명에서 신발이 상용화되기 전에, 인간의 발은 상당히 튼튼하고, 유연성이 있고 강했다. 그러나 대략 사만 년 전에, 추운 날씨와 평평하지 않은 보행로에서 발을 보호하기 위해 동물과 식물로 만든 물질로 발을 감싸기 시작하자 우리의 발은 변하기 시작했다. 신발의 사용으로 인해 우리 발이 변했을 뿐 아니라, 놀랍게도 그것은 오늘날 발의 부상이 증가하는 것에도 책임이 있는 듯하다.

우리 조상의 작은 네 개의 발가락들이 크기 면에서 줄기 시작한 시기는 바로 이 기간이었다. 인간이 자신들의 발을 더 감싸기 시작하면서 걸을 때 지면을 움켜쥐는 강한 발가락들의 필요성이 줄어들게 되었다는 것은 발자국이나 화석으로 입증되었다. 이것은 발에 가해지는 압력이 줄어드는 직접적인 결과를 낳았다. 그래서 오늘날 인간의 발은 우리 조상들의 발보다 더 상처받기 쉽다. 이 외의 흥미로운 것은 이러한 변화가 과학자들이 한 때 생각했던 것처럼 진화의 결과가 아니라는 점이다. 과학자들은 우리 조상들의 발만큼 튼튼해지도록 발을 단련할 수가 있다는 것을 알아냈다.

지면에 있는 날카로운 물체와 추운 날씨로부터 발을 보호하는 신발은 확실히 발을 안전하게 지켜주지만, 달리기를 할 때 신발을 신는 것은 운동선수의 활동에 치명적인 부상의 위험을 증가시킨다고 스포츠 물리학자들은 주장한다. 남아프리카와 호주에서 걸출한 경주자 중 몇몇은 운동화를 신지 않는다. 그들의 발은 외관상 옛 조상들의 발과 훨씬 더 유사하다. 그들의 발은 더 크고, 거칠고, 발의 근육이 매우 발달되어 있다. 과학자들은 강화되면서 커진 근육의 크기로 인해, 그들의 발은 오늘날의 발보다 부상을 덜 입게 되는 경향을 띤다고 생각한다.

신발류는 달릴 때 흔히 일어나는 발목 염좌의 발생을 증가시킨다고 알려져 왔다. 신발이 발을 지면에서 들어올리기 때문에, 발목을 심하게 비틀거나 구부리면 발목에 부상을 입는다. 맨발 경주자는 이러한 문제점을 갖고 있지 않다. 게다가 무거운 신발로 달리는 것은 발이 지면을 딛는 방식에 영향을 미친다. 신발을 신게 되면, 발의 뒤꿈치로 땅을 딛으려 하고 이로 인해 더 무리가 가게 땅을 딛게 된다. 이러한 동작의 반복으로 무릎 부상을 야기할 수 있다. 맨발 경주자들은 발바닥의 둥근 부위로 지면에 좀 더 가볍게 착지하는 경향이 있고, 이로 인해 부상의 빈도를 줄이게 된다. 그러므로 운동화는 그 이점에도 불구하고, 유익하기보다는 해를 끼칠 수 있다.

문 1 | 첫 번째 단락에 따르면, 발이 변화한 원인이 무엇인가?
Ⓐ 사람들이 발을 보호하기 위해 발을 감쌌기 때문에
Ⓑ 사람들이 지면에 있는 날카로운 물체를 밟았기 때문에
Ⓒ 발뼈가 점차 약해졌기 때문에
Ⓓ 너무 많은 압박이 맨발에 종종 가해졌기 때문에

해설 | 여러 위험으로부터 발을 보호하기 위해 발을 감싸기 시작하면서 발이 변화했다는 내용이 나온다.

문 2 | 두 번째 단락에서 우리 조상의 발에 대해 추론할 수 있는 것은?
Ⓐ 예전의 발가락 크기는 현재보다 더 다양했다.
Ⓑ 오늘날의 발보다 길었으나 폭이 좁았다.
Ⓒ 발바닥은 훨씬 더 단단하고 두꺼웠다.
Ⓓ 발의 구조가 (오늘날과는) 훨씬 달랐다.

해설 | 예전엔 발바닥이 지면에 직접 닿았으므로 더욱 단단했었음을 유추할 수 있다.

문 3 | 주어진 문장이 두 단락에 들어갈 수 있는 4개의 네모〔■〕를 살펴보시오.

This was a direct result of less stress being placed on the foot.

문장이 들어갈 가장 적절한 곳은?
단락에 문장이 들어갈 한 개의 네모〔■〕를 클릭하시오.

해설 | 발에 가해지는 압력이 준 것은 발가락이 직접 지면을 움켜쥘 힘이 덜 필요하게 되면서이므로 this는 Ⓒ의 앞 문장을 가리킨다.

문 4 | 다음 중 두 번째 단락의 하이라이트 된 문장의 핵심 내용을 가장 잘 표현한 것은? 틀린 보기는 본문의 내용을 심각하게 바꾸거나 핵심적인 내용을 누락시킨 것이다.
Ⓐ 신발은 발이 날카로운 물체와 추운 날씨로 인해 다치는 것을 막아줄 수 있지만, 달리기로 인한 부상으로부터 발을 보호할 수 없다.
Ⓑ 신발은 날카로운 물체와 추운 날씨로부터 발을 보호할 수 있으므로, 운동선수의 활동에 상당히 중요하다.
Ⓒ 신발 착용은 달리는 동안 부상당할 가능성을 증가시킬 수 있지만, 일반적으로 발이 매우 시리게 되는 것으로부터 보호한다.
Ⓓ 신발이 발을 안전하게 보호할지라도, 신발을 착용하고 달리는 것은 심각한 부상을 더 빈번하게 일으킬 수도 있다.

해설 | protecting them from ~ cold temperature는 safety의 부연으로 생략되고, that is fatal to athlete's performance는 injury에 대한 부연설명으로 less important information이다. 따라서 문장의 핵심은 Ⓓ가 된다.

문 5 | 세 번째 단락의 they가 가리키는 것은?
Ⓐ 남아프리카인의 발
Ⓑ 조상들의 발
Ⓒ 경주자의 발
Ⓓ 과학자의 발

해설 | 발 근육을 키운 것은 남아프리카와 호주의 걸출한 경주자들이다.

문 6 | 글쓴이가 세 번째 단락에서 남아프리카와 호주의 걸출한 경주자들을 언급한 이유는 무엇인가?
Ⓐ 그들이 신발을 신지 않기 때문에 더 잘 달릴 수 있다는 것을 보여주기 위해
Ⓑ 맨발 경주자들이 부상을 당할 가능성이 적다는 것을 예시하기 위해
Ⓒ 몇몇의 걸출한 경주자들이 달리는 동안 신발을 신지 않는 원인을 설명하기 위해
Ⓓ 운동화를 신는 다른 경주자들의 발과 비교하기 위해

해설 | 맨발로 달리는 선수들의 예를 들어 부상의 위험이 적다는 것을 보여주고 있다.

문 7 | 네 번째 단락에서 글쓴이가 발목 염좌에 대해 이야기하는 바는 무엇인가?
Ⓐ 맨발 경주자에게 더 흔하게 나타났다.
Ⓑ 신발 사용으로 인해 발생할 수 있는 한 가지 결과이다.
Ⓒ 고대인들은 발목 부상이 상당히 드물었다.
Ⓓ 신발을 신지 않으면 더 빨리 회복된다.

해설 | 신발로 인해 발목 염좌의 발생 빈도가 잦아졌다고 글쓴이는 말하고 있다.

문 8 | 신발에 대한 글쓴이의 의견은 무엇인가?
Ⓐ 맨발 훈련의 효과를 명백히 밝히기 위해 더 많은 연구가 이뤄져야 한다고 느낀다.
Ⓑ 사람들이 신발을 신지 않고 걷거나 달리는 것을 훈련해야 한다고 생각한다.
Ⓒ 운동화 디자인에 사용되는 진보된 기술에 깊은 감명을 받고 있다.
Ⓓ 신발을 신고 달리는 것은 신발을 신지 않고 달리는 것보다 더 많은 부상을 일으킨다고 확신하고 있다.

해설 | 글쓴이는 신발때문에 발이 약해져서 부상을 당할 가능성이 크다고 주장하고 있다.

문 9 | 적절한 보기를 골라 관련 있는 그룹과 짝지으시오. 두 개의 보기는 제외됩니다.
Ⓐ 발이 혹독한 기후에서 건조해지는 것을 막는다.
Ⓑ 경주자가 발의 위치를 감지할 수 있도록 한다.
Ⓒ 사람이 날카로운 물체를 밟는 것을 막는다.

ⓓ 발바닥에 발생하는 피부 문제를 증가시킨다.
ⓔ 추운 날씨에 발이 보온될 수 있도록 한다.
ⓕ 달리는 동안 사람의 발목에 가해지는 압박을 줄인다.
ⓖ 발바닥의 둥근 부위를 이용하여 더 가볍게 땅에 착지하도록 한다.

해설 | 신발을 신으면 날카로운 물체나 추운 날씨에 발을 보호해 주지만 맨발로 걸을 때보다 발과 관절에 더욱 무리가 생긴 다고 설명하고 있다.

〔10~19〕

1692년, 미국 북동부에 있는 매사추세츠 주의 세일럼이라는 작은 마을에, 미국 역사상 지금까지도 잘 알려진 사건인 세일럼 마녀재판이 일어났다. 열아홉 명의 사람들이 주술을 부린다고 고발당하여 교수형에 처해졌고, 100명이 넘는 사람들이 구속되었다. 이러한 비극에는 여러 가지 원인이 있었다.

주요 원인은 그 마을의 정치적 긴장이었다. 세일럼은 성장하고 있는 마을이었으나, 마을 사람들이 그 성장 방식에 대해 합의하지 못했다. 마을이 계속 성장하고 있었기 때문에 어떤 사람들은 기존의 마을을 파괴하고 다시 만들기를 원했다. 반면 다른 사람들은 세일럼을 그대로 유지하기를 원했다. 이러한 의견의 불일치는 마을 사람들 간의 긴장을 낳았다. 이후에 이것은 사람들이 서로 거리낌 없이 배신하게끔 하였다. 마을 사람들은 어떠한 비난이 가해져도 믿게 되었다.

그러므로 두 명의 어린 소녀, Betty Parris와 Abigail Williams가 알 수 없는 병을 앓게 되어 바닥에 쓰러져 울부짖는 것과 같은 이상한 행동을 하게 되었을 때, 마을에 있는 누군가가 주술을 부린 것이라고 의심을 받았다. 소녀들은 그들에게 이러한 짓을 한 마녀의 이름을 자백하도록 강요받았다. 그들은 세 명의 이름, 노예인 Tituba, 집 없는 떠돌이 여성인 Sarah Osborne, 그리고 교회에 다니지 않는 노파인 Sarah Goode을 말했다. 그 여성들이 재판에 회부되었을 때, 오로지 노예 여성만이 주술을 부렸다고 자백했다. 그 이유는 그녀가 소녀들과 함께 점치는 놀이를 했을 때, 순진하게도 자신이 마녀의 특기를 갖고 있을지도 모른다고 생각했기 때문이다. 다른 여성들은 결백하다고 주장했음에도 불구하고, 세 여성 모두는 교수형에 처해졌다.

그러나 이것은 단지 서막에 불과했다. 첫 번째 재판은 마녀재판에 대한 또 다른 주요 원인인 광기를 일으켰다. 마을 사람들은 세일럼이 마녀에 의해 침략당했고, 그들에 의해 통제되고 있다고 확신하게 되었다. 그들의 미신적인 믿음은 그들을 이성적으로 생각하지 못하게 만들었다. 소녀들의 원인을 알 수 없는 병이 결국 호전되지 않자, 그들은 마을에 사는 더 많은 마녀들의 이름을 밝히도록 또 다시 압력을 받았다. 그들은 더 많은 마녀들의 이름을 대기 시작했다. 그 마녀들은 흔히 그들 가족의 적들이었다. 그리고 Abigail과 Betty가 진실을 말했는지에 의심을 표시한 사람들은 마녀의 혐의를 받고 감옥에 보내졌다. 마을 사람들 간의 이러한 두려움으로 그들은 그 소녀들을 비판하지 못했다. 이러한 광란 상태가 끝났을 때, 열아홉 명의 사람들은 죽었고, 더 많은 사람들이 여러 해 동안 감옥에 수감되었다.

문10 | 두 번째 단락의 intact와 가장 의미가 유사한 것은?
ⓐ 안전한
ⓑ 성장하는
ⓒ 평화로운
ⓓ 온전한

해설 | 앞에 대조되는 문장에서 break off가 단서가 되어, intact가 '그대로인, 변하지 않은'의 의미임을 알 수 있다.

문11 | 두 번째 단락의 this가 가리키는 것은?
ⓐ 불일치
ⓑ 긴장
ⓒ 마을
ⓓ 고소

해설 | 마을 사람들이 서로 배신하게 한 것은 '의견 불일치로 일어난 긴장' 때문이다.

문12 | 두 번째 단락에 따르면 세일럼 사람들 사이에 긴장을 가져온 원인이 무엇인가?
ⓐ 마을이 더 많은 인구로 성장하게 되면서 마을을 어떻게 분리해야 하는지에 관한 불일치
ⓑ 지도자들에 의해 조성된 미래 정치에 관한 마을 사람들 간의 불신
ⓒ 마을의 발전에 대해 의견이 엇갈리는 두 정치인 간의 고소
ⓓ 마을이 점점 더 성장하면서 마을을 발전시키는 더 나은 방법에 대한 논쟁

해설 | 두 번째 단락의 두 번째 문장에서 세일럼 사람들 사이에 조성된 긴장의 원인을 간략하게 설명하고 있다.

문13 | 주어진 문장이 단락에 들어갈 수 있는 4개의 네모[■]를 살펴보시오.
문장이 들어갈 가장 적절한 곳은?
[That's because as she played fortune-telling games with the girls, she naively thought she might have had the special talents of a witch.]
단락에 문장이 들어갈 한 개의 네모[■]를 클릭하시오.

해설 | she는 흑인 노예 여성을 말한다. that's because ~ 이하는 노예 여성이 주술을 부렸다고 고백한 이유이므로,

Ⓒ 자리에 문장이 삽입되어야 한다.

문14 | 세 번째 단락에 따르면, 다음 중 사실이 아닌 것은?
Ⓐ 마녀라고 주장된 세 여성 중 한 명은 자백했다.
Ⓑ 마녀라고 호명된 세 여성들은 교수형 당했다.
Ⓒ 사람들은 두 소녀가 앓고 있던 병의 원인을 실제로 알지 못했다.
Ⓓ 두 소녀는 그들을 아프게 한 마녀의 이름을 정말로 알고 있었다.

해설 | 두 소녀가 마녀의 이름을 정말로 알고 있었다는 사실은 언급 되지 않았다.

문15 | 네 번째 단락의 overrun과 가장 의미가 유사한 것은?
Ⓐ 방문 받은
Ⓑ 저주받은
Ⓒ 침략 당한
Ⓓ 패배당한

해설 | or 다음에 있는 control로 보아 overrun이 '침략하다'의 의미임을 유추할 수 있다.

문16 | 네 번째 단락에서 글쓴이가 두려움을 언급한 이유는 무엇인가?
Ⓐ 마을 사람들의 생각과 행동에 대한 이유를 제시하기 위해
Ⓑ 소녀들이 마녀이야기를 지어낸 이유를 설명하기 위해
Ⓒ 마녀 사냥에 대한 주요 원인들을 비교하기 위해
Ⓓ 광기가 마녀사냥의 궁극적인 원인이라는 결론을 제시하기 위해

해설 | 마을 사람들이 이성적으로 판단하지 못하고, 소녀들에 대해서도 비판하지 못한 이유를 언급하기 위해서이다.

문17 | 다음 중 네 번째 단락의 마녀 재판에 대해 추론할 수 있는 것은?
Ⓐ 마녀 재판 기간에 아팠던 많은 소녀들은 마녀의 이름을 밝히도록 강요받았다.
Ⓑ 두 소녀는 두 번의 재판 이후에 다른 마녀들의 이름을 밝히지 않았다고 비난을 받았다.
Ⓒ 마녀 재판은 세일럼 마을 사람들을 황폐화 시켰다.
Ⓓ 사람들은 재판 중에 두 소녀가 어느 누구를 마녀라고 지목했든 간에 믿었다.

해설 | 마녀 재판으로 많은 사람들이 죽고 투옥되었다는 내용으로 마을 사람들이 많이 지치고 힘들어 했음을 추론할 수 있다.

문18 | 세일럼 사람들에 관한 글쓴이의 의견은 무엇인가?
Ⓐ 그들은 신념에 대한 적절한 명분을 갖고 있었다.
Ⓑ 발전은 그들 간의 갈등을 야기했다.
Ⓒ 그들은 정치적 논란에 너무 깊숙이 관련되었다.
Ⓓ 그들은 당시에 이성적으로 처신하지 못했다.

해설 | 미신에 대한 믿음과 투옥되는 것에 대한 두려움 등으로 마을 사람들은 이성적인 판단을 하지 못했다.

문19 | 지문에 대한 간단한 요약을 위한 도입 문장이 아래에 제시된다. 가장 중요한 내용을 표현한 3가지 대답을 선택하여 요약을 완성하시오. 몇몇 문장들은 단락에서 언급되지 않았거나 중요하지 않은 내용을 표현해서 요약에 들어갈 수 없다.

세일럼 마녀 사냥이라는 비극에는 수많은 원인이 있었다.
Ⓐ 마을의 잠재적 성장에 대한 불일치가 낳은 긴장은 그 사냥의 근본적인 원인이었다.
Ⓑ 두 소녀에게 동의하지 않는 사람들은 마녀로 간주되어 사형을 선고받았다.
Ⓒ 마을에 있던 두 소녀들에게 마녀라고 고발당했던 세 명의 여성들의 재판으로 이 사냥이 시작되었다.
Ⓓ 마을 사람들로 하여금 이성적인 생각과 행동을 하지 못하게 한 미신적인 믿음과 통제할 수 없는 두려움이 또 하나의 이유였다.
Ⓔ 세일럼에 영향을 받았던 근처의 다른 마을들이 자신들의 마을에 있는 마녀를 고발하고 재판하기 시작했다.
Ⓕ 마을 인구가 증가하자, 마을의 몇몇 구성원들은 세일럼에서 분리되어 자신들의 마을을 건설하기 원했다.

해설 | 많은 사람들이 죽고 투옥된 마녀 사냥은, 정치적 긴장으로 서로 믿지 못하던 마을에 살던 두 소녀의 고발로 시작하였고, 사람들의 광기로 인해 확산되었다.

[20~30]
폴리오(소아마비) 바이러스는 인간의 신경계에 침투한다. 걷지 못하고, 수족을 쓰지 못하게 되고, 인공 호흡 장치를 착용하고 살아가도록 하고, 심지어 사망할 수도 있는 것이 폴리오가 인간에 미칠 수 있는 영향이다. 그것은 오랜 옛날부터 존재해왔다. 고대 이집트 시대에는 폴리오로 인해 다리를 절고 있는 사람들이 그려진 그림들이 있다. 서반구에서 가장 최근에 폴리오가 창궐했던 시기는 20세기의 전반기였다. 이 전염병의 절정기인 1952년에 거의 60,000명의 사람들이 매해 폴리오에 걸렸고, 3,000명이 그로 인해 사망했다.

그러나 Jonas Salk에 의해 발명되었던 폴리오 백신은 1955년에 상용화되었다. 1979년에 폴리오는 미국에서 소멸하였다. 1991년이 되자 서반구에서는 자연적으로 발생하는 폴리오는 없어졌다. 이 질환은 백신 때문에 근절되었다. 그러나 폴리오는 나머지 세계에서는 여전히 흔한 전염병이었다. 그러므로 1988년 세계 보건 기관들은 지구상에서 폴리오를 완전히 근절하리라는 목표를 세웠다.

이러한 노력은 매우 성공적이었다. 매해 전 세계 어린이들이 폴리오 예방접종을 받는다. 1988년 목표가 설정된 이후, 2004년까지 전 세계적으로 발병하는 폴리오는 거의 99% 소멸하였다. 그러나 폴리오에 대한 근절 수단이 있음에도, 지구상의 20개국에서는 여전히 폴리오가 발병한다

는 보고가 있다. 의료진이 이들 국가의 국민에게 백신을 투여하고 이 질병을 근절하려는 목적을 달성하는 것을 어렵게 하는 전쟁과 자금 조달의 부족과 같은 몇 가지 장애물이 있다.

첫 번째 문제점은 정치적 불안정이다. 이것은 폴리오가 여전히 발병하는 20개국 중 거의 모든 국가들에 해당하는 가장 공통적 특징 중 하나이다. 폭력과 전쟁으로 인한 혼란은 물자와 서비스가 이런 나라들에 쉽게 전달되는 것을 방해한다. 특히 찾아가기 어려운 시골 지역은 더 심하다. 이런 상황으로 인해, 의사들은 이들 국가에 백신을 투여하는 것이 거의 불가능하다.

두 번째 문제점은 자금이다. 모든 사람들은 폴리오를 근절하는 것이 긍정적인 목표라는 것에는 동의한다. 그러나 세계 보건 기관들이 예방접종을 추진하기 위한 투자에 필요한 자금을 모금하는 것은 힘들다. 이것은 폴리오가 상당수의 지역에서 근절되었기 때문에, 사람들은 이에 대해 더 이상 생각하지 않기 때문이다. 그리고 사람들이 그에 대해 생각하지 않는다면, 기금이나 그 질병과 싸우는 데 도움이 될 자원을 기부하지 않을 것이다. 따라서 이 질병에 대한 대중의 인식을 높이는 것이 폴리오를 근절시키고자 하는 목표를 이루는 데 큰 도전이 된다.

문20 | 첫 번째 단락의 antiquity와 가장 의미가 유사한 것은?
Ⓐ 고대
Ⓑ 근대
Ⓒ 선사 시대
Ⓓ 중세

해설 | Ancient Egyptian times로 antiquity가 '고대'를 의미한다는 것을 유추할 수 있다.

문21 | 폴리오의 결과로 언급되지 않은 것은?
Ⓐ 호흡 장애
Ⓑ 보행 능력 상실
Ⓒ 기억 상실
Ⓓ 사망

해설 | 첫 번째 단락에선 폴리오 바이러스로 인해 신체상의 장애를 설명하고 있으며, 기억 상실에 대한 언급은 없다.

문22 | 첫 번째 단락에서 글쓴이가 고대 이집트를 언급한 이유는?
Ⓐ 이집트인들이 탁월한 폴리오 치료법을 보유했다는 것을 암시하기 위해
Ⓑ 그 질병이 최초로 이집트에서 발견되었다는 것을 말하기 위해
Ⓒ 폴리오가 오래된 질병이라는 주장에 대한 예를 들기 위해
Ⓓ 폴리오가 과거에 다른 영향을 미쳤다는 것을 지적하기 위해

해설 | 폴리오가 오래된 질병이라는 것을 설명하기 위해 이집트 시대의 그림을 예로 들어 설명하려 하고 있으며 이집트에서 최초로 발견되었다는 설명은 아니다.

문23 | 두 번째 단락의 eradicated와 가장 의미가 유사한 것은?
Ⓐ 늦추어졌다
Ⓑ 제한되었다
Ⓒ 근절되었다
Ⓓ 변형되었다

해설 | 뒤에 대조되는 However polio was still a common ~에서 eradicate가 '박멸하다'의 의미임을 유추할 수 있다.

문24 | 두 번째와 세 번째 단락에서 글쓴이는 폴리오 백신을 어떻게 소개하는가?
Ⓐ Salk가 최초의 백신을 발명한 방법을 설명하면서
Ⓑ 폴리오를 감소시킨 효능을 설명하면서
Ⓒ 백신이 인체에 어떻게 작용하는지를 예를 들어주면서
Ⓓ 폴리오와 해결하기 어려운 다른 질환과의 차이를 비교하면서

해설 | 백신이 나오게 된 배경이나 몸에서의 작용 또는 다른 백신과의 비교는 언급되지 않았고 백신의 효능에 대해 자세히 설명하고 있다.

문25 | 다음 중 세 번째 단락의 폴리오 예방접종에 대해 추론할 수 있는 것은?
Ⓐ 폴리오의 수효가 감소한 이후에 계속해서 백신 접종 가격이 상승했다.
Ⓑ 1990년대에 전 세계에 충분한 백신 접종을 공급하기 위해 많은 액수의 기금이 모였다.
Ⓒ 세계에서 폴리오 바이러스를 근절하기 위해 많은 폴리오 백신이 발명되었다.
Ⓓ 백신에 함유된 몇 가지 성분이 성인에게 안전하다고 충분히 입증되지 않았다.

해설 | 2004년도에는 polio가 많이 없어져서 기금이 줄었지만 그전에는, 특히 1990년 즈음에는, 많은 기금으로 백신을 공급했다는 점을 추론할 수 있다.

문26 | 다음 중 세 번째 단락의 하이라이트 된 문장의 핵심 내용을 가장 잘 표현한 것은? 틀린 보기는 본문의 내용을 심각하게 바꾸거나 핵심적인 내용을 누락시킨 것이다.
Ⓐ 전쟁과 자금 부족으로 사람들은 이들 국가에 백신을 전달하여 그들의 목적을 달성하기 어렵다.
Ⓑ 이들 국가에 백신을 위한 기금을 모금하는 것을 어렵게 하는 전쟁이 있기 때문에 질병은 사라지지 않을 것이다.
Ⓒ 폴리오를 근절하겠다는 목표는 몇몇 국가에 백신을 전달하는 것을 어렵게 하는 난점으로 인해, 완수되지 않았다.
Ⓓ 이들 국가에 의료진이 백신을 유입하는 것은 모금을 방해하는 몇 가지 요인으로 인해 어렵다.

해설 | wars and lack of funding은 몇 가지 장애의 예이므로 생략하고, medical personnel도 부연 설명이다.

문27 | 네 번째 단락의 This가 가리키는 것은?
Ⓐ 백신 재고분의 부족

Ⓑ 폭력과 접근의 어려움
　　　Ⓒ 백신을 필요로 하는 사람 수
　　　Ⓓ 의료 활동이 가능한 의사의 부족

해설 | 백신을 배포하는 것을 어렵게 하는 것은 폭력과 특정 지역에의 접근하기 어려움 때문이다.

문28 | 주어진 문장이 첫 번째 단락에 들어갈 수 있는 4개의 네모〔■〕를 살펴보시오.
　　　문장이 들어갈 가장 적절한 곳은?
　　　〔And if people aren't thinking about it, they aren't very likely to donate funds and resources to help fight it.〕
　　　단락에 문장이 들어갈 한 개의 네모〔■〕를 클릭하시오.

해설 | And는 앞에 설명의 부가적 설명을 할 때 쓰는 접속사로 사람들이 폴리오에 대해 심각하게 생각하지 않는다는 설명 다음인 ■에 주어진 문장이 들어가야 한다.

문29 | 다음 중 폴리오를 제거하는 데 대해 장애물로 언급되지 않은 것은?
　　　Ⓐ 가기 어려운 장소에 대한 접근 부족
　　　Ⓑ 아이들이 기꺼이 접종을 받지 않으려고 하는 것
　　　Ⓒ 전쟁과 관련된 폭력
　　　Ⓓ 백신 접종 기금의 부족

해설 | 접근이 어렵고, 전쟁, 자금 부족이 장애물로 언급되고 있다.

문30 | 지문에 대한 간단한 요약을 위한 도입 문장이 아래에 제시된다. 가장 중요한 내용을 표현한 3가지 대답을 선택하여 요약을 완성하시오. 몇몇 문장들은 단락에서 언급되지 않았거나 중요하지 않은 내용을 표현해서 요약에 들어갈 수 없다.

　　　몇 세기에 걸쳐 인간에게 엄청난 해를 끼친 이후, 폴리오는 몇몇 국가를 제외하고는 지구상에서 거의 사라졌다.
　　　Ⓐ 폴리오 백신은 Jonas Salk 박사에 의해 20세기 중반에 개발되었고 아이들에게 효익이 있다고 입증되었다.
　　　Ⓑ 백신이 개발되고, 신종 폴리오를 감소시킴으로써 서양에서 효과가 있다고 입증되었다.
　　　Ⓒ 20세기 후반까지 폴리오는 세계 대부분의 지역에서 근절되었지만, 여전히 몇몇 국가에서는 위협적인 병이다.
　　　Ⓓ 백신의 접종 가능성과 비용이 부족하여 폴리오가 발병했다고 보도되는 몇몇 국가들이 있다.
　　　Ⓔ 전쟁은 의사와 물자가 고립된 지역에 조달되는 것과 그 국가들에 충분한 백신이 공급되기 위해 필요한 기금을 모금하는 것에 방해가 된다.
　　　Ⓕ 국가의 불안정한 상태와 그 질병의 근절을 위해 모금되는 자금의 부족은 폴리오를 완벽히 제거하는 것을 방해한다.

해설 | 백신의 개발로 고대부터 있어온 폴리오를 거의 근절시키긴 했으나, 몇몇 나라는 정치적 불안정과 기금의 부족으로 폴리오 백신을 공급받을 수 없어 폴리오는 여전히 어떤 나라들에게는 위협이 되고 있다는 것이 지문의 핵심 내용이다.

NEXUS makes your next day
www.nexusEDU.kr | 책에 대해 궁금한 사항은 넥서스에듀 홈페이지 1:1 고객상담 게시판을 이용하세요.

NEXUS TOEFL® iBT Reading Series의 특징

1 지문을 분석·정리하는 학습 훈련 강조
2 학습 스킬의 체계적인 구성
3 다양한 테마의 독해 지문 및 관련 어휘 학습
4 중요한 리딩 스킬의 누적 활용
5 iBT 실전에 맞춘 단계별 연습 문제

NEXUS TOEFL® iBT Series의 구성

Reading	Starter	Level 1	Level 2	Level 3
Listening	Starter	Level 1	Level 2	Level 3
Writing		Starter	Level 1	Level 2
Speaking		Starter	Level 1	Level 2

www.nexusEDU.kr
넥서스 초·중·고등 사이트

	초1	초2	초3	초4	초5	초6	중1	중2	중3	고1	고2	고3
Writing				공감 영문법+쓰기 1~2								
						도전만점 중등내신 서술형 1~4						
			영어일기 영작패턴 1-A, B · 2-A, B									
			Smart Writing 1~2									
Reading					Reading 101 1~3							
					Reading 공감 1~3							
					This Is Reading Starter 1~3							
						This Is Reading 전면 개정판 1~4						
						This Is Reading 1-1 ~ 3-2 (각 2권; 총 6권)						
						원서 술술 읽는 Smart Reading Basic 1~2						
								원서 술술 읽는 Smart Reading 1~2				
								[특급 단기 특강] 구문독해 · 독해유형				
Listening						Listening 공감 1~3						
						The Listening 1~4						
						After School Listening 1~3						
						도전! 만점 중학 영어듣기 모의고사 1~3						
									만점 적중 수능 듣기 모의고사 20회 · 35회			
TEPS						NEW TEPS 입문편 실전 250+ 청해 · 문법 · 독해						
							NEW TEPS 기본편 실전 300+ 청해 · 문법 · 독해					
								NEW TEPS 실력편 실전 400+ 청해 · 문법 · 독해				
									NEW TEPS 마스터편 실전 500+ 청해 · 문법 · 독해			

이것이 THIS IS 시리즈다!

THIS IS GRAMMAR 시리즈
▷ 중·고등 내신에 꼭 등장하는 어법 포인트 분석 및 총정리

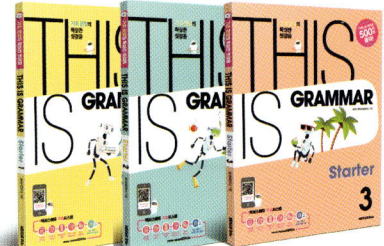

강남인강 강의교재

THIS IS READING 시리즈
▷ 다양한 소재의 지문으로 내신 및 수능 완벽 대비

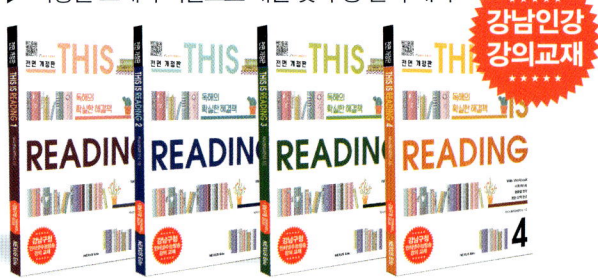

강남인강 강의교재

THIS IS VOCABULARY 시리즈
▷ 주제별로 분류한 교육부 권장 어휘

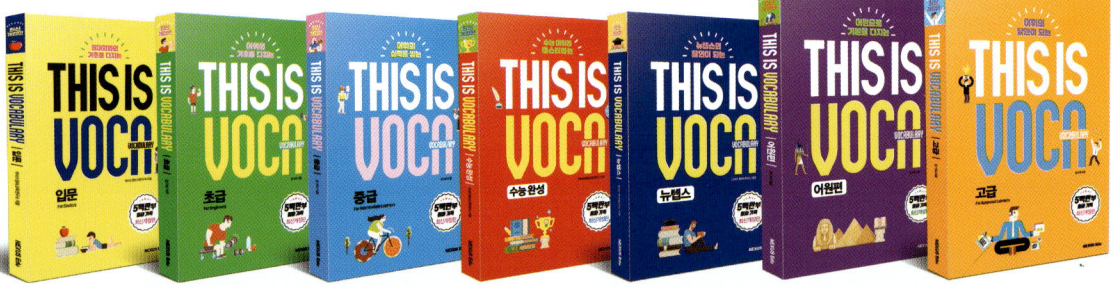

THIS IS 시리즈

무료 MP3 및 부가자료 다운로드
www.nexusbook.com
www.nexusEDU.kr

THIS IS GRAMMAR 시리즈
- **Starter 1~3**   영어교육연구소 지음 | 205×265 | 144쪽 | 각 권 12,000원
- **초·중·고급 1·2**   넥서스영어교육연구소 지음 | 205×265 | 250쪽 내외 | 각 권 12,000원

THIS IS READING 시리즈
- **Starter 1~3**   김태연 지음 | 205×265 | 156쪽 | 각 권 12,000원
- **1·2·3·4**   넥서스영어교육연구소 지음 | 205×265 | 192쪽 내외 | 각 권 10,000원

THIS IS VOCABULARY 시리즈
- **입문**   넥서스영어교육연구소 지음 | 152×225 | 224쪽 | 10,000원
- **초·중·고급·어원편**   권기하 지음 | 152×225 | 180×257 | 344쪽~444쪽 | 10,000원~12,000원
- **수능 완성**   넥서스영어교육연구소 지음 | 152×225 | 280쪽 | 12,000원
- **뉴텝스**   넥서스 TEPS연구소 지음 | 152×225 | 452쪽 | 13,800원